Time, Reality & Experience

ROYAL INSTITUTE OF PHILOSOPHY SUPPLEMENT: 50

EDITED BY

Craig Callender

CAMBRIDGE
UNIVERSITY PRESS

PUBLISHED BY THE PRESS SYNDICATE OF THE UNIVERSITY OF CAMBRIDGE
The Pitt Building, Trumpington Street, Cambridge, CB2 1RP,
United Kingdom

CAMBRIDGE UNIVERSITY PRESS
The Edinburgh Building, Cambridge CB2 2RU, United Kingdom
40 West 20th Street, New York, NY 10011–4211, USA
477 Williamstown Road, Port Melbourne, VIC 3207, Australia

Printed in the United Kingdom at the University Press, Cambridge
Typeset by Michael Heath Ltd, Reigate, Surrey

*A catalogue record for this book is available
from the British Library*

Library of Congress Cataloguing-in-Publication Data

Time, reality & experience/edited by Craig Callender.
p. cm.—(Royal Institute of Philosophy supplement, ISSN
1358–2461; 50)
Includes bibliographical references and index
ISBN 0-521-52967 0 (pbk.)
1. Time—Philosophy. I. Title: Time, reality, and experience. II.
Callender, Craig, 1968. III. Series.
BD638.T566 2002
115—dc21   2002067445

ISBN 0 521 52967 0 paperback
ISSN 1358-2461

Contents

Preface v

Notes on Contributors vii

When Time Gets Off Track 1
JAN FAYE

Burbury's Last Case: The Mystery of the Entropic Arrow 19
HUW PRICE

Zeno's Arrow and the Significance of the Present 57
ROBIN LEPOIDEVIN

Presentism, Ontology and Temporal Experience 73
L. NATHAN OAKLANDER

A Presentist's Refutation of Mellor's McTaggart 91
PHILIP PERCIVAL

Time and Degrees of Existence: A Theory of 'Degree
Presentism' 119
QUENTIN SMITH

McTaggart and the Truth about Time 137
HEATHER DYKE

On Absolute Becoming and the Myth of Passage 153
STEVEN F. SAVITT

Time Travel and Modern Physics 169
FRANK ARNTZENIUS AND TIM MAUDLIN

Freedom from the Inside Out 201
CARL HOEFER

On Stages, Worms and Relativity 223
YURI BALASHOV

Contents

On Becoming, Cosmic Time and Rotating Universes 253
MAURO DORATO

How Relativity Contradicts Presentism 277
SIMON SAUNDERS

Can Physics Coherently Deny the Reality of Time? 293
RICHARD HEALEY

Rememberances, Mementos, and Time-Capsules 317
JENANN ISMAEL

Preface

In the past decade the philosophy of time seems to have experienced a renaissance across all of its various sub-fields. With this activity in mind, the Royal Institute of Philosophy agreed to let me organize its annual conference around the title, **Time, Reality and Experience**. Held at the London School of Economics on 27-8 Sept 2000, the conference brought together philosophers and scientists interested in time from all over the world. The conference was truly international, with speakers coming from nine different countries across three different continents. In many cases, prominent philosophers of time met each other for the first time. The conference was also wide-ranging in terms of its approach to philosophy of time, balanced between studies of time as it is found in science and more traditional analytic philosophy of time. In all, I felt it a great success.

The London conference was a cause of this book, but it was not the source of all that is in it. Professor Anthony O'Hear of the Royal Institute charged me with producing a good collection in philosophy of time, regardless of the origin of the papers. To round out the volume, I then searched for more good unpublished papers in philosophy of time—and found them. I heard two at a wonderful conference (**Real Time and its Quantum Roots**, 12–14 April, 2001) organized by Richard Healey and held at the University of Arizona. They were papers by Richard himself and Jenann Ismael on the—dare I say 'timely'—topic of timelessness in quantum gravity. Then L. Nathan Oaklander kindly brought to my attention a paper by Philip Percival, who was an active member of the audience at the London conference. The last paper I found while browsing on the internet. There I happened upon an outstanding contribution on time travel by Frank Arntzenius and Tim Maudlin. Though already published online, I felt it also deserved a home on good old-fashioned paper. I'm indebted to Richard, Jenann, Philip, Frank and Tim for allowing me to include their excellent papers.

For financial support of the London conference, I gratefully acknowledge the generosity of the Royal Institute of Philosophy, the British Society for the Philosophy of Science, and the LSE's Centre for Philosophy of Natural and Social Sciences. I also thank the London School of Economics and its Department of Philosophy, Logic and Scientific Method for its moral and physical support of the conference. Damian Steer also deserves thanks for designing a beautiful conference website and helping me with all the

v

Preface

practical necessities on the days of the conference. For giving me a quarter away from teaching during this time, I thank the AHRB for a research leave award. Finally, I'm very grateful to all the contributors to this volume and/or the conference for writing such stimulating papers.

Craig Callender
Department of Philosophy
University of California, San Diego
La Jolla, CA 92093
USA

Notes on Contributors

Jan Faye is Senior Lecturer at the Department of Education, Philosophy and Rhetoric, University of Copenhagen.

Huw Price is currently Professor of Logic and Metaphysics in the Department of Philosophy at the University of Edinburgh. He also has a continuing association with the University of Sydney, where he holds a Personal Chair in Natural Metaphysics in the Department of Philosophy.

Frank Arntzenius is Professor of Philosophy at Rutgers University.

Tim Maudlin is Professor of Philosophy at Rutgers University.

Carol Hoefer is Senior Lecturer in Philosophy at the London School of Economics.

Quentin Smith is Professor of Philosophy at the University of Western Michigan.

Heather Dyke is Lecturer at the Department of Philosophy, University of Otago.

Philip Percival is Lecturer at the Department of Philosophy, University of Glasgow.

Nathan Oaklander is Professor of Philosophy, University of Michigan-Flint.

Robin LePoidevin is Professor of Philosophy at The University of Leeds.

Simon Saunders is Lecturer in Philosophy of Science at the University of Oxford. He is a Fellow of Linacre College and a Member of the Philosophy and Physics Faculties.

Steve Savitt is Professor of Philosophy at The University of Georgia.

Yuri Balashov is Assistant Professor of Philosophy at the University of Georgia.

Mauro Dorato is Associate Professor for the Philosophy of Science.

Richard Healey is Professor of Philosophy at the University of Arizona.

Jenann Ismael is Assistant Professor of Philosophy at the University of Arizona.

When Time Gets Off Track

JAN FAYE

I

Over the last forty years, philosophers have argued back and forth about backward causation. It requires a certain structure of time for something as backward causation to be not only possible but also to take place in the real world. In case temporal becoming is an objective feature of the world in the sense that the future is unreal, or at least ontologically indeterminate, it is impossible to see how backward causation can arise. The same difficulty does not hold with respect to forward causation. For even though it is assumed according to one dynamic view of time, the instant view or presentism, that merely present events exist—and past events therefore are no longer real or have become ontologically indeterminate—such a view can still maintain that past events once were there to cause present events. Future events, however, are still to come, and being indeterminate or nothing at all, they cannot cause any events in the present. In other words, causation backwards in time can occur only if we think of time as static; that is, no objective becoming exists, and the world consists of tenselessly occurring future events that exist in the same sense as past and present events. Backward causation requires the so-called full view, or possibly the half-full view, of time.

It has been argued that another dynamic theory of time may allow for the logical possibility of backward causation. In his *Time and Reality* (1995) Mauro Dorato says that the empty view of the future, the position taking both past and present events to be real and ontologically determinate in contrast to future events, may be consistent with backward causation. It could respond to the fact that no traces of the future have been discovered by claiming that this empirically proves the future to be empty. Against such an argument one might still want to hold that the empty view as a dynamic view of objective becoming does not logically open up for the existence of future events. The lack of future traces thus could not be used as an empirical proof of objective becoming. In other words, the reality of the future is to my mind necessary for backward causation to take place, but this does not mean that the reality of future events would suffice for future events to be causes of present events. The future may be real but not processes going back in time.

1

I think that causality is first and foremost a common-sense notion which has no 'natural' physical interpretation. Thus, one may attempt to associate it with different physical notions of processes. Four different suggestions have been put forward: (i) the causal link can be identified with the transference of energy; (ii) it can be identified with the conservation of physical quantities like charge, linear, and angular momentum; (iii) it can be identified with inter-action of forces; or (iv) it can be identified with the microscopic notion of interaction. But it appears with respect to all four sugges-tions that they involve descriptions that are invariant under the time reversal operation.

No empirical evidence seriously indicates processes going back-wards in time. This does not, however, exclude an inquiry into the physical nature of such processes—whether they exist or not. Today, physicists do not regard the positron-electron creation and annihilation as an electron going back and forth in time, a sugges-tion which Richard Feynman once forwarded as a possible interpre-tation of the positron. The Bell type experiments have by some been interpreted as if quantum events could be connected in such a way that the past light cone might be accessible under non-local interaction—not only in the sense of action at a distance but even as backward causation. But these experiments could be interpreted in many other ways, and as long as we do not have positive results of *post factum* experiments, that is, a type of experiment where the effect depends on something that happens later, little can be said in favour of causal processes going backwards in time.

What is common to most of the discussions concerning possible physical cases of backward causation is that the processes in ques-tion are thought to be quite similar to those going forward in time. In fact, it is nearly always taken for granted that the difference between forward and backward causal processes has something to do with a difference between their boundary conditions due to their time reversal symmetry, and that the overwhelming number of forward causal processes—with respect to backward causal processes—depend on an unequal distribution and realization of these boundary conditions.

Recently, Huw Price has in his *Time's Arrow and Archimedes' Point* (1996) strongly advocated such a view based on the agency theory of causation. He suggests that the causal asymmetry is an anthropocentric matter; in nature we do not meet such an asymmetry. Says Price: 'I shall be presenting the agency account of causal asymmetry as a more sophisticated version of Hume's con-ventionalist strategy. I shall argue that that it is our de facto temporal orientation as agents that requires that we choose the relevant conventions as we do.' (p. 158)

I shall challenge such an understanding of advanced action in terms of a temporal symmetry of causal processes by claiming that such a view leads to an inconsistency. I think Price is wrong; we observe many sequences in nature which are time asymmetric and which can be described completely non-anthropocentrically. Price has turned the whole argument upside down: manipulation does not conventionally define a causal asymmetry, it provides us with *knowledge* of a causal orientation. He may not believe in precognition, but the fact is that we could discover it quite easily by manipulation. For the sake of the argument, think of a person who is always capable of saying in advance what will be the result of a randomly selected card drawn from a deck of cards. If such a situation really took place, I am sure that even he would agree that the later selection of a card is the cause of the previous prediction regardless of his conventionalist strategy. I shall, contrary to Price, argue that the causal orientation exists objectively independent of any human agent.

Furthermore, my claim suggests that our idea of such an objective causal direction can be identified within modern physics. I shall propose an approach to defining *retarded* actions in terms of positive mass and positive energy as well as *advanced* actions in terms of negative mass and negative energy—a view taking causal processes to be asymmetric in time. According to such an alternative understanding, particles which could possibly manifest themselves as going backwards in time would belong to a different category than those which actually travel forward in time.

Not until the beginning of the twentieth century did it make sense to imagine something as having a negative energy density or negative mass. First the theory of relativity, and later quantum mechanics, opened up for the theoretical possibility that mass and/or energy could exist in two opposite forms very much as other physical attributes such as the electric charge. Little attention, however, has been paid to how negative mass and energy can be understood in relation to positive mass and energy, and whether the possible existence of negative mass and energy would have any influence on our view on time and cosmology. Even today a basic philosophical understanding of negative mass and energy is still missing.

In modern physics we find two theoretical indications of negative mass and/or energy: (i) the solutions of the four-momentum vector do have both positive and negative values; and (ii) the zero-point energy of the quantum vacuum fluctuates: according to Heisenberg's indeterminacy principle, the energy density of a field must fluctuate randomly around the zero-point energy. Some indirect effects of these fluctuations have in fact been observed, namely the Casimir effect and the squeezed vacuum state, both phenomena are explained in terms of negative energy.

II

What, then, is the basic challenge? I take it to be this: On the one hand, our everyday concept of causality is such that causes are considered to be causally prior to their effects; on the other hand, the most fundamental processes of physics are time reversal invariant. How should we face this dichotomy? The standard interpretation attempts to solve the dilemma by claiming that the causal direction of reversible processes is not objective. But the consequences drawn by the claim vary. The observed direction is said to depend on (i) the statistics of *de facto* irreversible processes or on (ii) a psychological projection of an orientation into the observation of these processes based on our experience of human action. How can we prove that the standard interpretation involves an inconsistency and that it arises because of the objectivity of the causal direction?

To address this question, we must consider which conditions one must meet in order to call the causal direction for objective. I take the claim of objectivity to be about empirical knowledge and therefore its justification must be based on experience and experiments. This claim is very much in line with Ian Hacking's pragmatic view that atomic particles are real if we can manipulate them. Moreover, I take the conditions of objectivity to be fulfilled if the order of the experimental outcomes is identical with respect to different observers having an opposite time sense. So in order to establish the objectivity of the causal direction in time, I shall investigate the results of a series of toy experiments.

Before we turn to these experiments, I want to clarify some further assumptions which I think are uncontroversial in the sense that they are acceptable even by the advocates of the standard interpretation.

First, we must distinguish between *process tokens* and *process types*. In the past much ambivalence and sloppy reasoning have resulted from the fact that no clear distinction was made between various descriptions of a process which is numerically the same, and of processes which were merely qualitatively identical with one another.

Second, we must distinguish between a *passive* time reversal operation and an *active* time reversal operation. The difference is that the passive transformation is one in which the same system is described by using the opposite coordinates, whereas the active transformation involves some physical translation, or rotation, of the system itself.

Third, we should also, as a consequence of the above distinctions, realize that the *passive* time reversal operation applies to process *tokens* by referring to the numerically same process with respect to two opposite time senses, but that the *active* time reversal operation applies to process *types* by referring to two numerically different tokens both belonging to the same kind.

Let us with these assumptions in mind set up the toy experiments. Imagine two boxes, Box 1 and Box 2 facing each other, both containing a shutter through which a particle can pass. At the beginning of each run of the experiment, one of the boxes contains a particle, but we do not know whether it is Box 1 which acts as the emitter and Box 2 as the receiver, or vice versa. Assume, too, that the particle is always placed in the same box—never in the other—but that we are not told which one. It is now our job to find out whether the particle goes from Box 1 to Box 2, or from Box 2 to Box I.

Take A to be the event that a particle is leaving or entering Box 1, i.e., A is a change taking place in Box 1, and take B to be the event that the particle is leaving or entering Box 2, i.e., B is a change taking place in Box 2. If no such activity occurs in the respective boxes irrespectively of whether they are open or closed, we shall call it $\bar{A}$ and $\bar{B}$. We can find out whether a particle has left or entered a box by weighing the box because of the loss or gain of the particle's energy E, therefore whether A or B corresponds with a decrease or an increase of energy.

Do we have some common sense criteria which reveal in which direction the particles are travelling? If so, are these criteria objective in the sense that even an observer of the opposite time sense can rely on the same criteria? The answer seems to be yes. We would say that A is the cause of B whenever:

(i) A happens even if Box 2 is closed,
(ii) B does not happen unless Box 1 is open,
(iii) $\bar{A}$ happens if and only if Box 1 is closed,
(iv) $\bar{B}$ may happen even if Box 2 is open.

5

Jan Faye

I hold that if our observations meet these criteria we have acquired knowledge of a causal direction between As and Bs.

Now, consider the assumption that the particles move from Box 1 to Box 2. To test this hypothesis we must run a series of four experiments in which we vary between opening and closing the shutters. By doing this we get four different combinations: (1) closed, closed; (2) open, open, (3) closed, open; and (4) open, closed. As shown in figure 1 we would experience four sets of events in these four cases $(\bar{A}, \bar{B})$; (A, B); $(\bar{A}, \bar{B})$; and $(A, \bar{B})$;

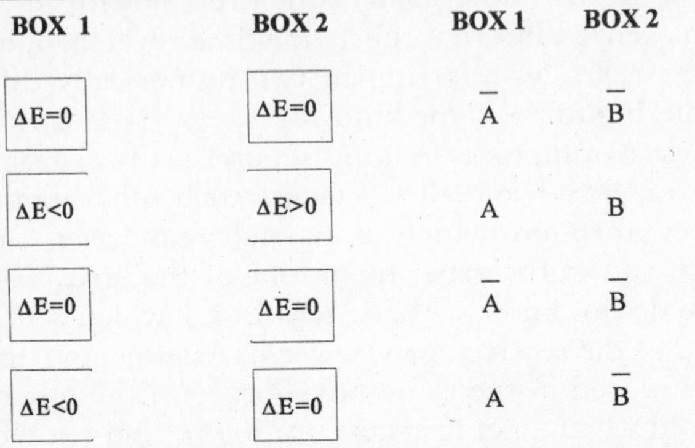

BOX 1	BOX 2	BOX 1	BOX 2
$\Delta E=0$	$\Delta E=0$	$\bar{A}$	$\bar{B}$
$\Delta E<0$	$\Delta E>0$	A	B
$\Delta E=0$	$\Delta E=0$	$\bar{A}$	$\bar{B}$
$\Delta E<0$	$\Delta E=0$	A	$\bar{B}$

Figure 1. A causes B (The normal oberver).

From this we can conclude that particles do in fact move from Box 1 to Box 2. The reason is that we have two As but only one B, and that one $\bar{B}$ appears even though Box 2 is open and Box 1 is closed; whereas one A appears when Box 1 is open and Box 2 is closed. In my opinion it is a series of experiments like these which justify our belief in the particles moving from Box 1 to Box 2.

In addition, we may notice that the cause A seems to coincide with a decrease of energy while the effect B seems to coincide with an increase of energy. Perhaps we could identify causation in physics with propagation of energy? We shall soon return to this point.

III

In the mean time we must find out whether our beliefs of the causal direction is about objective matters or not. We shall investigate how an observer with the opposite time sense of ours (a counter observer) would describe the situation. As I said, there are two very different ways of understanding time reversal invariant, and I shall argue that it is *only the passive operation which corresponds with a description according to the observer with the opposite view of time.*

One way of understanding time reversal invariant is as an *active* transformation of the original process under consideration so the particles now move from Box 2 to Box 1. The active time reversal operation is illustrated in figure 2.

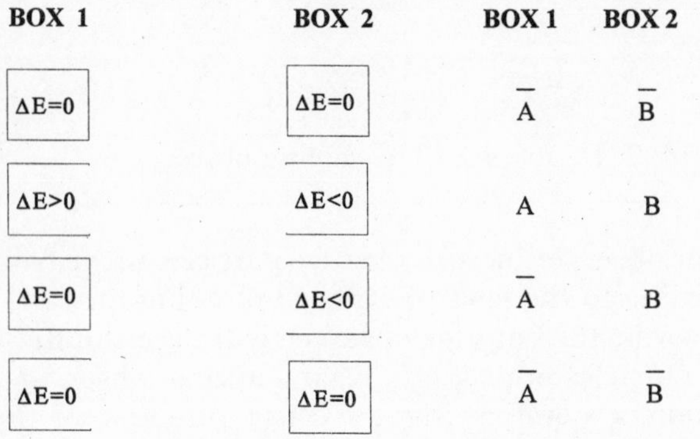

BOX 1	BOX 2	BOX 1	BOX 2
ΔE=0	ΔE=0	$\bar{A}$	$\bar{B}$
ΔE>0	ΔE<0	A	B
ΔE=0	ΔE<0	$\bar{A}$	B
ΔE=0	ΔE=0	$\bar{A}$	$\bar{B}$

Figure 2. B causes A (The normal observer)

Here the situation is such that *B* is now the cause of *A* based on exactly the same reasoning as before, and *B* can also be, or so it seems, identified with a loss of energy and *A* with a gain of energy. The problem for the standard interpretation is that this description does not give us the opposite description of the *same tokens* according to a different time sense. It presents rather a description of different tokens with respect to the same time sense as ours.

Thus, the second way of understanding time reversal invariant is as a *passive* transformation of the original process in question. So what gives us the description of the opposite time sense is the passive time reversal operation with respect to the same tokens. Figure 3 shows how the standard interpretation will describe the situation.

The counter observer with the opposite time sense will see *B* as a loss of energy and *A* as the gain of energy. Hence it seems as if Box 1 is now acting as the receiver and Box 2 as the emitter. This is similar to the situation where we noticed the active time reversal operation described (apart from the fact that Box 1 will now receive a particle, not from Box 2, but from the environment or the infinity). Thus the standard interpretation draws the following conclusion

BOX 1	BOX 2	BOX 1	BOX 2
$\Delta E = 0$	$\Delta E = 0$	$\overline{A}$	$\overline{B}$
$\Delta E > 0$	$\Delta E < 0$	A	B
$\Delta E = 0$	$\Delta E = 0$	$\overline{A}$	$\overline{B}$
$\Delta E > 0$	$\Delta E = 0$	A	$\overline{B}$

Figure 3. B causes A (The counter observer)

about the counter observer: he will observe particles move from Box 2 to Box 1 according to the laws of nature but going forward in his time. In other words, the counter observer will describe the causal direction of the particles opposite to what a normal observer would do. The conclusion is therefore that the causal direction of the very same tokens cannot be objective.

I believe, nonetheless, that this analysis is flawed. The experiment provides the counter observer with no criteria for making such a judgement. He will face a situation where Box 2 is open but no changes take place in this box unless Box 1 is open; whereas Box 1 may be open and still undergo a change without Box 2 being open. How then can the counter observer claim that Box 2 is the emitter? He cannot! In my opinion even the counter observer must admit that the causal direction is objective because he will ascribe the process with the same orientation as the normal observer. He will, like the normal observer, observe *two As* in Box 1 and only *one B* in Box 2. Furthermore, he will realize that even though Box 2 is open, it is not always the case that a change happens (no loss of energy) in that box. A change happens in Box 2 only if Box 1 is open; but in Box 1, if it is open, a change happens regardless of whether or not a change happens in Box 2; that is, regardless of whether Box 2 is open or not. But this combination of events *formed the exact criteria* that the normal observer used to reason that the particles were moving from Box 1 to Box 2. So the counter observer will see the same experimental pattern as the normal observer, and, by using the same criteria, reach the same conclusion as the normal observer about the direction of the process. We can therefore conclude that the particles move *objectively* from Box 1 to Box 2. According to the counter observer, however, the propagation is oriented backwards in his time as opposed to forward in time for a normal observer.

Apart from the temporal orientation, the normal observer and the counter observer will also differ with respect to the ascription of physical properties to the particles. We should be aware of the fact that the theory of relativity yields two solutions of the four-momentum vector with respect to energy: (i) positive energy solutions, and (ii) negative energy solutions. As a consequence, Feynman's propagator formalism usually integrates over all positive energies into the future and over all negative energies into the past. These different solutions can easily be understood as the time sense reversed description of one and the same particle. Feynman himself suggested, based on this formalism, that a positron could be interpreted as a negative energy electron going backwards in time. As the above thought experiment shows this is a false idea. Nothing of relevance is changed in the experiment if one replaces the particles with positrons or any other kind of anti-particles. Instead we should think of the positive energy solutions as how the normal observer will describe a *retarded* particle (the usual common particles or their anti-particles) and of the negative energy solutions as how the counter observer will describe such a retarded particle. (As illustrated in figure 4 and 5.)

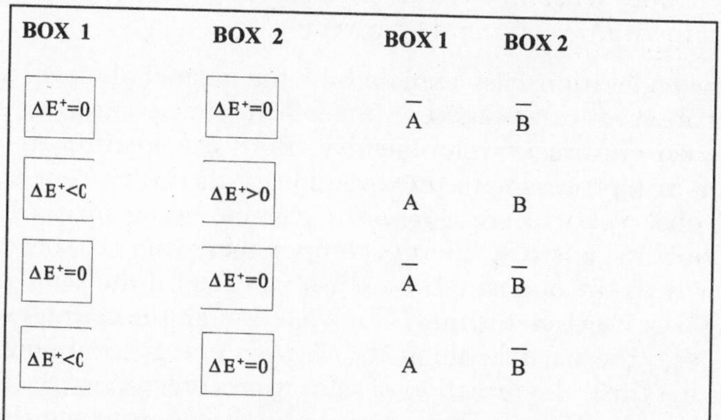

BOX 1	BOX 2	BOX 1	BOX 2
$\Delta E^+ = 0$	$\Delta E^+ = 0$	$\bar{A}$	$\bar{B}$
$\Delta E^+ < 0$	$\Delta E^+ > 0$	A	B
$\Delta E^+ = 0$	$\Delta E^+ = 0$	$\bar{A}$	$\bar{B}$
$\Delta E^+ < 0$	$\Delta E^+ = 0$	A	$\bar{B}$

Figure 4. A causes B (The normal observer)

The objective interpretation connects energy and the time reversal operations in the following way:

(a) The *passive* time reversal operation turns a *positive* energy particle with *positive mass* into a *negative* energy particle with *negative mass*, or vice versa, by viewing the *same* process token from the *opposite* frame of time sense.

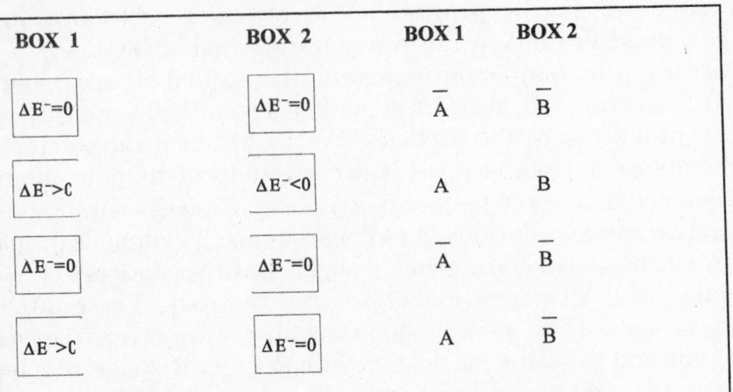

BOX 1	BOX 2	BOX 1	BOX 2
$\Delta E^-=0$	$\Delta E^-=0$	$\overline{A}$	$\overline{B}$
$\Delta E^->C$	$\Delta E^-<0$	A	B
$\Delta E^-=0$	$\Delta E^-=0$	$\overline{A}$	$\overline{B}$
$\Delta E^->C$	$\Delta E^-=0$	A	$\overline{B}$

Figure 5. A causes B (The counter observer)

(b) The *active* time reversal operation turns a *positive* energy particle with *positive mass* into a *positive* energy particle with *positive mass* (or a negative into a negative) by providing a description of *another* process token seen from the *same* frame of time sense in virtue of reversing the particle's three momentum vector and spin vector.

These two operations also explain how the normal observer and the counter observer can—based on their different perspectives—agree that the causal direction is objective. Both can identify the causal direction of a process with the direction of its positive energy. So a normal observer will see a *retarded* particle going forward in her time along its positive energy component, whereas the counter observer with the opposite time sense will regard the same particle as going backwards in his time. For even though the counter observer will 'see' the particle along its *negative* energy component forward in his time, the direction of causation coincides with the *positive* energies backwards in his time—the direction which the common criteria point out *is* the causal direction.

IV

I want to make some further comments on the interpretation of the above experiment and on backward causation in general.

First of all, the sceptic may, as Lars-Göran Johansson has pointed out to me, raise the following objection: it seems to me that your criteria rest on a false assumption which invalidates your conclusion. Think of a photon instead of a particle with a rest mass. According to the toy experiment a photon may leave Box 1 even if it is not absorbed by Box 2. That means that there must be some environment functioning as absorber. This environment can just as well emit a photon. Hence, a photon may very well be absorbed in Box 2 even if Box 1 is closed; that is, we may have an event B without an A. So the above conditions (i) and (ii) are incompatible in the settings of current physical theory. But this is devastating for your argument, since the asymmetry between cause and effect in your model now build upon the assumption that the effect, viz. the absorption of energy (in the normal case), may occur even though the 'cause', viz. the emission of energy from Box 1, has not occurred, whereas the cause, the emission of energy, cannot occur without the effect. If this asymmetry is dismissed, you have no ground, in your model, to tell what is cause and what is effect, independently of the time ordering.

Now, the sceptic may continue his criticism by saying: you could, indeed, add as an explicit criterion for the entire experiment that the environment is a perfect black body; however, would such a response not undermine your argument, too? For there are not real perfect black bodies, and so this model cannot even be used as a thought experiment showing the possibility for an objective time ordering.

How can this sceptical challenge be met? One should be aware of a couple of things. The sceptic is not presenting a case based on the original tokens. The case where Box 1 is closed and Box 2 is open but receives a photon from the environment is different from the original case in which Box 1 was closed and Box 2 open but did not receive a particle. We can also in the latter case find out whether Box 2 is absorbing or emitting a photon by looking for the gain or the lost of weight. So what the sceptical objection amounts to is a request for an explanation of how the following series of event tokens can be excluded: $(\bar{A}, \bar{B})$; (A, B); $(\bar{A}, B)$ and $(\bar{A}, B)$. For if the toy experiment produces such a series of events, we will not be able to use the above criteria to find the causal order.

A solution is, I think, within our range. Although it is possible that Box 1 may be closed and Box 2 is open but nevertheless receive a photon, it may not be as likely a situation as the case where Box 2 receives no photon. We can solve the problem by imagining (a combination of) three possibilities:

1. We may think of the environment as a black-body. But, again, there are no perfect black-body absorbers.

2. We can argue that the experiment has been designed so that probability of Box 2 containing a photon depends on whether Box 1 is open or closed. With respect to Box 2 we have: P(photon in box 2 | box 1 is open) ≫ P(photon in box 2 | box 1 is closed), whereas with respect to Box 1 we have: P(photon in box 1 | box 2 is open) = P(photon in box 1 | box 2 is closed). We have not thereby excluded that the environment could emit a photon which appears in Box 2 even though Box 1 is closed.

3. Run the experiment within four time intervals ΔT_n, n = 1,2,3, 4, during which one or two boxes will be open (if they are going to be open) and be weighed. The length of the intervals will be around $2\, l/c$, long enough for a photon to travel back and forth between the two boxes, but short enough for any photon from the environment to play an active role in the experiment, that is, its probability would be very low.

The sceptic will most certainly reply that such a response misses the point. The core idea of the proposed refinement is to claim that probabilities for emission and absorption depend on earlier events but not on later events. This is problematic when talking about photons, i.e., electromagnetic quanta. Let us look at the world from the point of view of the photon for a while. As it travels with the speed of light, all distances are reduced to zero which means that in a sense a photon is present everywhere at each moment of time. That is another way of saying that the environment must be taken into account as absorber or emitter when only one box is open. In this context an important feature of quantum field theory is that the probability for excitation of an atom at one point starts increasing at the very same moment a quantum is emitted from another atom at another place, independently of their distance. (See G. Hegerfeldt (1994)). The fatal consequence for my argument being applied to photons seems to be that the situation becomes symmetric in excitation/deexcitation so that the probability for a photon being present in Box 1 is not independent of the opening/non-opening of Box 2. In short, one runs into trouble by assuming a particle view of photons.

But, as we have seen, it is not really necessary to use photons. We have considered particles with rest mass and my argument certainly goes through. This raises, however, an interesting problem. For if we regard photons as particles, we arrive at a very different conclusion about the asymmetry of emission and absorption than we do when taking particles with rest mass into account. What does this mean? Is my argument and the common understanding of quantum field theory consistent with one another? This is still something to consider.

I think there is no problem here. It might very well be that the environment can act as emitter of photons and therefore that one photon may occur in Box 2 even though Box 1 is closed. But one has to remember that by observing the thought experiment both the normal observer and the counter observer see the same token processes which means that if the counter observer watches that a change takes place in Box 2, in spite of the fact that Box 1 is closed, so will the normal observer. An unwanted situation like this may be avoided by a long series of experiments or by increasing the number of the photons to work with a beam instead of single photons at a time. It seems after all possible to establish the suggested asymmetry of emission and absorption between Box 1 and Box 2.

A second objection may be raised against my notion of an active transformation by not accepting the expression: 'the active transformation involves some physical translation or rotation of the system itself.' Here I seem to speak of translations and rotations in physical space, but what has that to do with time reversals?

The passive time transformation is 'one in which the same system is described by using the opposite coordinates.' This applies to the time reversal operator utilized in quantum mechanics. My interpretation of this operation seems to rest on a confusion of two things: the change of time coordinates is a change of representation of the time relations 'before' and 'after', not an exchange of before and after. Normally we represent the times of events in such a way that if the event a occurs before event b, the time of a is represented by a smaller number than the time of b. Time reversal is reversal of this convention: later times are represented by smaller numbers. (the time relation ... earlier than ... is represented by the numerical relation ...>...) It is not a reversal of the real ordering before-after, or of the perception of the real ordering of events. It could not possibly be because in a mathematical theory one must represent everything 'real' with mathematical entities such as numbers and functions and no operation on these entities can by itself, i.e., without further interpretative assumptions, be taken to represent something extra-mathematical such as a real change of time direction.

I do not believe, however, that I conflate two things when talking about time reversal: It has been argued by many philosophers and scientists that the time reversal of mechanical processes should be understood as if the planets suddenly changed their momentum in the opposite direction around the sun. This is what I mean by the active transformation. I don't think that the example says anything

Jan Faye

about time reversal. It represents, as I pointed out long ago, a case of motion reversal by involving two different tokens of the same process type and the illustration with the planets rests on the ambiguity between types and tokens.

When it comes to the passive transformation, it is correct to distinguish the difference between the exchange of representation of a system and what can be called the exchange of before and after. In fact, this is what I am trying to argue when I claim that the causal direction of the process token is objective with respect to observers with opposite time. We have therefore two questions to answer: (i) Is the reversal of time merely a subjective convention? And if it isn't, what then does it represent?

What I want to say is this: One may exchange the temporal representation of the system by changing the mathematical representation of the time relations 'before' and 'after'. Nonetheless, a philosopher like Price takes this to mean that the physical laws themselves are time symmetric. It is only the distribution of boundary conditions which makes a temporal asymmetry between before and after.

Contrary to this view, I believe that the opposite mathematical representations should be interpreted as if they were descriptions made by observers moving opposite one another in time. If one wants the representation to reflect how observers with opposite time senses will represent the time reversed situation, one also needs to change the sign of energy as a reflection of their different observations. But this is not a real change of before and after because, in my vocabulary, the causal direction is objective by being constituted by the positive energy component.

Some people may have difficulties in understanding what is meant by saying that time goes backwards, entirely or for a particular person. Would a person with a reversed sense of time die before he is born? What is then meant by the terms 'dying' and 'being born'? Would such a person remember what will happen tomorrow but not what he had for breakfast the very same morning? And would he say that he remembers the future, or would he say: 'I, as everybody else, can only remember what has passed. It is only that what I call the past, you call the future?' Surely, the issue is not about what words we use!

I think that some of these questions reflect real difficulties in our understanding of what a person with a differing time sense means: but I also think that they are based on our common ways of seeing things. A counter observer will, of course, see his life as we experience ours. He will see himself grow older and eventually die. But a

14

normal observer (as we are) will certainly 'observe' such a person becoming younger and eventually being born.

One may also question the proposal of seeing causation in physics as something that has to do with energy transference. Against the idea of identifying the causal direction of a physical system with the flow of positive energy through time, I have been confronted with two objections that I shall address here.

Phil Dowe has argued that in a static world in which a physical system S contains the same amount of positive energy at t_1 and t_2— say, S is a single particle which is represented by a straight world-line—no information about the energy can tell us whether t_1 or t_2 is later than the other, and *ipso facto* it makes no sense to talk about the flow of energy from t_1 to t_2. I think the point is well taken. Apparently to say that the same amount of energy in the system S is propagating from t_1 to t_2 also requires a dynamic flow of becoming. I even think that the objection can be phrased in more general terms. As long as we describe the energy from the *internal* perspective of S itself, and no redistribution of energy takes place within S, we cannot point to what may determine the transference of energy from t_1 to t_2, because the fact that the energy is the same at two different moments does not involve any direction.

I take, however, the right response to be this: the positive energy merely endures between t_1 and t_2, hence no causal changes take place during this interval. From its own perspective S does not experience any lapse of time, t_1 will be identical with t_2, and therefore it will not causally move between t_1 and t_2. Thus, a physical system—or the entire world for that matter—described from its own internal perspective exists timelessly unless its energy is redistributed within itself. But from an *external* perspective of S, as soon as S occupies two different places, x_1 and x_2, at t_1 and t_2 we have a transference of energy. Assume that we find that at t_1 the energy is positive in x_1 and zero in x_2, and that at t_2 the situation is reversed, then we know that a transference of positive energy took place between t_1 and t_2, and by using the above experiments we can get to know in which direction this flow happens; that is, from t_1 to t_2, or vice versa.

Another objection is due to Huw Price. One may, he says, refuse to accept the above interpretation by arguing that the sign of energy merely builds on a convention. How can the direction of causation be identical with the direction of positive energy in case we can replace a positive description with a negative one? We merely call positive energy negative and negative energy positive. Indeed we might. But this linguistic fact does not suffice to refute the interpretation suggested. It can be compared to the choice we can make between various geometries for the description of the physical space. Such a selection is also based on a convention. But when the convention first has been established, we must stick to the choice we once made. Let me remind you of Carnap's remarks about the conventionalist view concerning the choice of geometries. As he points out: 'Because Poincaré said the choice was a matter of convention, his view became known as the conventionalist view. In my opinion, Poincaré meant that the choice was made by the physicist *before* he decided which method to use for measuring length. After making the choice, he would then *adjust* his method of measurement so that it would lead to the type of geometry he had chosen. Once a method of measurement is accepted, the question of the structure of space becomes an empirical question, to be settled by observation.' (p. 160) This is precisely to say what the identification of the causal direction with the propagation of positive energy is all about.

Finally, we are now in a position to grasp how a notion of backward causation should be accommodated into physics. Since positive mass and positive energy states forward in time can be identified with the causal direction of processes forward in time, it means that positive mass and positive energy states backwards in time can be associated with processes propagating backwards in time. A counter observer will, according to his time sense, *see* such processes of *advanced* particles moving forward in his time. If a normal observer were going to see such processes of advanced particles, they would *appear* to her as having negative masses and as a series of negative energy states succeeding one another forward in her time. In spite of this the normal observer is forced by the choice of convention to admit that the advanced particles really go backwards in her time through their positive energy states.

In my opinion whether backward causal processes exist or not is an objective question which in principle can be settled by experiments. It is neither a matter of convention, nor is it a matter of subjective projections, or even a matter of the violation of *de facto* irreversibility like entropy and expanding outgoing waves. The existence of backward causation will prove itself, I suggest, whenever we observe a violation of the conservation of energy. Only then do we see time gets off track.

Acknowledgement: I wish to thank Mauro Dorato and Lars-Göran Johansson for their critical comments and suggestions to an earlier version of this paper.

References

Carnap, Rudolf 1966. *Philosophical Foundations of Physics*. New York, London: Basic Books.

Dorato, Mauro 1995. *Time and Reality*, Bologna: Clueb.

—— 1998. 'Becoming and the Arrow of Causation' (unpubl.)

Faye, Jan 1989. *The reality of the future*. Odense: Odense University Press.

—— 1997a. 'Is the Mark Method Time Dependent?', in Jan Faye, Uwe Scheffler & Max Urchs (eds) *Perspectives on Time. Boston Studies in the Philosophy of Science,* **189**, Dordrecht: Kluwer, 215–36.

—— 1997b. 'Causation, Reversibility and the Direction of Time', in Jan Faye, Uwe Scheffler and Max Urchs (eds) *Perspectives on Time*, 237–66.

Hegerfeldt, G. 1994a. 'Causality Problems for Fermi's Two-atom System', *Phys. Rev. lett.* **72**, no. 5, 596–99.

—— 1994b. 'Remark on Causality and Particle Localization.' *Phys. Rev. D,* **10**, no. 10, 3320–21.

Price, Huw 1996. *Time's Arrow and Archimedes' Point*. Oxford: Oxford University Press.

Burbury's Last Case: The Mystery of the Entropic Arrow

HUW PRICE

Does not the theory of a general tendency of entropy to diminish [sic[1]] take too much for granted? To a certain extent it is supported by experimental evidence. We must accept such evidence as far as it goes and no further. We have no right to supplement it by a large draft of the scientific imagination. (Burbury 1904, 49)

1. Introduction

Samuel Hawksley Burbury (1831–1911) was an English barrister and mathematician, who favoured the latter profession as loss of hearing increasingly curtailed the former. The Bar's loss was Science's gain, for Burbury played a significant and perhaps still under-rated part in discussions in the 1890s and 1900s about the nature and origins of the Second Law of Thermodynamics. One commentator of the time, reviewing Burbury's *The Kinetic Theory of Gases* for *Science* in 1899, describes his role in these terms:

> [I]n that very interesting discussion of the Kinetic Theory which was begun at the Oxford meeting of the British Association in 1894 and continued for months afterwards in *Nature,* Mr. Burbury took a conspicuous part, appearing as the expounder and defender of Boltzmann's H-theorem in answer to the question which so many [had] asked in secret, and which Mr Culverwell asked in print, *'What is the H-theorem and what does it prove?'* Thanks to this discussion, and to the more recent publication of Boltzmann's *Vorlesungen über Gas-theorie,* and finally to this treatise by Burbury, the question is not so difficult to answer as it was a few years ago. (Hall 1899, 685)

In my view, however, it is at best half-right to describe Burbury as a defender of the H-Theorem. In some respects, he was the leading advocate for the prosecution. The crucial issue arising from Culverwell's (1890a, 1890b, 1894) enquiry was the source of the

---

[1] By 'entropy' here, Burbury seems to mean the quantity H of H-Theorem fame, which diminishes as a gas approaches equilibrium.

time-asymmetry of the H-Theorem, and while Burbury put his finger on the argument's time-asymmetric premise, he himself fingered it—in true forensic spirit—as an object of considerable suspicion. A decade later, as the quotation with which we began indicates, he still wasn't convinced that we are *entitled* to assume it; and in their important survey article of 1912, Ehrenfest and Ehrenfest note his continuing dissent on the matter (1959, 42; 95, n. 168). Indeed, in reading Burbury's work from the late 1890s and 1900s, one gets the sense that the issue of the basis and justification of the Second Law remained *the* great intellectual puzzle of his later life.

Later in the paper I want to return to Burbury's contribution to the debate of the 1890s. I want to endorse his scepticism about our present entitlement to assume that entropy will continue to increase, and I want to show that in one important respect, his contribution to the debate has been systematically misunderstood. (In uncovering this misunderstanding, I shall argue, we undermine one widespread conception of what it would take to account for the Second Law.)

However, the main task of the paper is to call attention to two kinds of objection to some well-known strategies for explaining the temporal asymmetry of thermodynamics. Neither of these objections is particularly novel, but I think that despite the long history of the problem, neither has received the prominence it deserves. As a result, in my view, the strategies concerned continue to enjoy more popularity than they merit.

In a more constructive vein, I want to locate the strategies I am criticizing within a kind of taxonomy of possible approaches to the problem of the thermodynamic asymmetry. In this way, I want to suggest that they are mistaken not only for the reasons identified by the two objections in question, but also for a more basic reason. In effect, they are trying to answer the wrong question. This may sound doubly critical, but the double negative yields a positive—given that the proposed strategies don't work, it turns out to be good news that we don't need them to work, in order to understand the thermodynamic asymmetry. In this respect, the present paper deals with a topic I have examined in more detail in other recent work (Price 2002): the issue as to the precise nature of the time-asymmetric explanandum presented to us by thermodynamic phenomenon.

1.1 Origins of the problem
The time-asymmetry of thermodynamics is associated with the Second Law. According to this principle, non-equilibrium systems progress monotonically towards equilibrium. Temperature differ-

ences decrease, energy concentrations dissipate, and entropy increases monotonically until equilibrium is reached.

In the latter half of the nineteenth century, having recognized and described this tendency as a phenomenological principle, physics sought to explain it in statistical mechanical terms. The Second Law turned out to be different from more familiar laws of physics in at least two ways. First, it was probabilistic rather than strictly universal in nature—exceptions were possible, though very unlikely. Secondly, and more interestingly for our present purposes, it was time-asymmetric—the phenomena described by the Second Law showed a clear temporal preference. Late in the nineteenth century, and especially in the debate mentioned above, physics began to see that the latter fact is rather puzzling, in the light of the apparent time-symmetry of the laws of mechanics. How could symmetric underlying laws give rise to such a strikingly time-asymmetric range of phenomena as those described by the Second Law?

More than a century later, there is surprisingly little consensus as to how this question should be answered. Late in twentieth century, indeed, a leading authority on the conceptual foundations of statistical mechanics could still refer to the puzzle of the time-asymmetry of the Second Law as the elusive object of desire. (Sklar 1995) In my view, the fact that a solution has remained elusive rests in part on some confusion about what we are actually looking for. It is unusually difficult to be clear about what precisely needs to be explained about the time-asymmetry of the Second Law. There are several competing conceptions of what the problem is, with the result that proponents of rival approaches tend unwittingly to be talking at cross-purposes.

In order to try to clarify matters, I proceed as follows. I focus first on the nature of the time-asymmetric phenomena that are the source of the problem. Here, I think, a few simple remarks do a great deal to help us keep the true object of desire in view, and to avoid issues which are not directly relevant to the puzzle of time-asymmetry. I then distinguish two major competing approaches to the explanation of these time-asymmetric phenomena—two approaches which differ markedly in their conception of what needs to be done to solve the puzzle.

Despite their differences, the two approaches do agree about one part of the puzzle—they both hold that an important contributing factor to the observed thermodynamic time-asymmetry is that entropy was much lower in the past than it is now. However, where-as one approach argues that this asymmetric boundary condition is the *sole* time-asymmetric source of the observed asymmetry of thermodynamic phenomena, the other approach is committed to the existence of a *second* time-asymmetry—a time-asymmetric lawlike generalization. So far as I know, the distinction between these two approaches has not been drawn explicitly by other writers. Without it, it is not easy to appreciate the possibility that many familiar attempts to explain the time-asymmetry of thermodynamics might be not *mistaken* so much as *misconceived*—addressed to the wrong problem, in looking for time-asymmetry in the wrong place.

In my view, the 'two-asymmetry' approaches are misdirected in just this way. In looking for a basis for a time-asymmetric generalization, they are looking for something the explanation of the phenomena in question neither needs nor wants. However, my main aim is not to argue that these approaches address the problem of the thermodynamic asymmetry in the wrong terms, but to show that they don't succeed in addressing it in their own terms—they fail by their own lights. Specifically, I shall raise two objections to the two-asymmetry approach. Neither objection applies to all versions of this approach. However, I shall note two characteristics, one or other of which seems a feature of any version of the two-asymmetry view. Each characteristic leaves the view in question open to one of my two objections. My claim is thus that any version of the two-asymmetry approach is subject to at least one of the two objections. Some, as we shall see, are subject to both.

As I said, however, I take these negative conclusions to be good news for the project of trying to understand the thermodynamic asymmetry itself. For they bolster the case—already strong, in my view, on simplicity grounds—for taking the one-asymmetry view to provide the better conception of what actually needs to be explained.

2. Three Preliminary Clarifications

I begin with three preliminary remarks about the nature of thermodynamic time asymmetry. The purpose of these remarks is to 'frame' the relevant discussion, as I see it, and explicitly to set aside some issues I take not to be of immediate relevance. I am aware, of course, that these judgements of relevance themselves are not uncontroversial, and that some readers will feel that I am ignoring the interesting part of the subject. But in territory thick with the criss-crossed tracks of previous expeditions, it is useful to all parties to mark out one's own course as clearly as possible. What follows are three assumptions that I shall take for granted in the remainder of the paper.

2.1 Numerical asymmetry not practical reversibility

It is common to characterize the time-asymmetry of thermodynamic phenomena in terms of the irreversibility of the processes by which matter tends to thermodynamic equilibrium. However, the term 'irreversible' is ambiguous. In particular, some writers interpret it in a very practical sense. The time-asymmetry of thermodynamics is hence thought to be tied to the practical difficulty of 'reversing the motions' in real systems. (Ridderbos and Redhead 1998 appear to take this view, for example, focusing on the contrast between most ordinary systems and those involved in the so-called spin-echo experiments, which do permit reversal of motions, at least to an unusual degree.)

In my view, this focus on practical reversibility mislocates the important time-asymmetry of thermodynamic phenomena. Consider a parity analogy. In a world containing handed structures of a certain kind, we may distinguish two sorts of question: (i) Can a left-handed example of such a structure be 'reversed' into a right-handed version, and vice versa? (ii) Is there a numerical imbalance in nature between the number of left-handed and right-handed examples? These two questions are logically independent—one can easily imagine worlds with any of the four possible combinations of answers.

Similarly in the temporal case, I think. The issue of the practical reversibility of a time-oriented phenomenon is logically independent of that of the numerical imbalance in nature between examples of the phenomenon in question with the two possible temporal orientations. Clearly, our world shows a vast numerical imbalance of this kind, for the kind of phenomena described by the Second Law. It is this numerical imbalance that is the primary puzzle, in my view, not the issue of the practical reversibility of individual systems.

2.2 A monotonic entropy gradient, not an increase or decrease

When we say that entropy always *increases,* or that entropy change is always *non-negative,* we presuppose a convention as to which is to count as the 'positive' direction on the temporal axis. If we reverse this convention, an increase is redescribed as a decrease, a non-negative change as a non-positive change. In one rather uninteresting sense, this means that the Second Law is itself a conventional matter—in its standard formulations, it depends on a convention concerning the labelling of the temporal axis.

Some people may feel that they can make sense of the view that the choice of labelling is not merely conventional—that one or other labelling is objectively correct, and that time itself is objectively 'directed' in this way. The point I wish to emphasize is that these are separate issues from that of the thermodynamic asymmetry. In particular, the objectivity of the thermodynamic asymmetry does not depend on the view that time itself is objectively directed (whatever that might mean).

Indeed, the thermodynamic asymmetry is easily characterized in a way which avoids the conventional choice of labelling altogether. We simply need to say that the entropy gradients of non-equilibrium systems are all aligned in the same direction, leaving it unspecified (and a conventional matter) whether they all increase or all decrease. (By way of analogy, we might describe a universe containing nothing other than a single hand as objectively 'handed', while regarding it as a conventional matter whether it contains a left hand or a right hand.)

2.3 'Entropy' is inessential

One source of complexity in discussions of the Second Law is the existence a variety of competing definitions of entropy. In view of this complexity, it is helpful to keep in mind that if necessary, the puzzling time-asymmetry of thermodynamic phenomena can be characterized without using the notion of entropy—at least if we are prepared to tolerate some loss of generality. We can describe the puzzle by being more specific—by listing some of the actual kinds of physical phenomena that exhibit a temporal preference; that occur in nature with one temporal orientation, but not the other. Warm objects cool down rather than heat up in a tub of ice, pressurized gas flows out from but not into a bottle, so on. (In all these cases the description presupposes the ordinary temporal labelling, in the way noted in Section 2.1.)

The notion of entropy may turn out to provide a useful way of generalizing over this class of phenomena, but doing without it wouldn't deprive us of a way of talking about the temporal bias displayed by real systems—which, after all, is the real source of the puzzle. I shall continue to use the term in this paper, but take it to be merely a place-holder for more specific descriptions of the relevant properties of time-asymmetric thermodynamic systems.

3. Two Models of the Origin of the Thermodynamic Asymmetry

In this section I distinguish two different explanatory models for the thermodynamic asymmetry. In my view, insufficient attention to this distinction does a great deal to explain the striking lack of consensus about this topic—in particular, it explains the major respect in which various participants in the debate have been talking at cross purposes.

3.1 The two-asymmetry view

As noted above, the nineteenth century attempt to reduce thermodynamics to statistical mechanics led to two realizations about the Second Law: first, that it is probabilistic rather than strictly universal in nature; and second, that it is time-asymmetric. As a result, the Second Law is commonly seen as a time-asymmetric probabilistic generalization, with a lawlike or quasi-lawlike character—a general constraint on the behaviour of matter, preventing or at least discouraging (in a probabilistic sense) entropy from decreasing, in the ordinary time sense.

What does 'lawlike' mean in this context? This question deserves more attention than I can give it here, but for present purposes the crucial feature seems to be *projectibility*. At the very least, for two-asymmetry views, the Second Law retains the status of a time-asymmetric generalization *on which we are entitled to rely*, in forming expectations about the future behaviour of matter. (As we shall see, it cannot have this status for one-asymmetry views.)

The nomological character of two-asymmetry approaches sometimes also shows up as the view that matter has a certain time-asymmetric *property*, or *disposition*—that of being 'thermodynamic' rather than 'anti-thermodynamic'. Thus Richard Feynman, in comments attributed to 'Mr X' in discussion reproduced in (Gold 1963), refers to 'the assumption that matter is thermodynamically "one-sided", in the ordinary sense that it damps when you try to shake it.' (Gold 1963, 17) Here it is the *property* which is thought of as projectible—the time-asymmetric disposition to absorb heat, disperse energy, and the like.

According to this picture, then, a large part of the task of explaining the observed thermodynamic asymmetry is a matter of finding a basis for a time-asymmetric nomological generalization or disposition—finding something that 'makes' entropy increase towards the future, which 'makes' matter thermodynamic, in the above sense. Whatever this basis is, it needs to be time-asymmetric itself. Otherwise, the generalization would hold in both temporal directions, and entropy could only be constant. (Damping becomes anti-damping under time reversal, so matter that damped in both time directions would be incompatible with the existence of shakers.)

However, it is crucial to note that even a time-asymmetric nomological constraint of this kind would not give rise to the observed thermodynamic asymmetry unless entropy were initially lower than its maximum possible value—unless there were something around to do the shaking, in Feynman's example. Otherwise, the effect of the constraint would simply be to maintain a state of equilibrium, with no observable entropy gradient, and no asymmetry. So in order to explain the observed time-asymmetry, according to this conception of the Second Law, we actually need *two* time-asymmetric ingredients: the asymmetry nomological tendency or generalization, and an asymmetric boundary condition, to the effect that entropy is low at some point in the past (again, in the ordinary time sense).

Diagrammatically, the observed time-asymmetry thus arises as follows, according to the two-asymmetry view:

Asymmetric boundary condition—entropy low in the past
+ Asymmetric lawlike tendency—entropy *constrained* to increase

---

Observed asymmetry.

As we shall see, these two-asymmetry views share the need for the first component—the asymmetric boundary condition—with their 'one-asymmetry' rivals. Their distinguishing feature is thus the attempt to find a basis for the second component—for a nomological time-asymmetry. (In practice, this is often seen as very much the more important aspect of the problem.)

In my view, the search for such a time-asymmetric principle or property is both misconceived and unsuccessful. It is unsuccessful in the light of one or both of the two objections I want to raise below to different versions of this two-asymmetry approach to the explanation of the thermodynamic asymmetry. And it is misconceived because there is a preferable alternative view of the origins of the observed time-asymmetry of thermodynamic phenomena, which—because it does not involve a time-asymmetric generalization in the first place—simply does not face the problem of a basis or explanation for such a generalization.[2]

[2] In Price 2002 I call the two-asymmetry view that the 'causal-general' approach, and the one-asymmetry view the 'acausal-particular' approach.

3.2 The one-asymmetry view

We noted that a nomological time-asymmetry is at best half of what we need to explain the observed asymmetry of thermodynamic phenomena. A constraint preventing entropy from decreasing does not yield an asymmetry unless entropy is low to start with. This low entropy past boundary condition is the second of the two-asymmetry approach's two asymmetries.

The essence of the alternative approach is that this low entropy boundary condition is actually the only asymmetry we need. There need be no additional *time-asymmetric* generalization at work in nature (at least in its thermodynamic manifestations), in order to account for the observed phenomena. This one-asymmetry approach originates in the late 1870s, in Boltzmann's response to Loschmidt's 'reversibility objections'. In essence, I think—although he himself does not present it in these terms—what Boltzmann offers is an alternative to his own famous H-Theorem. The H-Theorem offers a dynamical argument that the entropy of a non-equilibrium system must increase over time, as a result of collisions between its constituent molecules. As Burbury made clear in the 1890s (see Section 7), the time-asymmetry of the argument stems from a time-asymmetric independence assumption. Roughly, it is assumed that the velocities of colliding particles are independent *before* they interact.

The statistical approach does away with this dynamical argument altogether. In its place it offers us a simple statistical consideration. In a natural measure on the space of possible microstates of a physical system, microstates which are such that the system approaches equilibrium over time vastly outnumber those in which it behaves in other way in the set of all microstates compatible with a give macrostate). In a sense, this is not so much an explanation for the behaviour of the system as a reason why no special explanation is necessary—a reason for thinking the behaviour unexceptional.

As Boltzmann himself notes (1877, 193), the statistical considerations involved in this argument are time-symmetric. For a system in a given non-equilibrium macrostate, most microstates compatible with that macrostate are such that the system equilibrates towards the past, as well as towards the future. In practice, of course, this is not our experience. The low entropy systems with which we are familiar typically arise from systems of even lower entropy in the past. For example, the temperature difference between a cup of tea and its environment arises from the greater temperature difference between the boiling kettle and its environment. Entropy seems to decrease towards the past, and Boltzmann's time-symmetric statistics render this behaviour exceptionally puzzling—in making it unsurprising that the tea cools down, they make it puzzling why there was ever such a concentration of heat in the first place.

Taken seriously, Boltzmann's statistical approach thus directs our attention to the fact that entropy was very low at some point in the past. This 'boundary condition' is time-asymmetric, as far as we know, but this is the only time-asymmetry in play, on this view. The observed time-asymmetry of thermodynamic phenomena is thus taken to arise from the imposition of an asymmetric boundary condition[3] on the time-symmetric probabilities of the Boltzmann measure. Diagrammatically:

Asymmetric boundary condition—entropy low in the past
+ Symmetric default condition—entropy likely to be high, *ceteris paribus*

Observed asymmetry.

3.3 Advantages of the one-asymmetry view

The immediate advantage of the one-asymmetry view is its relative simplicity, or theoretical economy. If it works, it simply does more (or as much) with less. The best response to such a claimed advantage would be to show that rival views do something more—and something worth doing, of course, for otherwise the extra expenditure is for nought. In this area, unfortunately, one's conception of what needs doing depends very much on very issue at stake. Proponents of two-asymmetry views take it that there is a time-asymmetric nomological generalization evident in thermodynamic phenomena, and hence take explanation of this generalization to be something worth paying for (in the coin of theoretical complexity). But this consideration will not move their one-asymmetry rivals, who deny that there is any such generalization at work.

Disputes of this kind are difficult to settle, because the two sides have such different views of what counts as winning. The best

---

[3] The use of the term 'boundary condition' here is intended to reflect the role the proposition in question plays in the explanation of the thermodynamic asymmetry, relative to 'local' dynamical constraints on the behaviour of matter. Thus, it reflects the view that the condition does not flow from those constraints, but needs to be given independently. It is not intended to exclude the possibility that the condition in question might come to be treated as lawlike by some future physics.

dialectical strategy is often to exploit one's opponents' own conception of what counts as losing—in other words, to show that their view fails by their own lights. This is the strategy I shall follow below, in arguing against the two-asymmetry view. First, however, I want to respond to what may seem an objection to the one-asymmetry approach.

3.4 A surprising consequence of the one-asymmetry view?

The probabilities involved in the statistical picture are time-symmetric. They imply that entropy is very likely to be high in the past, as well as in the future. Yet entropy seems to have been extremely low in the past. Doesn't this amount to a strong disconfirmation of the view, by any reasonable standards? In other words, doesn't it give us good grounds for thinking that the Boltzmann measure is inapplicable to the real world?

It seems to me that there are two possible strategies available to one-asymmetry view, in response to this objection:

(i) *The no asymmetry strategy.* This involves saying that the Boltzmann measure is not erroneous, because the past low entropy is just a fluke—the kind of possible though extremely unlikely outcome explicitly permitted by the Boltzmann probabilities. This sounds like simply thumbing one's nose at the canons of confirmation theory, but Boltzmann himself suggests a way of making this option less unappealing than initially it seems. In an infinite universe, even very low entropy states may be expected to occur occasionally, simply by random fluctuation. If creatures like us can only exist in appropriate proximity to such fluctuations, then it is not surprising that we find ourselves in an otherwise unlikely kind of world.[4] (Since this approach does away altogether with the need for an additional time-asymmetric restriction on the Boltzmann probability measure, it is genuinely a 'no asymmetry' approach: on the global scale, it tells us, there is no thermodynamic asymmetry!)

(ii) *The ceteris paribus strategy.* The second approach takes the Boltzmann probabilities to be merely 'default' expectation values, to be used in the absence of overriding factors—and the past low entropy boundary condition, as yet not fully understood, seems

---

[4] The closest Boltzmann seems to come to making this anthropic proposal explicit is in his (1895, 415). I am grateful to Jos Uffink for pointing out to me that it is not nearly as obvious that Boltzmann actually had this point in mind as tradition has tended to assume.

to be one such factor. In other words, the Boltzmann measure tells us what is likely to be the case, other things being equal—and we know of one relevant respect in which other things are not equal, namely, the low entropy past.

Note that the one-asymmetry approach cannot avail itself of a third escape strategy, that of claiming that the Boltzmann probabilities are reliable only in one direction. If the probabilities become asymmetric in this way, we no longer have a one-asymmetry view.

Thus for the one-asymmetry approach the choice seems to be between (i) and (ii). Option (i) is now widely regarded as unworkable. There are two major problems. The first is that if this suggestion had been true, we should not have expected to find any more order in the universe than was already known to exist, for that was certainly enough to support us. The second is that it is much easier for a fluctuation to 'fake' historical records, by producing them from scratch, than by producing the real state of affairs (of even lower entropy) of which they purport to be records. On this view, then, historical records such as memories are almost certainly misleading.[5]

Option (ii) has a surprising consequence. Given that the Boltzmann probabilities are time-symmetric, it implies that they have must the same 'default' status towards the future as towards the past, and hence that they cannot give us grounds for confidence that entropy will not decrease in the future. All we can reasonably say is that it is very unlikely to decrease, other things being equal—i.e., *in the absence of the kind of overriding factors which make it decrease towards the past*. In other words, statistical arguments alone do not give us good grounds for confidence that the Second Law will continue to hold. The statistics cannot rule out (or even give us strong grounds for doubting) the possibility that there might be a low entropy boundary condition at some point in the future, as there seems to be in the past. (In order to clarify this possibility, we need to understand more about the reasons for past boundary condition.)

[5] For more details, see Price 1996, ch. 2, and Albert 2000, ch. 4. I believe that the point was made originally by C. F. von Weizsäcker 1939, in a paper which appears in English translation as §II.2 in von Weizsäcker 1980. Von Weizsäcker notes that 'improbable states can count as documents [i.e., records of the past] only if we presuppose that still less probable states preceded them.' He concludes that 'the most probable situation by far would be that the present moment represents the entropy minimum, while the past, which we infer from the available documents, is an illusion' (1980, 144–5).

In other words, the one-asymmetry view leads us to the kind of open-mindedness about the future thermodynamic behaviour of the universe that Burbury himself seemed to recommend (for somewhat different reasons, as we'll see), in the passage with which we began. In my view this is a major 'sleeping' consequence of Boltzmann's statistical approach to the thermodynamic asymmetry—'Boltzmann's Time Bomb', as I call it in Price 2002—which has been triggered by the recent discovery of the cosmological origins of the low entropy past.

Some people may feel that this consequence of the one-asymmetry view is a reason for preferring its rival—better time-asymmetric probabilities than probabilities whose predictions can't always be trusted. In my view, this reaction is a case of shooting the messenger. If this is what our best theory of the origins of the thermodynamic asymmetry tells us, shouldn't we take it seriously, rather casting around for an alternative theory? (It is not as though we have any good *independent* reason to reject the conclusion.)

Why is the one-asymmetry approach the best theory? In part because it is simpler, and in part because the alternatives are fatally flawed. Justifying the latter claim brings me to the main task of the paper, which is to lay out some objections to the two-asymmetry approach.

4. Two Kinds of Two-asymmetry View

I want to raise two objections to the two-asymmetry view. Neither objection applies to all versions of the two-asymmetry view, but all versions are subject to one objection or other, and some versions are subject to both. In order to make things clear, I need a simple taxonomy of possible views. For completeness, I include the one-asymmetry view. I'll present the taxonomy as a decision tree, as in Figure 1. Answers to a few simple questions lead to one to one or other of the four possible positions I want to distinguish.

The first issue is whether we need a second asymmetry at all—whether the explanation of thermodynamic phenomena requires a time-asymmetric nomological generalization, in addition to low entropy past boundary condition. One-asymmetry approaches deny this, of course, and hence occupy position **A** on the tree.

Next, two-asymmetry approaches may usefully divided into two broad (though non-exclusive) categories, depending on their view of the source of the second asymmetry. One category comprises a group of approaches which seek a source for the second asymmetry

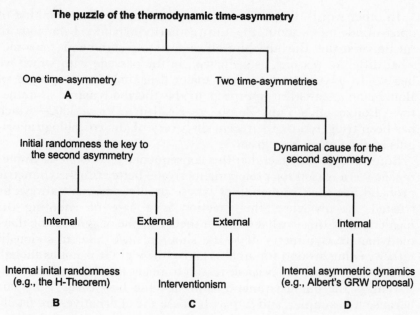

The puzzle of the thermodynamic time-asymmetry

One time-asymmetry **A**

Two time-asymmetries

Initial randomness the key to the second asymmetry

Dynamical cause for the second asymmetry

Internal

External

External

Internal

Internal inital randomness (e.g., the H-Theorem) **B**

Interventionism **C**

Internal asymmetric dynamics (e.g., Albert's GRW proposal) **D**

Figure 1. Four possible views of the origin of the themodynamic arrow.

in some asymmetric 'boundary condition', involving randomness, independence, or 'lack of correlation', in the initial motions of the microscopic constituents of matter. More precisely, these approaches take the second asymmetry to rest on the fact that there is such randomness or lack of correlations in the *initial* but not the corresponding *final* conditions. Approaches of this kind may be further sub-divided according to their answer to the following question. Is the 'internal' randomness of the microscopic motions of the constituents of a system sufficient (position **B**), or do environmental influences play a crucial role, as held by interventionist approaches (position **C**)?

The second broad category of two-asymmetry approaches comprises views that seek a dynamical *cause* for the second asymmetry—in other words, some identifiable factor dynamical without which entropy would not be constrained to increase. Again, views of this kind may usefully be sub-divided according to their view of the 'location' of this cause. For some views it essentially involves an external influence (position **C**). For others it is a feature of the *internal* dynamics of normal systems—i.e., it would normally be present even in a completely isolated system (position **D**).

Interventionism thus turns up in both broad categories. On the one hand, the interventionist's external influences comprise an identifiable *cause*, without which (according to the interventionist) entropy would not necessarily increase. On the other, it turns out to be crucial that these external influences are suitably *random*, uncorrelated with the internal motions of the systems on which they exert an influence.

Interventionism thus provides the obvious overlap between the two broad second-level categories of two-asymmetry approaches identified in Figure 1. In principle, these categories might also turn out to be non-exclusive for a more subtle reason, namely that 'initial randomness' itself might be held to be a dynamical cause for the second asymmetry. This possibility will be clarified below. For the time being, I want to discuss causal approaches and initial randomness approaches separately. As I have said, I want to raise two objections to two-asymmetry approaches. The first objection is to causal approaches, and hence applies to options **C** and **D**. The second is to the initial randomness approach, and hence applies to options **B** and **C**. Interventionism at least thus turns out to be doubly at fault, by my lights, being vulnerable to both objections. And if there is a further region of overlap between the causal and initial randomness approaches, the same will be true there.

5 The Counterfactual Confinement Problem

Causal approaches seek a dynamical factor responsible for the general tendency of entropy to increase—some factor without which entropy would not increase, at least with the observed regularity. As we noted, this factor needs to be time-asymmetric, for otherwise entropy would be constrained to be constant (non-decreasing in both directions).

One version of such an approach is interventionism, which takes the cause to be provided by influences from the external environment 'coming at haphazard' (in the words of Burbury (1894, 320), who seems to have been one of the first to suggest this idea). For the moment, let's ignore the role of 'haphazardness', or randomness, and focus on the external nature of these influences. I want to call attention to the implied counterfactual claim:

(5a) If there were no such external influences, the observed phenomena would be different—entropy would not increase monotonically, in the observed fashion.

This counterfactual seems part and parcel of what it means to say that the observed increase in entropy is *caused* by such external influences.

If we accept that we need a dynamical cause for observed monotonic increase in entropy, but reject interventionism, then the alternative is to locate the cause in some asymmetric feature of the internal dynamics of matter. A recent example of such a view is David Albert's (1994, 1998, 2000) suggestion that the collapse mechanism in the GRW interpretation of quantum theory provides such an asymmetry. The details of this proposal need not concern us here, but again I want to call attention to the implied counterfactual:

(5b) If there were no such asymmetric mechanism, the observed phenomena would be different.

In his 1994 paper, Albert accepts this counterfactual claim, at least implicitly, in taking seriously the objection that if his suggestion were correct, entropy would not increase in systems containing too few constituents to allow the GRW mechanism to have its effect:

> [T]he collapse-driven statistical mechanics ... will entail that an extraordinarily tiny and extraordinarily compressed and *absolutely isolated* gas will have *no lawlike tendency* whatever to spread out.

> It can hardly be denied, therefore, that runs strongly counter to our intuitions. [sic]

> What it does *not* run counter to, however (and *this* is what has presumably got to be important, in the long run) is our empirical experience. (1994, 677)

In a later paper, Albert accepts the counterfactual claim explicitly, saying that it is

> perfectly right ... that anybody who claims that one or another causal mechanism called M is what actually underlies the tendencies of the entropies of thermodynamic systems to increase must also be claiming that if that mechanism were not *operating* then would *be* no such tendencies. (1998, 16)

Let us think about what this means. In a deterministic world, on this view, thermodynamic systems would not behave as they normally behave. Deterministic coffee would not grow cold, Newtonian cider would not need bottling. More precisely, if it were true that the observed thermodynamic behaviour is *caused* by some asymmetric indeterministic mechanism in the dynamics, then a means for turning off this mechanism would be a means for turning off the general tendency to equilibration. Useful as this might prove in practice, our present concern is with plausibility. Do we have good grounds for thinking that such counterfactuals are true? Similarly in the interventionist case. Is it really plausible that temperatures would not equalize in a completely isolated laboratory?

In the remarks quoted above, Albert says that these counterfactuals do not 'run counter to ... our empirical experience', and on the assumption that the mechanism in question (GRW, or random external influences) does obtain in the world of our empirical experience, this is quite true. But it is true in the trivial sense that in virtue of having an antecedent which is contrary to fact, *every* strictly *counter*factual conditional does not run counter to empirical experience. For strict counterfactuals especially, then, not running counter to experience is a very long way from being supported by experience (and, *pace* Albert, the latter is what has *really* got to be important, in the long run).

Albert also suggests that the issue is whether a gas has a 'lawlike tendency ... to spread out', and this seems to me to be a little misleading. The lawlike character of what we observe is disputable. Indeed, it is precisely the point at issue. As I have noted, one-asymmetry approaches to the thermodynamic arrow differ from their two-asymmetry rivals mainly in denying that there is any asymmetric *nomological* generalization or disposition of matter to be explained. The real issue is not whether the gas would have a lawlike tendency to spread out, but simply whether it would spread out. It is not enough for these causal views to claim that a world without the cause in question would differ *solely* in modal respects.

These approaches thus require that the causal factor 'makes a difference'—that it alters the behaviour of matter in some way. Note especially the burden of proof. It is the proponents of these causal views who need a justification for the counterfactual claims (5a) and (5b). Their opponents need only say that they see no reason to accept such counterfactuals. Hence it is not sufficient for the causal view to object that its opponents have no basis for a contrary counterfactual claim. Thus Albert 1998 responds to the present objection as follows: 'If the GRW-theory is right, then there simply *are* no [Boltzmann-like probability distributions over initial conditions]; and so (of course) there would be no such distributions to fall back on in the event that one were to entertain a counterfactual sort of GRW-theory with the spontaneous localizations removed.' However, my point is that it is Albert who needs to justify the counterfactual (5b), not his opponents who need to refute it.

This objection seems to me to be very powerful, and it has a long history, at least as applied to interventionism. I'm not sure who first noted that it seemed implausible to claim that temperatures would not equalize, or gas not disperse, in a genuinely isolated system, but the point is certainly well known. Yet interventionism continues to attract supporters. This sort of situation is common in science and philosophy, of course, but it is often a sign that the two contending theories are operating with different conceptions of the nature of the problem. One way forward is to try to clarify the common task— to step back from the various proposed solutions, and ask what the problem actually is.

The debate about the asymmetry of thermodynamic phenomena seems to me very much in need of this kind of clarification. The approaches I have criticized in the section—interventionism, and the asymmetric internal dynamics view—seem to me to be take for granted that thermodynamic phenomena present us with a distinctive *lawlike* regularity, for which we need to find a basis. Once this is taken for granted (and it is accepted that the Second Law of Thermodynamics cannot simply be a primitive law, inexplicable in terms of any more basic feature of matter), it implies that there is *something* more basic, without which the regularity in question would not obtain. The task then is just to discover what that 'something' actually is. Against this background, the present objection is bound to seem more of an issue of detail than an objection of principle.

However, the background assumption is not compulsory. There is an alternative view of the phenomena, according to which equilibration towards the future is not a nomological regularity. On the contrary, it is the product of a weaker, *time-symmetric,* default condition on the behaviour of matter, in combination with a single time-asymmetric constraint (the low entropy past boundary condition). On this view—the one-asymmetry view—what happens towards the future is simply *not* the manifestation of a time-asymmetric nomological constraint.

Of course, what happens in the other direction—towards the past—is not in accordance with the time-symmetric default condition. Hence it does call for explanation, on this view. Thus there is a time-asymmetry in the phenomena, something puzzling in the behaviour of matter—but the puzzle is the way it behaves towards the past, not the way it behaves towards the future. In other words, the one-asymmetry approach takes interventionism and the asymmetric internal dynamics view to be trying to answer a question which doesn't need addressing.

It would be naive to hope that this kind of second-order point will be suddenly convincing, where the first-order objection has failed for so long. However, it does seem to me important to clarify the debate in this way. To a considerable extent, rival approaches to the thermodynamic asymmetry are not offering different answers to the same question, but answers to different questions. In order to make progress, we need first to recognize these competing conceptions of the nature of the problem—competing views of what an answer to the puzzle of the thermodynamic time-asymmetry would look like. In particular, we need to distinguish between the one-asymmetry and two-asymmetry conceptions of the nature of the task.

6. The Use and Abuse of Initial Randomness

I now turn to those versions of the two-asymmetry approach which attribute the general tendency of entropy to increase to a characteristic of the initial microstates of interacting matter—to 'initial randomness', or 'lack of initial correlations'. (In Price 1996 I called it the 'Principle of the Independence of Incoming Interactions', or PI^3.) Again, this assumption needs to be time-asymmetric, applying to initial conditions but not to final conditions. Otherwise, it yields no asymmetry.

Figure 1 gave us two kinds of example of such views. One was interventionism, which relies on the assumption that the incoming influences exerted on a thermodynamic system by the external environment are uncorrelated with the microstates of the system itself. The incoming influences are assumed to 'come at haphazard'. In this case the time-asymmetry is held to reside in the fact that the outgoing connections *to* the external environment do not 'go at haphazard', for otherwise, as just noted, the argument yields no asymmetry. In other words, it needs to be held that the system is correlated with its environment after their interaction, in a way in which it is not correlated beforehand.

The second version of this initial randomness approach is the one exemplified by the grandfather of would-be derivations of the Second Law, the H-Theorem itself. This differs from interventionism in that the initial randomness invoked is essentially an 'internal' matter, not dependent on a contribution from the environment. Burbury's great contribution to the discussion of the H-Theorem in the 1890s was to put his finger on the time-asymmetric assumption in question. It is the famous 'assumption of molecular chaos', or the *stoßzahlansatz*—roughly, the principle that the velocities of inter-acting molecules are independent *before* they collide. As we shall see in a moment, it was Burbury who pointed out why the correspond-ing condition could not be expected to hold *after* collisions.

My discussion of these initial randomness approaches is in two parts. I begin (Section 7) by examining the historical and theoreti-cal basis of some assumptions typically associated with this approach, from which it derives much of its appeal. This examina-tion reveals a surprising foundational lacuna, apparently obscured from view, at least in some quarters, by some longstanding errors of interpretation of early arguments in the field (including especially those of Burbury himself).

In the second stage, in Section 8, I want to treat the initial randomness approach in a more abstract way, paying particular attention to issues of explanatory and epistemological structure. I distinguish several possible forms the approach may take, and argue that all forms fall victim to one or other of several sub-problems. The main distinction is between (i) those versions of the approach which claim that our grounds for believing the entropy will contin-ue to increase are that we have prior justification for believing in initial randomness (in some appropriate form); and (ii) those which take the epistemology to run the other way—which take the relevant initial randomness principle to be known by inference from an inde-pendently justifiable belief that entropy will continue to increase. I argue that in different ways, both versions suffer from the problem that their assumed epistemology is ungrounded—the required pri-mary beliefs are simply not justifiable, by ordinary scientific stan-dards. The latter approach also suffers from another problem. The initial randomness assumption it invokes turns out to come in weak-er and stronger forms. In weaker forms the proposed explanation of entropy increase turns out to be question-begging in its epistemol-ogy, and to introduce no genuine second time-asymmetry, of the kind the two-asymmetry view requires. In stronger forms it runs out to be vulnerable to the counterfactual containment problem.

These objections may seem surprising, for the initial randomness assumptions have an apparent naturalness and plausibility. This is strikingly exemplified in what for more than a century has often been seen as one of the key problems in the thermodynamics of non-equilibrium systems—that of dealing with objections to the H-Theorem which turn on the claim that the assumption of molecular chaos cannot continue to hold over time, because the molecules of a gas become correlated as they interact. On this view, as Ridderbos puts it, the central problem in non-equilibrium statistical mechanics [is that] equilibrium can only be obtained and entropy can only increase for those systems for which an appropriate analogue of the Stoßzahlansatz can be shown to hold. That is, a necessary condition for the approach to equilibrium is that the system has to get rid of correlations which are continually being built up dynamically by the interactions between the constituents of the system. (1997, 477)

A number of authors—e.g., Bergmann and Lebowitz (1953), Blatt (1959), Ridderbos and Redhead (1998)—have suggested that interventionism provides a solution to this 'central problem'. Where does the time asymmetry come from, on this view? From the fact, it is claimed, that the incoming influences 'from the environment' are uncorrelated, whereas the corresponding 'outgoing influences' are correlated, *in virtue of the interaction between system and environment*. As Ridderbos and Redhead put it:

This is why the argument cannot be applied in the reverse time direction to argue that equilibrium will be approached into the past; in the ordinary time direction the 'incoming' influences are the influences from the environment on the system, and these are uncorrelated, but in the reversed time direction the 'incoming' influences are the influences the system exerts on its environment and these will be correlated. (1998, 1261)

This tradition thus seems committed to the following two principles:

(6a) Particle motions are independent *before* interactions—i.e., if the particles concerned have not interacted in their common past.

(6b) Interactions *give rise to* (or in general *increase*) correlations.

These principles are logically independent, in the sense that neither implies the other. Yet each is clearly time-asymmetric, and necessarily so, if both are to be maintained. For each principle is incompatible with the *time-inverse* of the other.

On the face of it, moreover, neither of these principles depends on the low entropy past. Thus, remarkably, this tradition seems to be committed to the existence of *three* independent time-asymmetries: (6a), (6b), and the low entropy past boundary condition. And the combination is of doubtful coherency. After all, if there is a dynamical reason for the accumulation of correlations in one direction due to interaction, and (as typically assumed in these discussions) the dynamics is time-symmetric, then how could it fail to be the case that correlations accumulate in both directions? Puzzling assumptions, then, but as we have seen, also very natural ones to contemporary intuitions.

How did the tradition get to this point? Where did this peculiar combination of assumptions come from? It turns out that in order to answer these questions, we need to return to Samuel Burbury's contribution to the debate about the H-Theorem in the 1890s.

7. Origins of an Orthodoxy

In his initial (1894, 1895) contributions the debate of the 1890s, Burbury points out that Boltzmann's proof of the H-Theorem relies on what Burbury calls 'Condition A' (later 'Assumption A'). This amounts to the assumption that the velocities of colliding particles are independent, before collisions. Burbury also points out that if this condition applied also to reverse motions, the H-Theorem would imply that the gas in question would also be approaching equilibrium in reverse, and this could only be true if the gas were already at equilibrium. So in a case in which the gas is not in equilibrium, and in which Assumption A does hold initially, the assumption is not true of the reversed motions at the end of the interval in question.

After Burbury's initial presentation of the point in his (1894) and (1895) letters to *Nature,* the argument is reproduced in many places both by Burbury himself (e.g., Burbury 1899, §39) and by others. In particular, it is reproduced by the Ehrenfests in their important survey article in 1912 (Ehrenfest and Ehrenfest 1959, 40; 85, n. 65).

Roughly stated, Burbury's observation might seem to amount to the principle that particle motions are not uncorrelated after collisions—i.e., to principle (6b). It seems to be interpreted this way by Ridderbos, among others:

> It was the Ehrenfests in their famous 1912 article [Ehrenfest and Ehrenfest 1959] who in a careful analysis of the Stoßzahlansatz pointed out the asymmetry which it contains; in general a distribution of molecules in a gas which satisfies the Stoßzahlansatz at an initial moment will fail to do so at a later moment *as a result of the correlations between the molecules which are built up dynamically as a result of the collisions.* (1997, 526, emphasis added.)

This interpretation is simply mistaken, however. The Burbury, Ehrenfest and Ehrenfest (BEE) argument that the *stoßzahlansatz* (or Assumption A) does not hold after a period of interaction relies on two assumptions: (i) that the gas in question is not in equilibrium, and (ii) that the condition does obtain at the beginning of the time interval in question. Given these assumptions, the H-Theorem implies that entropy increases over the time interval in the forward time sense, and hence that it decreases in the reverse time sense. From the latter fact, a second application of the H-Theorem, and *modus tollens,* we may infer that Assumption A does not obtain at the end of the time interval.

Note the crucial role of the assumption of initial non-equilibrium. Far from revealing a general tendency for correlations to accumulate *as a result of collisions,* the BEE argument turns on nothing more than this: Assumption A fails in the reverse motion *because* entropy was low in the past. Not only is this not a *result* of interactions; it seems independent of whether there actually are any interactions!

The BEE argument thus supports neither (6a) nor (6b). It provides no basis for the view that there is an asymmetrical tendency for interaction to give rise to correlations in the 'forward' time sense, as (6b) asserts. And it gives us no a priori justification for assuming that Assumption A does hold at any given 'initial' moment, as (6a) maintains. On the contrary, in fact. Since our reason for thinking that Assumption A does not hold later is that we know that entropy was low earlier, we might think—by symmetry, as it were—that we are not justified in assuming with (6a) that Assumption A holds earlier, until we know whether entropy is low later. Clearly, this thought has the potential to undermine any proposal to make (6a) our *reason* for thinking that entropy will not decrease in the future. (More on this in a moment.)

It is worth noting that Burbury himself seems to regard Assumption A as unrealistic, and indeed, in the remark I quoted at the beginning, offers what seems a lone voice of caution about our right to assume that entropy will continue to increase. However, even the astute Burbury does not seem to doubt that we are justified in assuming (6a) for the case of incoming influences from an external environment. His caution about Assumption A seems to be based on the intuition that interactions within all but an ideally rarefied gas will induce violations of Assumption A (due to the production of 'velocity streams', for example). He does not seem to see that there is a more basic puzzle about the origin of the asymmetry in the assumption of independence for initial but not for final motions.

The BEE argument is not the only reason for thinking that the *stoßzahlansatz* cannot continue to hold over an extended time period. A more basic reason is first noted, so far as I am aware, by J. H. Jeans:

> The effect of this assumption [i.e., Assumption A] is to enable us to regard certain probabilities at any given instant as independent, and we then assume not only that the probabilities at a later instant are *inter se* independent, but also that they are independent of the events which took place at any earlier instant. This assumption cannot be logically reconciled with the fact that the motion of the system is continuous in time, *i.e.*, that the events which occur at any instant depend on those which occurred at a previous instant. (1903, 598)

Jeans calls this an a priori argument that Assumption A cannot continue to hold over a time interval. He then goes on to give a second argument, which he terms a posteriori. This latter argument is essentially the BEE argument. And Burbury, in turn, immediately adopts Jeans' a priori argument, endorsing it, for example, in (1903, 530) and (1904).

Does Jeans' a priori argument support (6a) and (6b)? Not at all, for it is not time-asymmetric. Nor incidentally, does it depend on the assumption that the constituents of the system in question actually interact. (As I noted, this is also true of the BEE argument.) In other words, Jeans' logical point cannot be the basis of a one-way tendency for correlations to be built up dynamically as a result of collisions.

I know of one more argument which might at first sight seem to support (6a) and (6b). Consider two particles, of initial momenta p and p'. If they interact with each other (and with nothing else), conservation of momentum ensures that their combined momentum after collision is $p + p'$. Doesn't this imply that the two particles are now correlated—that their momenta cannot vary independently?

However, a moment's reflection reveals that this simple argument cannot provide a basis for (6b) and (6a). For one thing, there is nothing time-asymmetric here. The argument applies equally well in reverse. Indeed, it applies not only at any earlier or later time, whether or not the particles collide; but also, in a sense, at the initial time itself. If we are given the total momentum, and told that there are only two particles, then, *relative to this information* the two momenta are not independent. The diachronic content of this argument is essentially that of Jeans' argument, viz., that in virtue of the determinism of the dynamics, a choice of the dynamical variables at any one time fixes those values at all other times (so long as the system remains isolated, of course).

Thus it seems to me that in so far as the tradition maintains that there is some time-asymmetric sense in which correlations accumulate as a result of collisions, it is simply mistaken. There is no sense in which the dynamics produces correlations in a forward time sense in which it does not also do so in the reverse time sense. As a result, the idea that the asymmetry of (6b) could bolster that of (6a)—could show why (6a) doesn't hold in reverse—is also without foundation. On the contrary, in fact. Our only relevant reason for thinking that there are correlations in *final* conditions are that we know entropy was low in the *past*. Far from showing us that there is a past–future asymmetry, this suggests that we cannot know whether there is such an asymmetry—whether, as (6a) claims, there are no corresponding correlations in *initial* conditions—until we know whether entropy is low in the *future*.

Perhaps even more damagingly, this brief excursion into the history of the initial randomness approach suggests that it provides no legitimate basis whatsoever for the nomological *second asymmetry* required by the two-asymmetry approach. At best, the asymmetry of micro-correlations is simply the *first asymmetry* re-described—the asymmetry of macroscopic boundary conditions, characterized in another way.

In order properly to evaluate these objections, however, it is necessary to bring their target more sharply into focus. It turns out that there are several subtle variants of the initial randomness approach, differently sensitive to these points. In the next section I want to look at the approach in abstract terms, paying close attention to matters of explanatory and epistemological structure—that is, in particular, to the issue of what is being taken as providing grounds for believing what. It turns out, I think, that while there are possible versions of the initial randomness approach which are not guilty of question begging, and which do genuinely introduce a second time-asymmetry, these versions have other problems. For one thing, they are subject to the counterfactual containment problem.

8 The Formal Structure of the Appeal to Initial Randomness

Let's begin with some terminology, to be read in conjunction with Figure 2. The propositions **HiEnt$_p$** and **HiEnt$_f$** say that there is a macroscopic condition of high entropy in the past and the future, respectively. **Ran$_f$** and **Ran$_p$** represent the corresponding microscopic conditions at the other end of time. Figure 2 depicts the combinations of these propositions and their negations we ordinarily assume to be true of the actual universe: $\neg$**HiEnt$_p$** and $\neg$**Ran$_f$**, and **HiEnt$_f$** and **Ran$_p$**.

Thus the two shorter double-headed arrows in Figure 2 represent logical implications (modulo the laws). Given the dynamical laws, a high entropy past (**HiEnt$_p$**) would imply and be implied by the corresponding kind of randomness in the future (**Ran$_f$**); and a high entropy future (**HiEnt$_f$**) implies and is implied by the corresponding kind of randomness in the past (**Ran$_p$**). (In particular, therefore, **Ran$_p$** is logically the *weakest* assumption that implies **HiEnt$_f$**.)

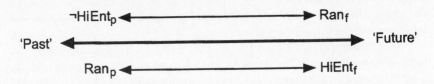

Figure 2. Macroscopic entropy and microscopic correlation

In the most abstract terms, then, the initial randomness approach is committed to the idea that a high entropy future is a consequence of, and is to be explained by, the fact that **Ran$_p$**—that is, by the randomness of the earlier microstates. Perhaps the true explanans is some stronger principle of which **Ran$_p$** is a consequence—more on this option below—but at any rate the later high-entropy macrostate is thought of as a consequence of the earlier microstate, and **Ran$_p$** is by definition the weakest condition which will do the trick.

8.1 Explanation and epistemology

The initial randomness approach thus takes **Ran$_p$** to explain **HiEnt$_f$**. It also seems natural to take $\neg$**HiEnt$_p$** to explain $\neg$**Ran$_f$**. Note that the 'intuitive' direction of explanation is past-to-future, in both cases. But this alignment in our explanatory intuitions should not be allowed to mask an important difference in the epistemological structures of the two claims, and hence a reason to be suspicious of the former. The grounds for suspicion turn on the issue of the justification the initial randomness approach takes us to have to accept that **HiEnt$_f$**.

In the case of the claim that $\neg$**HiEnt$_p$** explains $\neg$**Ran$_f$** the epistemology is relatively unproblematic. Our grounds for thinking that $\neg$**Ran$_f$**—i.e. that there are microscopic correlations in the future—

are simply that we have observed that the universe is highly ordered now and in the past. Epistemological inference thus follows the explanatory arrow, and all is well because the past state of affairs—the assumed explanans—is an observable matter.[6]

In the other case, however, the epistemology turns out to be problematic. To see why, let us note first that there are two broad possibilities. The first is that the epistemology does follow the explanatory arrow (taken to be past-to-future), so that our grounds for thinking that $\mathbf{HiEnt_f}$ are that we have independent reason for thinking that the required microscopic randomness ($\mathbf{Ran_p}$) obtains now (or in the past). The second is the converse possibility—our grounds for thinking that $\mathbf{Ran_p}$ obtains now and in the past are that we have independent reason to believe that entropy does not decrease in the future (from which past randomness follows as a logical or at least abductive consequence). Let us call these possibilities *past-to-future inference* and *future-to-past inference,* respectively. I want to show that both are problematic, though for different reasons.

8.2 Past-to-future inference?

This version of the initial randomness approach requires that we have grounds for believing that $\mathbf{Ran_p}$ obtains, other than by inference from the fact that it is required for $\mathbf{HiEnt_f}$. In what could these grounds consist?

The first option is that we might observe $\mathbf{Ran_p}$ directly. However, it is not difficult to see that this is not possible, at least in general. Just as it becomes impossible, in practice, to detect the correlations associated a system's low-entropy past—to tell, for example, whether a particular equilibrium sample of gas had a specified non-equilibrium state at a given earlier time—so it is impossible to make such determinations with respect to the future. (Among the factors which make this kind of observation impossible, in real systems, is the fact that measurements would be required across an entire spacelike hypersurface of the past light cone of the relevant segment of future spacetime.) Thus there is no prospect whatsoever of

---

[6] For present purposes I ignore the sceptical issue concerning our entitlement to believe our apparent evidence for a low entropy past, stemming from von Weizsäcker's observation (see Section 3.4 above) that if Boltzmann's probabilities are our guide, then it is much easier to produce fake records and memories, than to produce the real events of which they purport to *be* records. Albert 2000, ch. 4, provides an excellent recent account of this sceptical point.

detecting directly the 'hidden' correlations which would be required for entropy to decrease in the future—nor, for the same reasons, of excluding them on observational grounds.

If our acceptance of $\mathbf{Ran_p}$ does not rest on direct observational grounds, then on what? Could there be some direct but non-observational reason for accepting $\mathbf{Ran_p}$? There seem to be two kinds of argument on offer at this point. One tries to appeal to the intuition above, that correlations are typically produced by interactions, and 'hence' that none are to be expected before interactions—incoming influences can be expected to be independent. However, we have seen that the history of the subject offers us no sound basis whatsoever for this appeal, or for the asymmetric principle about interactions on which it relies.

The second kind of argument appeals to statistical considerations. It claims that failure of $\mathbf{Ran_p}$ would require highly improbable coordination among the microscopic motions of matter, in order to give rise to $\neg\mathbf{HiEnt_f}$. However, in the absence of an independent reason for thinking that the statistics are time-asymmetric, we have no reason to think that the correlations required to give rise to $\neg\mathbf{HiEnt_f}$ are any more unlikely than those required to give rise to $\neg\mathbf{HiEnt_p}$. Since the latter obtains *despite* these statistical considerations, we have very good reason to doubt the general reliability of statistical reasoning in this context. (After all, it fails in one case out of a possible two.)

It might be objected that we do have good reason—very good reason—to think that the relevant statistical arguments are reliable past-to-future, namely, that they perform so well in predicting the past-to-future behaviour of many real systems. However, in so far as it claims to offer us a reason to believe $\mathbf{Ran_p}$, this argument involves an inductive step. In effect, it relies on the claim that we are justified in expecting this statistical success to continue. As such, the claimed inference to $\mathbf{Ran_p}$ thus becomes indirect, and future-to-past (on which more in a moment).

Thus it appears that the epistemology of the claimed explanation of $\mathbf{HiEnt_f}$ by $\mathbf{Ran_p}$ cannot follow the explanatory arrow. Unlike in the case of the explanation of $\neg\mathbf{Ran_f}$ by $\neg\mathbf{HiEnt_p}$, our grounds for accepting the future explanandum cannot be that we have independent grounds to accept the past explanans. If we have good reason to believe the supposed explanandum at all, then, it must be on some basis more direct. Let us now turn to that possibility.

8.3 Future-to-past inference—a direct case for HiEnt$_f$?

In this version, the initial randomness approach is the view that we are led to some sort of initial randomness principle by abductive inference from the prior discovery that entropy will continue to increase. It is the view that in some form, initial randomness is the best explanation for this independently established fact about the physical world.

I want to raise two kinds of objection to this proposal. The first echoes Burbury's point, from the quotation with which we began. We simply *don't* have particularly strong reasons for believing that entropy will continue to increase, at least in the distant future. However, although the sentiment is Burbury's, the present justification for it depends on considerations of which Burbury could not have been aware. It depends on our current understanding of the nature of the past low entropy boundary condition, and hence on modern cosmology.

Within the last thirty years or so, cosmology has offered us a plausible hypothesis as to the origins of the observed low entropy. Briefly, everything seems to turn on the fact that matter was very smoothly distributed, soon after the Big Bang. This is a very highly ordered condition for a system dominated by gravity, and seems to supply a low-entropy 'reservoir' which supplies the entire thermodynamic gradient we observe in our region. (This story is very well told by Penrose 1989. On its links to the present issue, see Price 1996, ch. 2, Price 2002.)

Given this reason to think that the low entropy past has cosmological origins, we also have some basis for thinking that the issue of future low entropy also turns on cosmological issues. In particular, if we are entitled to believe that entropy will not decrease in the future, then it must be because we are entitled to believe—on cosmological grounds—that there is no future low entropy condition, of the same kind as the past condition. There seem to be two possible routes to such a belief. One would be theoretical, and turn on the question as to whether our best cosmological models excluded the possibility (or at least the likelihood) of such a future condition. The other would be observational, at least in part, and turn on the issue of what *present* manifestations there might be of such a future boundary condition. At present, both routes are best very inconclusive. (I shall say more about the latter possibility in a moment.) As it stands, then, Burbury's cautious agnosticism remains the appropriate attitude. In other words, it is very far from clear that there is an explanandum (**HiEnt$_f$**) in need of the kind of explanans (**Ran$_p$**) this approach takes initial randomness to offer.

I shall also argue that even if we did have good reason for thinking that entropy will continue to increase, this wouldn't count in favour of the initial randomness approach, which would still fall victim to the following dilemma. Depending on what is meant by initial randomness, it is either (i) a condition too weak to support a non-trivial two-asymmetry approach to the thermodynamic asymmetry; or (ii) a condition that, in being stronger than necessary, is subject to an analogue of the counterfactual containment problem.

8.3.1 Why HiEnt$_f$ isn't presently observable

If entropy were to decrease on a large scale at some time in the future, would that fact be detectable now? If we assume determinism, then in one sense, of course, it would be observable in principle to a Laplacian ideal observer. As we have already noted, however, there is no prospect whatsoever of this sort of microstate-based observation being possible for real observers in real systems. If it were possible, moreover, then it would count as direct observation of Ran$_p$, and hence as a basis for a past-to-future inference. The possibility we have now to consider is different. It is that there might be macroscopic evidence now as to whether entropy continues to increase in the future.

This possibility is not as bizarre as it might at first sound. There seem to be quite good grounds for thinking that certain kinds of future low entropy boundary conditions would have observable consequences now—and hence that at least to some extent, we can have observational evidence that those boundary conditions do not obtain in the future. The kind of evidence concerned is very much the kind of evidence we have of the low entropy past. Essentially, the latter evidence consists in low entropy 'remnants'—in systems that had not yet had time to reach equilibrium, following the low entropy condition in the past. (Stars and galaxies are striking examples of such remnants.)[7]

In an exactly analogous way—and proceeding on the same assumptions, applied in reverse—future low entropy conditions might well be expected to have manifestations now. These would be systems that, in the reverse time sense, have likewise not had sufficient time to equilibrate.

This possibility has been discussed in the literature in connection

---

[7] Again, I am ignoring von Weizsäcker's sceptical difficulties about inference to the past.

with a proposal made by Thomas Gold 1962, that the universe might be globally symmetric in entropy terms, with a low entropy future endpoint. The question of the advanced effects of such a boundary condition has been addressed in variations of the Ehrenfest two-urn models, with two-time boundary conditions. (See, for example, Cocke 1967 and the references in Schulman 1997, 156.) The upshot of these investigations is that such a boundary condition at a time T_f is not expected to be detectable before $T_f - t_{relax}$, where t_{relax} is the relaxation time of the relevant physical processes. Beyond that relaxation time, the system behaves in a manner macroscopically indistinguishable from one which lacks the future boundary condition. (The predictions assume a statistical measure that is symmetric, before application of boundary conditions. However, the conclusion concerning detectability outside the relaxation time seems likely to apply even in asymmetric background measures.)

Thus it seems that even a very large low entropy future boundary condition, comparable in magnitude to that in our past, might be undetectable now, so long as it is sufficiently far away. How far away is sufficiently far away? The issue depends on the relaxation time of the relevant real physical processes. This question has been discussed a little in recent years (e.g., in Gell-Mann and Hartle 1994; see also Price 1996, ch. 4), but the relevant issues remain open. At any rate, it is clear that at present there is no strong observational case for saying that there isn't a low entropy boundary condition in the future.

It might be thought that there is easier observational route to the conclusion that **HiEnt_f**. Can't we simply get there by induction from the observed present behaviour of matter? We observe that the Second Law holds now, with great consistency. Isn't that a reason to believe that it will continue to hold in the future? In other words, doesn't induction give us our explanandum (and abduction then our explanans)?

The problem is that induction depends on the assumption that the future will be like the past in the relevant respect. It is therefore question-begging to try to use it to exclude the contrary hypothesis. In other words, induction is powerless to exclude a theoretically well-motivated hypothesis to the effect that the future will not be like the past. (This is simply a more localized version of Hume's point, viz., that we can't use inductive methods to justify induction.) Indeed, as I noted in Section 3.1, the issue between the one-asymmetry and two-asymmetry views seems to come down to that as to whether there is a *projectible* (or induction-supporting) generalization to the effect that entropy will continue to increase. There is no prospect of settling this issue by induction.

8.3.2 Why initial randomness would be in trouble, even if $HiEnt_f$ were observable

Suppose for a moment that we did have good theoretical or observational grounds for believing $HiEnt_f$. Would we be justified in making an abductive inference to Ran_p? Yes, at least on some conceptions of explanation. Since Ran_p is by definition equivalent to $HiEnt_f$, given the relevant laws, it follows that Ran_p is an initial condition sufficient to imply $HiEnt_f$, given the laws. If this is held to be sufficient for explanation, then Ran_p can indeed explain $HiEnt_f$.

Unfortunately for the two-asymmetry approach, however, such an explanation does not conform to the two-asymmetry model. Ran_p implies $HiEnt_f$, but the implication is logical, not nomological. So long as $HiEnt_f$ is a factlike matter, so too is Ran_p. After all, the one-asymmetry view also accepts that Ran_p. On this view, the default expectation is for both Ran_p and Ran_f (or equivalently, both $HiEnt_f$ and $HiEnt_p$); and the single asymmetry is the constraint which supplies $\neg HiEnt_p$ (or equivalently $\neg Ran_f$).

Thus if abductive inference is to get us anywhere useful from $HiEnt_f$, from the two-asymmetry approach's point of view, it has to get us to something stronger than Ran_p. Call such a stronger proposition $*Ran_p$. In effect, the initial randomness approach will then be committed to the counterfactual

(8a)   If not $*Ran_p$, then (probably) not $HiEnt_f$.

For if $HiEnt_f$ were held to be likely to occur anyway, even in the absence of $*Ran_p$, the supposition that $*Ran_p$ could hardly be required to *explain* $HiEnt_f$.

But why should we accept (8a)? We know it is *logically* possible that Ran_p (and hence $HiEnt_f$) should obtain without $*Ran_p$. (By definition, Ran_p is sufficient for $HiEnt_f$, and $*Ran_p$ is logically stronger than Ran_p, so failure of $*Ran_p$ does not entail failure of Ran_p.) This version of the initial randomness approach will therefore need to argue on non-logical grounds that if $*Ran_p$ failed, so too would Ran_p—the result would not simply be a world in which Ran_p obtained anyway.

The dialectical position of the initial randomness approach here is the same as that of causal versions of the two-asymmetry theory. As we saw in Section 5, those approaches are committed to the claim that if the causal mechanism in question did not operate—if a system were truly isolated from its environment, if there were no GRW collapse, or whatever—thermodynamic systems would not behave as they are observed to behave. In effect, this amounts to the idea that entropy needs to be *prevented* from decreasing—that the initial condition of the universe is such that entropy will decrease, unless something intervenes. The one-asymmetry approach challenges this idea, arguing that the observed phenomena can be construed as the product of a single time-asymmetric constraint (the low entropy past) on an otherwise symmetric space of possibilities. Unless we are given some reason to rule out this conception of the origin of the phenomena in question, the causal approach is not entitled to its counterfactuals. While the one-asymmetry model remains a viable possibility, in other words, we cannot be justified in claiming that without the second asymmetry, the relevant phenomena would have been different.

All this transfers to the present case. Given the supposition that **HiEnt$_f$**, the one-asymmetry approach will propose that the resulting past–future asymmetry—the fact that **HiEnt$_f$** but not **HiEnt$_p$**—reflects only one-time asymmetry, that of the low entropy past boundary condition. In order to make a case for (8a), and hence for a second asymmetry in the form of ***Ran$_p$**, the initial randomness approach needs a reason to disallow this one-asymmetry proposal. No such reason seems to have been forthcoming.

8.3.3 Summary: The case against nomological initial randomness

The argument against an appeal to a 'strong' form of initial randomness may be summarized in this way. If ***Ran$_p$** were to be justified on theoretical grounds, these grounds would need to be time-asymmetric (since otherwise they would equally give us ***Ran$_f$**, and hence **HiEnt$_p$**). A time-asymmetric theoretical assumption of this kind might be justified if we already knew **HiEnt$_f$**, and therefore sought an explanation of this known fact. But (i) this is not our situation—on the contrary, we are still looking for some reason to believe **HiEnt$_f$**. And (ii) even if we did have such reason, ***Ran$_p$** wouldn't be necessary, since we have no reason to think that situation is not merely the result of symmetric Boltzmann probabilities, subject to a single time-asymmetric boundary condition.

8.3.4 Is the argument too strong?

It might be objected that the last objection proves too much. If it worked, wouldn't it show that nomological explanations are always too strong? For isn't the possibility always open that the same phenomena would have occurred without the law in question?

This is an interesting point, which raises issues which go far beyond the scope of this paper. In my view, the counterfactual containment argument does pose a general problem for some strongly realist conceptions of the nomological realm. For present purposes, however, what matters is something that seems to distinguish the use of argument in the thermodynamic context from possible general uses.

In the present context, we have a relatively clear alternative to the two-asymmetry approach's conception of the origins of the relevant thermodynamic phenomena. That is, we have clearly in view a means by which the same phenomena could have arisen, without a nomological asymmetry. Assuming a deterministic dynamics, all it takes is for the initial microstate of the universe to be 'normal', in the sense of Boltzmann's measure, in the space of possibilities compatible with the initial macrostate. Hence the onus is on the proponent of a two-asymmetry view to convince us that without the nomological asymmetry supposedly in question—GRW collapse, external influence, ***Ran$_p$**, or whatever—the initial microstate would not have been of that kind. (As I noted in Section 5, there is no corresponding onus on opponents of the two-asymmetry approach to *defend* the Boltzmann measure. Proponents of the two-asymmetry approach are obliged to justify the relevant counterfactual, and hence to *exclude* the Boltzmann measure, but opponents can simply afford to be agnostic.)

A familiar argument for realism about nomological necessity is that without it, observed regularities become incredible coincidences. The implicit counterfactual claim is that without real necessities, the regularities in question would probably fail. Whatever we think about the merits of this argument, it is better than the analogous defence of nomological asymmetry in the thermodynamic case. There may perhaps be a prima facie case that regularities in general would fail without laws. Post-Boltzmann, there isn't even a prima facie case that thermodynamic systems would equilibrate differently without a nomological constraint. Boltzmann showed us that there is at least one plausible measure on the space of possible initial microstates under which the observed phenomena are highly likely, even in the absence of a nomological constraint. In doing so, he placed the ball squarely in the court of defenders of nomological asymmetry. To make their view stick—to return the ball— defenders of that view need a reason to rule out Boltzmann's measure. So far as I know, there has been no serious, let alone *successful,* attempt to do so. (Once again, the point is not that

Boltzmann's measure is a priori *right*, but simply that it is a serious contender, which has not been shown to be *wrong*.)

8.4 Conclusion

When disambiguated, the initial randomness approach turns out to be unable to provide a satisfactory explanation of the second asymmetry, of the kind the two-asymmetry approach requires. The faults of the approach depend on the precise form in which it is presented to us.

If it is offered in the spirit of a justification for believing that entropy will continue to increase, then it fails because there is no good reason to believe that the required condition of initial randomness does obtain. (It is not observable, and statistical arguments are unreliable, by parity of reasoning.)

If it is offered to us in the spirit of an inferred explanation of something independently determinable, then again the approach fails. In this case, the problem is both that the explanandum is not independently justifiable, and that even if it were, the proposed explanans would be either (i) too weak for the two-asymmetry approach, in not supplying a nomological second asymmetry, or (ii) unnecessary.

9. Starting in the Wrong Place

The failings of the two-asymmetry approach seem to boil down to two points. The first is an epistemological failing, a vulnerability to a modern version of Samuel Burbury's objection. It simply hasn't been adequately established that on a global scale, the relevant phenomena are as the two-asymmetry approach takes them to be. That is, it hasn't been established that entropy will continue to increase. We saw that what has been added since Burbury's time is the cosmological case for regarding this as an open question. Burbury was rightly suspicious of the crucial assumption (the assumption that he himself had first identified) of the leading argument for thinking that entropy will continue to increase. The cosmological connection supplies an independent reason for holding open the possibility that it will not do so.

The second failing is methodological. Even if we grant the relevant phenomena, the two-asymmetry approach has failed to establish that the explanation of those phenomena requires something either nomological or time-asymmetrical (in addition, that is, to the low entropy past boundary condition). To make this case, the two-asymmetry approach needs to defend the kind of counterfactual we identified at (5a), (5b) and (8a), and thus to exclude the alternative one-asymmetry conception of the origin of the asymmetric phenomena in question. No such defence has been offered.

In my view, these two failings are symptoms of a more basic failing, that of asking the wrong question to start with. The two-asymmetry approach begins with the question: Why does entropy go up towards the future—why is matter engaged in this 'uphill' journey? The one-asymmetry approach begins instead with the question: Why does entropy go down towards the past—why does the matter begin its journey at such a 'low' spot? It is true that by one-asymmetry lights these are in a sense the same question: the journey is uphill *because* it starts in a low place. All the same, the latter version puts the emphasis in the right place—it brings to the foreground the crucial puzzle.

By two-asymmetry lights, the questions are not the same. A reason why matter cannot go 'downhill' is not automatically a reason why its journey must start at a low place. Hence the need for two asymmetries, in this picture—and so much the worse for this approach, as we have seen.

In my view, a great but still under-appreciated consequence of Boltzmann's contribution to our understanding of the thermodynamic asymmetry is that it directs our attention 'backwards' in this way. It show us that if our interest is in the time-asymmetry, the proper focus of our attention is the condition of the universe in what we regard as its past, rather than some intrinsically time-asymmetric characteristic of its current journey.

Thus the crucial question is why entropy is so low in the past, and as noted in Section 8.3, modern cosmology has given this issue a remarkably concrete form. But this question arises from an even more basic one, which isn't essentially time-asymmetric: Why isn't entropy almost always high, as the time-symmetric Boltzmann measure would lead us to expect? We'll still need to answer this latter question, even if—as we currently have no very strong reason to disbelieve, in my view—entropy turns out to decrease in the distant future, and the 'end' of the universe is as peculiar as its 'beginning'.[8]

[8] Early versions of some of this material were presented at a conference in Groningen in September, 1999, at the Royal Institute of Philosophy Conference at LSE in September, 2000, and in talks in Utrecht, College Park and Tucson in April, 2001. I am grateful to participants for discussions on those occasions; and indebted to David Atkinson and Craig Callender for comments on earlier drafts, amongst much else.

References

Albert, D. 1994. 'The Foundations of Quantum Mechanics and the Approach to Thermodynamic Equilibrium', *British Journal for the Philosophy of Science*, **45**, 669–677.

——1998. 'The Direction of Time', paper presented to the Annual Meeting of the Eastern Division of the APA, Washington, D.C., December, 1998.

Bergmann, P. G. and Lebowitz, J. L. 1955. 'New Approach to Non-equilibrium Processes', *Physical Review*, **99**, 578–87.

Blatt, J. M. 1959. 'An Alternative Approach to the Ergodic Problem', *Progress in Theoretical Physics*, **22**, 745–56.

Boltzmann, L. 1877. 'Über die Beziehung zwischen des zweiten Hauptsatze der mechanischen der Wärmetheorie' ('On the Relation of a General Mechanical Theorem to the Second Law of Thermodynamics'), *Sitzungsberichte, K. Akademie der Wissenschaften in Wien, Math.-Naturwiss*, **75**, 67–73 (reprinted in Brush 1966).

—— 1895. 'On Certain Questions of the Theory of Gases,' *Nature*, **51**, 413–15.

—— 1964. *Lectures on Gas Theory*, Berkeley: University of California Press.

Brush, S. 1966. *Kinetic Theory. Volume 2: Irreversible Processes*, Oxford: Pergamon Press.

Burbury, S. H., 1894. 'Boltzmann's Minimum Function', *Nature*, **51**, 78.

—— 1895. 'Boltzmann's Minimum Function', *Nature*, **51**, 320.

—— 1899. *The Kinetic Theory of Gases*, Cambridge: Cambridge University Press.

—— 1903. 'Mr J. H. Jeans' Theory of Gases', *Philosophical Magazine, Series 6*, **6**, 529–35.

—— 1904: 'On the Theory of Diminishing Entropy', *Philosophical Magazine, Series 6*, **8**, 4349.

Cocke, W. 1967. 'Statistical Time Symmetry and Two-Time boundary Conditions in Physics and Cosmology', *Physical Review*, **160**, 1165–1170.

Culverwell, E. 1890a. 'Note on Boltzmann's Kinetic Theory of Gases, and on Sir W. Thomson's Address to Section A, British Association, 1884', *Philosophical Magazine*, **30**, 95–99.

—— 1890b. 'Possibility of Irreversible Molecular Motions', *Report of the British Association for the Advancement of Science*, **60**, 744.

—— 1894. 'Dr. Watson's Proof of Boltzmann's Theorem on Permanence of Distributions', *Nature*, **50**, 617.

Ehrenfest, P. and Ehrenfest, T. 1959. *The Conceptual Foundations of the Statistical Approach in Mechanics*. English translation by M.J. Moravcsik (Ithaca, NY: Cornell University Press). Dover edn. 1990 (NewYork: Dover Publications).

Gell-Mann, M. and Hartle, J. 1994. 'Time Symmetry and Asymmetry in Quantum Mechanics and Quantum Cosmology,' in Halliwell, Perez-Mercader, and Zurek (1994), pp. 311–45.

Gold, T. 1962. 'The Arrow of Time,' *American Journal of Physics,* **30** 403–10.

Gold, T. (ed.) 1963. *The Nature of Time.* Ithaca: Cornell University Press.

Hall, E. H. 1899. Review of S. H. Burbury, *The Kinetic Theory of Gases* (Cambridge: Cambridge University Press, 1899), *Science, New Series,* **10**, 685–88.

Halliwell, J., Perez-Mercader, J. and Zurek, W. (eds), 1994. *Physical Origins of Time Asymmetry,* Cambridge: Cambridge University Press.

Jeans, J. H. 1903. 'The Kinetic Theory of Gases developed from a New Standpoint', *Philosophical Magazine, Series 6,* **5**, 587–620.

Lebowitz, J. 1993: 'Boltzmann's Entropy and Time's Arrow', *Physics Today,* **9:93**, 32–8.

Price, H. 1996. *Time's Arrow and Archimedes' Point: New Directions for the Physics of Time,* New York: Oxford University Press.

—— 2002: 'Boltzmann's Time Bomb', *British Journal for the Philosophy of Science,* **53**, 83–119.

Ridderbos, T. M. 1997. 'The Wheeler-Feynman Absorber Theory: A Reinterpretation?', *Foundations of Physics Letters,* **10**, 473–86.

Ridderbos, T. M. and Redhead, M. 1998. 'The Spin-echo Experiments and the Second Law of Thermodynamics', *Foundations of Physics,* **28**, 1237–70.

Schulman, L. 1997. *Time's Arrows and Quantum Measurement,* Cambridge: Cambridge University Press.

Sklar, L. 1995. 'The Elusive Object of Desire: in Pursuit of the Kinetic Equations and the Second Law', in Savitt, S., (ed.), *Time's Arrows Today.,* Cambridge: Cambridge University Press, 191–216. Originally published in Fine, A. and Machamer, P., (eds), *PSA 1986: Proceedings of the 1986 Biennial Meeting of the Philosophy of Science Association,* vol. 2.

von Weizsäcker, C. 1939. 'Der zweite Hauptsatz und der Unterschied von der Vergangenheit und Zukunft,' *Annalen der Physik (5 Folge),* **36**, 275–83.

—— 1980. *The Unity of Nature,* New York: Farrar Straus Giroux.

Zeno's Arrow and the Significance of the Present

ROBIN LEPOIDEVIN

I. Introduction

Perhaps the real paradox of Zeno's Arrow is that, although entirely stationary, it has, against all odds, successfully traversed over two millennia of human thought to trouble successive generations of philosophers. The prospects were not good: few original Zenonian fragments survive, and our access to the paradoxes has been for the most part through unsympathetic commentaries. Moreover, like its sister paradoxes of motion, the Arrow has repeatedly been dismissed as specious and easily dissolved. Even those commentators who have taken it seriously have propounded solutions with which they profess themselves to be perfectly satisfied. So my question is: will Zeno's Arrow survive into the millennium just begun?

I certainly hope so. What I want to do in this paper is argue, not simply for its preservation, but also for its creative reconstruction. Every generation needs to reinvent the wheel. Arguments, conundrums, paradoxes have to be rediscovered and re-presented in the contemporary idiom. Philosophy of time has of course moved on since Zeno's day, but that is not to say that the Arrow cannot speak to the kinds of issues that are now engaging us.

At the end of a characteristically detailed and illuminating commentary, Jonathan Barnes offers the following observation:

> It is usually supposed that Zeno's paradox carries with it some philosophical theory about the nature of time; and Zeno's commentators regularly adduce rival theories in the course of their reflexions about it. My discussion has shown the falsity of that common assumption. ... The paradox, as we should expect and desire, is innocent of any such theories: it presupposes only the two harmless and common notions that there are instants, as well as periods, of time; and that things move, if at all, at instants. (Barnes (1982), p. 285)

As a purely exegetical remark, this may be above reproach, although I am persuaded by Jonathan Lear's remarkable discussion of the topic (Lear (1981), (1988)) that the best reconstruction of the

Robin Le Poidevin

argument gives prominence to the notion of the present moment, as Barnes does not. I want to build on Lear's insight and offer a version of the paradox that explicitly incorporates a theory of time, thus (to my mind) increasing its interest and power. I cannot seriously present the result as what Zeno originally intended, but we should not expect, and need not insist, that reinvented wheels should conform to the original blueprint.

II. First reconstruction: no motion in an instant

Although, as remarked above, our sources are not sympathetic ones, they tend to converge in their accounts of the Arrow, which should give us hope. The most argumentatively explicit account is that of Simplicius:[1]

> The flying missile occupies a space equal to itself at each instant, and so during the whole time of its flight; what occupies a space equal to itself at an instant is not in motion, since nothing is in motion at an instant; but what is not in motion is at rest, since everything is either in motion or at rest: therefore the flying missile, while it is in flight, is at rest during the whole time of its flight. (Lee (1936), p. 53.)

This suggests the following reconstruction:

(1) If x moves throughout a period T, then x moves at each instant of T.

For each instant t of T:

(2) x is either at rest or in motion at t.
(3) x occupies a space equal to itself at t.
(4) If x occupies a space equal to itself at t then x is not in motion at t.

From (3) and (4):

(5) x is not in motion at t.

From (1) and (5):

(6) x does not move throughout T.

Finally, from (2) and (6):

(7) x is at rest throughout T.

[1] For sources and commentary, see Lee (1936), Barnes (1982) and Kirk, Raven and Schofield (1983). For discussion, see Ross (1936), Owen (1957), Vlastos (1966), Grünbaum (1967), Salmon (1970) and Sorabji (1983).

The crucial term of art here, of course, is 'instant'. For the premises to be remotely plausible, we need to interpret this as an *indivisible* point of time, not further resolvable into smaller items. If there can be nothing smaller than an instant, then whatever takes place within an instant cannot be differentiated into distinct states obtaining in smaller moments. (I postpone until the next section the question of whether these indivisibles have any duration.)

Having settled that point of interpretation, let us begin by indicating some general lines of attack.

Aristotle's objection, which would threaten (2), that if one cannot speak of something's being in motion at an instant, one cannot properly speak of its being at rest at an instant either, can be conceded without damaging the argument. (2) and (7) do not contribute anything of value, since (6) is quite shocking enough on its own. So we need to look at (1), (3) and (4).

Aristotle has another, more worrying objection: '[the conclusion] follows from the assumption that time is composed of moments: if this assumption is not granted, the conclusion will not follow.' (*Physics* 239b30–3) The premise this observation is most relevant to is (1), since one could defend (1) on the basis that there is nothing to *T* other than the instants within it, and what is not true of any instant cannot, be true of the period. But this rationale is dubious whether or not we suppose time to be composed of instants. For to infer a property of the whole from a property of the parts is commit the fallacy of composition. Perhaps, then, we should present (1) as an application of the following principle:

If *x* is *F* throughout *T*, *x* is *F* at every instant of *T*.

Now, clearly, for most properties, this principle is perfectly acceptable: green, cubic, composed of copper, at 10 degrees C, etc. Nor is this list confined to monadic properties. It seems just as acceptable when applied to relational properties: being three yards from a heat source, reflecting light, being an object of perception, etc. The principle, then, is a plausible one, and seems to embody neither the fallacy of composition nor the assumption that Aristotle locates in Zeno's argument. (It may be, however, that Aristotle's reasoning behind his remark that time is not composed of moments is damaging in a different way to the argument; we return to this below.) (1), then, will only be vulnerable if there is any good reason to doubt that the general principle above applies to the property of being in motion.

What of (3)? A moving object occupies a succession of different positions and so, in a sense, occupies (although not all at once) a volume of space that is greater than its own—i.e. that whose boundaries are defined by the object's surface. Of course, the volume of an object will be defined as that which it occupies at an instant, so it is trivially true that an object, whether moving or not, occupies at an instant a space equal to its volume. (3), then, seems secure. But what is inferred from this, namely that a moving object is not moving at an instant, seems far from trivial. The most obviously controversial premise, then, is (4).

However, before proceeding, we need to look at the suggestion that the argument depends on a further, tacit, assumption about the nature of instants.

III. Atomism: the hidden premise?

Why does Aristotle suppose the Arrow to depend on the premise that time is composed of instants? As we saw in the previous section, it is possible to defend (1) without recourse to such an assumption, and indeed explicit appeal to it would invite the charge of fallacy. Now it may be that Aristotle takes Zeno to be making a fairly obvious blunder, but there is a more interesting possibility.

It is uncontroversial that the argument depends on realism about instants. There must be such things as instants, not simply as logical fictions, but as independently existing entities, for there to be truths about what is the case at those instants. But this realism may imply something about the topological structure of time. Let us imagine that the indivisible instants of time at which the Arrow occupies a space just its own size have a small, but non-zero duration. Then periods of time would be composed of such 'time atoms', and the number of such atoms in a period would determine its length (assuming that each atom has the same duration). Time atoms would be the fundamental unit from which periods were built up. So a discrete topology for time is compatible with—indeed implies—realism over instants. But now suppose instead that time is not discrete but continuous, so that each period of time were indefinitely divisible. What implications would this have for instants? This is what I take to be Aristotle's answer to that question: Although time is continuous, we avoid the consequence that would appear to flow from this, namely that each period contains an infinite number of instants, by the assumption of *finitism*. Nothing is *actually* infinite (there is no infinitely large object, for example), but only *potentially* infinite. So, for example, numbers are infinite only in the sense that, however high a number one has counted to, one can always count to a higher number. The process of counting has no limit built into it. Similarly, a length is infinitely divisible only in the sense that, however many divisions you have made, you can always make more. The process of dividing has no limit. But the divisions do not exist independently of one making them, so the potentially infinite divisibility of a length does not imply the actual existence of an infinite number of divisions within that length.[2] And as with length, so with time: a period of time is infinitely divisible, but only potentially so. Durationless instants do not exist independently of their being marked in some way. This view of the divisibility of space and time provides Aristotle with an answer to two other Zenonian paradoxes of motion, the Dichotomy and the Achilles. Both paradoxes start from the assumption of the continuity of time and space, and derive the unpalatable conclusion that motion involves achieving the impossible: the traversal of an infinite number of sub-distances in a finite length of time. Aristotle dissolves the paradoxes by denying that divisions have any independent existence. Admittedly, Aristotle only explicitly applies this to spatial divisions, but the same reasoning leads to a similar conclusion concerning temporal divisions.

This, then, is my conjecture: Aristotle, quite correctly, takes the paradox to depend on realism about instants. But he takes this realism to imply a discrete topology for time, which he expresses as the view that time is composed of instants. So attributing to Zeno the premise that time is composed of instants is simply an expression of the fact that the Arrow depends on the real existence of instants.

Whether or not this reconstruction of Aristotle's thinking holds water, it is certainly true that a number of commentators have attributed an atomistic premise to Zeno. Lee (1936), for example, takes it as obvious that this is an assumption (even if an implicit one) without, however, giving his reasons for thinking so. There is something attractive about the suggestion. For one thing, it presents a pleasingly symmetrical picture of the overall dialectic of Zeno's four famous paradoxes of motion. The Dichotomy and Achilles show that motion is impossible if space and time are continuous; the Arrow and Stadium show that motion is impossible if space and time are discrete. Since motion is impossible without time, and time must either have a discrete or continuous structure,[3] motion is impossible.

[2] See *Physics*, Book III, Chapters 6 and 7. Hussey (1983), pp. 14–18.

[3] I ignore here, since it does not affect the argument, the possibility that time might be merely *dense*: that is, isomorphic to the series of rational, rather than real numbers. See Newton-Smith (1980) for a discussion of the distinction between continuity, density and discreteness.

Barnes calls this picture 'a neat fantasy', and I am inclined to agree. What matters is that an instant is indivisible, thus permitting no motion within it. But this does not conflict with a continuist topology: it merely implies that if time is continuous, an instant must be defined as having no duration whatsoever. For Barnes, then, the argument need make no topological assumptions. This does not, of course, provide an answer to the objection to instants raised by Aristotle's finitism. If there is no actual infinite, how can there be an infinite number of actual instants in any period? Perhaps finitism can be reconciled with instants and the continuum, however, by appeal to Aristotle's conception of the actual infinite as that which exists *all at once*. A continuum of real spatial points would count as an actual infinite by this definition, whereas a continuum of temporal points would not, as the points are successive and not simultaneous. (It has to be admitted, however, that this move somewhat weakens the case for attributing to Aristotle the thought that Zeno's Arrow depends on a discrete structure for time.)

Even if realism about instants can be reconciled with the continuum, the Arrow can legitimately be challenged as follows: why should we take realism about instants seriously, when we can say everything we want to say about time using only the language of intervals? Temporal order, metric and topology can all be expressed in terms of intervals. And we can construct instants out of intervals by treating them as the notional lower limit of nested intervals.[4] So why introduce instants when, as the Arrow shows, they lead to difficulties? Well, there is one instant at least whose existence is hard to impugn: the present moment. What happens to Zeno's Arrow when we build reference to the present into the reconstruction?

IV. Second reconstruction: no motion in the present

The most effective answer to our first reconstruction of the Arrow is to produce an account of motion (and of change in general) that is both plausible and which undermines at least one of the premises. The obvious candidate for such an account defines change as follows: change consists in the instantiation at different times of incompatible states of affairs. Thus, for example, just as heating consists in an object's (or region's) being at different temperatures at different times, so motion consists in an object's occupying different places at different times. This approach to motion we will call, after Russell (but also somewhat contentiously), the *static*

[4] See Newton-Smith (1980), pp. 134–8.

account of motion. There are two ways in which one might take the static account as undermining the Arrow. One is to take it as falsifying (1). One could concede that there is no such thing as motion (or change in general) at an instant, but merely the occupancy of a particular position (or state), and insist that motion is attributable to an object only over a period of time. By analogy, an extended object may be ten foot wide without it being true that all its parts are ten foot wide. This is Russell's response to the Arrow.[5] It is a rather surprising response, however, since there is a kind of motion that seemingly obliges us to talk of motion at an instant, namely acceleration. If an object accelerates continuously through a period, it surely has a different velocity at each successive instant. One could, perhaps, insist that this is merely a theoretical abstraction, but it would have to go hand in hand with the view that instants themselves are theoretical abstractions. A much more plausible approach takes our analysis of motion to undermine premise (4). There is no need to deny that objects can move at an instant, but they do so only in a derivative sense. An object is in motion at *t* iff it occupies different positions at times immediately preceding and/or immediately succeeding *t*. What is true at an instant thus depends in part on what is true at other times. So from the indisputable fact that an object necessarily occupies a space just its own size at *t*, it does not follow that an object cannot be in motion at *t*.

The game is not yet up, however, for we can provide another reconstruction of the Arrow, one that brings out the limitations of the static account of motion.

A feature of Aristotle's reconstruction of the Arrow, and of his discussion of time in general, is the phrase 'in the now' (εν το νυν). Jonathan Lear has suggested that, by interpreting *nun* as 'moment', commentators like Owen, Vlastos and Barnes have overlooked the significance of the *nun*: it is the *present* moment and not merely some arbitrary instant. Lear's own reconstruction of the paradox goes as follows:

(1) Anything that is occupying a space just its own size is at rest.
(2) A moving arrow, while it is moving, is moving in the present.
(3) But in the present the arrow is occupying a space just its own size.
(4) Therefore in the present the arrow is at rest.
(5) Therefore a moving arrow, while it is moving, is at rest.

(Lear (1988), p. 84)

[5] See Russell (1903), pp. 467–73. His definition of motion is given on p. 473. For a discussion of the Arrow, see pp. 350–2.

Robin Le Poidevin

Recall one objection to the first reconstruction: that we could avoid talk of indivisible instants altogether in favour of intervals, and in so doing make irrelevant the alleged fact that nothing moves at an instant. But turning the focus of the argument onto the present moment explains why the moment in question must be an indivisible instant and not a period. For if the present were divisible into different parts, some would be earlier than others, and so not present. But every part of the present must itself be present, which is to say, of course, that the present has no earlier and later parts.

Another feature of Lear's reconstruction is that he talks, not of what is happening *at* the present, but *in* the present (this being the literal translation of '$\epsilon\nu$ το νυν'). This certainly makes the premises somewhat more plausible, for we could happily concede that nothing moves in (i.e. within the space of) the present. It is not immediately obvious how this helps, however, because we could still insist that the crucial question is what is true of the arrow *at* an instant, and, as Barnes points out,[6] commonsense dictates that it is true to say of the arrow that it is moving at an instant of time. It moves *at* an instant by virtue of that instant being part of a period *in* which the arrow is continuously in motion.

Nevertheless, the second reconstruction does represent a significant advance on the first. The most powerful objection to the first reconstruction is constituted by the static analysis of change: something moves in an instant by virtue of its position both at that instant at other times. So talk of motion at an instant is derivative: its truth depends on what is happening over a period of time. It is this move that is challenged by the second reconstruction. For what is true in the present should not be derivative, but *fundamental*. It is the privileged status of the present that insulates present fact from past and future fact. The static analysis of change makes expressions like '*x* moves in the present' temporally hybrid, turning what purports to be a simple statement about the present into a complex statement about past, present and future. But, we may imagine the champions of the present arguing, '*x* moves in the present' is a simple statement about the present, and should not be taken as elliptical for something else. Here is how Lear presents the moves:

> To Zeno's incredulous question, 'So you think that an object can be moving solely in virtue of positions it has occupied in the past and will occupy in the future?', one would simply answer 'yes.' This would be the response of someone who did not wish to

[6] See Barnes (1982), pp. 280–1.

incorporate the notion of a present duration into his scientific theory of time. (Lear (1988), p. 90)

I think Lear is quite right, by which I mean I think he has constructed a much more effective argument than one which talks merely of instants. I also think he is right that the Arrow is most problematic for those who accord a special status to the present, and that one effective response (although one which requires a revision to our ordinary view of time and change) is to dethrone the present and treat it as a merely perspectival feature of our temporal descriptions. But he moves rather too fast. We need a more explicit account of what it is to treat the present as somehow special, and we also need to be clear why this should imply anything about the nature of change and motion. Before embarking on this, however, we should consider whether there is a plausible alternative to the static account of motion, implied in the suggestion that '*x* moves in the present' is a simple assertion about what is presently the case.

V. The dynamic account of motion

The static account of motion, recall, goes as follows:

> An object moves at a time by virtue of its position at that time *and* its position(s) at other times.

The contradictory of this should be something like the following:

> *The dynamic account of motion*: an object's motion at a time is independent of the object's position at other times.

This is not, however, a single account, but the common denominator of a number of accounts. For example, the statement above leaves it an open matter whether an object's motion at a time is an intrinsic property of that object or a relation between that object and simultaneously existing objects or places. It is also an open question whether the account arises from a demotion of instants to a logical construction from intervals, as canvassed in §III. Introducing greater specificity and detail into the dynamic account would produce the following variants:

(i) It is an intrinsic property of an object that it is in motion at a particular time, the property in question being a disposition of the object to be elsewhere than the place it is.

(ii) Motion at an instant consists in the object both being, and not being, in the place where it is.

(iii) Events, including those involving motion, are primitive, not decomposable into series of states. Similarly, intervals are primitive, not decomposable into series of instants. So talk of 'motion at a time' must always be interpreted as motion in an arbitrarily small interval.

Account (i) falls victim, I think, to the following counterexample: a stationary object is struck at t by a rapidly moving one, as a result of which (causation being successive and never simultaneous) it begins to move *after t*. Though the object is *disposed* to be elsewhere at t, as a result of its being subjected to a force at that moment, we would count t as the last moment of rest, rather than the first moment of motion. (i) would also conflict with the (more contentious) assertion that constant motion is always relative to some other object or objects.

Account (ii) is, most commentators would admit, very strange. Priest (1987), who offers an imaginative and sympathetic reconstruction of it, describes it as the 'Hegelean' account of motion, on the basis of the following admittedly very explicit remark of Hegel's:

> ...motion itself is contradiction's immediate existence. Something moves not because at one moment of time it is here and at another there, but because at one and the same moment it is here and not here. (Hegel (1840), quoted by Priest (1987), p. 219)

To take it seriously is, in effect, to embrace dialetheism, the view that there are true contradictions, and that contradictory states of affairs can actually obtain.[7] Even the dialetheist is not going to countenance all contradictions, however, but only those for which there are compelling reasons. Since the arguments of this paper tacitly employ the Law of Non-Contradiction, which dialetheism rejects, however, I cannot without hypocrisy leave logical space for the Hegelean account. No doubt it deserves proper consideration, but here I will simply point out that it is contradictory, and hope that by abandoning it on those grounds I have not lost all my readers.

We are left, then, with (iii). It certainly undermines the first reconstruction of the Arrow, for reasons already rehearsed. Does it undermine the second? Let us reserve judgement for the time being, and return to Lear's contention that the key concept in an understanding of the Arrow is that of the present. Now there is more than one way to take the present seriously, the most obvious being to take

---

[7] For an extended exposition and defence of dialetheism, see Priest (1987).

66

it as the temporal location of all that is real. So let us now consider its effect on Zeno's paradox.

VI. The consequences of presentism

The word 'presentism' is often used to describe the view that only what is present is real (elsewhere (1991) I used the term 'temporal solipsism', but here I follow convention). I take this to imply the following theses:

(a) Where the domain of quantification is concrete objects, the existential quantifier ranges only over those objects that are located in the present moment.
(b) The truth-makers of past- and future-tensed token sentences are present facts.

And, as a consequence of (a) and (b):

(c) Primitive relations obtain only between contemporaneous objects.

One way of expressing presentism is to say that all truths, fundamentally, are present truths. What was and will be the case obtains only by virtue of what is now the case. This is a much more substantial position than the trivial thesis that any propositions of the form

It was the case that p

and

It will be the case that p

are equivalent to, respectively,

It is now the case that (it was the case that p)
It is now the case that (it will be the case that p)

Presentism is essentially an ontological thesis, restricting reality to a single time. It is hard to think of a way in which the present moment could be taken more seriously. If Lear is right, then, about the importance of the present moment to the Arrow, presentism should have implications for the treatment of motion. In particular, we should expect that 'x moves in the present' cannot, on a presentist reading, be treated as elliptical for a statement about past and future positions.

However, at first sight, presentism seems rather to *favour* the static analysis, insofar as it conflicts with the rival to that analysis. According to the version of the dynamic account which we were left with at the end of the last section, an object's being in motion is a primitive event, not further analysable in terms of objects, properties and times. Now for these primitive events to exist, on the presentist reading, they must be capable of existing in the present. But events, being changes, are not instantaneous items: they take up time. So, at best, what exists in the present are *parts* of events. The idea of events having parts that are not themselves events, however, conflicts with the primitive status of events. To the question, what are these parts? the obvious answer seems to be: instantaneous states of an object. Presentism is therefore incompatible with primitivism about events. Thus we come back to the static analysis.

So why should we suppose there to be any conflict between presentism and the static analysis? For the presentist, all fact is present fact. This implies, then, that x's moving in the present is simply a present fact, or collection of present facts. This is at least formally consistent with the static analysis. The presentist can allow that x was in a different position from the one it now occupies, but has to insist that this is made true by present fact. So one set of present facts makes true 'x was at s_1', another set makes true 'x is at s_2', and yet another set 'x will be at s_3'. Thus present fact can, in principle, make it true that x is moving, even when we understand motion in terms of the static analysis.

It is clear that we will have to look a little deeper if we are to discern the kind of difficulty Lear was alluding to. The problem, I think, has to do with the extent to which the present is capable of making determinate past states of affairs. Firstly, anything less than a fully deterministic universe will leave some propositions concerning the past without a determinate truth-value (this feature is peculiar to presentism, of course). Secondly, it is not even clear that the presentist is in a position to build determinism into their world view.

Let us look at these points in turn. What presentism requires, in order to guarantee the truth of propositions concerning the past location of objects, is the classical determinist picture, expressible as follows:

> Given the conjunction of all laws, for any two times, t and t', the total state of the universe at t is logically compossible with only one total state at t'.

This particular formulation is not, however, essential to the classical position. We could, for example, have avoided explicit reference to laws, treated determinism as a property of theories rather than the universe, and replaced reference to total states of the universe by reference to models of those theories, as follows:

> The conjunction of all true theories is such that if any two models of that conjunction are isomorphic at any point, they are isomorphic at all other points.[8]

The appeal to truth here is essential. Even if determinism is a feature of theories, the fact (if it is a fact) that the conjunction of all true theories is deterministic will depend on a feature of the world. Any non-realist interpretation of theories, or doubts whether there could be such a thing as the conjunction of all true theories, represent a departure from the classical picture.

Both formulations above, note, are time-symmetric: the state at one time determines both later *and* earlier states. Some statements of classical determinism are not time-symmetric, and make only the future depend on the present, but it is clear that the presentist requires the past to be determined too.

Even with determinism (of the relevant sort) in place, however, problems remain, which brings us to the second point. Since presentism confines reality to a single, durationless point, it cannot build in to the description of the total state of the universe at a given time reference to motion, for this imports states at times other than the present. All that is available to the presentist is the position of objects, their various states, and the forces acting upon those objects. Is this enough to determine earlier and later positions? Consider the following two cases:

(i) The substantivalist conception of space as an entity existing independently of its contents is correct. Consequently, there is such a thing as absolute motion (this being simply motion relative to space itself). Now consider a universe of objects in absolute, but not relative, unidirectional and non-accelerating motion. Can the position at any one time of those objects determine earlier and later positions? No.

(ii) The substantivalist conception of space is not correct, and all motion is relative to other contents of space. Now consider a (relatively simple) universe in which the forces on certain objects at a particular moment cancel each other out, so there is no resultant force on those objects in any one direction. Can the state of the objects at that moment determine their earlier and later positions? No.

[8] See Butterfield (1998) for different formulations of determinism and discussion of associated difficulties.

Robin Le Poidevin

It seems, then, that we can say, first, that classical determinism cannot accommodate absolute motion, if it is built on presentist assumptions;[9] and secondly, that at least in a range of cases, presentism cannot even account for the relative motion of objects. Consequently, the presentist can only adopt the static analysis of motion (and change in general) on pain of an unacceptable level of indeterminacy. On the other hand, since we have already ruled out treating change in terms of primitive events, it is not clear what other account is now available to the presentist.

Our third and final reconstruction of the argument can be presented as follows:

> (A) The dynamic account of motion: an object's motion at a time is an irreducible property, independent of the object's state at other times.
> (B) The static account of motion: an object moves at a time by virtue of its position at that time and at other times.

> (1) If motion is possible, then either (A) or (B) is the correct account of it.
> (2) If presentism is true, (A) is false.
> (3) If presentism is true, (B) is false.

From (1), (2) and (3):

> (4) If presentism is true, motion is impossible.

What further conclusion we draw from (4) I leave to the reader.[10]

I have tried to provide some more detailed argument for Lear's suggestion that what we have called the static account of motion is only available to 'someone who did not wish to incorporate the notion of a present duration into his scientific theory of time.' There is, I have argued, a conflict between presentism and the static account. But is the choice of positions limited to presentism on the one hand and an elimination of the present in favour of a pure-

[9] Priest (1987), p. 217, notes a tension between classical determinism and the static account. That tension, however, could be resolved by a small revision to the classical account, as follows: states of the universe at arbitrarily (but non-zero) intervals determine states at other times. This move, of course, is blocked by presentism.

[10] I cannot resist adding another twist, however. Consider the following paradox, as formulated by Owen in his discussion of Aristotle's conception of time: 'Only the present is real, yet the present is never a stretch of time. ... Moreover time is a function of change ... but nothing can be changing at a present moment. How can time be real?' (Owen (1976), p. 309: page reference to the reprinted version.)

ly tenseless conception of time on the other? Is there no room for a view that takes tense to be part of the world, rather than simply our representations of it, and yet which does not restrict reality to the present? For reasons I have articulated elsewhere ((1991), Chapter 2), I believe the answer to this question to be 'no'. Treating tense as real can only lead to contradiction unless one assumes presentism.

Our final reconstruction of the Arrow would horrify Barnes (and perhaps Zeno, too). But then an Arrow purged of any but the most minimal theoretical content is vulnerable, as we have seen, to rather obvious objections. To strengthen the Arrow, we need to engage with theory. If one of history's most ancient paradoxes is to survive into the new age, that's the deal.

References

Barnes, Jonathan 1982. *The Presocratic Philosophers*, revised edition, London: Routledge and Kegan Paul.

Butterfield, Jeremy 1998. 'Determinism and Indeterminism', in Edward Craig (ed.) *The Routledge Encyclopedia of Philosophy*, London: Routledge, pp. 33–9.

Grünbaum, Adolf 1967. *Modern Science and Zeno's Paradoxes*, Connecticut: Wesleyan University Press.

Hegel, G. W. F. 1840. *Lectures on the History of Philosophy*, trans. E. S. Haldane, London: Kegan Paul.

Hussey, Edward 1983. *Aristotle's Physics, Books III and IV*, Oxford: Clarendon Press.

Kirk, G. S., Raven, J. E., and Schofield, M. 1983. *The Presocratic Philosophers: A Critical History with a Selection of Texts*, 2nd edition, Cambridge: Cambridge University Press.

Lear, Jonathan 1981. 'A Note on Zeno's Arrow', *Phronesis*, **26**, pp. 91–104

—— (1988) *Aristotle: The Desire to Understand*, Cambridge: Cambridge University Press.

Lee, H. D. P. 1936. *Zeno of Elea*, Cambridge: Cambridge University Press

Le Poidevin, Robin 1991. *Change, Cause and Contradiction*, London: Macmillan.

Newton-Smith, W. H. 1980. *The Structure of Time*, London: Routledge and Kegan Paul.

Owen, G. E. L. 1957. 'Zeno and the Mathematicians', *Proceedings of the Aristotelian Society*, **58**, pp.199–222; reprinted in Owen (1986), pp. 45–61.

—— 1976. 'Aristotle on Time', in P. Machamer and R. Turnbull (eds), *Motion and Time, Space and Matter*, Columbus: Ohio State University Press, pp. 3–27; reprinted in Owen (1986), pp. 295–314.

—— 1986. *Logic, Science and Dialectic*, ed. Martha Nussbaum, London: Duckworth.

Robin Le Poidevin

Priest, Graham 1987. *In Contradiction: A Study of the Transconsistent*, Dordrecht: Nijhoff.

Ross, W. D, 1936. *Aristotle's Physics*, Oxford Clarendon Press.

Russell, Bertrand 1903. *The Principles of Mathematics*, Cambridge: Cambridge University Press.

Salmon, Wesley 1970. *Zeno's Paradoxes*, Indianapolis: Bobbs-Merrill.

Sorabji, Richard 1983. *Time, Creation and the Continuum*, London: Duckworth.

Vlastos, G. 1966. 'A Note on Zeno's Arrow', *Phronesis*, **11**, pp. 3–18.

Presentism, Ontology and Temporal Experience

L. NATHAN OAKLANDER

In a recent article, 'Tensed Time and Our Differential Experience of the Past and Future,' William Lane Craig (1999a) attempts to resuscitate A. N. Prior's (1959) 'Thank Goodness' argument against the B-theory by combining it with Plantinga's (1983) views about basic beliefs. In essence Craig's view is that since there is a universal experience and belief in the objectivity of tense and the reality of becoming, (that he identifies with 'the presentist metaphysic') 'this belief constitutes an intrinsic defeater-defeater which overwhelms the objections brought against it.' (1999a, 519) An intrinsic defeater-defeater is a belief that enjoys such warrant for us that it simply overwhelms the defeaters brought against it without specifically rebutting or undercutting them. Thus, Craig claims that an effete philosophical argument like McTaggart's paradox is nothing more than 'an engaging and recalcitrant brain teaser whose conclusion nobody really takes seriously.' (1999a, 532) It is difficult to reconcile this statement with Craig's own writings elsewhere. For Craig has vigorously argued in at least two other articles that 'hybrid A-B theorists like McCall, Schlesinger, and Smith [who give ontological status to both A-properties and B-relations] are in deep trouble' (1998, 127) since they are all effectively refuted by McTaggart's Paradox (cf. Craig 1997). It is not Craig's inconsistency regarding the significance of McTaggart conundrum that I want to draw attention to, however. Rather I wish to raise a different issue.

Presentists such as Prior and Craig (and A-theorist's generally) maintain that one motivation, and for some the primary motivation for adopting presentism is 'the desire to do justice to the feeling that what's in the past is over and done with, and that what's in the future only matters because it will *eventually* be present.' (Zimmerman 1998, 212; my emphasis). As Craig puts it, '[O]nly on the A-theory; with its ontological distinctions between past, present, and future can differential attitudes toward events ... be rationally justified.' (1999a, 530) He claims that one is rationally justified in feeling relief concerning the cessation of a painful experience because

L. Nathan Oaklander

> [O]n a presentist metaphysic the experience was *once* real and now no longer is. ... (Analogously, dread about some future painful event is appropriate because, although not yet real, it *soon* will be, ...). (1999a, 521–22)

In these passages the phases '*eventually* will be present,' 'once real' and 'it soon will be' seem to imply the existence of temporal relations. For, 'once' in this context means, 'at some *earlier time*,' 'soon' means 'at a relatively short *time later*,' and 'eventually' means 'at a relatively distant *later time*.' Thus, to explain our differing attitudes of dread and relief it would appear that in addition to the existence of the present time (and present experiences), earlier and later times (and earlier and later experiences) must be real too. As Craig himself says, 'When I feel relief, what I am relieved about can be analysed as a *complex fact* that it is now and that the relevant event *is earlier than now*.' (1999a, 523; my emphasis)

With this background the main question I wish to explore in this paper can be stated as follows: Can an ontological analysis that specifies the constituents of the complex fact that *it is now and the relevant event is earlier or later than now* be given that is consistent with presentism? *Prima facie* the answer to this question is 'no' because in order for there to be a temporal relation between two events there must *be* the two events that stand in that relation. Indeed, this is a truism that is even accepted by some presentists. Consider, for example, the following statement by John Bigelow, whose views I discuss in detail below:

> It is; I maintain, an a priori truth that a two-place relation can only be manifested when it holds between two things, and in order for this to be so there must be two things which stand in the relation. And in saying 'there must be' two things which stand in the relation, one is really asserting that 'there must exist' two things—one is committed to the existence of those things. The principle of the existence entailment of relations is an a priori truth. (1996, 39)

Since relief involves a temporal relation between a present belief or feeling, and something else that is not present (what I believe or am relieved about), it follows that some things/events/times exist that are not present. To avoid this conclusion presentists must provide an ontological reduction of temporal relations, but it is not clear that they have the resources available to accomplish that task. Thus, we are led to ask, what is the truth-maker or, to use Robin Le Poidevin's turn of phrase, 'that bit of reality' (1999b, 149) that is the ontological ground of the complex fact that one event (or time) is earlier or later than the present event or time? If presentists cannot give an adequate answer to that question then far from rationally justifying our different attitudes toward earlier and later events, they render those attitudes mysterious.

The importance of giving an adequate ontological assay of temporal relations is highlighted by another concern. Presentism has been claimed to border on the trivial or the absurd. It is trivial if it is taken to assert, 'The only things that exist now (i.e. at present) are those that exist at present.' (Zimmerman 1998, 209) And it is absurd if it is taken to mean what David Lewis takes it to mean, namely, that for the presentist nothing changes because it rejects persistence altogether by maintaining that there are no past or future times, but only this present moment. (1986, 202–3) In response to the triviality objection a presentist may claim that their view does not assert the tautology that only the present exists at present, but that only the present exists *simpliciter* or just plain exists. To exist *simpliciter* does not mean to exist now, or to exist at time t, but simply to exist (or to happen) without temporal qualification.[1] But if only the present moment exists without qualification, then in order to generate change the presentist must introduce tensed propositions that change their truth value at different *times* depending on what exists *simpliciter* at those times as time passes. Of course, if a tensed proposition changes its truth-value at different times, then there must *be* those times at which the proposition changes, and in order to be genuine *times* they must be members of temporal series whose generating relation is earlier/later than. But if there exists only *one* time, the present time, then how can any time be earlier or later than another and how can a proposition or anything else *change* from *one time to another*?

How, in other words, can it be true, as it obviously in some sense is, that

(PC) There are (at least) two different times, one at which I am bent, another at which I am straight?

[1] It seems, therefore, that the presentist is committed to Tooley's (1997) distinction between what *actual simpliciter* and what is *actual as of a time*. For if what exists *simpliciter* is all that exists, and if only the present moment exists *simpliciter*, then Lewis is right and we have no past or future. For a critique of the conjunction of the notions of actual *simpliciter* and actual as of a time, see Le Poidevin (1998b, 2001), Oaklander (1999a), Smith (1999a) and Mellor (1998).

L. Nathan Oaklander

In response to this question a presentist may offer a paraphrase that captures what is meant by (PC) but does not involve direct reference to non-present times. Thus, for example, Dean Zimmerman says that (PC) can be taken as a tenseless statement expressing a disjunction of tensed propositions:

> Either I was bent and would become or *had previously* been straight, or I was straight and *would become* or had previously been bent, or I will be bent and will have been or be *about to become* straight, or I will be straight and will have been or be about to become bent. Surely this tensed disjunction is true if (PC) is true; furthermore, it contains no mention of anything like a non-present time. So given the presentist's desire to avoid ontological commitment to non-present times, this tensed statement provides a perfectly sensible paraphrase of my conviction that I can persist through change of shape. (1998, 215; emphasis added)

I shall avoid the question of whether Zimmerman's paraphrase captures what is meant by (PC)[2] and concentrate on the question, 'Does it avoid ontological commitment to non-present times?' It certainly does not avoid commitment to temporal relations and, on the face of it, temporal relations presuppose the existence of earlier and later (i.e., non-present) times. Included in his analysis of (PC) are the phrases 'had *previously* been straight,' and 'about to become bent.' The former phrase has the sense of 'was at some *earlier time* straight' and the latter means, 'at a short *time later* becomes (or will become) bent.' Furthermore, the concept of *temporal* becoming, if it is to be the ground of *temporal* change, that is, change in a given direction, must account for my becoming straight *before* becoming bent or *vice versa*. Thus, the presentist must provide an account of temporal relations, and to provide such an account is to specify what there is in the world, independently of minds, that is the truth maker of judgments asserting that two entities stand in a temporal relation. If an adequate account is not forthcoming then not only are our different attitudes toward earlier and later events left unexplained, but Lewis's objection, that for the presentist nothing changes, is vindicated. In what follows I shall consider several recent versions of presentism that attempt to respond to the challenge of providing an adequate ontological ground of temporal relations and argue that none of them is successful.

Each of the philosophers I shall discuss, William Craig, John Bigelow and Robert Ludlow, all avowed presentists, acknowledge

[2] And I shall also avoid diagnosing why Zimmerman characterizes his paraphrase of (PC) as both a 'tenseless statement' and a 'tensed statement.'

their debt to Prior, but for one reason or another find his particular explication of presentism wanting. Prior's views have also recently received extensive critical discussion by other A-theorists such as Craig (1997, 27–29), Smith (1986; 1993, 158–169; 1999b, 248–249, 2002), and Tooley (1997, 165–70, 232–8), as well as by B-theorists such as Le Poidevin (1991, 36–57), Mellor (1998, 70–81) and Oaklander (1984, 90–104). For that reason there will be only an incidental discussion of Prior's views on time in this paper.

Let me then first consider Craig's various versions of presentism to see if any of them can make sense of the notion of events standing in temporal relations. According to Craig,

> [T]he A-theorist denies the very reality of past and future events, but he does not deny that some events are objectively past or others future—he just parses such statements to mean that 'It was the case that e_1 exists' and 'It will be the case that e_2 exists' are true. (1999a, 534)

On the face of it, to deny the reality of past and future events, and to affirm that some events *are* objectively past and future is an explicit contradiction. Thus, to avoid that contradiction we need to ask of Craig's paraphrase of statements about past and future events, what is it that makes them true? To that he responds:

> [C]orresponding to past/future-tense propositions are tensed facts or states of affairs that presently obtain, e.g., its being the case that e will occur [or it being the case that e did occur]. But e [or e'] itself is not presently existent or real. Though equally unreal, past and future events are properly regarded differentially by us due to the direction of time. ... [O]n the A-theory the impossibility of backward becoming entails the propriety of differential attitudes toward earlier and later events. (1999a, 534)

One problem with this analysis is that if neither e_1 or e_2 nor the properties of pastness and futurity exist, then what could be the foundation of the difference between the tensed facts that e_2 *will occur* and e_1 *did occur*? And what could be the truth-maker for the state of affairs that e_1 is earlier than e_2?

Perhaps Craig would attempt to specify a tensed fact by appealing to the properties or a description that one associates with the purportedly past or future event. He could then claim that the difference between a past and future tensed fact is that in one case the defining properties of e_2 *will be exemplified*, presently obtains whereas in the other case the defining properties of e_1 *once was exemplified*, presently obtains. However, I don't think this gambit

works. For unless one explains (or specifies) the ontological correlate of 'will be exemplified' and 'was exemplified,' there really is no
basis for the difference in the temporal location of either of these
facts. In other words, if there is no grounding of the past and future
tenses in the complex fact that e_2 will be exemplified and e_1 was
exemplified, then there is no basis for determining whether e_1 is
exemplified *before* e_2 is exemplified or *vice versa*.

Furthermore, I do not see how, as Craig says, the direction of
time can be the basis of the difference between past and future tense
states of affairs. On the A-theory, the direction of time is based on
the changing truth of past and future tense propositions. That is, on
the A-theory the direction of time is grounded in the fact that an
event is *first* future, *and then* present *and then* past rather than the
other way around. As Prior puts it,

> We all know what it is to wait for something.... What we're wait-
> ing for *begins by being future*; it *hasn't yet* come to pass. *Then a
> time comes* when it does come to pass—when it's *present*, and we're
> aware of its presentness, and there's no mistaking it. *And then* it's
> past.... (1996, 50; my emphasis)

In other words, on the A-theory the direction of time is grounded in
an event/thing/time being future *before* it is present and being present *before* it is past.[3] Thus, the difference between past and future
events (or times), and the temporal relations that hold between them,
cannot be based on the direction of time because the direction of
time is based on the distinction between past and future tensed facts
and their temporal relations to the present. Furthermore, Craig's
claim that 'on the A-theory the impossibility of backward becoming
entails the propriety of differential attitudes toward earlier and later
events' (1999a, 534) is question begging. Without a prior account of
the ontological difference between past and future tensed facts, and
a grounding of temporal relations, Craig is not entitled to assume
that backward becoming is impossible.

---

[3] Prior seems to be making essentially the same point when he says: 'I
believe that what we see as a progress of events is a progress of events, *a
coming to pass* of one thing *after* another, and not just a timeless tapestry
with everything stuck there for good and all.' (1986, 104) I should note,
parenthetically, that Prior's claim that what we see as a progress of events
(one thing occurring *after* another) is, on the B-theory, 'just a timeless
tapestry with everything stuck there for good and all,' is a common mis-
characterization that depends on viewing time from a God-like third person point of view and not the subjective first-person temporal point of
view that B-theorists believe in.

Presentism, Ontology and Temporal Experience

Nor can Craig appeal to causation to ground the direction of time and the impossibility of backward becoming since the A-theorist has just as much problem with causal *relations* as he or she does with temporal relations because some present events are caused by non-present events. After all, why believe, for example, that my presently having lines around my eyes, or my presently having relatively little hair on the top of head, is evidence that I have aged over the past twenty years unless present evidence is causally related to the past which thereby must exist? In other words, if only the present exists how could the past be causally related to it?

In his article, 'Is Presentness a Property?' Craig realizes that the presentist needs to somehow ground the relational aspect of time since he says,

> on a presentist ontology past and future events/things/times are not real or existent and, hence, do not exemplify properties like pastness and futurity ... The A-theorist thus agrees with the B-theorist that pastness and futurity are relational predicates, but he will differ in *anchoring these relations in what is non-relationally present.* The construal of pastness and futurity as relational predicates should not be taken to mean that these are relational properties inhering in events. Rather such ascriptions should be parsed as asserting that the entity in question *did* or *will* exist. (1997, 29; my emphasis)

Again, this move seems to me unavailing. To assert that e_1 did exist and e_2 will exist says nothing more than that e_1 is past and e_2 is future. Since, however, 'is past' and 'is future' do not name temporal monadic properties or relational properties of events or times, Craig's paraphrase tells us nothing about the ontological difference between past and future tensed facts or about how temporal relations are to be 'anchored' in what is non-relationally present.

In adopting a presentist metaphysics Craig expresses his sympathy with Prior's view that to be present is simply to exist. He recognizes, however, that the treatment of 'was' and 'will be' and the past and future tenses as 'tensed operators' analogous to the sentential operator of negation, or the modal operator of possibility 'raises a host of questions for ontology. [And it] makes one suspicious that the ontological questions concerning tense ascriptions cannot be so neatly circumvented as Prior hoped.' (1997, 31) This seems to me to be quite true. Even if 'It was the case that ' and 'It will be the case that' are tensed operators analogous to sentential operators like negation (see Hinchliff, 1996), there remains the ontological question concerning whether or not there are past and future tensed facts. Although Russell allegedly caused a riot at Harvard when he lectured about negative facts, Russell (1918) believed and argued that negative facts exist. He is not alone, Gustav Bergmann (1964), Reinhardt Grossmann (1992), Herbert Hochberg (1969) and others have agreed and argued that there are conjunctive and general facts as well.[4] Hence, while treating the past and future tenses as operators does not imply that there are future and past tensed properties or facts, it does not rule them out either. Nor can treating the past and future tenses as *primitive* operators *eo ipso* avoid ontological commitment to past and future individuals and A-properties. Since even if the tenses are conceptually primitive one can still ask what entities do those primitives stand for? I shall return to this point in my discussion of Peter Ludlow.

In another paper 'McTaggart's Paradox and the Problem of Temporary Intrinsics,' Craig (1998) attempts to explicate the ontology of presentism 'by allowing tensed states of affairs to be constituents of possible worlds. ... Tensed possible worlds which did, do or will obtain are tensed actual worlds. ... A tensed actual world at t is the world which obtains when t's being present obtains' (1998, 126), but *when* does t's being present obtain? Judging from his comments it appears that t's being present obtains *before* t*'s being present obtains (for any later t*), since Craig maintains that

> The tensed history of any possible world W will be all the tensed possible worlds constituted by the states of affairs entailed by W and each *successive* t's being present in W. (1998, 126; emphasis added)

Thus, to explain *when* possible worlds obtain he appeals to *succession*, but since the appeal to succession implies the reality of B-relations one of whose terms is non-present, this particular explication does not answer the question of how a presentist ontology can consistently account for the relational aspect of time. It simply assumes that it can.

In his reply to my critique (1999b) Craig claims that his characterization of presentism in terms of possible worlds did not mean to '*found* [or ground] the objectivity of temporal becoming, but simply to provide a language in which to formulate such notions.' (1999b, 320) If, however, the appeal to possible worlds being actual at times that are present is not intended to explicate what makes relational temporal statements true, then it does not address the fundamental

---

[4] For an argument against negative facts that is also a precursor of one version of the new tenseless theory of time see Oaklander and Miracchi (1980).

problem with the ontology of presentism. For it does not provide an ontological explanation of how there can *be* objectively earlier and later times if all that exists is present.

Finally, in another recent publication on time, 'The Extent of the Present,' Craig maintains that the present is neither instantaneous nor atomic, but is a pre-metrical notion that denotes some arbitrarily selected finite interval. He continues,

> Any temporal interval which is contextually taken to be the present interval is susceptible of being conceptually divided into shorter temporal phases which will be past, present, and future, respectively. ... The present minute can thus be analysed into a past phase composed of seconds *earlier than* the present second, a present phase which is the present second, and a future phase composed of the *later* seconds remaining in the minute. (2000a, 179)

Thus, to avoid Augustine's problem of a durationless present, Craig claims that an interval can be present as a whole even if it is composed of parts some of which are past and some of which are future.

It does seem to me that one advantage of this account is that it looks like it has a chance of grounding the existence of past and future tensed facts, as well as temporal relations between past, present and future individuals in terms of what 'presently' exists.[5] The disadvantage is that Craig's latest account is not compatible with presentism, as his comments on the 'present' make clear. He says that,

> ... an interval may be present *simpliciter* even though we can divide it into sub-intervals which are not every one present. Thus, the present minute is *qua* minute present *simpliciter*, but if we divide it into seconds, then only one second is *qua* second present *simpliciter*. If any sub-interval of an interval is present, then the whole interval is as such present (2000a, 184).

If the present exists *simpliciter*, it would seem to be composed of phases some of which exist *simpliciter*. And if past and future phases *are temporally related* to the sub-interval that is present, and

[5] I say that Craig's view looks like it has a chance to succeed, but it cannot in fact succeed even if he countenances the full range of A-properties and B-relations. For the most elaborate and carefully crafted A/B ontology of tensed time is to be found in Smith. (1993 and 1994) However, in Oaklander (1996) I argue that Smith's version of the A-theory cannot account for events having their A-properties successively. Smith's view also receives a trenchant criticism in Nerlich (1998). I should note, however, that in his paper for this volume Smith (2002b) has modified his views in the light of criticism.

the entire interval exists because it is *as such present*, then it seems to me that we have a tenselessly existing series whose sub-intervals successively become present as time flows. This is the A-B ontology that Craig claims is 'incoherent.' (2000a, 165) Whether it is coherent or not, it is certainly not presentism.

For these reasons I do not think that Craig's various explications of presentism have met the challenge to give an adequate ontological assay of the complex fact that, say, an unpleasant visit to the dentist is *earlier than* a present memory of it, that is consistent with presentism. It should be noted, however, that Craig has several forthcoming articles and books on time in which he refines and defends presentism. Perhaps in one of those writings a more plausible version of presentism is to be found.[6]

I shall turn next to two other recent attempts (the first by John Bigelow and the second by Peter Ludlow) to deal with the challenge to presentism of what Bigelow aptly calls 'the argument from relations.' Bigelow attempts to ground truths about past and future individuals and the temporal relations between them by means of properties that *are presently exemplified*. He says that in order to meet the argument from relations,

> [W]e do not need to suppose the existence of any past or future things, only the possession by present things of properties and accidents expressed using the past and future tenses. ... Present things have present properties and these are the ontological ground of the past, the future and the passage of time. (1996, 46) These properties may include things like the property of being burdened with a certain sort of past, or (as Leibniz put it) being pregnant with a certain sort of future. (1996, 47)

On Bigelow's view, presently instantiated properties are the ground of the difference between the past and the future, and of temporal relations. No temporal relation ever in fact holds between things that exist at different times, since at any given time the ground of temporal relations are properties that are presently exemplified by the world as a whole at that time. Thus, Bigelow says,

> [O]ne of the things that exist is the whole world, the totality of things that exist. The world can have properties and accidents, just as its parts may have. It is a present property of the world that it is a world in which Helen was abducted, and the Trojans were conquered. (1996, 46)

[6] Craig's books on time (2000b, 2000c, 2001) have appeared since the completion of this paper.

And in discussing causal relations that, like temporal relations, purport to connect present events with events that are not present, he says:

> [T]he causal relation does not, in fact, ever hold between things that exist at different times. At any given time the causal relation holds between properties, perhaps between world properties, each of which is present and is presently instantiated. (1996, 46)

But can presently exemplified world properties of the sort Bigelow introduces account for the difference between the past and the future without introducing past and future individuals? Can they account for the relational aspect of time? And is the positing of such properties consistent with presentism? I do not think any of these questions can be answered affirmatively.

Bigelow says that there are presently exemplified properties that are expressed by the past and future tenses, but he never makes clear what it is exactly that makes these properties *tensed*. To bring the issue into sharper focus suppose at any given time both Helen was abducted and Helen will be abducted are presently exemplified. (That is, suppose that Helen was abducted, rescued and will be abducted again.) What is the difference in these presently exemplified properties expressed by the past and future tenses? How does the fact that the world exemplifies the one differ from the fact that the world exemplifies the other? And finally, how do those properties or facts provide an ontological ground of temporal relations and the passage of time? Unfortunately, Bigelow does not directly answer these questions, and it does not seem to me that he can unless he countenances the non-relational temporal properties of pastness and futurity. However, positing the existence of *pastness* and *futurity* as constituents of past and present tensed world properties is problematic. For if there is a full range of tensed properties then presumably there are past and future individuals as well. To see why note that if the world presently exemplifies the property of being such that the birth of my first grandchild will be past, then that event *exists* in the future when it exemplifies pastness. And if the world exemplifies the property of being such that the birth of my first child was future, then that event exists in the past when it exemplifies futurity. Thus, if some events did exemplify futurity and others will exemplify pastness, then *there are* non-present, i.e., past and future times/events/things that exemplify those properties. For that reason, if Bigelow posits the existence of pastness and futurity to account for what is expressed by the past and future tenses, then he must jettison presentism.

L. Nathan Oaklander

On the other hand, if tensed properties don't exist, then the difference between what is expressed by past and future tensed propositions remains mysterious, and there is no basis for the passage of time. For, if I understand Bigelow's position correctly, the passage of time requires that a future tensed proposition is true (and thus that a *future* tensed property is presently exemplified) *before* a past tensed proposition is true (and thus that a *past* tensed property is presently exemplified). If, however, pastness and futurity are not constituents of the properties expressed by the past and future tense, then there is no difference between past and future tensed facts, and for that reason, there can be no basis for the passage of time and the direction of becoming.

There is a further problem closely connected with the previous one. It is not clear how Bigelow would handle the problem of ordering events (or things) that are both past or both future. In other words, since Lincoln's assassination is past and Kennedy's assassination is past, then on Bigelow's view, the world presently exemplifies the properties of Kennedy was assassinated and Lincoln was assassinated. What, then, is the ground of the fact that Kennedy was assassinated *after* Lincoln was assassinated? The typical move of introducing degrees of pastness or futurity is not open to a presentist who rejects the properties of pastness and futurity. Moreover, introducing properties such as being past by a certain degree would not be sufficient to order the properties, and hence the terms that exemplify those properties, unless there was a temporal relation between the properties, or unless the property itself was complex that included a relation. That is, if we order the events by means of the world property that say, Lincoln's assassination *was more past* then Kennedy's assassination, we are clearly reintroducing temporal relations as basic entities back into the ontological analysis of temporal facts. Finally, the attempt to order past events by appealing to a property such as Kennedy was assassinated 27 years ago whereas Lincoln was assassinated 135 years ago is questionable since, once again, it is not at all clear that different temporal intervals from the present can be accounted for in this manner without presupposing either temporal relations or temporal properties such as pastness and futurity. (For further discussion of this issue see, Le Poidevin (1999a, 30–35) and Tooley (1997, 166–70.)

I have one final point concerning Bigelow's world properties gambit. If one accepts the full range of A-properties, as I believe Bigelow is committed to doing by introducing tensed properties such as *Helen was abducted* and *Bush will be elected*, then, as I suggested above, he must accept past and future events/thing/times in addition to the present events/things/times. Bigelow says things that drive him perilously close to explicitly espousing such a view. Consider the following passages:

> The past no longer exists; yet there is a sense in which the past can never be lost: the world will always be one with the property of having once been thus and so. Likewise the future does not exist yet; yet there is a sense in which the future will be what it will be: the world has always been one with the property of being a world which is going to be thus and so. At any given time, you can grasp truths which transcend your present and describe the world *sub specie aeternitatis*, from the standpoint of eternity. (1996, 47)

And again,

> From the standpoint of presentism the rival theory four-dimensionalism, is just a partial picture of reality. It only acknowledges the eternal truths about what was, is or will be. The things it acknowledges to be true are indeed true as far as they go, but they are all accommodated as an abstracted, logical consequence of what is real according to the presentist. (1996, 48)

Bigelow is correct in saying that his view implies that four-dimensionalism is a *partial* picture of reality. It is, however, not an abstracted logical consequence, but a metaphysical commitment resulting from his acceptance of past and future tensed properties. If we add to this partial picture of reality the view that Bigelow also wishes to endorse, namely, that 'the true Present, the world, is not identical with eternity. The world is rather a changing ground for unchanging truths' (1996, 48), then we get a version of the moving NOW A-theory that, whether immune to dialectical difficulties or not, is certainly incompatible with presentism.

I want to conclude my critique of presentism with a brief discussion of Robert Ludlow's version of that doctrine as found in his recent book, *Semantics, Tense and Time: An Essay in the Metaphysics of Natural Language* (1999). Like virtually all contemporary presentists, Ludlow's work takes its cue from Prior's writings on time and tries to answer two difficulties that Prior's logical analysis of tense sought to resolve. The first is McTaggart's paradox and the second is the problem of temporal anaphora. The elegance of Ludlow's own view of time is that it allegedly provides a common solution to both problems. The weakness, I submit, is that it fails in both attempts.

The problem of temporal anaphora is that of specifying, within a presentist framework, the semantic value of implicit or explicit temporal anaphors such as 'then' that seem to refer to non-present times and events. For example, 'Sam addressed Bill. Bill didn't respond then.' McTaggart's problem or paradox rests on the claim that every event is past, present and future, which is absurd. Of course, it has seemed to many that this absurdity need not trouble us because we can say either that

(1) Every event is past at *one time*, present at *another time* and future at a still *different time*.

Or, that

(2) Every event is future *before* it is present and present *before* it is past.

Or, as Prior has said, that

(3) Every event either *is* future and *will be* present and past, or *has been* future and is present and *will* be past, or *has been* future and present and *is* past. (Prior 1967, 5–6)

Each of these ways of avoiding the original absurdity results in a statement that removes any explicit contradiction in temporal attributions, but whether they involve anything more than a verbal solution to an ontological problem is debatable. Since the first alternative presupposes the existence of *past* and *future times* and the second presupposes the existence of *temporal relations*, both are an anathema to the presentist. Thus, the third option is clearly the one a presentist must take, but it gives rise to the following question: How is one to analyse the tenses? More specifically, what are the truth-makers of each of the conjuncts in each disjunct? Is there some analysis of the tenses that avoids collapsing the third alternative into a variation of one of the first two? For example, can one analyse 'event *e* has been present' in such a way that it avoids an ontological commitment to either a past *time* at which *e* is present or to *e*'s occurring *earlier than* a present moment?

Ludlow thinks that the A-theory has presentist resources available to answer these questions since he believes that we can

treat the standard B-theory predicates 'before and 'after' as composed out of more basic A-series relations. The idea here would be that a sentence like [I ate before I left the house] would have a logical form in which 'before' is treated as composed of a past-tense morpheme and a simple when-clause. (1999, 126)

I do not need to go into details here. The overall point is that we can eliminate reference to times and temporal relations between them by giving the semantics for 'before' and 'after' in terms of the predicates 'past', 'present', 'future' and the relational predicate 'when.' If this can be done then McTaggart's paradox cannot get off the ground. To quote Ludlow

> To illustrate, take a proposition like [] [∃e) e is the dying of Queen Anne] []

> That proposition was future and is now past, but we can't overlook the temporal anaphora. There is an implicit when-clause, so that what we actually have is that the proposition was future (say, when Queen Anne was born) and it is past (say, as I write these words). There is not even the illusion of a contradiction if we remember to include the temporal anaphora. (1999, 134)

The question I have concerning Ludlow's response to McTaggart's argument is this: 'What is the ontological significance of the tenses and the 'when' clause?

Ludlow notes that,

> If this gambit is to work, 'when' cannot mean 'at the same time'; it must be taken as a kind of *primitive*, just as PAST, PRES, and FUT morphemes are. That is, 'when' must be understood as being more fundamental than the B-series conception of simultaneity. (1999, 112; my emphasis)

What does 'primitive' mean in this context? One would think that in doing the metaphysics of time, to take something as primitive is not only an epistemological notion, but an ontological notion as well. When one is attempting to reduce temporal relations to some ontologically more basic entity or entities, to take something as primitive should imply ontological commitment to what is referred to by that primitive term. A primitive is thus what is unanalysable in terms of simpler constituents. However, for Ludlow primitives do not name simple constituents of complex facts since he says, '[M]y A-theory of tense will regard tenses as being *predicates* of proposition like objects.' (1999, 112; my emphasis) And he claims that predicates, including I would surmise, relational predicates such as 'when' are non-referring expressions that do not denote non-relational or relational properties construed either as Platonic entities, or as extensions (i.e., sets of objects). Indeed, he maintains that properties are 'very poor candidates for our ontology.' (1999, 46) If, however, there are no A-properties referred to by the tenses, and there are no temporal relations referred to by the language that

L. Nathan Oaklander

expresses them, then what exactly is Ludlow's ontology of *time?* What is the ground, in the sense of the truth-makers, for the world being *temporal?* Ludlow says that we can avoid taking 'times' as being points in the sense of B-series metaphysics, by treating 'times as sets of when-clauses' (1999, 128), that he claims are temporal conjunctions. But he never explains what is that bit of reality that makes a 'when' clause a *temporal* conjunction?[7]

Although Ludlow clearly seems to be partial to desert landscapes he is, he says, 'still after a theory that delivers language-to-world connections. The point here is that properties and extensions (sets of objects) don't have to be part of that picture.' (1999, 46) Perhaps not, but if properties and presumably relations are not to be included in reality, then I fail to see how the rest of his very sophisticated semantical theory can specify what there is in the world that is the truth-maker of judgments asserting that two entities stand in a *temporal* relation. Without such an account the question, Can an ontological analysis that specifies the constituents of the complex fact that *it is now and the relevant event is earlier or later than now* be given that is consistent with presentism? has yet to be given an affirmative answer. And without an affirmative answer, our differential attitudes toward earlier and later events remain a mystery on presentist metaphysics, and the existence of change remains without an adequate foundation.[8]

References

Bergmann, Gustav 1964. 'Generality and Existence', in *Logic and Reality*. Madison: University of Wisconsin Press, 64–84.

Bigelow, John 1996. 'Presentism and Properties', in James E. Tomberlin (ed.), *Philosophical Perspectives* 10: *Metaphysics*, 1996. Cambridge, MA and Oxford, UK: Blackwell: 35–52.

[7] Ludlow believes that evidence for his view is gleaned from some psychological studies that 'have noted that a particular sense of 'when' emerges before the child has a notion of temporal order and simultaneity'. ([1999: 141) He mentions 'Cromer's (1968, 100) fascinating conclusion that 'perhaps the ability to 'date' an event by *a contemporaneous event* is more 'primitive' than the notion of serial ordering' (Ludlow 1999, 141), but by appealing to *a contemporaneous event*, i.e., one occurring at the same time, the study has not eliminated the B-relation of simultaneity, but has presupposed it.

[8] An earlier version of this paper was read at the Conference on Time, Reality and Experience at the London School of Economics, in London, on September 28, 2000.

Presentism, Ontology and Temporal Experience

Broad, C. D. 1938. *An Examination of McTaggart's Philosophy.* Cambridge: Cambridge University Press.

Craig, William Lane 1997. 'Is Presentness a Property?' *American Philosophical Quarterly* 34, 27–40.

—— 1998. 'McTaggart's Paradox and the Problem of Temporary Intrinsics', *Analysis* 122–7.

—— 1999a. 'Tensed Time and Our Differential Experience of the Past and Future', *Southern Journal of Philosophy* **37**, 4, 515–37.

—— 1999b. 'Oaklander on McTaggart and Intrinsic Change', *Analysis* **59**, 4, 319–20.

—— 2000a. 'The Extent of the Present', *International Studies in the Philosophy of Sciences* **14**, 2, 165–85.

—— 2000b. *The Tensed Theory of Time—A Critical Examination.* Dordrecht: Kluwer Academic Press.

—— 2000c. *The Tenseless Theory of Time—A Critical Examination.* Dordrecht: Kluwer Academic Press.

—— 2001. *Time and the Metaphysics of Relativity.* Dordrecht: Kluwer Academic Press.

Cromer, R. F. 1968. *The Development of Temporal Reference During the Acquisition of Language.* Ph.D thesis, Harvard University.

Grossmann, Reinhardt 1992. *The Existence of the World—An Introduction to Ontology.* New York: Routledge.

Hinchliff, Mark 1996. 'The Puzzle of Change', in James E. Tomberlin (ed.), *Philosophical Perspectives* 10: *Metaphysics*, 1996. Cambridge, MA and Oxford, UK: Blackwell: 119–36.

Hochberg, Herbert 1969. 'Negation and Generality,' *NOUS* 3, 325–43.

Le Poidevin, Robin 1991. *Change, Cause and Contradiction: A Defense of the Tenseless Theory of Time.* London: Macmillan.

—— (ed.) 1998a. *Questions of Time and Tense.* Oxford: Clarendon Press

—— 1998b. 'Review of Michael Tooley's *Time, Tense and Causation*', British Journal for the Philosophy of Science **49**, 365–69.

—— 1999a. 'Egocentric and Objective Time', *Proceedings of the Aristotelian Society.* New Series 99, 19–36.

—— 1999b. 'Can Beliefs Be Caused By Their Truth-Makers? *Analysis* **59**, 3, 148–56.

—— 2001. 'Reply To Smith and Tooley', in L. Nathan Oaklander (ed.), *The Importance of Time.* Dordrecht: Kluwer Academic Publishers, 285–91.

Lewis, David 1986. *On the Plurality of Worlds.* Oxford: Blackwell.

Ludlow, Peter 1999. *Semantics, Tense, and Time—An Essay in the Metaphysics of Natural Language.* Cambridge: MA: Massachusetts Institute of Technology.

Mellor, D. H. 1998. *Real Time II.* Routledge: London.

Nerlich, Graham 1998. 'Time As Spacetime', in Robin Le Poidevin (ed.), *Questions of Time and Tense.* Oxford: Clarendon Press, 119–34.

Oaklander, L. Nathan and Silvano Miracchi (1980), 'Russell, Negative Facts, and Ontology', *Philosophy of Science*, **47**, 434–55.

L. Nathan Oaklander

—— 1984. *Temporal Relations and Temporal Becoming: A Defense of a Russellian Theory of Time*. Lanham, MD: University Press of America.

—— and Smith, Quentin (eds.) 1994. *The New Theory of Time*. New Haven, Conn.: Yale University Press.

—— 1996. 'McTaggart's Paradox and Smith's Tensed Theory of Time', *Synthese* **107**, 205–21.

—— 1999a. 'Review of Michael Tooley's *Time, Tense and Causation*', *Mind* **108**, 407–13.

—— 1999b. 'Craig on McTaggart's Paradox and the Problem of Temporary Intrinsics', *Analysis* **59**, 4, 314–18.

—— (ed.) 2002. *The Importance of Time*. Dordrecht: Kluwer Academic Publishers.

Plantinga, Alvin 1983. 'Reason and Belief,' in Alvin Plantinga and Nicholas Wolterstorff (eds), *Faith and Philosophy*. Notre Dame, IN: University of Notre Dame Press, 39–63.

Prior, Arthur 1959. 'Thank Goodness That's Over', *Philosophy* **34**, 12–17.

—— 1967. *Past, Present and Future*. Clarendon, Oxford, UK.

—— 1968. *Papers on Time and Tense*. Clarendon, Oxford UK.

—— 1970. 'The Notion of the Present', Studium Generale **23**, 245–48.

—— 1996. 'Some Free Thinking About Time', in B. J. Copeland (ed.), *Logic and Reality, Essays on the Legacy of Arthur Prior*. Oxford: Clarendon Press.

Russell, Bertrand 1918. *The Philosophy of Logical Atomism*, in Robert Charles Marsh (ed.) (1964), *Logic and Knowledge: Essays 1901–1950*. London: George Allen & Unwin, 177–281.

Smith, Quentin 1986. 'The Infinite Regress of Temporal Attributions', *The Southern Journal of Philosophy* **24**, 383–96. Reprinted in L. Nathan Oaklander and Quentin Smith (eds.), *The New Theory of Time* (1994).

—— 1993. *Language and Time*. New York: Oxford University Press.

—— 1999a. 'Review of Michael Tooley's *Time, Tense and Causation*', *The Philosophical Review* **108**, 123–27.

—— 1999b. 'The 'Sentence-Type Version' of the Tenseless Theory of Time', *Synthese* **119**, 233–51.

—— 2002a. 'Reference to the Past and Future', in Alexandar Jokic and Quentin Smith (eds.), *Time, Tense and Reference*. Cambridge, MA: MIT Press.

Smith, Quentin 2002b. 'Time and Degrees of Existence: A Theory of "Degree Presentism",' in Craig Callender (ed.), *Time, Reality and Experience*, Cambridge: Cambridge University Press, 119–36.

Tooley, Michael 1997. *Time, Tense and Causation*. Oxford: Clarendon Press.

Zimmerman, Dean 1998. 'Temporary Intrinsics and Presentism', in Peter van Inwagen and Dean Zimmerman (eds), *Metaphysics, The Big Questions*. Oxford: Blackwell, 206–19.

A Presentist's Refutation of Mellor's McTaggart

PHILIP PERCIVAL

For twenty years, D. H. Mellor has promoted an influential defence of a view of time he first called the 'tenseless' view, but now associates with what he calls the 'B-theory.'[1] It is his defence of this view, not the view itself, which is generally taken to be novel. It is organized around a forcefully presented attack on rival views which he claims to be a development of McTaggart's celebrated argument that the 'A-series' is contradictory. I will call this attack 'Mellor's McTaggart.' Although it has received much critical attention, it has not been well understood. For one thing, it has changed over the years in a way that is little appreciated. Whereas Mellor's (1981) original version amounts to a dilemma each horn of which contains a single strand of argument, later statements (1986, 1998) of the first horn contain a second strand of argument unannounced. I shall be concerned to disentangle these strands. I shall also show them to have been largely anticipated by Gareth Evans (1979). However, my main aim is not the clarification of Mellor's McTaggart, but its refutation. I shall show that there is a rival to Mellor's view of time against which the first horn of the dilemma begs the question both as originally presented, and as supplemented. This rival is a 'Priorean' version of the 'presentist' doctrine that only what is present exists. Although Prior himself gave McTaggart's own argument short shrift, in refuting Mellor's development of it I do not merely resurrect Prior's moves. Mellor's McTaggart introduces specifically semantic considerations. It focuses not as McTaggart did on presentness and futurity etc., but on the truth-values of tokens of propositions in which presentness and futurity etc. are (said to be) ascribed. Consequently, its refutation requires an answer, from the perspective of a presentist metaphysics, to a question which came to the fore only after Prior's death. The question is this: How should semantic theory be developed in the light of the need for a theory of linguistic understanding? Though Evans (1979) flirted with the issue of how this question should be answered from a presentist perspective, the

[1] See, respectively, Mellor (1981) and Mellor (1998).

Philip Percival

answer he articulates is wrong. I shall do no more than sketch the correct answer. That is all a refutation of Mellor's McTaggart requires.

Before Mellor's McTaggart can be refuted (section III), it must first be clarified. This is a matter of clarifying the conclusion Mellor wishes to establish (section I), and the argument by which he tries to establish it (section II). Clarifying the conclusion to Mellor's McTaggart is in some ways the hardest task. It is a messy and laborious business, and I bid the reader to be patient.

I 'Tensed' vs. 'Tenseless' views of time

I.i A (philosophical) defect in Mellor's terminology—Mellor (1981: 4) opposes a 'tenseless' view of time to a 'tensed' view, and then claims that his semantic development of an argument due to McTaggart reveals the tensed view to be inconsistent. His later dissatisfaction with this terminology stems from the fact that whereas the terms 'tensed' and 'tenseless' apply primarily to language, the debate he has in mind concerns the nature of (temporal) reality. Still, although his earlier terminology is potentially misleading in this respect, Mellor's (1998: xi) current employment of the alternative terms 'B-theory' and 'A-theory' redeems matters only at the cost of an unpalatable blandness. I will revert to Mellor's original talk of 'tensed' and 'tenseless' views of time.

According to the tensed view of time, 'tense' is real. The tenseless view denies this: it holds tense unreal. But what is it the reality of which is thereby disputed? Primarily, 'tense' is a feature of language: verbs can take a variety of grammatical forms, or 'tenses.' With respect to this primary meaning there can be no question of a metaphysical debate over 'tense': tense in this sense is a real feature of language. However, if grammatical tense is not the issue, perhaps it is a guide to what is. In particular, one might wonder whether grammatically tensed sentences, or uses of such sentences, successfully represent the world as having a certain feature, to be called 'tense.' The debate between the two views of time might then be taken to dispute not the reality of grammatical tense, but its function, and what the successful exercise of that function involves. Perhaps the tensed view should be characterized as holding that grammatical tense successfully serves a representational function—representing a feature, to be called 'tense,' which (some part of) reality possesses—while the tenseless view should be characterized as denying this. However, though this characterization would be closer to the mark, it would be fundamentally wrong. Firstly, even if the debate between the tensed and tenseless views may be characterized as concerning the representational function of certain sentence-types, these sentence-types are not singled out by their employment of grammatical tense: containing a grammatically tensed verb is neither necessary nor sufficient for being of the type in question. Secondly, the debate over the reality of tense should not in any case be characterized as turning on whether the world has some feature, 'tense,' which the tensed view takes to be represented by (uses of) the disputed sentence-types. To understand the debate between tensed and tenseless views of time, one needs to understand why these two misconceptions are such.

Let's begin with the first misconception. According to Mellor (1981, 1986), the disputed sentence-types are distinguished not by their employment of grammatically tensed verbs, but by the fact of their being 'tensed.' But what is it for a sentence-type to be 'tensed'? Having said that

> TENSES ... [are] ... temporal positions in McTaggart's *A* series, 'that series of positions which runs from the far past through the near past to the present, and then from the present through the near future to the far future,'

Mellor (1986: 167) answers this question by saying that

> [A] thought, statement or sentence ... [is] ... TENSED if it explicitly or implicitly ascribes a TENSE to something, its TENSE being the TENSE is ascribes.[2]

However, this characterization of the sentences of the dispute class —the 'tensed' ones—is disastrous. Firstly, since the tenseless view of time holds that in a non-grammatical sense, 'tense' is unreal, it is wildly obfuscatory to begin an argument to this conclusion by insisting that there are entities which, in a non-grammatical sense, are 'tensed.' Secondly, the characterization of 'tensed' representations as those which 'ascribe' a 'tense' to something conflicts with Mellor's own view of time. His view is not an 'error-theory.' The view that 'tense' is unreal is not the view that all token utterances of sentence-types like e.g. 'The great day is finally present' are false: on the contrary, utterances of this sentence on the (great) day in question are held to be true. Yet if the sentence ascribes a tense to

[2] Cf. Mellor (1981: 4), and Le Poidevin and Mellor (1987). Mellor (1986) only capitalizes 'tense' to emphasize its distinctness on his usage from grammatical (verbal) tense. In discussing his views I drop this practice.

something, when in reality nothing has any tense, no utterance of it could be true: ascribing something which nothing possesses results in falsehood.[3] Thirdly, allowing a representation to be 'tensed' even if it ascribes a tense to something only 'implicitly,' and then presupposing, as Mellor does, that there are representations, i.e. the 'tenseless' ones, which are not tensed, begs the question. In the case of sentences (rather than representations of other kinds), the contrast he intends is between sentences like 'At last the exam is in the past' and 'Bush ate fish yesterday' on the one hand, and sentences like 'World War II exists in the past, or the present, or the future' and 'Bush eats dates at noon on Christmas Day, 2004' on the other. But while sentences of the latter kind do not specify the tense of anything explicitly, it is a moot point whether they do so implicitly. Suppose, as some think, that future entities are unnameable. In that case, wouldn't any sentence containing 'World War II' 'implicitly' say that World War II is either past or present? Or again, suppose, as some think, that future contingents lack truth values. In that case, wouldn't even an 'eternal' sentence like e.g. 'Bush reads at t' 'implicitly' say that t is past or present?

Let's leave the issues raised by the unsatisfactoriness of Mellor's characterization of 'tensed' representations for the moment and turn to the second misconception. I claim that the debate between the tensed and tenseless views should not be construed as a debate over whether there is a feature of the world—'tense'—which commonplace talk of temporal matters often represents (parts of) the world as having. This claim might be thought presumptuous, since it flies in the face of Mellor's explicit definitions to the contrary. Having characterized the 'tense' of something other than a representation as its A-series position, in *Real Time* Mellor says (p. 4) that the tensed view holds, whereas the tenseless view denies, that

> Distinctions and transitions of tense ... reflect nonrelational differences between past, present and future things (events, facts, etc.) ... Futurity, temporal presence and pastness ... [are] ... real nonrelational properties which everything in time successively possesses, changing objectively as it exchanges each of these properties for the next ... [properties which] ... are ... much like (e.g.) temperatures.

[3] This objection is not undermined by Mellor's (1998) new terminology. It is equally applicable to a strategy which begins an argument for a non error-theoretic view that there are no 'A-facts' by characterizing sentences or propositions etc. belonging to the class of 'A-sentences or A-propositions' as those which explicitly or implicitly state A-facts.

A Presentist's Refutation of Mellor's McTaggart

In *Real Time II*, the debate between the 'A-theory' and the 'B-theory' is characterized similarly (p. 2):

> The question is, what makes a statement like '*e* is past' true when it is true, namely at any time later than *e* ? There are two answers to this question. One is that at any such time *e* has the property of being past. This is what I call the '*A*-theory' view. My own '*B*-theory' view is that what makes '*e* is past' true at any time *t* is the fact that *e* is earlier than *t*.

To be sure, Mellor is setting his own agenda, and introducing novel technical terms to describe it. Nevertheless, this isn't to say he can define those terms as he pleases. In defining them he is trying to capture an opposition between the view of time he subsequently defends, and a view of time which he takes to be refuted by his development of McTaggart's argument against the reality of the A-series. His initial characterization is therefore subject to a retro-spectively imposed norm: it should characterize *these* views. But it doesn't, and to this extent his official characterization of the debate at the heart of *Real Time* (and its successor) is mistaken. There are two reasons why this is so.

Firstly, as Mellor knows all too well, no one opposes his view of time more strongly than Arthur Prior. Yet Prior (1967: 18) holds that '"Is present", "is past", etc. are only quasi-predicates,' which do not designate properties ('like temperatures'), and which are to be analysed by means of sentential operators like 'it was the case that.' Prima facie, therefore, on Mellor's official characterization, the tenseless view he is concerned to promote is embraced by his most formidable opponent! Mellor (1981: 95; cf. 1998: 75) tries to avoid this anomaly by dismissing the significance of Prior's employment of temporal (sentential) operators on the grounds that it is 'tantamount to regarding P[astness], N[owness] and F[uturity] as properties, not of events, but of tensed facts.' If this were so, his characterization of the tensed and tenseless views would indeed classify Prior's metaphysics correctly. Despite holding that e.g. 'is past' is a 'quasi-predicate,' which does not designate a property of events, Prior's employment of temporal (sentential) operators would commit him to the view that e.g. pastness is a non-relational property (of some facts), and, hence, to the reality of tense and the tensed view of time. However, Mellor's diagnosis of Prior's employment of temporal operators is too controversial to bear the burden being placed upon it. In part, this is because an ontology of facts is itself controversial. But even if this ontology is admitted, Prior's doctrine of temporal operators has good reason to resist

95

Mellor's recommendation. On Mellor's diagnosis, the metaphysical import of Prior's employment of temporal operators has e.g. the joint truth of 'Bush is reading' and 'It was the case that (Clinton is reading)' requiring the existence of two facts, the second being different from the first in two respects: it involves Clinton rather than Bush, and it possesses not the property of being present, but the property of being past. But Prior would resist this attribution as strongly as I (and many others) would resist the idea that the joint truth of 'Bush is reading at noon on Christmas Day, 2002' and 'It might have been the case that (Bush is walking on the moon at noon on Christmas Day, 2002)' requires the existence of two facts, the second differing from the first in two respects: it involves walking where the other involves reading, and it possesses the property of being possible instead of the property of being actual. One might object that in the absence of a positive account of what a temporal operator like 'It was the case that' does if it does not designate a property of facts, an attempt to resist Mellor's attribution fails. However, I think it wrong to insist on forcing sentential operators, temporal or otherwise, into the mould of the classical ontology of entities and their properties and relations. Nor is Mellor any longer in a position to insist on it. In replacing *Real Time*'s view that e.g. 'Bush is reading at t' has the form 'Reading (Bush, t)' by *Real Time II*'s view that it has the form 'at t (Bush, reading),' he now invokes sentential operators which cannot be forced into this mould.[4] (On his latest view, 'at t' designates not a property (of a fact) but a 'temporal location' (of a fact).)

Mellor intends a debate on which the 'tenseless' view of time is essentially opposed to Prior's view. Prior's denial that e.g. 'pastness' is a property ('like temperature') affords one reason for seeking an understanding of the claim that 'tense is real' on which tense can be held real even though it is not a non-relational property, and, a fortiori, not a property determinations of which are designated by e.g. 'is past' or 'it was the case that.' A second reason for seeking such an understanding is provided by *Real Time II*'s rewriting of *Real Time*'s discussion and development of McTaggart's argument to include a discussion of Tooley's (1997) view of time.[5] Because Tooley's view does not advert to non-relational properties of presentness etc., Mellor (1998: 81) classifies it, using his new terminology, as a 'B-theory.' Yet Tooley's view is also held to be refuted by the semantic development of McTaggart's argument against the

---

[4] See respectively chapters 7 and 8 of Mellor (1981) and Mellor (1998).

[5] See chapters 7 and 6 respectively of these works. The additional material in question is to be found in Mellor (1998: 81–3).

reality of the A-series. Once more, then, Mellor's central thesis, as defended by the McTaggartian argument which is the lynchpin of both *Real Time* and its successor, is seen to be stronger than the thesis that there are no non-relational properties of pastness, presentness and futurity by which the 'tenseless' view of time is officially characterized.

Mellor's characterization of the thesis that tense is real, and hence of the tensed view of time, as the thesis that there are entities which possess temporally variable non-relational properties of pastness, presentness and futurity, captures an important object of debate. But his dispute with Prior and Tooley, and his employment of Mellor's McTaggart against them, reveals this debate to be less deep than the one at the real heart of *Real Time* and its successor. Although one might retain Mellor's characterization of the thesis that 'tense' is unreal, and hence of the debate between the 'tensed' and 'tenseless' views of time, and introduce new terminology to capture the deeper one, so doing would miss something philosophically. In effect, in *Real Time* the phrase 'the tenseless view' is used in two ways that are assumed to coincide. As characterized officially, it signifies the thesis that nothing has non-relational properties of pastness, presentness and futurity. But it is also employed to signify a view which this thesis is implicitly assumed to entail, notwithstanding the fact that this latter view explicitly conflicts with the respective views of Prior and Tooley. In recognizing this assumption, and including additional material in which a view like Tooley's is critically discussed for the first time, *Real Time II* is obliged to choose, in effect, between *Real Time's* two uses of 'the tenseless view.' As we have seen, when introducing the term 'B-theory' as an alternative to 'the tenseless view,' Mellor chooses to retain the official characterization. But this choice results in the absurdity of there being no term in *Real Time II* for the (stronger) view of time which is carried over from its predecessor, and which is now explicitly defended by the central (McTaggartian) argument of the two books.

A better alternative corrects this anomaly. The phrase 'the tenseless view of time' should be employed to signify a view of time which (i) *Real Time* took it to signify (albeit not officially), which (ii) is defended in *Real Time* and its successor, and which (iii) *Real Time* implicitly assumes, and *Real Time II* explicitly argues, to be proven correct by Mellor's McTaggart. This view of time holds more than the weaker thesis that nothing in reality has non-relational properties of pastness, presentness or futurity. *Real Time II's* term 'B-theory' can be retained, as defined by Mellor, for this weaker thesis. The 'tenseless' view of time then amounts to 'B-theory' *plus something extra.*

The next question is: what is the additional feature which turns a mere B-theory into the full-blown tenseless view of time?

I.ii The tenseless view—Cursory reflection reveals the crucial additional feature in virtue of which Mellor (1981) takes his 'tenseless' view to be stronger than his own official characterization. Like the explicit conclusion of the semantic development of McTaggart's argument against the reality of the A-series in *Real Time II*, it is characterized most generally not as the rejection of non-relational properties of presentness etc., but as the rejection of a view of (a kind of) temporal change, and hence of temporal reality, which is entailed by, but does not require, the existence of such properties. In terms of an ontology of (truthmaking) facts, the rejected view is easily stated. It is simply the view that the facts change over time.[6] Since an ontology of facts would suggest, as in the Tractatus, that reality comprises the facts, this view quickly becomes the view that reality itself (so to speak, conceived as a whole) changes over time.

Following the terminological recommendation of the previous section, temporally changing facts can be called 'tensed' facts; unchanging ones, 'tenseless' facts. The terms 'A-fact' and 'B-fact' can then be retained as defined in *Real Time II*: 'A-facts' are facts which involve, or which possess, non-relational properties of pastness, presentness, or futurity. 'B-facts' neither involve, nor possess, such properties. Clearly, if there are A-facts, then there are tensed facts. But the status of the converse entailment is unclear. Prima facie, temporal change in the facts needn't involve 'A-facts.' If it does involve them, it might perhaps be a matter of temporal variation in the properties of eternally existing A-facts: after all, as we have seen, Mellor himself attributes to Prior the idea that futurity, presentness, and pastness are properties which facts successively possess. More plausibly, however, it might be a matter of facts coming to exist or ceasing to exist (i.e. the presumption being that existence is not a property). Again, one variant of this alternative holds that the facts which do this include such A-facts as

---

[6] Cf. Mellor's (1981: 103) claim that '[Because] tenses cannot change ... The world can[not] ... grow by the accretion of facts as they become present.' See too Mellor's (1998: 81) claim that 'McTaggart's proof disposes of more than A-facts [i.e. facts involving non-relational properties of pastness, presentness or futurity]. It disposes also of the idea ... that even B-facts need not exist at all times.'

an event's having a non-relational property of presentness: such a fact would not have existed until the event became present, and would cease to exist when the event becomes past. But other variants hold that even B-facts come into, or go out of, existence, or both, with the passage of time. On Tooley's view for example, the passage of time amounts to the successive expansion of reality as new B-facts of this kind come into, only then to remain forever in, existence. By contrast, someone sympathetic to Dummett's (1969) anti-realism about the past might have facts ceasing to be with the passage of time (as they cease to be knowable), but never coming to be (since mere futurity cannot undermine the following decision procedure: wait around).[7] Finally, a Priorean presentist might have a fact—e.g. Bush is sitting down—successively coming and ceasing to be as Bush goes about his daily business.[8]

By contrast, on the view of time which Mellor defends, and which he takes his development of McTaggart's argument against the reality of the A-series to establish, the facts don't, and hence reality (as a whole) doesn't, change over time in any of these ways. Mellor's official characterization notwithstanding, *this* is what *Real Time* eventually uses the phrase 'the tenseless view' to signify. Since *Real Time II* both continues to uphold this view of time, explicitly, and to take Mellor's McTaggart to establish it, it is a pity that the official characterization is retained in the terminological shift to 'B-theory.' The consequence that neither *Real Time* nor its successor contain a term by which their view of time is signified stems from *Real Time's* presumption that if there are no non-relational properties of futurity, presentness or pastness, then the facts don't change over time. Judging by the rewriting of Mellor's McTaggart in *Real Time II*, Tooley opened Mellor's eyes in this respect. But a more sensitive reading of Prior might have opened them earlier.

It might seem that we are in a position to define the 'tenseless' view of time: it is B-theory's rejection of non-relational properties of pastness, presentness, or futurity, plus the view that B-facts are

[7] See too Dummett (1981: 382–400). The relation between Dummett's debate regarding realism about the past and Mellor's debate regarding the tenseless view is considered in Yuval Dolev (2000).

[8] As we have seen, Prior resists properties of pastness, presentness or futurity. On this conception, 'Bush is sitting down' would be a B-fact which lacks times as constituents. Mellor (1998) himself advocates B-facts of this kind. But his view is very different from Prior's. Mellor takes these B-facts to be unchanging, and gives them unchanging 'temporal locations' 'at' dates. Given an ontology of facts, Prior would take e.g. 'Bush is sitting down' to be a changing fact *which has no temporal location.* (For Prior, 'dates' are logical constructions out of propositions.)

unchanging over time. However, there is reason to be cautious at this juncture, since an ontology of facts is controversial: there are those who deny the existence of facts.[9] We should at least try to find an alternative characterization of the 'tenseless' view from which Mellor's ontological presupposition is absent.

The obvious alternative, which Mellor's own practice encourages, is to couch the debate in terms of truth conditions.[10] For there is hope that talk of truth conditions does not presuppose novel entities. Truth conditions are said to be possessed by sentences, or by utterances of sentences, and to 'obtain.' But for 'snow is white' to have the 'property' of having the truth condition it does might amount to nothing more than that according to the 'canonical' theorem for 'snow is white' in the theory of truth for English which does best by certain criteria, 'snow is white' is true iff snow is white. Likewise, for this truth condition to 'obtain' might amount to nothing more than that snow is white. So we can adopt the following proposal. The dispute between A-theory and B-theory turns on whether the truth conditions of tokens of propositions like 'The great day is present' or 'Bush is sitting down' involve non-relational properties of presentness, pastness or futurity: A-theory says they do, while B-theory denies this. The 'tenseless' view of time then adds to B-theory the claim that the truth conditions of token propositions are 'tenseless' in the sense that the obtaining of such tokens' truth conditions is not a matter which varies over time. The 'tensed' view of time denies this: it holds that some token propositions have truth conditions that are 'tensed' in so far as whether their truth conditions obtain is a matter which varies over time.

In what follows, I focus on this latter formulation. In its terms, Mellor takes his semantic development of McTaggart's argument against the reality of the A-series to show that no token proposition can have tensed truth conditions.

II Mellor's McTaggart

II.i The original version—Mellor's McTaggart (1981) is best articulated as a dilemma. Mellor himself develops the dilemma with

[9] Cf. Lowe (1987b: 539) who declines to enter the dispute over whether there are tensed 'facts' on the grounds that he 'can find little use for this notion.'

[10] This is the focus of the discussion in e.g. Lowe (1987a, 1987b, 1992); Mellor (1981, 1986); Paul (1997); Priest (1986); and Smith (1994). (However, Mellor himself doesn't see truth conditions as an escape route from an ontology of facts: for him, the truth condition of something is that some fact obtain.)

A Presentist's Refutation of Mellor's McTaggart

respect to a sentence-type '*e* is past' (where *e* is some event), but so as to emphasize that the tensed view which is really being attacked is not committed to the supposition that there are non-relational properties of pastness, presentness, and futurity, I prefer to use an atomic sentence-type containing a present tense verb, such as 'Bush is sitting down.' Nothing of substance, except greater generality, turns on this choice. Many will agree that if any sentence-type is such that tokens of it have truth conditions the obtaining of which is a matter which varies over time, this one does. Those who deny this can substitute some other sentence-type they deem a better candidate for the distinction of having tensed truth conditions. The argumentation of Mellor's dilemma is structural, and they will have no difficulty in applying it to the sentence-type of their choice.

For any sentence-type S, let S be 'non-indexical with respect to time' if the truth conditions of a token utterance of S do not depend on that token's temporal location, and let S be 'indexical with respect to time' otherwise. 'Bush is sitting down' is either indexical with respect to time or it is not. Mellor's McTaggart (1981) as originally developed first argues that the tensed view of time cannot accommodate the thesis that this sentence-type is non-indexical with respect to time. It then argues that the tensed view of time cannot accommodate the thesis that this sentence-type is indexical with respect to time. More particularly, Mellor (1981) propounds the following dilemma:

First Horn—Suppose 'Bush is sitting down' is non-indexical with respect to time. Since it contains no non-temporal indexicals, this is to say that all of its token utterances have the same truth conditions. In that case, all of its tokens have the same truth-value irrespective of their temporal locations. But this is impossible. Since what inclines the tensed view to say that utterances of this sentence-type have tensed truth conditions in the first place is recognition of the fact that this sentence-type is temporally sensitive, and, hence that the truth-value of a token utterance of it depends in part on the token's temporal location, it would result in some token utterances ending up both true and false. It is therefore incoherent to suppose that 'Bush is sitting down' is non-indexical with respect to time.[11]

[11] Compare the statement in Mellor (1981: 100–1) that 'any attempt to state in a tensed meta-language the one tensed fact that makes all ... true tokens [of "e is past"] true is bound to fail. The alleged fact would by definition have to make all tokens of the type true, regardless of their A-series position, whereas in fact some are always true and others always false.'

Philip Percival

Second Horn—Suppose 'Bush is sitting down' is indexical with respect to time. In that case, the truth conditions of token utterances of it are given by some such clauses as[12]

Date—A token *u* of the sentence-type 'Bush is sitting down' uttered at t [is] true if and only if Bush [is] sitting down at *t*

or

Token-Reflexive—A token *u* of the sentence-type 'Bush is sitting down' [is] true if and only if *u* [is] uttered simultaneously with Bush's-sitting-down.

However, the truth conditions such clauses specify are *tenseless*: Whether such truth conditions obtain is not a matter which varies over time. For each time *t*, whether or not Bush is sitting down at *t* is not a matter which changes over time; for each utterance *u*, whether *u* is simultaneous with Bush's-sitting-down is not a temporally variable matter. The thesis that the sentence-type 'Bush is sitting down' is indexical with respect to time is therefore incompatible with the supposition that token utterances of it have tensed truth conditions.[13]

II.ii Later versions—The semantic development of McTaggart's argument against the reality of the A-series in chapter 6 of *Real Time* has recently appeared, rewritten, as chapter 7 of *Real Time II*. In a preface, Mellor acknowledges many revisions, supplements, and changes of opinion. In particular, he relates that the rewriting of *Real Time's* chapter 6 contains an additional section which attempts to refute what is said to be 'Michael Tooley's (1997) ... theory ... [which] admits only B-facts while denying ... that they exist at all times.' In the terminology I have recommended, this additional section supplements the second horn of the original dilemma: it amounts to a further argument to the effect that if e.g.

---

[12] In placing certain occurrences of 'is' in the clauses which follow within brackets, I follow Lowe (1998). My reasons for so doing will become clear in a moment. I am enriching Mellor's (1981) second horn a bit, since that argument is committed to the Token-Reflective account and does not recognize the alternative, which I have called 'Date,' by which it is replaced in *Real Time II*. I do so because the switch from 'Token-Reflexive' to 'Date' does not affect the original second horn's form of argument, and is therefore relatively superficial.

[13] Cf. Mellor (1981: 101).

the sentence-type 'Bush is sitting down' is indexical with respect to time, the truth conditions of its tokens, or the facts in virtue of which true tokens of it are true, are indeed tenseless. Since I am concerned to undermine the first horn of Mellor's dilemma, I won't go into this supplement to the second one.[14]

However, although Mellor does not acknowledge the fact, *Real Time II* also contains additional material which supplements the first horn. The argument in this material emerged in Mellor's (1986) interchange with Graham Priest. While Priest (1986) mistakenly reads it into *Real Time's* presentation of Mellor's McTaggart, Mellor's (1986: 170–1) reply happily takes it on board and endorses it. Curiously, Mellor (1988: 80–1) returns to form and omits it from his statement of the first horn of his dilemma. But with Mellor's (1998: 78) publication of *Real Time II* it is thoroughly assimilated:

> [C]onsider two tokens, *a* and *b*, of '*e* is past', one earlier than *e* and one later. Suppose for example that *e* is Jim's race [at 4.30] on 2 June ... Then if *a* and *b* are both made true by the A-fact that *e* is past, <u>they must both be true when this *is* a fact and false when it is not. So at 4p.m., when *e* *is* still future, *a* and *b* must both be false; and at 5p.m., when it is past, they must both be true</u> ... Yet [these truth values] are obviously wrong. To say *before* Jim's race that it is past is to produce a token of '*e* is past' that is and always will be false. Similarly, to say *after* his race that it is past is to produce a token that is and always was true ... Once we distinguish propositions from their tokens, it is obvious that tokens of an A-proposition, unlike the proposition itself, <u>do *not* change their truth values over time</u> (my underlining).

As presented originally, the first horn of Mellor's McTaggart claims that supposing a sentence like e.g. 'Bush is sitting down' to be non-indexical with respect to time has the absurd consequence that all tokens of this sentence-type, whatever their temporal location, have the same truth value. I will call this the argument 'within' time. By contrast, this later presentation adds the further claim that this supposition has the absurd consequence that each

---

[14] Lowe (1987a,b; 1992, 1998) attacks the second horn of Mellor's McTaggart, arguing that it is wrong to presume, as Mellor does, that the truth-conditions of token utterances which are specified by Date or Token-Reflexive are tenseless: on the contrary, he suggests, Date and Token-Reflexive specify tensed truth-conditions provided the occurrences of '[is]' they contain are read not as tenseless verbs of the same kind as the one which occurs in e.g. 'two plus five is seven,' but as a disjunction 'is, was, or will be' of *tensed* verbs (Lowe 1998: 44–5).

token is such that its truth value switches between truth and falsity over time. That is:

> *The supplement to the first horn*—Suppose 'Bush is sitting down' is non-indexical with respect to time. In that case, since it contains no non-temporal indexicals, all of its token utterances have the same truth conditions. It follows that the truth condition of a token utterance of this sentence-type must be (something like) *that Bush is sitting down*. So it must be a truth condition the obtaining of which varies over time in the following way: with the progression of time, it obtains, it does not obtain, it obtains ... If the obtaining of a token utterance's truth condition varies over time in this way, so too must its truth value switch between true and false. But this is absurd. It contradicts the basic semantic fact that the truth value of a token utterance does not vary over time in this way.

I will call this the argument 'over' time.[15]

II.iii An untenable response—Priest (1986) accuses the first horn of Mellor's McTaggart of begging the question. To assume that the truth-value of a token utterance of a sentence-type like 'Bush is sitting down' depends on the token's temporal location is, he suggests, to take the tenseless view for granted. However, Mellor's (1986) immediate reply that this just won't do is surely correct. It

---

[15] This development in the first horn of Mellor's dilemma has not received the recognition it deserves, and the relation between the two strands of argument is not always properly appreciated. As we have seen, Priest conflates the two strands of argument, and in a way Mellor does too. Robin Le Poidevin is also a case in point. Le Poidevin (1991; chs. 2–3) holds that Mellor's (1981) argument against the tensed view of time illuminates McTaggart's Paradox (1927), that only (Prior's) doctrine of 'presentism' (or 'temporal solipsism' as Le Poidevin calls it) can resist this argument, and that presentism is nevertheless refuted by an argument in Evans (1979). So, since the latter argument is precisely the argument 'over' time, by which Mellor (1986, 1998) supplements *Real Time*'s original presentation of the first horn, in my terms Le Poidevin (1991) claims that the argument 'within' time illuminates McTaggart, that it can be resisted only by presentism, and that presentism is refuted by the supplementary argument 'over' time. Yet despite reiterating his earlier claim that presentism provides 'the only way for the tensed theorist to escape McTaggart's paradox' when he returns to the topic, Le Poidevin (1998) imports the supplementary argument into Mellor's McTaggart. (Since he implies that he has not changed his mind either as to the force of the supplementary argument, or as to the degree to which Mellor's argument illuminates McTaggart's, this is at best disconcerting and at worst contradictory.)

ought to be clear as day that the truth-value of a token utterance of e.g. 'Bush is President of the U.S.' depends on the token's temporal location. Everyone should agree that, pragmatic features aside, all goes well when Jones speaks the words 'Bush is President of the U.S.' during Bush's Presidency. But it is equally uncontroversial that all did not go well when Jones spoke those words in November 1997, and to insist as Priest does that no harm is done if the two utterances are given the same truth value is damningly obfuscatory. As Mellor (1986) observes, the link between the truth of an utterance and its correctness should be preserved. Semantically, the two utterances of 'Bush is President of the U.S.' are not on a par. Similarly, it just won't do to suggest, as Priest (1986) does, that nothing is untoward if a semantic theory has the consequence that the truth value of some utterance of e.g. 'Bush is sitting down' switches between truth and falsity with the passage of time. The link between the truth of an utterance of some sentence-type, and the correct use of that sentence-type, is obvious, and one cannot just accept, as Priest's proposal would have us do, that whether or not a specific token utterance involves a correct use of the sentence-type employed switches over time. As Evans (1979) points out, prima facie, if the normative status of utterances one might make is temporally variable in this way, one would be at a loss as to what to say.

II.iv An alternative strategy—Pace Priest, the difficulty with the first horn of Mellor's dilemma is not that a question is begged when certain consequences are deemed to be incoherent: these consequences are indeed absurd. Rather, the difficulty is that, pace Mellor, these consequences do not follow. Specifically, the mere supposition that e.g. 'Bush is sitting down' is non-indexical with respect to times need not have either of the (absurd) consequences respectively claimed by the arguments 'within' and 'over' time: it need have neither the consequence that all tokens of this sentence-type have the same truth value, nor the consequence that the truth-value of a token of this type changes from true to false, and vice-versa, as Bush goes about his daily business. As I am about to explain, the view of time on which this supposition lacks these consequences is a 'Priorean' presentism.

III. Mellor's McTaggart refuted

III.i Prior's presentism—According to Arthur Prior, 'the present simply *is* the real considered in relation to two species of unreality, namely the past and the future.'[16] This is a version of 'presentism,' the thesis that only what is present exists.[17] Whatever other versions of presentism might say, this version is not the thesis that there is a non-relational property, 'presentness,' which all and only existing things possess. Rather, on my understanding (at least), it couples the thesis that everything that exists is picked out by the phrase 'everything that presently exists' with the thesis that pastness and futurity are significant operations on existence, in that (i) what exists might not have existed before and might not exist subsequently; and, more contentiously, (ii) what exists might include neither what did exist nor what will exist.

The key to understanding Prior's presentism is provided by his sympathy for the scholastic doctrine that

> 'Socrates is sitting' is a complete proposition, *enuntiabile*, which is sometimes true, sometimes false; not an incomplete expression requiring a further phrase like 'at time t' to make it into an assertion.[18]

For it is but the shortest of steps from this doctrine to the thesis that temporality is an operation on propositions expressed by sentential-operators like 'it was the case that' etc., and hence to the discipline of tense-logic.

In effect, the scholastic doctrine of propositions and the doctrine of temporal operators together announce that Prior declines to think of temporality in the way that David Lewis thinks of modality. David Lewis views a true modal sentence like '◊(There are talking donkeys)' as being true in virtue of the same sort of thing—namely, talking donkeys (albeit non-actual ones)—as the sort of thing—namely, (actual) donkeys—that a true atomic sentence like 'There are donkeys' is true in virtue of. But most of us do not think like this. We think of the modal sentence as being true in virtue of something altogether different—the existence of abstract talking donkeys, or of certain things doing duty for talking donkeys, or of certain things representing talking donkeys, if we are anti-modalists and either Ersatzers or fictionalists about possible worlds, or, if we are modalists, the existence of some irreducible fact (speaking loosely) of the form: ◊(There are talking donkeys). *Pace* Lewis, for us the actual simply *is* the real considered in relation to one species of unreality, namely the (merely) possible.

Prior thinks of temporality, and hence of that in virtue of which

[16] Prior (1970: 245).
[17] Cf. Bigelow (1996: 35).
[18] Prior (1967: 15–16). Cf. Geach (1949).

temporal propositions like 'it will be the case that (there are conscious computers)' and 'it was the case that (there are dinosaurs)' are true, in the same way most of us think of modality. These propositions are not held to be true, if true, in virtue of the sort of thing that the atomic sentences 'there are computers' and 'there are reptiles' are true in virtue of. Rather, they are held to be true in virtue of the existence of something doing duty for, or representing, conscious computers and dinosaurs. Or better still, they are held to be true in virtue of such brute, irreducible facts as that: it will be the case that (there are conscious computers) and it was the case that (there are dinosaurs).

Accordingly, Prior's presentism is the temporal analogue of a modalism about possibility which is by no means unattractive. In holding that pastness and futurity are operations on propositions, it can deny that presentness, pastness and futurity are properties. It might also endorse e.g. Lowe's (1987b: 539) suggestion that an ontology of facts is obscure and by no means essential to the tensed view.

Prior (1967: ch. 1) himself had little time for McTaggart's paradox. He saw McTaggart's claim that if time exists, every event is past, present, and future as a crass falsehood encouraged in part by McTaggart's failure to recognize that complex tenses are expressed by sentential operators, not by predicates. However, Prior himself had no occasion to respond to the charge that it is incoherent to suppose that token utterances of temporally sensitive sentence-types[19] have tensed truth conditions, and while more recent authors who favour the tensed view have shown some sympathy for Prior's metaphysics, I know of no attempt to develop a Priorean account of the truth conditions of token utterances which expressly and self-consciously rebuts Mellor's semantic development of McTaggart's argument.[20]

---

[19] I.e. sentence-types the correct use of which is sensitive to time of utterance.

[20] I came close to so doing in an earlier paper (Percival (1989)). In trying to build on what I took to be natural thoughts about the modal analogue of Mellor's McTaggart, I suggested that Prior might try to resist Mellor's dilemma by distinguishing evaluations of token utterances for 'truth' from evaluations of them for 'truth-at-a-time.' What follows develops and corrects those inchoate thoughts. See too Percival (1990). For further exploration of the modal analogue of the debate between the tenseless and tensed views of time, and for discussion of the possibility of arguments which distinguish the temporal and modal cases, see Percival (1991, 1992, 1994).

Philip Percival

III.ii Evans's anticipation of Mellor—How then might one who thinks that

> 'Socrates is sitting' expresses a complete proposition, *enuntiabile*, which is sometimes true, sometimes false; not an incomplete expression requiring a further phrase like 'at time *t*' to make it into an assertion

approach the task of giving truth conditions for token utterances of temporally sensitive sentence-types? He should start with a clause for atomic sentence-types on which clauses for complex sentences involving tense operators can be built recursively. The obvious place to look for such a clause is the model theory of tense logics. Deleting the reference to a model, for an atomic sentence, X—'it is raining,' say—this will include some such clause as:

(1) For any time t, $\text{true}_t(X)$ iff it is raining at t,

and the clause

(2) For any time t, and any sentence S, $\text{true}_t('P'(S))$ iff there is a time t', earlier than t such that S is $\text{true}_{t'}$

for the past-tense operator 'P.' Can these clauses be interpreted by the Priorean presentist so as to yield his own account of the truth conditions of token utterances of such sentence-types? Given the practice we have followed hitherto of identifying the 'correct' employment of a sentence-type with the truth of a token utterance, this question engages the discussion in Evans (1979). For Evans (1979) rightly ponders the significance such clauses have for the 'correctness or incorrectness,' or 'semantic values,' of token utterances. As he says, any semantic theory worth its salt must combine with knowledge of the world to guide the production and assessment of token utterances.

The most radical interpretation of these clauses Evans considers, which he labels 'T_1,' connects 'true_t' with the correctness/semantic value of token utterances via the claim

(6) $(S)(u)(t)[Of(S,u) \rightarrow (\text{Correct-at-}t(u) \leftrightarrow \text{true}_t(S))]$

Evans then observes that the effect of (6) is that clauses such as (1) and (2) are interpreted in such a way that

> All utterances of the same type have the same semantic value ... [but] an utterance is not to receive a single assessment as correct or incorrect, but rather an assessment which varies with time ... the evaluation of an utterance as correct or incorrect depends

upon the time the *evaluation* is made (and so the evaluation varies) (p. 348)

I hope this remark seems familiar! Once token truth is identified with token correctness, Evans's characterization of the consequence of using (6) to interpret (1) and (2) coincides with the consequence we have already seen to be drawn from the supposition that e.g. 'Bush is sitting down' is non-indexical with respect to time in Mellor's (1986, 1998) presentation of his dilemma's first horn. This is the consequence that all tokens of this sentence-type have the same truth value whatever their temporal location, and this truth value switches between true and false as time ('the time of evaluation') progresses and Bush goes about his daily business. Moreover, like Mellor, Evans rejects this consequence, and hence T_1. Unlike Mellor, however, he does not protest at the supposition that all tokens of a sentence-type like 'Bush is sitting down' have the same truth value whatever their temporal location. He merely protests that (p. 349):

> If a theory of reference permits a subject to deduce merely that a particular utterance is now correct, but later will be incorrect, it cannot assist the subject in deciding what to say, nor in interpreting the remarks of others.

Even more striking, from our point of view, is the fact that Evans discerns T_1, and hence this unpalatable consequence, in Prior's metaphysics, and in particular in Prior's sympathy for the scholastic doctrine about propositions (above). Evans's point, of course, is that this doctrine appears likewise to warrant the conclusion that token utterances of e.g. 'Socrates is sitting' do not admit a stable evaluation as correct or incorrect (nor, hence, as true or false), but instead switch between correct and incorrect (and hence between true and false) with the passage of time depending on whether Socrates is sitting. All that seems needed to mediate the passage from the scholastic doctrine about propositions to this conclusion about token utterances is the attractive assumption that

(*) For all token utterances u, the truth condition of u is met if and only if the proposition it expresses is true

In short, Evans (1979), which Mellor has never acknowledged, anticipates even the later, supplemented version of the first horn of Mellor's (1986, 1998) semantic development of McTaggart's argument.

III.iii An alternative presentist semantics—Notwithstanding the attractiveness of Evans's thought that Prior's scholastic doctrine of propositions entails radical token truth value variability (between truth and falsity) over time, I no longer think it has this consequence. On a presentist reading (*) does not combine with the scholastic doctrine about propositions to give switches in the truth value of a token utterance between true and false, while combining (6) with clauses like (1) and (2) does not yield the sort of semantic clauses that Prior's presentism demands. Combining (6) with (1) and (2) yields semantic clauses such as the following:

(6*) (u)(t)[Of('Bush is President of the U.S.,' u)→ (True-at-t(u)↔Bush is President of the U.S. at t)]

However, clauses such as these are not at all in keeping with Prior's philosophy of time. It is no more in keeping with that philosophy to specify the truth conditions of token utterances of sentence-types involving tenses like 'it will be the case that' by quantifying over times than it is in the spirit of a modalism according to which there are primitive modal operators to explain the truth conditions of '◊S' by quantifying over possible worlds. Admittedly, quantification over times does play a fundamental role in the model-theoretic semantics for tense-logics which Prior pursued. Ultimately, however, I believe his metaphysics obliges him to think of such model theories as no more than heuristic devices.[21] Far more natural, in the light of the scholastic doctrine of propositions, is a clause like this:

(T) (u)[Of('Bush is President of the U.S.,'u)→(True(u)↔Bush is President of the U.S.)]

Clauses like this seem to be the explicit target of the first horn of Mellor's dilemma, and they seem an implicit target of Evans's anticipation of it. For such clauses give all token utterances of a given temporally sensitive sentence-type the same truth conditions. Accordingly, this clause seems to support the absurd consequence the two of them detect in the supposition that e.g. 'Bush is President of the U.S.' is non-indexical with respect to time. That (T) ascribes all token utterances of this sentence-type the same truth conditions, and, hence, the same truth value, appears to conflict with the assumption that being temporally sensitive, the correct use of this sentence-type, and hence the truth value of a token utterance of it, depends on the token's temporal location. Moreover, although Bush is President of the U.S., he soon won't be. And this fact seems to

---

[21] See Percival (1990).

combine with (T) to yield the consequence that while token utterances of 'Bush is President of the U.S.' *are* true, they *will be* false.

Nevertheless, these objections to (T) miss the point of Prior's metaphysics. I will address them in turn.

The argument within time—For Prior the quantifier in (T) does not range over tokens having different temporal locations. According to Prior, only the present is real. Part of what this comes to is that the first-order universal quantifier ranges over only presently existing entities. In that case (T) does not assign tokens of 'Bush is President of the U.S.' having different temporal locations the same truth conditions, and hence the same truth values. It only assigns truth conditions to the existing, *present* tokens over which its quantifier ranges.

On the other hand, there is an obvious objection to the suggestion that reading (T) this way deflects the argument 'within' time. An argument to the effect that a weak reading of (T) has only weak consequences is beside the point. On such a reading, (T) is too weak to serve as a semantic theory! A semantic theory for a natural language must capture a speaker's grasp of the truth conditions of token utterances, and speakers do know the truth conditions of a token utterance of e.g. 'Bush is President of the U.S.' which is not located in the present once the temporal location of the token is given to them. I know not only what the truth conditions of a present utterance of that sentence-type are; I also know what the truth conditions of an utterance tomorrow of it will be, and what the truth conditions of a past utterance of it were. On Prior's reading of its quantifier, (T) does not capture this knowledge. The fact that (T) survives the argument within time is therefore irrelevant.

However, while I endorse the viewpoint which underlies this objection, I do not accept that it shows that (T) can only achieve the generality semantic theory demands if its quantifier is construed as ranging over non-present tokens, thereby leaving it vulnerable to the argument over time. It is not the case that in order to capture a speaker's knowledge of the truth conditions of non-present token utterances a semantic theory must quantify over token utterances other than present ones. This is readily seen by reflecting on the modal analogue. My grasp of English equips me to understand actual token utterances of the sentence-types of English. In particular, given relevant information regarding the context of utterance, I can assign truth conditions to actual token utterances. But I can do more: I can understand equally well, and assign truth conditions to, token utterances that are non-actual. No one addressed to me yesterday the words 'you are wearing a blue shirt.' However, in virtue of my grasp of English, I know that had anyone addressed those words to me, their utterance would have been true if and only if I had then been wearing a blue shirt. Here then is semantic knowledge which appears to go beyond knowledge of the truth conditions of actual utterances. Is this to say that semantic theory cannot proceed by quantifying over all actual token utterances and assigning truth conditions to them; that it must quantify over non-actual token utterances too? Unless the metaphysics of modality is much more straightforward than is generally believed, it is not to say this! On one respectable view, there are no non-actual objects. On this view, far from being obligatory, quantifying over non-actual token utterances so as to capture a speaker's grasp of the truth conditions of non-actual token utterances is not an option. Rather, a speaker's grasp of this much is captured by embedding quantifiers which actually range over actual objects in a necessity-operator thus:

> Necessarily, (u) [Of('Bush is President of the U.S. on Christmas Day 2002,' u)→(True(u)↔Bush is President of the U.S. on Christmas Day 2002)]

Since Prior assimilates time to modality as conceived by the modalist, a Priorean semantics for the tenses will treat the temporal case similarly. Speakers of English know the truth conditions of non-present token utterances, and a semantics for English must capture this knowledge. But this is not to say that such a semantics is obliged to quantify over non-present token utterances. On the contrary, from the point of view of Prior's presentism, so doing is not even an option: there are no such utterances. Rather, grasp of the truth conditions of non-present token utterances is captured by embedding the clause which quantifies over present token utterances in a temporal operator, thereby strengthening (T) to:

> (TT) Always, (u) [Of('Bush is President of the U.S.,' u)→ (True(u)↔Bush is President of the U.S.)]

Using this clause, I can capture what I know about the truth conditions e.g. of yesterday's utterances. What needs to be captured is the knowledge that a token utterance yesterday of 'Bush is President of the U.S.' was true iff Bush was President of the U.S. yesterday. On the view that I am recommending, this knowledge just *is* knowledge of a sort of instance of (TT), namely:

(TTY) Yesterday, (u) [Of('Bush is President of the U.S.,' u)→ (True(u)↔Bush is President of the U.S.)]

Suppose that I know that yesterday, someone uttered 'Bush is President of the U.S.' I can put this knowledge together with my knowledge of English and knowledge of current affairs to deduce that this utterance was true, i.e. that yesterday, someone produced a true token utterance. For we have

Yesterday, $(x)(Fx→.Gx↔p)$; Yesterday, $∃xFx$;
Yesterday, p |- Yesterday, $∃x(Fx\&Gx)$

(TT) does consistently what Mellor says cannot be consistently done: it assigns all token utterances of a temporally sensitive sentence-type like 'Bush is President of the U.S.' the same tensed truth conditions, and it does so while respecting the undeniable semantic fact that the truth condition, and hence the truth value, of a token utterance of such sentence-types depends on the temporal location of the token.

As originally presented, then, the first horn of Mellor's (1981) McTaggart doesn't even engage (TT) and the doctrine that only what is present exists. Hence, it begs the question against Prior; hence it begs the question against the tensed view of time. But what about the additional argument 'over' time by which Mellor (1986, 1998) supplements the first horn?

The argument over time—As we have seen, Le Poidevin (1991) effectively concedes that presentism can accommodate the argument 'within' time while insisting that it is refuted by the argument 'over' time.[22] But Le Poidevin's evaluation of this supplementary argument is wrong. A further consideration exposes it as a simple fallacy. Suppose Bush is President of the U.S., and that Tomorrow(Bush is not President of the U.S.). One cannot use (TT) to obtain directly from this the consequence that all token utterances of 'Bush is President of the U.S.' will have a truth value tomorrow different from the truth value they have now: one needs the assumption that they will tomorrow be utterances of 'Bush is President of the U.S.' Admittedly, for any token utterance of 'Bush is President of the U.S.' for which it holds that tomorrow, it will be (a token) of 'Bush is President of the U.S.,' we can derive both that this utterance is true (from T), and that it will be false (from TT). However, the assumption that token utterances persist over time isn't forced upon the presentist as a matter of logic, and nor do I

[22] See above, footnote 15.

think he should accept it. Certainly, e.g. marks on a page do persist through time in this way. But a charge simply that presentism has the consequence that the truth values of certain sentence tokens switch between true and false with the passage of time is vacuous. As Mellor insists, that they do so is undeniable on any view. Take an unattended electronic clock which has stopped and which continues to display the words 'it is now 17.00 hours.' During the temporal interval in which it persists, this display switches from being false to being (briefly) true every twenty four hours. Similarly, a shop sign saying 'Closed' left forgotten in a shop window switches its truth value as the shop opens and closes.[23] Accordingly, whether or not the truth value of a sentence token of a sentence-type like 'Bush is President of the U.S.' switches its truth value in this way during the temporal interval in which it persists is not what is at issue. What is at issue, rather, is whether it switches its truth value at times at which it does not persist.

This issue is best addressed by focusing not upon token sentences, but upon token utterances. Token utterances are the primary objects of semantic evaluation. Though they are often effected by producing sentence tokens, they are nevertheless distinct from them. If I write the words 'I love you' on a piece of paper and push it through a grating on a prison visit, the primary object of evaluation—my utterance—is not identical to that inscription. If three years later, the inmate to whom these words are addressed takes a crumpled piece of paper from her pocket and thinks 'no you don't, not any more,' she is not questioning the sincerity of my utterance, three years previously, whatever the consequences of her remark for the token of the sentence-type 'I love you' which she holds in her hand.

What is at issue is whether or not presentism is committed to the doctrine that the truth value of a token utterance of a sentence-type like 'Bush is President of the U.S.' switches between true and false with the passage of time. (TT)—namely

Always, (u) [Of('Bush is President of the U.S.,' u)→(True(u)↔Bush is President of the U.S.)]

---

[23] Cf. Mellor's (1981: 99) remark that 'long-lasting thing tokens can vary in truth-value during their lifetimes—e.g. a token of "e is past" printed before e will start off false and end up true.' (Actually, I think Mellor's treatment of this sort of case is unduly simplistic: once made, the distinctions between 'true' and 'true in L,' and between 'thing' token and token utterance, suggest a subtler treatment. (See Percival (1994: 203–5).) Nothing hangs on these subtleties.)

—has this commitment if token utterances exist over time. But for the presentist they don't. Everyone can agree that they don't persist over time. Token utterances are acts which, like winning the lottery, are instantaneous. The verbs which describe them are 'success verbs.' But to equate existence with present existence, as the presentist does, is to say that entities exist only while they persist. So the fact that token utterances don't persist over time will be taken by the presentist to indicate that they do not exist over time. For the presentist, just as it cannot be the case that Bush is sitting down iff Candorice is swimming except when Bush and Candorice exist, and hence except at times during which they persist, neither can it be the case that some token representation r is true iff Bush is sitting down except when r exists, and hence at times at which r persists. It follows that (TT) does not commit the presentist to supposing that the truth value of a token utterance of e.g. 'Bush is sitting down' switches between true and false over time depending on Bush's actions. On the contrary, such an utterance has a truth value only at times at which it exists, and hence at times at which it persists. Therefore, since such an utterance is momentary, it has only one truth value.

IV Conclusion

Mellor's McTaggart, and in particular its first horn, only appears forceful if doctrines which are central to Prior's presentism—namely, the related doctrines that only present objects exist and that only present objects fall within the range of the first-order quantifier—are ignored. Whatever (the temporal variability of) the semantic properties of persisting tokens of sentence-types like 'Bush is President of the U.S.,' the fundamental objects of semantic evaluation, and, hence, the fundamental bearers of the 'correctness' predicate (which I have read as a truth-predicate), are not tokens of sentence-types, but token utterances of sentence-types. These are more or less instantaneous. For the presentist, to suppose that fifty years ago there existed a token of 'Bush is President of the U.S.' is not to suppose that some token utterance of this type exists and has certain truth conditions. It is to suppose that: fifty years ago (there is something which has certain truth conditions). My knowledge of English includes implicit knowledge of what those truth conditions were. For I know that: fifty years ago, for all u, [Of('Bush is President of the U.S.,' u)→(True(u)↔Bush is President of the U.S.). Knowing a little history, I can work out that: fifty years ago, all utterances of 'Bush is President of the U.S.' are false. This does not contradict the fact that: all utterances of 'Bush is President of the U.S.' are true. Nor does it have the consequence that there is some token representation which has truth values at times at which it does not persist. Nor, hence, does it have the consequence that there are cases of temporal variability in token truth value other than the trivialities of the kind Mellor acknowledges, such as a token of a temporally sensitive sentence-type having different truth values at different times at which it persists. Prior's presentism is therefore untouched by Mellor's McTaggart.

Is this slight of hand? I've exchanged Mellor's official definition of the 'tenseless' view for something stronger, thereby weakening the tensed view. Moreover, I've couched his semantic version of McTaggart's argument against the A-series in terms of a sentence, 'Bush is sitting down,' which does not include a predicate which appears to ascribe pastness, presentness or futurity. Haven't I changed the goalposts, and thereby missed the point?

Not at all. These manoeuvres were conducted on Mellor's behalf. To see this, consider Mellor's own example, '*e* is past.' Mellor claims that it is contradictory to suppose that all tokens of this sentence-type are made true by the one A-fact that e is past: not only would so doing give all tokens of this sentence-type the same truth value, contrary to the fact that this sentence-type is what I have called 'temporally sensitive', the truth value which all tokens of it are given at any one time would also switch over time, e.g. from false to true in the case in which *e* starts off future and becomes present and then past, contrary to the fact that token truth value does not change in this way. However, it is easy to see that these claims beg the question against the presentist semantics I have sketched on behalf of Prior. In keeping with (TT) we have: Always, (u)[Of('*e* is past,' u)→(True(u)↔*e* is past)]. On the assumption that it is a fact that *e* is future, this truth condition has the consequence that all tokens of '*e* is past' are false. However, this consequence does not engage entities which merely will or did exist, and, hence, which will fall or which fell within the scope of the quantifier in the future or in the past. A fortiori, contrary to the first horn of Mellor's dilemma as originally presented—what I have called the argument 'within' time—it does not engage any merely future tokens of '*e* is past' that Mellor says are true. To be sure, on the assumption that e.g. it is a fact that two days hence (*e* is past), it will also follow that two days hence (all tokens of '*e* is past' are true). Again, however, this further consequence only engages those existing tokens of '*e* is past' which, e.g. being scrawled on a blackboard, persist for at least two days. This small subset of tokens will indeed be true two days hence, even though they are false now. But this consequence is not absurd. (At any rate, it is a consequence which Mellor himself believes.) By contrast, since existing token utterances of '*e* is past,' and other similarly short lived tokens of it, will not persist for the next two days, the fact that two days hence (all tokens of '*e* is past' are true) says nothing about them. A fortiori, contrary to the argument by which the first horn of Mellor's original dilemma is eventually supplemented—what I have called the argument 'over' time—it does not say about them that two days hence they will have a truth value different from the one they have now. Therefore, on a presentist semantics, the supposition that token utterances of a sentence like '*e* is past' have tensed truth conditions is not contradictory. It has neither the consequence that some token utterance of this sentence-type is both true and false (*pace* the argument 'within' time), nor that some token utterance of this sentence-type which is false will become true at some later time at which it does not persist (*pace* the argument 'over' time). Accordingly, Mellor's semantic development of McTaggart's argument against the A-series fails to engage Prior's presentist metaphysics. The tensed view of time survives it unscathed.[24]

References

Bigelow, J. 1991. 'Worlds enough for time,' *Noûs* **25**, 1–19.
—— 1996. 'Presentism and properties,' *Philosophical Perspectives* **10**, 35–52.
Dolev, Y. 2000. 'Dummett's anti-realism and time,' *European Journal of Philosophy* **8**, 253–76.
Dummett, M. 1960. 'A defence of McTaggart's proof of the unreality of time,' pp. 351–57 of M. Dummett (1978).
—— 1969. 'The reality of the past', pp. 358–74 of M. Dummett (1978).
—— 1978. *Truth and Other Enigmas*, London, Duckworth.
—— 1981. *Frege: Philosophy of Language*, 2nd edition, London, Duckworth.
Evans, G. 1979. 'Does tense-logic rest upon a mistake?' pp. 343–63 of his *Collected Papers*, Clarendon Press, Oxford.
Geach, P. 1949. Critical Notice of Julius Weinberg, *Nicolaus of Autricourt*, *Mind* **58**, 238–45.

[24] I would like to thank Yuri Balashov, Craig Bourne, Jim Edwards, Jonathan Lowe, and Nathan Oaklander for helpful comments. I am grateful to the Arts and Humanities Research Board for funding research leave during which this paper was completed.

Lowe, E. J. 1987a. 'The indexical fallacy in McTaggart's proof of the unreality of time,' *Mind* **96**, 62–70.

—— 1987b. 'Reply to Le Poidevin and Mellor,' *Mind* **96**, 539–42.

—— 1992. 'McTaggart's paradox revisited,' *Mind* **101**, 323–26.

—— 1998. 'Tense and persistence,' pp. 43–59 of R. Le Poidevin (1998).

McTaggart, J. M. E. 1927. *The Nature of Existence*, Cambridge, Cambridge University Press.

Oaklander, L. N. and Smith Q. (eds) (1994), *The New Theory of Time*, Yale University Press, New Haven.

Poidevin, R. Le and Mellor, D. H. 1987. 'Time, Change, and the "Indexical Fallacy",' *Mind* **96**, 534–38.

—— 1991. *Change, Cause and Contradiction*, Clarendon Press, Oxford.

—— 1998. *Questions of time and tense*, Clarendon Press, Oxford.

Mellor, D. H. 1981. *Real Time*, Cambridge University Press, Cambridge.

—— 1986. 'Tense's tenseless truth conditions,' *Analysis* **46**, 167–72.

—— 1988. 'I and now,' *Proceedings of the Aristotelian Society* **89**, 79–94.

—— 1998. *Real Time II*, Cambridge University Press, Cambridge.

Paul, L. A. 1997. 'Truth conditions of tensed sentence-types,' *Synthese* **111**, 53–71.

Percival, P. 1989. 'Indices of Truth and Temporal Propositions,' *Philosophical Quarterly* **39**, 190–97.

—— 1990. 'Indices of truth and intensional operators', *Theoria* **57**, 148–72.

—— 1991. 'Knowability, actuality, and the metaphysics of context-dependence,' *Australasian Journal of Philosophy* **69**, 82–97.

—— 1992. 'Thank goodness that's non-actual,' *Philosophical Papers* **21**, 191–213.

—— 1994. 'Absolute truth,' *Proceedings of the Aristotelian Society* **94**, 189–213.

Priest, G. 1986. 'Tense and truth conditions,' *Analysis* **46**, 162–7.

Prior, A. N. 1967. *Past, Present, Future,* Clarendon Press, Oxford.

—— 1970. 'The notion of the present,' *Studium Generale* **23**, 245–8.

Smith, Q. 1994. 'The truth conditions of tensed sentences,' pp. 69–76 of L. N. Oaklander and Q. Smith (eds) (1994).

Time and Degrees of Existence: A Theory of 'Degree Presentism'

QUENTIN SMITH

1. Introduction

It seems intuitively obvious that what I am doing right now is more real than what I did just one second ago, and it seems intuitively obvious that what I did just one second ago is more real than what I did forty years ago. And yet, remarkably, every philosopher of time today, except for the author, denies this obvious fact about reality. What went wrong? How could philosophers get so far away from what is the most experientially evident fact about reality?

The concept of a degree of existence (of being more or less real) went out of fashion with the rise of analytic philosophy early in the 20th century, specifically, with Russell's 1905 article 'On Denoting', for in 1904 and earlier years he and G. E. Moore held a sort of Meinongian theory of degrees of existence (subsistence and existence are distinguished, with existence being a higher degree of being than subsistence). Early work by Frege also rejected the notion of degreed existence and implied that existence is an all or nothing affair; either something exists or it does not exist, and it makes no sense to talk about it existing to some degree.

Most (but not all) philosophers from Plato to Meinong have held doctrines of degrees of existence. Unfortunately, however, they also denied this obvious temporal fact about reality, for they explained degrees of reality in other ways than the way we know it (as being more or less distant from the present). Indeed, they typically held (at least from Plato to Hegel and Bradley) that a being that does not exist in time at all is what is most real. Time, they often said, is unreal. Philosophy has been and still is a flight from temporal reality. There are a large number of reasons why philosophers have denied the obvious nature of reality, most of them being logically independent of one another. It would take a book to discuss all these reasons, and so I shall instead concentrate in this essay on explaining and defending the logical coherence the most obvious of all experientially obvious facts.

Being temporally present is the highest degree of existence. Being past and being future *by a merely infinitesimal amount* is the second highest degree of existence. Being past *by one hour* and being future *by one hour* are lower degrees of existence, and being past *by 5 billion years* and being future *by 5 billion years* are still lower degrees of existence. The degree to which an item exists is proportional to its temporal distance from the present; the present, which has zero-temporal distance from the present, has the highest (logically) possible degree of existence.

These degrees are quantifiable in terms of their opposites, degrees of nonexistence. The present has a zero degree of nonexistence. What is one second past has a one second degree of nonexistence, and what is two seconds past has a greater degree of nonexistence, namely, a two second degree of nonexistence.

There is a difference of degree and not of kind between the present and what is no longer present or not yet present. This is shown by the fact that our present mental state includes temporal parts that are past by 1/millionth of a second, etc., and this small degree of pastness is such a high degree of existence that we cannot experientially distinguish it from present existence, 100% existence. These *degrees of existence* are immediately given in our phenomenological experience. I believe this theory is logically coherent unless one misinterprets it by assigning a different meaning to 'degree of existence' or 'degree of nonexistence' than I have assigned it.

2. The Types of Tensed Theories of Time

Philosophers of time today are either tensed theorists or tenseless theorists. The theory of degrees of existence is a type of tensed theory of time, what is most accurately called (in today's parlance) 'degree presentism', to indicate that every item is distanced from the present to some degree (amount of time). This is the first time the phrase 'degree presentism' has been used. But I can think of no more accurate name for this theory. The A-theory or tensed theory of time can be divided into five kinds (at least):

i. The three-dimensional equal reality theory. The tensed theory McTaggart articulated is such a theory; the theory he articulated (but did not endorse) implied that future events, present events and past events are equally real. Richard Gale and George Schelesinger held different versions of the three-dimensional equal reality theory. They differed from McTaggart's formulation in several ways, however; for example, they argued B-relations are analysable into A-properties. The problem with this theory is that the past no longer exists, whereas the present does exist, and this entails the present has a higher existential status than the past, not an equal status.

ii. C. D. Broad held a two-dimensional equal reality theory. He held that present events and past events are equally real, but that the future is nothingness, i.e. that it is not the case that there is a future. Broad avoided answering such questions as: why am I preparing a lecture for tomorrow if there is no future? And when I expect the mailperson to arrive in the room in the next few minutes, what am I expecting if it is not the case there is anything I am expecting? And what are weather reports about? Are they about nothingness itself? If so, maybe Heidegger was on to something. Craig [2000a; 2002] holds that future tense sentence-tokens corresponds to presently existing, abstract states of affairs. This seems problematic since most future tense sentence-tokens (e.g., 'the sun will explode in 5 billion years') are about concrete things or events, not abstract objects. Further, all of these sentence-tokens are not about something that is wholly in the present and only in the present, but something that is not yet present. Craig would be better off if he either claimed that no future tensed sentence-token is true (it is without truth value or has the value of false) or else reductively analysed the future tense into something nontemporal, such as modals, as does Ludlow [1999].

What is distinctive about these two or three dimensional equal reality theories is that present events do not have greater reality than past and future events or that present events are the only real events. Presentness is neither identical with existence nor logically equivalent to existence, since events exist regardless of whether they are past or present (e.g., on Broad's theory). For example, Broad writes: 'There is no such thing as ceasing to exist; what has become exists henceforth for ever.' [Broad, p. 88]. However, even apart from the problems I have briefly mentioned above, it is beyond imagining what my dying is if it is not my ceasing to exist, so Broad's philosophy at the very least needs some elaboration if it is not to seem manifestly false.

The equal realities are versions of the standard contemporary 'all or nothing' theory of existence; i.e., either a particular exists or it does not exist, and there is no in between state where it exists to some degree and does not exist to some degree.

iii. Degree presentism. This is the theory of temporal degrees of existence that I shall defend in this essay. This theory is a presentism since it holds that what exists in the maximal or perfect degree of existence is only what is present. It is degreed since it holds that the past and future are not wholly unreal, but are real to some less than maximal degree. When I remember and expect things, I am not remembering and expecting nothing at all. The past and future exist to some degree, but to a lesser degree than the present. To say that Socrates exists to some degree does not mean, for example, that as he recedes into the past he first loses a hand, then a leg, then his head, etc.; what it means is that as he recedes into the past his distance from the present increases, e.g., from being 2,400 years from the present to being 2,4001 years from the present. I am not merely stipulating that 'degree of existence' means 'distance from the present'; I claim that this is how we experience existence, as something with degrees, and thus that degree of existence = distance from the present accurately describes our immediate acquaintance with existence and time. If you deny that this is how you experience existence, it is consistent for me to explain this fact by saying that 'you are in the grip of a (false) theory' and this prevents you from recognizing experienced existence and time. Alternatively, I could take on the larger project of arguing at length that every other theory of time and existence is either logically invalid or empirically disconfirmed. But here I am taking the first step of arguing that degree presentism is a logically consistent theory, and thus that the 'hand wave dismal' of the concept of degrees of existence that began with Russell's 1904 'On Denoting' has just as much argumentative support that Russell gave his 'all or nothing' theory in his 1904 article (i.e., no support at all—he 'refuted' Meinong by 'calling him names', e.g., by saying he 'lacks a robust sense of reality'.) It is not without interest that 20th century theories of existence have their original 'justification' in an insult.

Thus, I do not agree with Tooley [1997: 233] when he writes about 'the position that Quentin Smith refers to as 'presentism' in his book *Language and Time* (New York: Oxford University Press, 1993). But Smith's usage seems very unfortunate, since presentism so understood, is compatible with the existence of past states of affairs See, esp., p. 165'. Tooley is correcting in citing the specific page where this view is expressed in some form. However, each sense of 'exists' I distinguish on this page gives presentness a maximal existential status and pastness and futurity a lower status, since the past or future exist in a nonmaximal sense, viz., I say on page 165 that they 'exist' in the sense that they are no longer present or are not yet present. What Tooley, Zimmerman, Craig, Ludlow, Markosian, Bigelow and others refer to as 'presentism' is only one version of presentism, namely, the solipsistic version, where presentness not only has the maximal existential status but the only existential status of any sort or degree whatsoever.

iv. Modal, solipsistic presentism. Only the present exists in any meaningful sense of 'exists' and it is the not the case that any past or future event or thing exists in any sense whatsoever. 'Modal' is used in the possible world sense, since the present is conceived as analogous to the actual world and the past and future to merely possible worlds. Prior originated this view and William Craig (2000a; 2002] developed the ontology of this view to the greatest extent. Most tensed theorists of time hold this view in recent times: it is held by Christensen, Lloyd, Levison, Wolterstorff, Chisholm, Zimmerman, Markosian, Bigelow and others. According to this theory, you have no past or future, since it is not the case that there is a past and future. I believe solipsistic presentism is logically self-contradictory. The main founder of solipsistic presentism, Prior, tellingly defines it in an implicitly self-contradictory way, a way endorsed by Craig, Zimmerman and other solipsistic presentists. Prior writes: '...the present simply is the real considered in relation to two particular species of unreality, namely the past and the future.' [Prior, 1998: p. 80]. If the real stands in relation to the unreal, the unreal is real, since only something real can stand in relation to something. Unreality can no more stand in relations than it can possess monadic properties. If one says that Prior means that a thinker is considering the present in relation to unreality, then my response is that the consideration is self-contradictory, since I cannot consistently consider the unreal to stand in a relation to the real. Further, there can only be multiple species of real things; unreality cannot be differentiated into 'two particular species', as Prior says. It is an implicit contradiction suppose that there is some differentia that differentiates one sort of nothingness from another sort of nothingness, since no differentia exist in nothingness or nonexistence. (More precisely, it is a contradiction that 'if everything is in the present, then something is in what is not present, viz., differentia and species'.) If one is a presentist, one is forced to be a degree presentist on pain of holding a logically self-contradictory theory (solipsistic presentism).

Notwithstanding this, Craig should be commended for recognizing some of the logical incoherencies that largely make up Prior's schematic ontology for solipsistic presentism; Craig begins by quoting Prior's statement '. . .the reality of the present consists in what the reality of anything consists in, namely the absence of a qualify-

Quentin Smith

ing prefix'.' In the next sentence Craig comments on Prior's quoted remark. 'This last remark [of Prior] illustrates the sort of conflation of semantics and ontology that so exasperates Smith, for the reality of the lamp before me on my desk does not consist in the absence of a qualifying prefix, since prefixes do not operate on lamps.' [Craig, 2000a: pp. 193–194]'. Degree presentism does not face such difficulties.

v. There is reductivist solipsistic presentism, a recent and novel view first articulated by Peter Ludlow in [1999], where he reduces the past and future tenses by proposing that they fall instead into the linguistic category of evidentials (for the past tense), which have evidence for the proposition expressed as their semantic relata; and modals (for the future tenses), which have dispositions as their semantic content. This theory seems promising, since it avoids the problem of how irreducibly past tensed sentence-tokens can be true if there is no past, or how irreducibly future tensed sentence-tokens can be true if there is no future. But this reductivist theory has problems of coherency of its own. For example, it has to overcome such objections as that 'Some space existed for which there is no evidence', which is contingently true or false, if reductively analysable in terms of evidentials, becomes the self-contradiction that there is evidence for some space for which there is no evidence. And 'A new spatial point p will come into existence in the future, even though nothing present has the disposition for this point's existence' is contingently true or false but is self-contradictory if it means that *something present has the disposition for a spatial point p's existence, even though nothing present has the disposition for this point's existence.*

By a tensed theory of time I mean a theory that takes tensed truths and tensed states of affairs to be basic. This way of defining a 'tensed theory of time' makes Michael Tooley's theory [1997] a tenseless theory of a dynamic time. Whether it is 'dynamic' in some intelligible sense in which other tenseless theories are not dynamic is a debatable question [Smith, 2000].

I have a limited goal in this essay; I aim merely to argue that degree presentism is logically unproblematic and is thereby theoretically preferable to modal solipsistic presentism. I discuss this modal solipsistic presentism since it is the most prevalent tensed theory of time and because it is, in my opinion, the most logically incoherent theory of time.

I make no attempt to answer critics of the tensed theory by tenseless theorists such as Oaklander [1996], Dyke [forthcoming], Graham Nerlich [1998] and D. H. Mellor [1998]. This would require several papers unto themselves. This paper is degree presentism versus modal solipsistic presentism.

3. Degree Presentism, Tenseless Exemplification, and Existence

Ironically, one of the main arguments of solipsistic presentism is that degree presentism is logically incoherent, whereas degree presentism holds that solipsist presentism is incoherent. One thesis of degree presentism is that there is no primitive, irreducible tenseless quantifier; there is no tenseless sense of 'exists' that cannot be analysed into more basic tensed senses of 'exists'. I did not develop a 'degrees of existence' theory in my 1993 book, *Language and Time*, but I still hold the view I state on page 165: *Language and Time*, namely that 'x exists' in the tenseless sense means 'x existed, exists or will exist', where the middle 'exists' is present tensed. This shows that some interpreters of *Language and Time*, such as William Craig, are wrong in imputing to me the doctrine that every event exists equally in a primitive, irreducible tenseless sense of 'exists'. Such a view is the way McTaggart conceived of the tensed theory of time, but I reject the idea that properties of futurity, presentness and pastness successively inhere in events that exist in an irreducible tenseless sense of 'exist'. Solipsistic presentists do not distinguish between the equal reality tensed theory of time, such as the one put forth by McTaggart or Gale, and the degrees of existence theory. But this is not to impute a misunderstanding of some text to these solipsists, for the degrees of temporal existence theory has not been formulated before, and so when I examine their critical comments, this is primarily for heuristic purposes, not to show that they have misunderstood some doctrine that neither I nor anybody has stated in some book, such as *Language and Time*.

Solipsistic presentists deny not merely that there are properties of pastness and futurity, but even (in some cases) that there is a property of presentness. A. N. Prior said '. . . the presentness of an event *is* just the event. The presentness of my lecturing, for instance, is just my lecturing.' [Prior, 1998: p. 81]. But this cannot be true, for if the presentness of event E is wholly identical with E, then 'E is present' means E is E. But it is not a tautology that E is present, but contingently true or false, whereas it is a tautological truth that E is E.

Quentin Smith

But what most troubles solipsistic presentists is the idea that past and future things and events possess properties. If they are past or future, they do not exist (i.e., are not present) and thus there is 'nothing there' to possess any properties, even properties of being past or future. In response, I think that this is the point where a degrees of existence theory can be introduced to clarify the apparent problems that nonpresent items possess properties.

Equally troubling to many philosophers is my earlier claim that nonpresent items presently possess properties. I held this view in *Language and Time*, and Oaklander [1996], Craig [2000a: pp. 189–217] and Zimmerman [1998: pp. 212] have all strongly objected to this theory. At first I thought they were wrong, but now I think they are on the right track (even if I don't agree with the details of their criticisms of *Language and Time*). This doesn't mean I accept the solipsistic presentism of Craig and Zimmerman or Oaklander's tenseless theory of time. Rather, I prefer to respond by developing a new version of the tensed theory of time, degree presentism.

I would first note that monadic predicates (predicates are linguistic items) of past and future events are abbreviations of relational predicates, for a nonmaximal degree of temporal existence requires every determination of a particular to be a relationship to the present, in relation to which the degree to which the past or future particular exists is determined. For example, Socrates does not presently have the nonrelational property of *being alive*. Nor does he presently have the relational property of *having been alive over 2,000 years earlier than the present time*. Socrates existed 2,000 years ago, so he cannot exemplify relational properties in the present. But this past Socrates can stand in relations to the present of being earlier than it.

Whatever had been F, *had been F*, not timelessly, not at the past time at which it was F (for at that time, the thing *is* (present tense) F rather than had been F), and not at the future time. Having been alive is analysable into the property of aliveness and the state S of the thing tenselessly being alive being earlier than the present time. It is the whole complex, the state S, that stands in this relation to the present, not the thing's tenseless *exemplification* of being alive. 'Pastness', 'was', 'have been', 'had been' and the like are analysable into the exemplification of the property F that the thing possessed at the time it was present, and the complex state S consisting of thing's exemplification of this property being related to the present time by the relation of being earlier than it. Here exemplification can be taken to have a primitive tenseless meaning (that is fine, since

I do not identify exemplification with existence). If it were tensed, we would have to ask if the thing's exemplification is past, present or future, and this would lead to an unpalatable infinite regress (the exemplification is present, and the exemplification of presentness is present, and so on ad infinitum), as Oaklander pointed out very insightfully in his [1996]). Socrates' having been alive is analysable into tenselessly exemplifying the property of aliveness, such that the state of Socrates' tenselessly exemplify this property is over 2,000 years earlier than the present.

This means, contrary to my theory in *Language and Time*, that Socrates does not presently possess the property of having been alive. It is not the case that Socrates lies in the past but that his EXEMPLIFICATION of having been alive lies in the present. Rather, according to my new theory of degrees of existence, the semantic content of 'having been' is that Socrates exemplifies (tenselessly) the relational property *being alive over 2,000 years earlier than the present time*. Socrates is past and his exemplification of properties is a tenseless 'tie' (to use Strawson's term) of the properties to Socrates, such that the tenseless exemplification is atemporal in the sense that it has no A-properties and stands in no B-relations. N-adic property-ties are not the kind of item that is tied to other n-adic properties. Property-ties are not monadic properties or relations, but are what 'ties' properties and relations to entities; in the more usual terminology, property-ties are not properties or relations but are things' *exemplifications* of properties and things' *standings in* relation. Since these 'ties' do not have A-properties or stand in B-relations, they are 'atemporal' in this sense, but they are 'temporal' in the sense that the property-ties belong to a state that has temporal n-adic properties

The complication of the tenses still preserves this relatedness to the present. For example, if I say that Thales had been dead before Socrates was born, we have two past tense expressions, each of whose semantic content includes a relation of being earlier than the present time. The state S composed of Thales' being (tenselessly) dead is earlier than the present time and is earlier than the state S' composed of Socrates' birth; in addition, the state consisting of Socrates' being born is earlier than the present.

The present is existence itself, *ipsum esse*. As many philosophers have suggested, existence does not neatly fall into any category of *what* exists. Existence is not a thing, event, property, relation, set, mathematical object, proposition, operator, and so on. It is unique. Since existence is the present, the same holds for the present. We may say that each maximal existent is *a presence* (something present)

Quentin Smith

and that the whole of maximal existents is *The Presence* (or, if you prefer, *the present*, or *the present time*). But these are primitive notions, just as Plantinga says possibility, actuality and necessity are primitive notions. You can understand them by examples or synonymous expressions, but they cannot be defined in terms of something else. (Craig [2000a] says existence is the 'act of exemplification' but since acts need subjects, 'act' is at best a metaphor, since nobody performs the act of exemplification (Craig presumably has in mind a deity). And existence cannot be exemplification, since 'exemplification exists' is a contingent truth and yet 'exemplification is an exemplification' is a logically necessary truth, and does not even imply that exemplification exists. The present tense sense of exists is the 'is' (present tense) in 'x is', or is 'a presence' in 'x is (tenselessly) identical with a presence'. Maximal existence is also conveyed in 'x is (tenselessly) simultaneous with the present' and 'x is (tenselessly) a part of The Presence'. Why should such basic notions as exists and presence need to be defined in order to be understood? They don't, since our ability to find false definitions of *exists* (present tense) and *presence* presupposes that we already understand the meaning of 'exists' and 'presence'. A maximal existent is a presence. (Craig accurately notes that this was my first theory of existence, in my 1986 book *The Felt Meanings of the World*. To Craig's credit, he said [2000a] that existence would be presentness if it were not for the fact that some things can exist timelessly. But the credit is only partial. Why should the possibility of timeless existence bar the identity existence with presentness? A timeless existent is a presence that (a) occupies only one instant, this instant being the present, and (b) belongs to a possible world in which there is only that instant—and thus no past or future instants.)

Note that my theory of degrees of existence implies that all predications are reducible to tenseless predications, involving only a tenseless copula 'is' or verb phrase (e.g., 'runs'). Every relation to the present, xRy, where y is the present, is such that x stands tenselessly in the relation R to the present. Since we have eliminated monadic properties of pastness and futurity, we need only one irreducibly tensed word to state our ontology, namely, the present tensed 'exists'. Actually, we can go further and have our entire ontology stated in tenseless language, for we can replace 'exists' by 'is (tenselessly) simultaneous with the present' and 'the present' is a noun phrase, whereas tense is (by definition) an adverbial modification of a verb.

But this does not mean we belong in Tooley's camp. For Tooley,

128

there are only tenseless facts. For me, there are only tensed facts (where 'tensed' now has the nonlinguistic, ontological sense of A-facts, as distinct from B-facts). Every fact includes a relationship to the present. This is why I call my theory a presentism, or, more fully, degree presentism.

What is present stands tenselessly in a relation of simultaneity to the present. For example, I am (tenselessly) simultaneous with the present. What of the question, *when* am I simultaneous with the present? This question is malformed, since the information about the temporal location of myself is already given in the question itself. If I am tenselessly simultaneous with the present, my temporal location (by definition) is the present time. The sentence 'the sky is blue' means that the sky tenselessly exemplifies blueness and the state S composed of the sky's blueness is simultaneous with the present. Blueness is a nonrelational property of the sky, but the state of the sky being blue stands in a relation of simultaneity to the present.

The fact that past and future individuals lack nonrelational properties reflects their ontological status as not fully real beings; in a sense, they are partial beings. Does this mean they have another part that is nonbeing? It seems absurd to say that something is partly a being and partly a nonbeing. I respond that this sentence can be interpreted in many different ways, and most of these ways result in the sentence being taken to express a self-contradictory proposition.

But there is a consistent way to interpret it. The sentence 'Socrates is partly a nonbeing or a nonexistent' means two things (a) he has no nonrelational properties, and (b) he lacks full being of the amount, 2, 400 years (to use an approximate date), which means he is temporally separated from the full being by 2,400 years.

The sentence 'Socrates is partly a being or existent' means (a) he has only relational properties and (b) he partakes of full being in the sense that he is not present but tenselessly stands in certain metric relation to the present, a relation of being distant from it to a certain amount. (I am a realist, not a conventionalist, about time's metric, so something's degree of existence is not a matter of an arbitrary convention.)

4. Does Degree Presentism Imply Past and Future Particulars are Nearly Bare Particulars?

Zimmerman objects to presentist theories that imply realism about the past and future. He criticizes the relevant parts of *Language and Time* by avowing that 'A painful headache cannot exist without being painful ... Plato cannot exist while having neither body nor soul. What's left of these past and future things and events is too thin... Neither Plato nor the headache has any of these ordinary intrinsic properties it displayed while present... Past and future things become nearly-bare particulars' [Zimmerman, 1998: p. 212].

Let us see if we can isolate the structure of this argument against degree presentism about the past or future. First, let us clear up Zimmerman's fallacies of equivocation upon 'exists' and 'is' before we get to the heart of the matter.

The quoted sentences can be reformulated in a coherent way by a degree presentist. Does degree presentism imply that a painful headache is not painful? No. A degree presentist would agree with everyone else that the statement 'a painful headache is not painful' is an explicit logical contradiction. What would a degree presentist say about painful headaches? He would say that a headache had been painful while it existed, but since the headache has passed away it is not now paining anyone. To derive a contradiction from degree presentism, we need to equivocate on tensed expressions. Notice that by saying 'a painful headache' the tense is omitted, so we do not know from this expression *when* this headache occurs—whether it is past, present or future. This is tantamount to treating it as tenselessly existing; we (or, rather, Zimmerman)imply it exists, but are omitting to say whether it existed, exists or will exist. Now if we say 'a painful headache is not painful' this conversationally implicates (in Grice's sense) that the 'is' is used tenselessly, since we are predicating a property of an event that we have identified as existing tenselessly. It is a clear contradiction to say, using the tenseless 'is' in the irreducible B-sense, that 'a painful headache is (tenselessly) not painful'.

But suppose we do not use misleading language and fallacies of equivocation to describe the theory of degrees of existence. Then we would say that the headache, although painful while it was present, is not now paining me, and it is not now paining me precisely because it is no longer present.

And certainly the degree presentist believes that Plato cannot exist without having a body and soul. This means that Plato cannot be present without at the same time having a body and mind. And it implies that if Plato had been present, then Plato had a body and mind while he had been present. But it certainly does not mean that Plato has an irreducible tenseless existence and lacks a body and mind while he tenselessly exists. And it certainly does not mean that Plato *is present* and *presently* has no body and mind. And it does not mean that when Plato was present, he lacked a body and soul. It is true that Plato is tenselessly earlier than the present by over 2,000 years, and his having a body and mind is tenselessly earlier than the present by exactly the same amount of time. But statements of this sort are supposed to be where the problem with the degrees of existence theory lie. Where is the problem?

I think with this new theory of degrees of existence I have avoided a main problem that Zimmerman, Oaklander and Craig have noted with the theory in *Language and Time*. I there held that past things presently exemplify monadic properties. This implies that the things are not present, but their exemplification of properties lies in the present. How could a thing lie in the past and its states lie in the present? Zimmerman, Oaklander and Craig are right; I should abandon this theory. Contra Craig, and more in line with Oaklander, this theory is not logically self-contradictory but is an implausible synthetic assertion; it may be considered as a synthetic a priori falsehood. Even if it not a synthetic a priori falsehood, but merely implausible, it seems preferable to adopt a more intuitively plausible theory. The degrees of existence theory implies that no nonpresent items presently exemplify properties. Rather past or future items tenselessly stand in relations to the present of being earlier than it to a certain degree or later than it to a certain degree.

Zimmerman, Oaklander and Craig will undoubtedly have something to say about whether or not this new theory is 'better' than the old theory, since Oaklander rejects the tensed theory of time and Zimmerman and Craig reject degree presentism. But for now, let us be sure we really have in fact solved the above-discussed problem that Zimmerman posed for any theory that the past and future are real in some sense.

Is there a contradiction in the degrees of existence theory I formulated?

Note there is no logical contradiction in the statement:

(1) x is no longer present but x tenselessly stands in relation to the present of being earlier than it to a certain degree.

A contradiction would be 'x wholly is no longer present and x wholly is present' or 'x tenselessly stands in relation to the present of being distant from it to a certain degree and x does not tenselessly stands in relation to the present of being distant from it to a certain degree'. But these contradictions and other contradictions cannot be derived from statement (1).

Let us focus on the distinction between past particulars that the solipsistic presentist calls 'nearly-bare particulars' and present particulars, which are 'fully clothed' and thus seem ontologically unproblematic to the solipsist. It is true that past particulars lack the 'ordinary intrinsic properties they display while present'. In what sense does this make past particulars nearly bare particulars in any ontologically problematic sense?

The unusual feature of degree presentism is summarized as this: Past (or future) particulars do not have nonrelational, monadic properties, but only stand in relations or have relational properties. Thus they are 'bare particulars' in the sense that they lack nonrelational, monadic properties. This 'bareness' is due the fact that these particulars are only partly real; they are partly unreal in the sense (among other senses) that they are bare in this respect.

The property of being past is, when ontologically analysed, a relational property. If something is past, it is past by two hours, or past by 7 minutes, etc. Past particulars are partly clothed in the sense that they have relations in which they stand to the present of being temporally distant from it to some degree (amount of time). 'Plato walked' means Plato tenselessly exemplifies walking over 2,000 earlier than the present. This temporal distance from the present is another sense is which past particular are partly unreal, for the present is existence, full reality, and past particulars acquire only a degree of existence by virtue of being earlier than the present, by virtue of standing in relation to existence of lacking existence by a partial amount of it (e.g. the amount, 2,000 years).

So we have this result: maximal existents have nonrelational monadic properties and also stand in relations. But particulars that exist to less than the maximal degree only stand in relations. This is one sense in which they are partly real and partly unreal. Let us ask ourselves again; does it involve a logical contradiction?

I believe it can be proven not to be a contradiction. For any present item x, and for each nonrelational or relational property F than a present item x can possess, x has F or x does not have F. This is the precise meaning of the phrase 'the present item x is a logically complete individual', i.e. satisfies the logically necessary criteria to exist in the tenseless sense (existed, exists or will exist).

Past items also meet this criterion. For any past item y, and for each nonrelational or relational property F than a past item y can possess, y has F or does not have F. The past item cannot have any nonrelational properties, and so it is does not have any such properties as being spatial, being mental, breathing, and the like. For each nonrelational property G, it lacks G. But for each relational property R, it either has R or lacks R. For each nonrelational property G it possessed when it was present, it possesses the relational property of having possessed G a certain amount of time ago. The past particular is bare of nonrelational properties, but this is a necessary condition of it being past to some degree; but it is clothed to a logically sufficient degree. That is, it meets all the logically necessary conditions to exist in a tenseless sense (to have existed, to exist or to exist in the future). This implies that the past item x is a logically complete individual.

But how can a particular exist to any degree without having the nonrelational property of being a particular? The answer is that it has a relational property of being a particular. It had been a particular (say) 150 years earlier than the present time, but it is false that it is (present tense) a particular. There is no such particular that occupies the present time. And since the particular tenselessly exemplifies its relational properties of being temporally distant from the present, none of the states of the particular are present.

This enables us to answer the problem Zimmerman formulated: He writes that the degree doctrine implies the following: 'Plato is still a substance, I suppose, but he doesn't talk or think or walk or sleep or have any spatial location' [Zimmerman, 1998: p. 212]. Now we can see two problems. First, does the degree presentist hold that Plato is still a substance, that is, is presently a substance? This, of course, would pose a problem, for it would then be the case that Plato is presently a substance but presently is not in space and, further, presently has no mind.

But no such substance occupies the present time. It is not the case that Plato is still a substance. The nonrelational property of being a substance is not presently possessed by Plato. Rather, Plato had been a substance while he existed, over 2000 years distant from the present time. Substantiality, like every other property possessed by Plato, characterizes Plato only in the sense that it is part of a relation Plato has to the present. The state of *Plato's tenseless exemplification of being a substance* is over 2,000 years earlier than the present.

What is it that is earlier than the present? It is not an existent. But if it is not an existent, how can it stand in a relation to an existent? The answer is that it does exist—to some degree. To say that 'x does not exist', where 'exist' means 'present', can be analysed as meaning x does not exist to the maximal degree but exists to a less than maximal degree. What is the particular that is receding from the present? It is neither a total nonbeing nor a total being. It is a partial existent, which is part way between total nonbeing and total being. Its partial nonbeing consists in its lack of nonrelational properties and its lack of full existence. The 'part of being' it lacks is identical with the interval of time that separates the being from the present (the present having complete, whole or maximal being). This theory is not absurd unless one attaches different senses to the terms 'partial being', 'degrees of existence', 'maximal existence' than I have given them in this essay. These phrases may have emotional associations with Bradley, Hegel, Aquinas, Plotinus, Plato and others, but that is not a problem with my theory, but a problem with your emotions.

This seems to be a plausible way to explain our phenomenological experience of time; for we do experience that uttering the beginning of this sentence is more real than A Cro-Magnon's grunt 35,000 years ago. And we experience tomorrow's visit to the dentist as more real than the day of our 85th birthday twenty or forty years from now.

Thus degree presentism is, in a sense, half-way between solipsistic presentism and the tenseless theory of time. Degree presentism denies that the past and future are nothingness (distinguishing it from solipsist presentism) and denies that the past and future are equally as real as the present (distinguishing it from the tenseless theory of time, as well as from the equal reality version of the tensed theory of time).

The problem raised by the solipsist for the degree presentist about nonexistents is a question-begging problem of the solipsist's own making. The solipsistic presentist assumes that existence is 'all or nothing' and then infers from this that there is nothing earlier than the present that could stand in any relation to the present. But this is tantamount to assuming at the outset of the debate that solipsistic presentism is true and degree presentism is false.

Semantics issue about reference remain to be discussed. The name Plato' refers to a maximal existent when used while Plato is present, but the name 'Plato' refers to a lesser degree existent, when Plato is no longer present. It is the same particular that is the referent, but a referent that exists to different degrees at different times.

What I said above needs to be made more precise. I said Plato is a particular. But is he? The answer is that Plato's substantiality, particularity and thinghood are only partly real, since they are over 2,000 years distant from what is wholly real, what is present. Plato had been a substance, had been a particular, had been something, over 2,000 years ago. Plato *is* a particular to a certain degree, namely, a degree that is over 2,000 years from the time when Plato's particularity was maximally existent. Is this unintelligible? No. It just means that Plato is (tenselessly) a particular 2, 400 years before the present time.

But there may be other problems for the degrees of existence theory, leading to logical contradictions. The solipsistic presentist may say that a particular *essentially* has *nonrelational* properties when it is present, but loses these essential properties when it becomes past. How can a particular lose an essential property? The answer is that the property is essential to the particular in the sense that the particular cannot be present without possessing the property. The particular is essentially a human, and being human is an essentially nonrelational property. When the particular becomes past, it possesses an essentially relational property, one that is the past-time version of the presently possessed property. Instead of it being true that x has the essentially nonrelational property of being human, it is now true that x tenselessly has the essentially relational property of *having been a human over 100 years earlier than the present*.

The problem of change may be pressed further. How can a particular *change* relational properties over time if the particular is not present? I see no problem here. As each second passes, a past particular loses one relational property and acquires a new relational property of being one second more remote from the present time.

What about other properties? Consider Plato existing or being present when 389 B.C.E. is present. William Craig [2002] believes the realist runs into problems here. When this time is present, Plato possesses the property of being alive. But how can Plato, as located in 389 B.C.E., also possess the property of being dead? How can Plato as located in 389 B.C.E be both alive and dead? First let us remove the fallacy of equivocation on 'is'. In the premise the 'is' is used in a tensed sense and in the conclusion it is used in a tenseless sense. The proper way to state this fact is that Plato as located in 389 B.C.E. was alive when 389 B.C. E. was present, but Plato as located in 389 B.C.E. is now dead since 389 B.C.E. is over 2,000 years earlier than the present.

Once this equivocation is removed, we can understand how Plato as located in 389 B. C. E. can change properties. The answer is trivial: By the passage of time. When Plato, as located in 389 B.C.E., is over 2,000 years earlier than the present time, then Plato-in-389 B.C.E. does not presently possess the property of being alive but instead tenselessly possesses the relational property of being dead for over 2,000 years. Plato-in-389 B.C.E. possesses the property of being alive when 389 B.C. E. is present, and does not possess this property when 2000 A.D. is present. Thus, one cannot deduce the contradiction that Plato-in-389 B.C.E. simultaneously possesses logically incompatible properties. (A more precise treatment of this issue could be given if we gave two analyses, one presupposing the

Quentin Smith

continuant theory of particulars and the second presupposing the temporal parts theory of particulars. But that is not necessary here.)

In conclusion, I think the intuitively plausible degrees of existence theory can be defended with respect to its logical coherency and solves more ontological conundrums than does modal, solipsist presentism.

References

Broad, C. D. 1998. (see *The Big Questions*)
Craig, William Lane. 2000a. *The Tensed Theory of Time*. Dordrecht. Kluwer Academic.
—— 2000b. *The Tenseless Theory of Time*. Dordrect. Kluwer Academic.
—— 2002. 'Presentism: A Defense' in Quentin Smith and Alex Jokic (eds), *Time, Tense and Reference*. Cambridge, MA. MIT Press.
Oaklander, Nathan L. 1996. 'Smith and McTaggart's Paradox'. *Synthese*.
Smith, Quentin 1993. *Language and Time*. New York. Oxford University Press.
—— 1986. *The Felt Meanings of the World: A Metaphysics of Feeling*. West Lafayette, Ind. Purdue University Press.
Van Inwagen, Peter and Dean Zimmerman. (1998), *The Big Questions*. Cornwall. Blackwell Publishers.
Prior, A. N. 1998. (see *The Big Questions*)
Zimmerman, Dean 1998. (see *The Big Questions*).

McTaggart and the Truth about Time

HEATHER DYKE

1. Introduction

McTaggart famously argued that time is unreal. Today, almost no one agrees with his conclusion.[1] But his argument remains the *locus classicus* for both the A-theory and the B-theory of time. I want to show how McTaggart's argument provided the impetus for both of these opposing views of the nature of time. I will also present and defend what I take to be the correct view of the nature of time.

McTaggart begins by noting that, when we think about when, in the temporal order of things, an event is located, there are two ways in which we can do this. On the one hand, we can locate an event as in either the past, the present, or the future. Once we have designated an event as occurring, say, three days ago, then every other event temporally related to that event will have some determinate location in either the past, the present, or the future. McTaggart called the series of events ordered in this way the A-series. But we can also locate events in time without reference to the past, present or future. We can locate events as temporally related to each other. We say that an event is earlier than, later than, or simultaneous with some other event. We can use these relations to order every event in a temporal series. McTaggart called the series of events generated in this way the B-series.

This claim of McTaggart's is an uncontroversial one about the ways in which, as a matter of fact, we think about the temporal locations and ordering of events in time. The A-series and the B-series are just two different ways of ordering the very same events and moments. For instance, the Great Exhibition of 1851 occupies an A-series location: it is 149 years in the past. It is also located in the B-series. It is, for example, 63 years earlier than the outbreak of World War I, which implies nothing about its location in the past, present, or future. By drawing this distinction between the A-series and the B-series, McTaggart has simply drawn our attention to the fact that we can represent the temporal ordering of events in these two different ways. But in the light of this distinction, genuinely substantial metaphysical questions arise: is one of these two ways of

[1] Sprigge (1992) is an exception.

137

representing the temporal ordering of events more fundamental than the other? Does one of them truly represent the nature of time?

One characteristic of the A-series, that the B-series lacks, is that events don't keep the same A-series position for very long. If an event is present, then very soon it will be past. An event that is already past is gradually becoming more past. The B-series, on the other hand, is what we might call a static ordering of events. If an event occurs two days earlier than another event, then those two events are forever related to each other in that way. So, the notion of the A-series involves what we might call A-series change, which has also been called the flow of time, or temporal becoming.

Having made this distinction between the A-series and the B-series, McTaggart proceeds to present his argument for the unreality of time. It consists of two theses: a positive and a negative thesis. The positive thesis is that, if time exists at all, it must involve an A-series. His argument for this depends on the claim that there could not be change unless the events and moments of time formed an A-series as well as a B-series. So, the A-series is essential for there to be change, and change is essential for there to be time. His negative thesis is that the notion of the A-series is self-contradictory, so it cannot be part of reality. The conclusion that McTaggart draws is that, since the A-series must exist if there is to be time, but the A-series cannot exist because it is a self-contradictory notion, time itself does not exist.

In general, philosophers have accepted one of McTaggart's theses and rejected the other. So, while they recognize that his argument is valid, they have thought it unsound. However, they have disagreed over which thesis to accept and which to reject. The A-theorists agree with his positive thesis, that the A-series is essential for the existence of time. A-theorists think that a description of time that does not make reference to the A-series is an incomplete description of temporal reality. Consequently, A-theorists reject McTaggart's negative thesis, that the notion of the A-series is self-contradictory. B-theorists, on the other hand, tend to accept McTaggart's negative thesis. The notion of the A-series is indeed self-contradictory, so the A-series cannot be part of reality. But they reject his positive thesis. They think that time can exist without its constituents forming an A-series. In particular, they argue that change is possible without the elements of time occupying A-series locations. So, the A-series is self-contradictory, but since it is not essential to time, time itself is real, but consists only of a B-series.

2. Why I reject McTaggart's positive thesis

McTaggart thinks that change is of the essence of time. There is a sense in which we all think this, since we all think that time is the dimension of change. Change occurs when something possesses incompatible properties at different times: a tree is fully clothed with leaves, and then bare, and then fully clothed once more. But McTaggart means something more than this. For him, time itself exhibits change. Times, and the events that occur at them, change from being future to being present to being past. When McTaggart claims that time is the dimension of change, he means that it is the dimension of A-series change.

Why does McTaggart think that the existence of change requires the existence of an A-series? He argues that if time consisted only of a B-series, change would not be possible. If all there is to time is B-series facts about the temporal relations between events, then there cannot be change, according to McTaggart, because B-series facts never change. Facts about the B-series relations between events are fixed; they do not change. The only way in which the characteristics of an event can change is if it changes from being future to being present to being past. McTaggart's charge against the B-theory can be put another way. If there is only a B-series so that all events are equally real, no matter when they occur, and no event ever changes its B-series location, then nothing really changes. Reality is a fixed and unchanging entity.

McTaggart's objections to a B-series account of change are, I submit, question-begging. He argues that nothing about a B-series ever changes, so the B-series cannot accommodate change. However, he assumes, for the sake of his argument, that change *means* A-series change. It may be true that the B-series itself never changes, but that doesn't mean that the constituents of a B-series cannot undergo change. It may be true, to use McTaggart's example, that if a poker is hot at one time and cool at a later time, nothing about those facts ever changes, but it doesn't follow that those facts do not constitute a change in the poker. McTaggart is assuming that the paradigm subjects of change are events. It is events that change from future to present to past. But a proponent of B-series change need not accept this assumption. She can argue instead that the paradigm subjects of change are objects. It is objects that change by having incompatible properties at different times.

To put my objection in another way, McTaggart's argument establishes nothing more than that without an A-series there cannot be A-series change. A B-theorist can accept this, because for her,

139

there is no A-series, and there is no A-series change. McTaggart's conclusion is a conditional. He claims to have established that if there is time, then there must be A-series change. But all that he has really established is that if there is an A-series, then there must be A-series change. This conditional is acceptable to a B-theorist, since for her it is true because both antecedent and consequent are false. If the existence of time depends on the existence of A-series change, then it would indeed follow that without an A-series there could not be time. But all McTaggart has established is that the existence of the A-series depends on the existence of A-series change.

3. Why I accept McTaggart's negative thesis

McTaggart's argument that the notion of the A-series involves a contradiction is deceptively simple, and strangely uncompelling on a first reading. His premises are that the A-series positions are incompatible, and that if the A-series exists, and with it A-series change, then every event occupies every A-series position. It follows from these premises that the A-series does not exist. The obvious response, as McTaggart notes, is that no event satisfies all of the incompatible A-series predicates at the same time, but only successively, and there is no contradiction in anything satisfying incompatible predicates at different times.

The obvious response, however, doesn't work. It says that nothing is ever past, present and future at once, but only at different times. There are two ways in which we can cash out this response. Are the different times at which an event is past, present and future, different times in the A-series or in the B-series? Taking the second option first, the response now goes as follows: of course nothing can be future, present and past. But something can be future at one time, t_1, present at a later time, t_2, and past at a still later time, t_3. This way of understanding the obvious response does indeed avoid the contradiction. But it is unacceptable to anyone wishing to retain a genuine A-series in her ontology. To say that an event, E, is future at t_1, present at t_2, and past at t_3, is to say no more than that E occurs at t_2, which is later than t_1 and earlier than t_3. The A-series claims collapse into B-series claims. By anchoring the possession of incompatible properties to different times in the B-series, the A-series, and A-series change, have fallen out of the picture. Qualifying the A-series claims in this way yields B-series claims, which do not change their truth-value as things change their A-series position.

All that is described by these qualified claims is a fixed and unchanging B-series.

So in order to avoid the contradiction, and retain A-series facts and change, a defender of the A-series must relativize the possession of the incompatible A-series predicates to different times in the A-series. Now the response goes as follows: of course nothing can be future, present and past. But something can be present now, while it *was* future and *will be* past. This move also succeeds in removing the contradiction, but it does so by introducing a set of second level temporal predicates, and while some of these are compatible with each other, there are some that are not. But if the A-series, and A-series change, are real, then every event possesses every second level temporal predicate, even the incompatible ones. So the contradiction has not been removed, merely shifted up to these second level temporal predicates.

What has happened is this. By saying that an event is present, was future, and will be past, we have described things as they are now. But because reality undergoes A-series change, things have not always been as they are now, and they won't remain as they are now. In order to incorporate A-series change into our description of A-series-involving temporal reality, we must recognize that the same event also will be future, and was past. But these second-level temporal predicates are incompatible with the ones we used to avoid the contradiction in the first place. So, relativizing the possession of incompatible A-series predicates to different times in the A-series cannot eliminate the contradiction.

4. An alternative expression of McTaggarts paradox

I often find that people are initially resistant to McTaggart's reasoning in establishing his negative thesis. I therefore wish to unearth the contradiction that he identified in a different way. Recall McTaggart's A-series. The properties of events by which they are ordered in the A-series are the properties of being past, being present and being future.[2] If we suppose that events really are ordered according to these A-series characteristics, then we must also admit that they change their A-series characteristics over time. An event, like the Sydney Olympics, was once in the remote future, and was recently in the near future. It is now in the present, will soon be in the recent past, and will gradually recede into the more

[2] There are also finer gradations of A-series locations such as being three weeks ago, being this week, and being two minutes hence.

remote past. The question for McTaggart, and for us, is: does time, in reality, exhibit these A-series characteristics? Do events really possess the characteristics of being in the past, present or future, and do they really change in respect of them over time?

Let's suppose that events really do possess these characteristics. In that case, we can plausibly suppose that they are properties in some sense. Indeed, this is a common way of ascribing an ontological status to these characteristics, by those who think they are real.[3] How do the properties of pastness, presentness and futurity differ from each other? One thing that we can say is that they have different extensions. The property of pastness applies to all those things that are earlier than the present moment. Presentness applies to all those things that are occurring simultaneously with the present moment. Futurity applies to all those things that occur later than the present moment. But now notice that I have presented a picture of temporal reality that is only accurate for a moment. We can distinguish between past, present and future, in terms of their extensions, but by doing so, we leave out the other feature of the A-series: the continual change from future to present to past that everything undergoes.

So we must try to distinguish between past, present and future in a way that accommodates A-series change. But accommodating A-series change removes our means of distinguishing between past, present and future. Because everything successively possesses every A-series property, it follows that the extensions of the properties of pastness, presentness and futurity are all exactly the same. They all apply to everything. And it is not simply that these properties have the same extensions as a matter of mere contingent fact. If A-series change occurs, then they necessarily have the same extensions, reinforcing the conclusion that there is no genuine distinction between them.

One could object that the extensions of these properties are not identical if there is a first or a last moment of time. A first moment of time is never future, and a last moment of time is never past. But this does not avoid the co-extensiveness objection. In that picture, the property of presentness is co-extensive with the property of being either past or future, or alternatively, of being non-present. My conclusion stands, as being present, and being non-present are necessarily co-extensive if A-series change occurs.

Here, then, is McTaggart's paradox in my terms. We can only distinguish between the properties of pastness, presentness and

---

[3] See for example, Smith (1993).

futurity *at* some moment of time. But this yields a static 'snap-shot' picture of tensed time, a picture that is patently false, because everything is constantly changing its A-series property. But as soon as we try to incorporate A-series change into the picture, we lose our means of distinguishing between the A-properties. The distinction between pastness, presentness and futurity collapses because everything successively possesses them all.

To put my point another way, to suppose that the A-series is real requires commitment to two theses. Firstly, one must hold that there is a real, observer-independent distinction between past, present and future. Secondly, one must hold that different distributions of past, present and future obtain at different times. But it seems that one cannot hold both of these theses. Marking the objective distinction between past, present and future requires leaving A-series change out of one's account because one can only distinguish between past, present and future at a particular moment of time. Holding the second thesis, that the distribution of pastness, presentness and futurity changes from moment to moment, involves relinquishing our grip on the first thesis, that there is an objective distinction between past, present and future. As the distribution between A-properties changes the distinction between them collapses, since they all apply to everything. The entire account thus collapses under the weight of this contradiction.

It follows that time cannot be such that its constituents form an A-series. To suppose that the A-series is real is to suppose that time has these two features: an absolute distinction between past, present and future, and a continual change in respect of this distinction that the constituents of time undergo. But time cannot possess both of these features, so the A-series is not real.

5. The A-theory's options

If, as I have argued, McTaggart's attack on the reality of the A-series succeeds, what options remain? One option is simply to deny that times and their contents form an A-series at all. There is no objective, observer-independent distinction between past, present and future; nothing really changes from being future to being present to being past. Taking this line involves explaining why, if there is no past, present, and future, we are misled by our experience into thinking that there is. But for many this sort of response will be unsatisfactory. What is needed, they argue, is not an error theory of our possession of A-series concepts, but an account of them that does not collapse in the face of McTaggart's paradox. I think there are two potentially viable options for those sympathetic to the A-theory, which I will briefly outline.

McTaggart himself suggests the first option when he says 'It is never true that [an event] *is* present, past, and future. It *is* present, *will be* past, and *has been* future.' (McTaggart (1927) 21). For McTaggart the explanation cannot stop here, since it merely introduces more complex tenses than the three simple ones, and because A-series change is continually occurring, every event has every complex tense, just as it has every simple tense, and some of them are incompatible. So, as we have seen, for McTaggart this line of response cannot avoid the contradiction. But an A-theorist could take issue with McTaggart's claim that the explanation cannot stop at this point. Take any event, E, that is happening now. We can say of E that it is present, was future, and will be past, and in saying this we do not contradict ourselves. What we have described is the present state of affairs. E has the property of being present. It also has the past tense property of being future, and the future tense property of being past. Provided the A-theorist is willing to concede that the present state of affairs is all that there is, she can avoid McTaggart's paradox.

There are some A-theorists, presentists, who are willing to make this concession,[4] and I grant that it does offer a way out of McTaggart's paradox, but whether it can constitute a viable metaphysics of temporal reality is another question. For many, commitment to the unreality of past and future will be too high a price to pay for avoidance of McTaggart's paradox. Those presentists who are willing to pay it must still show us that their picture of the world is coherent, and coheres with our experience. And it is not obvious that they can do this. The presentist's response to McTaggart effectively involves denying that A-series change takes place. Certainly the presentist can talk about events that will be present, and events that will, in a week's time, be two weeks past, and this way of talking gives the impression that A-series change is consistent with the presentist picture. But all these expressions really convey is that every event is located somewhere in the A-series, and that, were a different moment present, they would be located elsewhere in the A-series. Presentism, it seems to me, cannot accommodate the change in A-series positions that events and times undergo, for as soon as it attempts to do so, it falls right back into McTaggart's paradox.

[4] For example, Prior (1970), Bigelow (1996), Craig (1998), and Hinchliff (1996).

The second A-theoretic response to McTaggart, that seems viable at first sight, is suggested by Dummett (1960). Dummett argues that what McTaggart's argument really shows is that there cannot be a complete description of reality independent of some perspective. According to Dummett, McTaggart implicitly assumes that there can be such a description. When that assumption is combined with his thesis that the temporal cannot be completely described without the use of A-series expressions, the contradiction quickly follows. If time is real, then the complete description of reality contains incompatible facts, viz., for any event E, E is past, present and future. McTaggart concludes that, since the complete description of reality cannot contain incompatible facts, time is not real. Dummett concludes instead that the false premise is the one that says that there can in principle be a complete description of reality. So time is real, but reality only contains some of the incompatible temporal facts.

If there can be no complete, observer-independent description of temporal reality, then one of two possibilities follows. Either temporal reality consists of two domains: that which we can consistently describe and that to which we can in principle have no epistemic access. If this is the right interpretation of Dummett, then the burden of proof lies squarely with him. Why should we think that there is any more to temporal reality than that to which we have epistemic access? Alternatively, we can interpret Dummett as arguing that the maximal consistent description of temporal reality that can be given from a particular temporal perspective describes all that there is. This alternative reduces to presentism. We can give a complete description of the A-series location of every event given a particular temporal perspective, and this would constitute a complete description of present fact. If present fact is all there is, then presentism is true. But if this is the right interpretation of Dummett, then he faces the same problem that I outlined above for the presentist.

6. Moving on from McTaggart

I think that time itself exists, but that the A-series doesn't. There are no characteristics of pastness, presentness or futurity. There is no flow of time. Nothing really changes from future to present to past. But all of our temporal experience seems to suggest that there is an A-series. How come we seem to be deceived by our experience on such a massive scale? In what follows I will present an account of our temporal experience that appeals only to the existence of a B-series.

The feature of our experience that is most suggestive of the existence of an A-series is that we talk about events as if they were located somewhere in the past, present or future. We say, for example, 'It's nearly 5 o'clock', which suggests that 5 o'clock is located in the proximate future, and will soon be present. We say 'World War II ended 55 years ago', which suggests that the end of World War II is located 55 years in the past. And when we say things like this, what we say is determinately either true or false. I will call sentences like this, which appear to locate events or times somewhere in the A-series, A-sentences. It is undeniable that many A-sentences are true when they are uttered, but what makes them true, if not the fact that a certain event or time is located somewhere in the A-series?

According to the B-theory of time, the fact that makes a sentence like 'World War II ended 55 years ago' true is the fact that the event that it is about (the end of World War II) is 55 years earlier than the utterance of the sentence.[5] All events stand in fixed and unchanging B-series relations to each other. Utterances of sentences are events like any other, so they stand in temporal relations to other events. In particular, they stand in temporal relations to the events that they are about. An A-sentence that appears to locate an event somewhere in the A-series will be true if and only if that event and the utterance of the A-sentence itself stand in the requisite temporal relation to each other. An A-sentence that locates an event in the present is true if and only if the utterance of the A-sentence and the event occur at the same time as each other. An A-sentence that locates an event in the future is true if and only if the event occurs *after* the utterance of the A-sentence. An A-sentence that locates an event in the past is true if and only if the event occurs *before* the utterance of the A-sentence. Facts about the temporal relations that obtain between events and utterances about them are sufficient to account for the truth of every true A-sentence.

The B-theory thus treats time in a way that is similar to our treatment of space. When I say that 'London is here' I am not attributing to London the property of being here. What makes my utterance true, if it is true, is that the utterance occurs *in the same*

---

[5] There are two different B-theoretic accounts of the facts that make A-sentences true: the date version and the token-reflexive version. I argue elsewhere (Dyke, forthcoming) that the token-reflexive version is preferable. For the sake of simplicity, I only discuss the token-reflexive account here.

place as London. Similarly, when I say that 'it is now Autumn', I am not attributing to Autumn the property of being present. What makes my utterance true, if it is true, is that the utterance occurs *at the same time* as Autumn.

A-sentences appear to change their truth-value over time. The sentence 'The train is now arriving' is true at some times and false at other times. According to the A-theory of time, the fact that A-sentences change their truth-value over time reflects the fact that events and states of affairs are continually changing their location in the A-series. The reason why the sentence 'The train is now arriving' is sometimes true and sometimes false, is because the fact that the train is now arriving is only a present fact at some times, but not at others. It is only when it is a present fact that the sentence is true. All this is denied by the B-theory of time.

The B-theory invokes the distinction between sentence-types and sentence-tokens. A sentence-type has a 'changing' truth-value if and only if some of its tokens are true and others false. Two tokens of the sentence-type 'The train is now arriving' might have different truth-values, but the truth-values they have are fixed and unchanging. The truth-value that any token of this type has depends on when it is produced. So, the claim that A-sentences change their truth-value over time is wrong. The fact of the matter is that some tensed sentence-types have some true and some false tokens. This gives the impression that the sentence-type itself is a determinate object with a changing truth-value, but sentence-tokens are the proper bearers of truth and falsity, and their truth-values are fixed and unchanging.

7. An objection to the token-reflexive version of the B-theory

The B-theory provides a token-reflexive account of the truth conditions of A-sentences. According to this account, a token of an A-sentence is true if and only if the event the A-sentence is about stands in the appropriate temporal relation to the token of the A-sentence itself. For example:

> For any token u of 'The train arrived 2 hours ago' u is true if and only if the train's arrival is 2 hours earlier than u.

The token-reflexive version is so called because the token itself constitutes part of its own truth conditions. It intuitively delivers the right truth conditions for tokens of A-sentences, but it has been criticized on the grounds that there are some circumstances where it delivers the wrong truth conditions.[6] For example, William Lane Craig (1996) argues that that 'The New B-theory can give no coherent account of the truth conditions of tensed sentences which are not tokened.' (Craig (1996) 18) He asks what the truth conditions are for a sentence like 'There are no sentence-tokens now.' Any token of this A-sentence-type would be false, because if the token existed, the time at which it existed would not be a time of which it is true to say that there are no tokens. However, it also seems to be the case that there are some times of which it *is* true to say that there are no tokens then. The point of this objection is that the sentence-type 'There are no sentence-tokens' can express something true even though no true token of it can ever be produced.

The force of this criticism stems from the intuition that truth, or what is true of the world, does not depend on what anybody happens to say. But the token-reflexive version seems to imply that truth depends on true tokens being produced. This criticism has been articulated in some depth by Quentin Smith (1993), so I shall address his statement of it. He says:

'If a normal A-sentence is used on some occasion to express something true, what the A-sentence expressed on that occasion would have been true then even if it had not been expressed.' (Smith (1993) 83)

Smith is appealing to an intuition that we have about the concept of truth. The intuition is that the way the world is does not depend on there being utterances expressing that the world is that way. Smith thinks that the token-reflexive theory is committed to the denial of this intuition because it gives truth conditions that can only be fulfilled when sentence-tokens are produced. I shall argue that the token-reflexive theory is not defeated by this objection.

Suppose an event occurs, and lasts for a certain amount of time. A forest fire starts at t_1 and burns itself out by t_2. During that period of time no one utters any sentence that expresses that the forest is now burning. Because the forest actually burns during this period of time, our intuition is that if someone had uttered such a sentence it would have been true. But how can the token-reflexive theory cohere with this intuition? I would explain it by putting forward the following counterfactual: between t_1 and t_2, if someone had uttered a token of the sentence-type 'The forest is now burning', that token would have been true. The reason why it would have been true is that its tenseless token-reflexive truth conditions would

---

[6] See, for example, Smith (1993), Craig (1996) and Mellor (1998).

have been satisfied. The truth conditions for a token of this sentence-type are:

> Any token u of 'The forest is now burning' is true if and only if the burning of the forest *is* simultaneous with u.

In order for these truth conditions to be satisfied two events must occur simultaneously: the burning of the forest and the production of a token of the sentence-type. Between t_1 and t_2 the forest burns so if, during that period of time, a token of the sentence-type is produced, its truth conditions would *ipso facto* be satisfied. However, if no such token is produced, the forest still burns during that period of time, but there is no token the truth or falsity of which we have to account for.

The project of providing truth conditions for A-sentence-tokens has both semantic and ontological significance.[7] On the one hand, it specifies what the world must be like in order for those tokens to be true. This is its ontological function. If the truth conditions of A-sentences only require the existence of B-facts, then that shows that A-facts are not needed to account for the truth of A-sentence-tokens. It also explicates how the truth or falsity of a sentence-token depends on what its semantic constituents mean when produced in a given context. This is its semantic function. If the project is successful it will show that the world need not be an A-world to account for the fact that we sometimes utter true and meaningful A-sentence-tokens, and it will also explain why the true A-sentence-tokens we utter are true. The provision of truth conditions makes perspicuous both the relationship between truth and reality, and that between truth and meaning.

The concept of truth is connected both to meaning and to reality. We might even say that it is ambiguous in that it has two distinct domains of application. Linguistic entities are capable of being true or false, and the world is that which makes true or false our utterances about it. Consider the difference between the predicate 'true' and the operator 'It is true that'.[8] The predicate 'true' applies to linguistic entities. It is sentence-tokens that can correctly be described as true or false. However, if we prefix a sentence with 'It is true that' we are making a claim about the world, not about the sentence. I can describe the sentence 'The forest is now burning' as true or false. But if I say 'It is true that the forest is now burning' I am making a

---

[7] Davidson (1986) recognizes both kinds of significance when he says 'The truth of an utterance depends on just two things: what the words as spoken mean, and how the world is arranged.' (Davidson (1986) 309)

[8] I am grateful to Colin Cheyne for suggesting this explanation to me.

claim about what the world is like; I am describing reality, not a sentence about it.

It is important to be clear, when expressing one's intuitions about truth, whether those intuitions are about the connection between truth and meaning or that between truth and reality. It is the connection between truth and reality that generates our intuition that truth is independent of the production of any sentence-tokens. The world is the way it is independently of what anyone happens to say about it. This is the intuition that Smith thinks the token-reflexive theory is unable to explain. His example constitutes a sentence-type, a token of which would have been true if it had been uttered at a certain time, but no such token was uttered. He argues that the token-reflexive theory cannot account for our intuition that this sentence expresses a truth whether or not a token of it is produced. But the token-reflexive theory can account for this intuition, simply by upholding the distinction between the ontological and the semantic aspects of truth. We have an intuition that the sentence 'The forest is now burning' is true between t_1 and t_2. The intuition can be explained by appealing just to the ontological aspect of truth. Between t_1 and t_2 *it is true that* the forest is burning, but if no sentence-token is produced, there is nothing to which we can ascribe the predicate 'true'. But reality remains the same whether or not sentences about it are produced.

Lastly, to return to the original challenge, I must explain how I would assign truth conditions to the sentence-type 'There are no sentence-tokens now' of which there can be no true tokens, even though *what it expresses* can be true. The general truth-conditional formula for this sentence-type is:

Any token, *u*, of 'There are no sentence-tokens now' is true if and only if *u* occurs at a time at which there are no sentence-tokens.

Now, consider some arbitrary token of that sentence-type. The time at which it is produced cannot be a time at which there are no sentence-tokens, so no true token of that sentence-type can be uttered. And the token-reflexive analysis explains why this is the case. However, if we turn now to the ontological aspect of truth, we can see that reality can be such that there are times at which it is devoid of sentence-tokens. That is all that is meant by the claim that there are times at which this sentence, or what it expresses, is true. It is, indeed, misleading to say that there are times at which this sentence is true. It is misleading in two ways. Firstly, it is ambiguous between sentence-types and sentence-tokens. As I have argued, it is sentence-tokens, not sentence-types that have truth-values, and there can be no times at which a token of this sentence can be true. Secondly, it equivocates between the semantic and the ontological aspects of truth. There are times at which *it is true that* there are no sentence-tokens, but there are no tokens of this sentence-type that can be described as *true*.

I have only dealt with one objection to the token-reflexive version of the B-theory of time, but it is, I believe, one of the most compelling. Those who reject this theory, very often do so on the grounds that it cannot account for the truth of unuttered propositions.[9] By restricting the application of the predicate 'true' to sentence-tokens, and by upholding the distinction between the semantic and the ontological aspects of truth, the problem for the token-reflexive theory evaporates. Furthermore, I hope to have deflected the criticism that the token-reflexive theory has the unacceptable consequence that the way the world is depends on what human beings happen to say about it.

8. Conclusion

My hope in presenting this paper has been to guide you all on a journey, starting from McTaggart's argument for the unreality of time, and finishing up with what I believe to be the truth about time. I think McTaggart was right to argue that our world cannot be an A-world: it cannot be a world in which anything is *really* past, present or future. But I think he was wrong to argue that our world has to be an A-world if time itself is to be a part of it. Our world is a B-world, in spite of the fact that we talk and think as if it were an A-world. Indeed, the fact that we live in a B-world can provide the best explanation for the truth of our true A-sentences.

References

Bigelow, J. 1996. 'Presentism and Properties', in James E. Tomberlin (ed.) *Philosophical Perspectives 10, Metaphysics*, (Oxford: Blackwell Publishers Ltd, 1996) 35–52.

Craig, W. L. 1996. 'Tense and the New B-theory of Language', *Philosophy* **71**, 5–26.

—— 1998. 'McTaggart's Paradox and the Problem of Temporary Intrinsics', *Analysis* **58**, 122–27.

[9] Mellor (1998), for example, rejects the token-reflexive theory in favour of the date theory for just this reason.

Davidson, D. 'A Coherence Theory of Truth and Knowledge', in Ernest LePore (ed.) *Truth and Interpretation: Perspectives on the Philosophy of Donald Davidson* (Oxford: Basil Blackwell, 1986) 307–19.

Dummett, M. 1960. 'A Defense of McTaggart's Proof of the Unreality of Time', *Philosophical Review* **69**, 497–504.

Dyke, H. (forthcoming, 2002) 'Tokens, Dates and Tenseless Truth Conditions', *Synthèse*.

Hinchliff, M. 1996. 'The Puzzle of Change' in James E. Tomberlin (ed.) *Philosophical Perspectives 10, Metaphysics*, (Oxford: Blackwell Publishers Ltd, 1996) 119–36.

McTaggart, J. M. E. *The Nature of Existence*, Vol II, (Cambridge: Cambridge University Press, 1927)

Mellor, D. H. *Real Time II*, (London: Routledge, 1998)

Prior, A. N. 1970. 'The Notion of the Present', *Studium Generale* **23**, 245–48.

Smith, Q. *Language and Time*, (New York: Oxford University Press, 1993)

Sprigge, T. L. S. 1992. 'The Unreality of Time', *Proceedings of the Aristotelian Society* **92**, 1–19.

On Absolute Becoming and the Myth of Passage

STEVEN F. SAVITT

In the literature on time in the twentieth century stemming from J. M. E. McTaggart's famous argument for the unreality of time,[1] two gems stand out. The first is C. D. Broad's patient dissection of McTaggart's argument in the chapter 'Ostensible Temporality' in his *Examination of McTaggart's Philosophy*.[2] Broad carefully, and to my mind persuasively, uncovers the root errors in McTaggart's argument. In addition he tentatively proposes that the features of time that he calls its transitory aspect can be explained in terms of a dynamic aspect of time that he calls *Absolute Becoming*.

The second gem is D. C. Williams' paper, 'The Myth of Passage,' a gloriously over-written rant against the idea that there is something active or dynamic to time over and above 'the spread of events in space-time'.[3] Broad is mentioned thrice as a proponent of this myth. His contrast of the transitory aspect of time to its extensive aspect and his invocation of Absolute Becoming are mentioned in Williams' survey of attempts to characterize passage. (102–4) A few paragraphs later Broad is specifically mentioned, along with Bergson and Whitehead, as trying but failing to escape 'the paradoxes of passage'. (106)

Broad clearly is on Williams' enemies list, and the general intent, as well as style, of Broad's chapter and Williams' paper could

[1] The argument first appeared in J. M. E. McTaggart's 'The Unreality of Time' *Mind*, New Series, No. 68 (October, 1908). A later version of this argument appears as Chapter 33 in McTaggart's *The Nature of Existence*, Vol. II (Cambridge University Press, 1927).

[2] 'Ostensible Temporality' is chapter 35 of Volume II of Broad's *Examination of McTaggart's Philosophy*, first published by Cambridge University Press in 1938 and reprinted, with the same pagination, by Octagon Books in 1976. References to Broad in the text will, unless otherwise specified, be to 'Ostensible Temporality'.

[3] Williams' paper first appeared in *Journal of Philosophy* **48** (1951). Page references in the text to this paper will be to the reprint in Richard Gale's *The Philosophy of Time* (Anchor Books, Doubleday and Company, Inc., 1967). The quote above appears on p. 99.

scarcely be more opposed. There is, nevertheless, an area of convergence, or even overlap, between the views of Broad and Williams that has not been remarked and that may help clarify the nature of passage. My aim in this paper is to indicate the nature and importance of this surprising common ground.

I. True and Literal Passage

In 'The Myth of Passage' Williams commends his view, 'the doctrine of the manifold', as an antidote to passage views, but he does little to describe this 'doctrine'. His most explicit statement of it comes in a later exchange with Milič Čapek.

> What I advocate as 'the doctrine of the manifold... is simply a philosophical acceptance, as an ultimate literal truth about the way things are in themselves, of the conception that nature, all there is, was, or will be, 'is' (tenselessly) spread out in a four-dimensional scheme of location relations which intrinsically are exactly the same, and hence in principle commensurate, in all directions, but which happen to be differentiated, in our neighbourhood at least, by the *de facto* pattern of the things and events in them—by the lie of the land, so to speak. We are all perfectly familiar with the fact that the prodigious difference of the vertical dimension of space, with its terrifying asymmetry of up and down, above and below, from all those comparatively indifferent directions we call horizontal, is not due to any intrinsic difference between vertical and horizontal distances but only to a certain characteristic complex of matter and force in our vicinity whose 'grain,' so to speak, runs one way and not the other. Just so, I argue, there is a somewhat more pervasive pattern of physical qualities and relations which constitutes the even more momentous oddity of the temporal direction, with its even more striking asymmetry of earlier and later, in contrast with all the so-called spatial directions. Very much as the singularities of arrangement which distinguish the vertical from the horizontal were explained by Descartes and Newton, so recent scientific attention to 'the direction of time' has begun the description of the arrangements which distinguish the temporal from the merely spatial.[4]

[4] Donald Williams, 'Physics and Flux: Comment on Professor Čapek's Essay' in *Boston Studies in the Philosophy of Science*, Volume II (Humanities Press, 1965): 465–66.

On Absolute Becoming and the Myth of Passage

It is a nice project, which I will engage in only superficially, to make sense of this doctrine. At some points Williams seems to take the equivalence of the four dimensions quite literally. He writes, for instance:

> It is conceivable, then, though perhaps physically impossible, that one four-dimensional part of the manifold of events be slued around at right angles to the rest, so that the time order of that area, as composed of its interior lines of strain and structure, runs parallel with a spatial order in its environment. It is conceivable, indeed, that a whole human life should lie thwartwise of the manifold, with its belly plump in time, its birth in the east and its death in the west, and its conscious stream perhaps running alongside somebody's garden path. (112)[5]

At other places he makes important claims that seem to me inconsistent with the above. For instance:

> The term 'the present' is the conventional way of designating the cross section of events which are simultaneous with the uttering of the phrase, and 'the present moves' only in that when similar words occur at successively different moments, they denote, by a twist of language essentially the same as that of all 'egocentric particulars' like 'here' and 'this', different cross sections of the manifold. (105)

In my view Williams would not be able to use the definite description 'the cross section of events' at some time t if there were not one distinguished (temporal) dimension of the manifold from which to locate a unique corresponding three-dimensional set of simultaneous events. So, while noting that Williams' official doctrine of the manifold runs at some points counter to it, I am going to write below as if Williams shared in a view about the structure of spacetime held more or less articulately by almost all the participants in the debate concerning passage stemming from McTaggart. In this view the basic elements of the spacetime ontology are instantaneous events.[6] These events may be sorted into equivalence classes of

[5] Consider the following remark of Julian Barbour's on page 242 of *The End of Time: The Next Revolution in Physics* (Oxford, 1999): 'The coordinates laid down on space-time are arbitrary. Since the coordinates include one used to label space-time in the time direction and all coordinates can be changed at whim, there is clearly no distinguished *label of time*.'

[6] Some use the term *event* to refer also to sets of events extended in space and time, like World War II. I prefer to use the term *process* for such sets of events. The events considered here have or occur at spatiotemporal locations and may have causal relations to one another. In spacetime theories, the spatiotemporal locations themselves are called events as well.

155

simultaneous events and these classes (which I will call *moments* or *times*, without wishing to prejudge any questions in the substantivalism/relationism controversy) can be completely ordered by the asymmetric and transitive binary relation *is earlier than* or its converse *is later than*.

The defining feature of events is that they happen. As Williams puts it:

> 'Taking place' is not a formality to which an event incidentally submits—it is the event's very being. World history consists of actual concrete happenings in a temporal sequence... (106)

Williams is a naturalist. The manifold reflects all and only what there (basically) is. It's hard to resist quoting his own way of putting it:

> I believe that the universe consists, without residue, of the spread of events in space-time, and that if we thus accept realistically the four-dimensional fabric of juxtaposed actualities we can dispense with all those dim nonfactual categories which have so bedeviled our race: the potential, the subsistential, and the influential, the noumenal, the numinous, and the nonnatural. But I am arguing here, not that there is nothing outside the natural world of events, but that the theory of the manifold is anyhow literally true and adequate to that world; true, in that the world contains no less than the manifold; adequate, in that it contains no more. (99)

Many (and Williams marshals an impressive list) have thought that the manifold missed an important extra ingredient of our world, the passage of time. 'This something extra...' writes Williams, 'is a myth: not one of those myths which foreshadow a difficult truth in a metaphorical way, but altogether a false start, deceiving us about the facts, and blocking our understanding of them.' (102) After burying the reader in a near avalanche of evocative quotations trying to express the idea of passage,[7] Williams comments that 'the instant one thinks about them one feels uneasy, and the most laborious effort cannot construct an intelligible theory which admits of the literal truth of any of them.' (104) Passage is, to repeat, 'an altogether false start'.

There is, however, a thread that runs through Williams' essay that has not drawn much comment. Consider the following remarks

---

[7] My favourite is from Santayana: 'The essence of nowness runs like fire along the fuse of time.'

■ [T]he theory of the manifold provides the true and literal description of what the enthusiastic metaphors of passage have deceptively garbled. (109)

■ [T]he dimensional theory accommodates what is true in the notion of passage, that is, the occurrence of events, in contrast with a mythical rearing and charging of time itself... (113)

■ There is passage, but it is nothing extra. It is the mere happening of things, their existence strung along in the manifold. (105)

It is not too difficult to see what Williams is getting at. Events in the manifold occur at times, some simultaneously, some earlier than others, some later. True and literal passage is the ordered occurrence of (simultaneity sets of) events in the manifold. If the manifold does have a temporal dimension (as I have argued it does, despite the occasional remark of Williams to the contrary), then it can accommodate or model or provide a representation of this true and literal idea of passage. Indeed, it can hardly avoid so doing. Is this true and literal passage, however, truly and literally passage— the real whooshy, zingy thing that is so salient in our experience? Keeping that question in mind, let us turn to the enemies list.

II. The Transitory Aspect of Temporal Facts

Whereas Williams barely mentions McTaggart's argument for the unreality of time, C. D. Broad's chapter 'Ostensible Temporality' is a full-dress exegesis and criticism of that argument.[8] McTaggart's argument is, in essence, this: there must be passage if there is to be change and there must be change if there is to be time; but passage is a self-contradictory notion, and hence there is no time.

Broad deals with this argument in great (excruciating, some would say) detail. In all this detail, it may be that the main thread of Broad's argument is occasionally lost. McTaggart, according to Broad, does present a way of construing passage—as events constantly changing with respect to properties like presentness, pastness, and futurity—that is indeed incoherent, but Broad argues that

[8] As only befits a chapter, Chapter 35 of Volume II, of a massive work entitled *Examination of McTaggart's Philosophy*.

there is a distinct notion of passage, Absolute Becoming, that is not.[9]

The route to Absolute Becoming starts in a distinction between those aspects of time in which it is like space (duration being like extension), which Broad calls *the extensive aspect of temporal facts*, and a peculiar aspect of time in which it seems very different from space, *the transitory aspect of temporal facts*.

> The third, and much the most puzzling, set of temporal characteristics are those which are involved in facts of the following kind. An experience is at one time wholly in the future, as when one says 'I am going to have a painful experience at the dentist's tomorrow.' It keeps on becoming less and less remotely future. Eventually the earliest phase of it becomes present; as when the dentist begins drilling one's tooth, and one thinks or says 'The painful experience I have been anticipating has now begun.' Each phase ceases to be present, slips into the immediate past, and then keeps on becoming more and more remotely past. But it is followed by phases which were future and have become present. Eventually the latest phase of this particular experience becomes present and then slips into the immediate past. There is the fact which one records by saying 'Thank God (on the theistic hypothesis) that's over now!' After that the experience as a whole retreats continually into the more and more remote past. [266–67]

McTaggart takes these facts at face value and treats passage as a kind of qualitative change—events changing with respect to properties like presentness, the various degrees of pastness, and the various degrees of futurity. Broad points out, however, that qualitative change requires the existence of some thing—in this case, an event—that changes its properties by persisting through time. Since events are by definition instantaneous, it is awkward to suppose also that they persist through time. In order to avoid this awkwardness,

[9] I find the essentials of this argument in section 1.22, 'Absolute Becoming,' of Broad's chapter. That section appears in part I, 'Independent Account of the Phenomenology of Time,' before McTaggart's argument officially enters the stage in Parts II and III, and hence it is easy to see how its importance might be overlooked. I ask those who doubt my reading of Broad to reflect on Broad's remark, which seems to appear out of the blue at the very end of his consideration of McTaggart's main argument, that '[t]he fallacy in McTaggart's argument consists in treating absolute becoming as if it were a species of qualitative change...' (317)

a defender of the idea that passage is a kind of qualitative change is inevitably tempted to suppose that events do persist (so they can change their properties) but that this persistence is not in ordinary time (in which they are instantaneous). The persistence must then be in a second temporal dimension: but if this second dimension truly is temporal, it too must admit of passage and the construction that boosted us from the first to the second temporal dimension bids fair to push us on to a third. Infinite regress beckons.

Broad's response was to propose that we not take the transitory aspect of temporal facts at quite face value:

> When one finds oneself launched on an endless series of this kind it is generally a sign that one has made a false move at the beginning. I think it is easy to see what the false move is in this case. The phrase 'to become present' is grammatically of the same form as the phrase 'to become hot' or 'to become louder'. We are therefore tempted to think that sentences like 'This event became present' record facts of the same kind as those which are recorded by sentences like 'This water became hot' or 'This noise became louder.' Now a very little reflection is enough to show that this is a mistake. (280)

The mistake is to treat passage as like qualitative change.[10] What kind of fact, then, *is* recorded by sentences like 'E became present' if not the acquisition by an event E of a new property? Here is Broad's answer:

> But a literally instantaneous event-particle can significantly be said to 'become present'; and, indeed, in the strict sense of 'present' only instantaneous event-particles can be said to 'become present'. To 'become present' is, in fact, just to 'become', in an absolute sense; i.e., to 'come to pass' in the Biblical phraseology, or, most simply, to 'happen'. Sentences like 'This water became hot' or 'This noise became louder' record facts of qualitative change. Sentences like 'This event became present' record facts of 'absolute becoming'.

Absolute becoming, as explained by Broad, is just the happening of events. Since events are located at various times or moments, they happen at various times or moments. Some events have happened, some are happening now, and others, we hope, will happen eventually. Some events occur simultaneously, some earlier than others,

[10] There is a parallel argument in the text that one should not treat passage as like motion either.

some later. Absolute becoming is the ordered occurrence of (simultaneity sets of) events. This is how Broad proposed that we should think of passage, and, as far as I can see, *there is no difference whatsoever between his understanding of absolute becoming and Williams' true and literal becoming.* Generally speaking, I think it is more useful to distinguish than to assimilate positions. In this particular case, however, the existence of a surprising common ground shared by a resolutely anti-passage philosopher like Williams and a stalwart (at least at this period of his life) pro-passage philosopher like Broad must be a significant clue to understanding the nature of temporal becoming.

Since Williams objected vociferously to Broad's absolute becoming, might it not be thought preposterous to propose that it is none other than his own true and literal becoming? Williams objects (106) that 'the extra idea of passage or absolute becoming' leads one to postulate an infinite hierarchy of times. Then Williams complains that absolute becoming 'involves the same anomalies of metahappening and metatime which we observed in the other version.' (107) Which other version Williams intends is not entirely clear, but if it is a version which treats passage as a sort of motion or as a kind of qualitative change, the argument is beside the point. Broad, as noted, agrees that treating passage as qualitative change or motion leads to contradiction or regress, and he proposes a different approach. Of course it is possible that Broad's own way of understanding passage leads to contradiction or regress too, but Williams does not address this possibility, relying on the old arguments against the old views. The burden of proof is on Williams at this point, but he does not shoulder this burden at all.

For a second problem with my irenic thesis that is bound to occur to many, note that Williams wrote, 'The statement that a sea fight not present in time nevertheless exists is no more contradictory than that one not present in space nevertheless exists.' (101) One would suppose that Broad differed here, that he would have denied the existence of tomorrow's sea fight.[11] Is that not an indication that

---

[11] Broad clearly did so in his treatment of time in *Scientific Thought*, in which he defended the idea that the future is nothing but that once an event becomes (or happens) then it continues to exist forever. I take Broad to have dropped the latter half of this view of absolute becoming by the time he wrote *Examination of McTaggart's Philosophy*, given his explicitly deflationary line that for an event to become absolutely is just for it to happen.

I find support for my claim, not just in the text of *Examination of*

On Absolute Becoming and the Myth of Passage

Broad 'took passage seriously' whereas Williams did not? How, then, could they have the same concept of passage?

I suggest that the alleged difference expressed in the previous paragraph is no difference at all, but merely a verbal confusion. There is an ordinary tensed sense of 'is' or 'exists' which, in the case of events, simply indicates that they are happening or occurring or that their appointed moment has arrived. Whatever time t it is now, both Broad and Williams agree that all and only those events that occur at t exist (that is, occur). Williams ought not be saddled with believing that tomorrow's sea fight occurs today.

In thinking of the sea fight, Williams probably slipped into using a tenseless sense of 'exist' in which an event EXISTS (as I will write to indicate the tenseless sense) if it has happened, is happening, or will happen. In this sense, tomorrow's sea fight does EXIST, and Broad should not be saddled with the view that it does not EXIST—that is, is not going to happen. If there is a difference between Broad and Williams about the existence of the past and future, then it lies much more deeply than this objection contemplates. If it lies deep, it may well be entirely unconnected to their *shared* view of passage.

III. Defending the Radical Middle

I propose that Williams' true and literal passage and Broad's Absolute Becoming is all there is to the passage of time. While I

McTaggart's Philosophy but also in Broad's later statement (on pp. 766–7 of 'A Reply to My Critics' in *The Philosophy of C. D. Broad*, edited by P. A. Schilpp (Tudor Publishing Company, 1959)) that though he once took seriously the idea of the world's history 'growing continually longer in duration by the addition of new slices,' he now lumped that idea in with the 'policeman's bulls-eye' metaphor as an inadequate way of trying to understand absolute becoming.

I have no idea, by the way, whether Williams ever noticed this passage and commented on it. Any information on this point would be greatly appreciated. In his earlier discussion of Broad's views on time in 'The Sea Fight Tomorrow' (in *Structure, Method and Meaning: Essays in Honor of Henry M. Sheffer*, edited by Paul Henle, Horace M. Kallen, and Suzanne Langer (The Liberal Arts Press, 1951)) Williams noted that Broad had indicated that his views in *Examination of McTaggart's Philosophy* differed in *some* ways from those of *Scientific Thought*. Williams quite understandably took it to be probable that the absolute becoming of the later work should be understood as the becoming of the earlier work, and I suspect that many readers have (mistakenly, in my view) read Broad through his eyes.

hope that my proposal will satisfy both sides in the dispute over the existence of passage, I fear it will be acceptable to neither. Where, the proponents of passage will ask, is the whiz and go in true and literal passage? How, the opponents of passage will wonder, can absolute becoming not engender paradox or inconsistency?

I have supposed that this investigation of the nature of passage takes place within a given presupposed background spacetime structure—that events can be partitioned into equivalence classes of simultaneous events that then can be completely ordered by an asymmetric and transitive relation such as *is earlier than*. The unease with my suggestion that true and literal passage is all there is to passage is that it comes close to merely pointing to this space-time structure, which, it is often said, is a changeless structure and so hopeless as a model for change or passage. It is always true to say, it will be objected, that the events that occur at t_0 occur at t_0, always true to say that the events that occur at t_1 occur at t_1, and always true to say that the events that occur at t_0 occur earlier than the events that occur at t_1, and so on. These unchanging facts are often illustrated by a picture like the one below, with two-dimensional planes replacing three-dimensional spaces for ease of illustration. Where in this picture, it may be asked, is passage?

My response to this critical question is that change is not in this picture but in what it is a picture of. One who asks it is confusing a

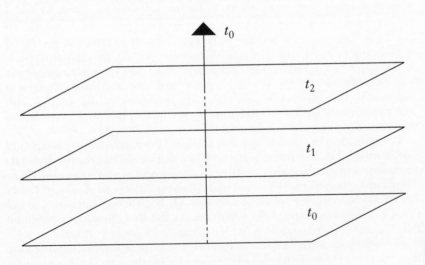

Successive sets of simultaneous events

static representation with a representation of stasis. If we learn from philosophers of mind that 'we must distinguish features of represent*ings* from the features of represent*eds*',[12] if we keep in mind that one dimension of this spacetime structure is supposed to represent time, that events occur at times, and that different events occur at different times, I think we should have no trouble in understanding that this static structure can represent a dynamic or unfolding world.[13] We do not need an animated picture to have a picture of animation. In my view, the call for animation in the model (rather than in what it is a model of) is an unnecessary duplication that is at the root of most of the paradoxes and regresses that are supposed to attend upon the idea of passage.[14]

In a very important paper, 'The Meaning of Time',[15] Adolf Grünbaum argued that becoming or passage is mind-dependent. But he explicitly contrasted passage with events happening seriatim. He wrote:

> It is... this occurring now or coming into being of previously future events and their subsequent belonging to the past which is called 'becoming' or 'passage'. Thus, by involving reference to present occurrence, becoming involves more than mere occurrence at various serially ordered clock times.[16]

Grünbaum adds that 'nowness, in the sense associated with becoming, plays no role as a property of physical events in any of the extant theories of physics.'[17] In the picture on the previous page

[12] *Consciousness Explained* by Daniel Dennett (Little, Brown and Company, 1991), p. 147.

[13] Palle Yourgrau (on p. 22 of *Gödel meets Einstein* (Open Court, 1999)) says that 'for Gödel, to spatialize time is to render it ideal (by robbing it of its characteristic mode of existence).' I think that Yourgau concurs in Gödel's view, and these two are but part of a chorus who have complained that spatializing time ignores its essential characteristic, passage. If what I say in the text is correct, however, one can do full justice to both the extensive aspect of time (that is, spatialize it) and to its transitory aspect, at least in the setting of classical spacetime.

[14] I am here consciously echoing the language of David Park in his essay 'The Myth of the Passage of Time' in *The Study of Time: Proceedings of the First Conference of the International Society for the Study of Time*, edited by J. T. Fraser, F. C. Haber, and G. H. Muller (Springer-Verlag, 1972). This paper originally appeared in *Studium Generale* **24** (1971): 19–30.

[15] In *Basic Issues in the Philosophy of Time*, Eugene Freeman and Wilfrid Sellars (eds.) (Open Court, 1971), pp. 195–228.

[16] 'The Meaning of Time', p. 195.

[17] Ibid, p. 211.

derived from classical physics, there is indeed no noweness to be seen. But, as I have claimed, it is all too easy to miss the becoming.

Grünbaum and I agree, I think, on what is the case. We agree that events occur at various serially ordered clock times, and we also agree that nowness is not a property that hops from event to event. What we disagree on seems close to emphasis, for I would drop the 'mere' in his second sentence and would then explain the absence of nowness from the mind-independent world by treating 'now' as an indexical, like 'here'.[18]

With respect to objections from the opponents of passage, who believe that the idea of passage involves paradox or regress, I have tipped my hand above. I think all such objections are objections to models of passage that construe it as a kind of motion or as qualitative change. Such objections, I believe, do not apply to the modest conception of passage as the successive happening of events advocated above.

Passage deniers might fret that the account of passage above is too modest—that it is, in fact, threadbare because it assumes too much or leaves too much unexplained. I identify passage with absolute becoming and Broad wrote, 'I do not suppose that so simple and fundamental a notion as that of absolute becoming can be analysed...' (281) As I understand Broad, he is saying that the happening of events is so fundamental a notion that it cannot be explained in terms of simpler or more basic ideas, and I have considerable sympathy with this claim. The authors of the entry on Time in *The Cambridge Dictionary of Philosophy* note, with disapproval I think, 'Broad attempted to skirt these perplexities [in giving an account of passage] by saying that becoming is *sui generis* and thereby defies analysis, which puts him on the side of the mystically inclined Bergson...' I've not noted a mystical streak in Broad, and I do think that one has to start somewhere, has to have some primitives. If and when I can say more about the happening of events, I will; but until then it does not seem to me either unreasonable or mystical or question-begging to start with it as a basic notion.[19]

[18] Of course, indexical expressions like 'now' can be used only in circumstances much like those that Grünbaum took to show that becoming is mind-dependent—especially if there is a close connection between conceptualization and possession of a language.

[19] Incidentally, if I can infer from the above remark that I have both Broad *and* Bergson on side for my account of passage, what more could I need to establish its *bona fides* to supporters of passage?

Passage affirmers may also find my account of passage too modest in another way. I suspect that J. J. C. Smart was not exaggerating when he wrote, at the conclusion of a chapter purporting to show that there was no genuine passage or becoming:

> In this chapter I have been defending the view of the world as a four-dimensional system of entities in space-time. Concepts such as 'past' and 'future' have been shown to be anthropocentric in that they relate to particular human utterances. My advocacy of the four-dimensional picture of the world is, therefore, among other things, part of the same campaign against anthropocentricity and romanticism in metaphysics that I have been waging elsewhere... It is surely no accident that romantic, vitalistic, and anti-mechanistic philosophies such as those of Bergson and Whitehead are also those which lay great emphasis on the alleged transitory aspect of time, process or absolute becoming. While I concede that our present notions of space and time may perhaps have to be revised, the idea of the world as a space-time manifold is nearer the truth than these romantic and obscure philosophical theories.[20]

When fancy verbiage, like 'Absolute Becoming', is stripped away, the notion of temporal becoming defended here is rather plain, homespun, humdrum, deflated, dowdy. There is no special connection between this sort of passage and either freedom, spontaneity, and emergence on the one hand or determinism, necessity, and reductionism on the other. It neither supports nor discourages romanticism and may therefore disappoint those who feel that passage must be portentous. It is root and branch neutral but, in my view, none the worse for that.

IV. Conclusions

I have argued that there is a kind of passage or temporal becoming espoused by at least one classic proponent of passage and admitted by at least one classic opponent of passage. This common or garden variety of passage is, I suggest, robust enough to satisfy those who insist on the dynamic or transitory aspect of time, yet weak enough to avoid any metaphysical or *a priori* objections. If this suggestion is correct, then one no longer need try to construe passage in terms

[20] Smart, J. J. C., *Philosophy and Scientific Realism* (New York: The Humanities Press, 1963), p. 148.

of qualitative change or motion.[21] If this suggestion is incorrect, then one is left with either the task of reducing this minimalist notion of passage even further to make it acceptable or, more likely, expanding it in some way that yet avoids the traditional metaphysical pitfalls.

Recognizing passage as no more (or less) than absolute becoming may help to solve some problems. I have suggested above, for instance, that it provides a helpful way for looking at questions about the reality of past and future (though I have by no means tried to provide a complete discussion of the issues involved). Also, in a recent paper,[22] Clifford Williams claims that Bergsonian intuition can not distinguish between classical passage and non-passage metaphysics. If these two ostensibly opposed metaphysics are each committed to a minimal common concept of transience, then it is no mystery why Bergsonian intuition should fail to find a difference.

Good solutions raise problems too. If it does turn out that absolute becoming is the best way to understand passage in the spacetime structure described at the beginning section III of this paper and presupposed throughout, then passage becomes mysterious again as soon as one turns to the spacetime of special relativity and, perhaps, to other more general spacetimes. Minkowski spacetime could scarcely be less hospitable to absolute becoming, since its geometry does not admit a unique partitioning into the sets of simultaneous events needed to occur successively.[23] General relativistic spacetimes most likely do not admit any privileged partitioning either. Can a differentiable manifold, then, provide 'the true and literal description of what the enthusiastic metaphors of passage have deceptively garbled', as Williams claimed his 'theory of the manifold' could?

[21] In any case, Broad's arguments against construing passage in these ways seem quite difficult to evade. McTaggart's own regress argument, however, may not be so formidable. I have tried to show why it fails in 'A Limited Defense of Passage', *American Philosophical Quarterly* **38** (2001), 261–70,.

[22] 'A Bergsonian Approach to A- and B-Time,' *Philosophy* **73** (1998): 379–93. See also his 'The Metaphysics of A- and B-Time,' *The Philosophical Quarterly* (1996): 371–81. I am in considerable sympathy with the ideas expressed in these papers, though I do not wish to express them in terms of Bergsonian intuition or in terms of opposition between A-theories and B-theories of time.

[23] I discuss the difficulties of importing the metaphysics of presentism into Minkowski spacetime in 'There's no time like the present (in Minkowski spacetime),' *Philosophy of Science* **67** (2000; Proceedings): S663-S574.

On Absolute Becoming and the Myth of Passage

This question seems to be the important and puzzling question concerning passage. I hope this paper helps to make it more central to philosophy of time in the 21st century than it was in the 20th.

Time Travel and Modern Physics

FRANK ARNTZENIUS AND TIM MAUDLIN

Time travel has been a staple of science fiction. With the advent of general relativity it has been entertained by serious physicists. But, especially in the philosophy literature, there have been arguments that time travel is inherently paradoxical. The most famous paradox is the grandfather paradox: you travel back in time and kill your grandfather, thereby preventing your own existence. To avoid inconsistency some circumstance will have to occur which makes you fail in this attempt to kill your grandfather. Doesn't this require some implausible constraint on otherwise unrelated circumstances? We examine such worries in the context of modern physics.

A Botched Suicide

You are very depressed. You are suicidally depressed. You have a gun. But you do not quite have the courage to point the gun at yourself and kill yourself in this way. If only someone else would kill you, that would be a good thing. But you can't really ask someone to kill you. That wouldn't be fair. You decide that if you remain this depressed and you find a time machine, you will travel back in time to just about now, and kill your earlier self. That would be good. In that way you even would get rid of the depressing time you will spend between now and when you would get into that time machine. You start to muse about the coherence of this idea, when something amazing happens. Out of nowhere you suddenly see someone coming towards you with a gun pointed at you. In fact he looks very much like you, except that he is bleeding badly from his left eye, and can barely stand up straight. You are at peace. You look straight at him, calmly. He shoots. You feel a searing pain in your left eye. Your mind is in chaos, you stagger around and accidentally enter a strange looking cubicle. You drift off into unconsciousness. After a while, you can not tell how long, you drift back into consciousness and stagger out of the cubicle. You see someone in the distance looking at you calmly and fixedly. You realize that it is your younger self. He looks straight at you. You are in terrible pain. You have to end this, you have to kill him, really kill him once and for all. You shoot him, but your eyesight is so bad that your aim is off. You do not kill him, you merely damage his left eye. He staggers off. You fall to the ground in agony, and decide to study the paradoxes of time travel more seriously.

Why Do Time Travel Suicides Get Botched?

The standard worry about time travel is that it allows one to go back and kill one's younger self and thereby create paradox. More generally it allows for people or objects to travel back in time and to cause events in the past that are inconsistent with what in fact happened. (See e.g. Gödel 1949, Earman 1972, Malament 1985a&b, Horwich 1987). A stone-walling response to this worry is that by logic indeed inconsistent events can not both happen. Thus in fact all such schemes to create paradox are logically bound to fail. So what's the worry?

Well, one worry is the question as to why such schemes always fail. Doesn't the necessity of such failures put *prima facie* unusual and unexpected constraints on the actions of people, or objects, that have travelled in time? Don't we have good reason to believe that there are no such constraints (in our world) and thus that there is no time travel (in our world)? We will later return to the issue of the palatability of such constraints, but first we want to discuss an argument that no constraints are imposed by time travel.

Topology and Constraints

Wheeler and Feynman (1949) were the first to claim that the fact that nature is continuous could be used to argue that causal influences from later events to earlier events, as are made possible by time travel, will not lead to paradox without the need for any constraints. Maudlin (1990) showed how to make their argument precise and more general, and argued that nonetheless it was not completely general.

Imagine the following set-up. We have a camera ready to take a black and white picture of whatever comes out of the time machine. The film is then developed and the developed negative is subsequently put in the time machine and set to come out of the time machine at the time the picture is taken. This surely will create a paradox: the negative will have the opposite distribution of black, white, and shades of grey, from the picture that comes out of the time machine. But since the thing that comes out of the time machine is the negative itself it we surely have a paradox.

However, it does not take much thought to realize that there is no paradox here. What will happen is that a uniformly grey picture will emerge which produces a negative that has exactly the same uniform shade of grey. No matter what the sensitivity of the film is, as long as the dependence of the brightness of the negative depends in a continuous manner on the brightness of the object being photographed, there will be a shade of grey that produces exactly the same shade of grey on the negative when photographed. This is the essence of Wheeler and Feynman's idea. Let us first be a bit more precise and then a bit more general.

For simplicity let us suppose that the film is always a uniform shade of grey (i.e. at any time the shade of grey does not vary by location on the film). The possible shades of grey of the film can then be represented by the (real) numbers from 0, representing pure black, to 1, representing pure white.

Let us now distinguish various stages in the chronological order of the life of the film (see Figure 0)

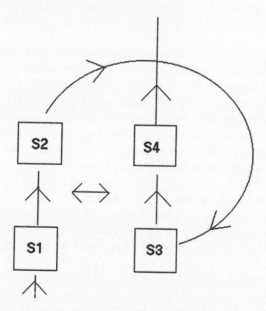

Figure 0

In stage S_1 the film is young; it has just been placed in the camera and is ready to be exposed. It is then exposed to the object that comes out of the time machine. (That object in fact is a later stage of the film itself). By the time we come to stage S_2 of the life of the film, it has been developed and is about to enter the time machine. Stage S_3 occurs just after it exits the time machine and just before it is photographed. Stage S_4 occurs after it has been photographed and before it starts fading away.

Let us assume that the film starts out, in stage S_1, in some uniform shade of grey, and that the only significant change in the shade of grey of the film occurs between stages S_1 and S_2. During that period it acquires a shade of grey that depends on the shade of grey of the object that was photographed. I.e. the shade of grey that the film acquires at stage S_2 depends on the shade of grey it has at stage S_3. The influence of the shade of grey of the film at stage S_3, on the shade of grey of the film at stage S_2, can be represented as a mapping, or function, from the real numbers between 0 and 1 (inclusive), to the real numbers between 0 and 1 (inclusive). Let us suppose that the process of photography is such that if one imagines varying the shade of grey of an object in a smooth, continuous manner then the shade of grey of the developed picture of that object will also vary in a smooth, continuous manner. This implies that the function in question will be a continuous function. Now any continuous function from the real numbers between 0 and 1 (inclusive) to the real numbers between 0 and 1 (inclusive) must map at least one number to itself. One can quickly convince oneself of this by graphing such functions. For one will quickly see that any continuous function f from [0,1] to [0,1] must intersect the line x=y somewhere, and thus there must be at least one point x such that f(x)=x. Such points are called fixed points of the function. Now let us think about what such a fixed point represents. It represents a shade of grey such that, when photographed, it will produce a developed film with exactly that same shade of grey. The existence of such a fixed point implies a solution to the apparent paradox.

Let us now be more general and allow colour photography. One can represent each possible colour of an object (of uniform colour) by the proportions of blue, green and red that make up that colour. (This is why television screens can produce all possible colours.) Thus one can represent all possible colours of an object by three points on three orthogonal lines x, y and z, that is to say, by a point in a three-dimensional cube. This cube is also known as the 'Cartesian product' of the three line segments. Now, one can also show that any continuous map from such a cube to itself must have at least one fixed point. So colour photography can not be used to create time travel paradoxes either!

Even more generally, consider some system P which, as in the above example, has the following life. It starts in some state S_1, it interacts with an object that comes out of a time machine (which happens to be its older self), it travels back in time, it interacts with some object (which happens to be its younger self), and finally it grows old and dies. Let us assume that the set of possible states of P can be represented by a Cartesian product of n closed intervals of the reals, i.e. let us assume that the topology of the state-space of P is isomorphic to a finite Cartesian product of closed intervals of the reals. Let us further assume that the development of P in time, and the dependence of that development on the state of objects that it interacts with, is continuous. Then, by a well-known fixed point theorem in topology (see e.g. Hocking and Young 1961, p. 273), no matter what the nature of the interaction is, and no matter what the initial state of the object is, there will be at least one state S_3 of the older system (as it emerges from the time travel machine) that will influence the initial state S_1 of the younger system (when it encounters the older system) so that, as the younger system becomes older, it develops exactly into state S_3. Thus without imposing any constraints on the initial state S_1 of the system P, we have shown that there will always be perfectly ordinary, non-paradoxical, solutions, in which everything that happens, happens according to the usual laws of development. Of course, there is looped causation, hence presumably also looped explanation, but what do you expect if there is looped time?

Unfortunately, for the fan of time travel, a little reflection suggests that there are systems for which the needed fixed point theorem does not hold. Imagine, for instance, that we have a dial that can only rotate in a plane. We are going to put the dial in the time machine. Indeed we have decided that if we see the later stage of the dial come out of the time machine set at angle x, then we will set the dial to $x+90$, and throw it into the time machine. Now it seems we have a paradox, since the mapping that consists of a rotation of all points in a circular state-space by 90 degrees does not have a fixed point. And why wouldn't some state-spaces have the topology of a circle?

However, we have so far not used another continuity assumption which is also a reasonable assumption. So far we have only made the following demand: the state the dial is in at stage must S_2 be a continuous function of the state of the dial at stage S_3. But, the state of the dial at stage S_2 is arrived at by taking the state of the dial at stage S_1 and rotating it over some angle. It is not merely the case that the effect of the interaction, namely the state of the dial at stage S_2, should be a continuous function of the cause, namely the state of the dial at stage S_3. It is additionally the case that the path taken to get there, the way the dial is rotated between stages S_1 and S_2 must be a continuous function of the state at stage S_3. And, rather surprisingly, it turns out that this can not be done. Let us illustrate what the problem is before going to a more general demonstration that there must be a fixed point solution in the dial case.

Forget time travel for the moment. Suppose that you and I each have a watch with a single dial neither of which is running. My watch is set at 12. You are going to announce what your watch is set at. My task is going to be to adjust my watch to yours no matter what announcement you make. And my actions should have a continuous (single valued) dependence on the time that you announce. Surprisingly, this is not possible! For instance, suppose that if you announce '12', then I achieve that setting on my watch by doing nothing. Now imagine slowly and continuously increasing the announced times, starting at 12. By continuity, I must achieve each of those settings by rotating my dial to the right. If at some point I switch and achieve the announced goal by a rotation of my dial to the left, I will have introduced a discontinuity in my actions, a discontinuity in the actions that I take as a function of the announced angle. So I will be forced, by continuity, to achieve every announcement by rotating the dial to the right. But, this rotation to the right will have to be abruptly discontinued as the announcements grow larger and I eventually approach 12 again, since I achieved 12 by not rotating the dial at all. So, there will be a discontinuity at 12 at the latest. In general, continuity of my actions as a function of announced times can not be maintained throughout if I am to be able to replicate all possible settings. Another way to see the problem is that one can similarly reason that, as one starts with 12, and imagines continuously making the announced times earlier, one will be forced, by continuity, to achieve the announced times by rotating the dial to the left. But the conclusions drawn from the assumption of continuous increases and the assumption of continuous decreases are inconsistent. So we have an inconsistency following from the assumption of continuity and the assumption that I always manage to set my watch to your watch. So, a dial developing according to a continuous dynamics from a given initial state, can not be set up so as to react to a second dial, with which it interacts, in such a way that it is guaranteed to always end up set at the same angle as the second dial. Similarly, it can not be set up so that it is guaranteed to always end up set at 90 degrees to the setting of the second dial. All of this has nothing to do with time travel. However, the impossibility of such set ups is what prevents us from enacting the rotation by 90 degrees that would create paradox in the time travel setting.

174

Let us now give the positive result that with such dials there will always be fixed point solutions, as long as the dynamics is continuous. Let us call the state of the dial before it interacts with its older self the initial state of the dial. And let us call the state of the dial after it emerges from the time machine the final state of the dial. We can represent the possible initial and final states of the dial by the angles x and y that the dial can point at initially and finally. The set of possible initial plus final states thus forms a torus. (See figure 1.)

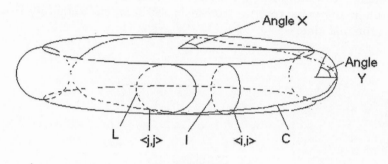

Figure 1

Suppose that the dial starts at angle I. The initial angle I that the dial is at before it encounters its older self, and the set of all possible final angles that the dial can have when it emerges from the time machine is represented by the circle I on the torus (see figure 1). Given any possible angle of the emerging dial the dial initially at angle I will develop to some other angle. One can picture this development by rotating each point on I in the horizontal direction by the relevant amount. Since the rotation has to depend continuously on the angle of the emerging dial, ring I during this development will deform into some loop L on the torus. Loop L thus represents the angle x that the dial is at when it is thrown into the time machine, given that it started at angle I and then encountered a dial (its older self) which was at angle y when it emerged from the time machine. We therefore have consistency if $x=y$ for some x and y on loop L. Now, let loop C be the loop which consists of all the points on the torus for which $x=y$. Ring I intersects C at point $<i,i>$. Obviously any continuous deformation of I must still intersect C somewhere. So L must intersect C somewhere, say at $<j,j>$. But that means that no matter how the development of the dial starting at I depends on the angle of the emerging dial, there will be some angle for the emerging dial such that the dial will develop exactly into that angle

175

(by the time it enters the time machine) under the influence of that emerging dial. This is so no matter what angle one starts with, and no matter how the development depends on the angle of the emerging dial. Thus even for a circular state-space there are no constraints needed other than continuity.

Unfortunately there are state-spaces that escape even this argument. Consider for instance a pointer that can be set to all values between 0 and 1, where 0 and 1 are not possible values. I.e. suppose that we have a state-space that is isomorphic to an open set of real numbers. Now suppose that we have a machine that sets the pointer to half the value that the pointer is set at when it emerges from the time machine.

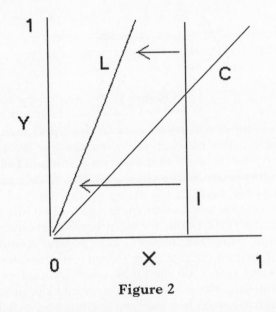

Figure 2

Suppose the pointer starts at value I. As before we can represent the combination of this initial position and all possible final positions by the line I. Under the influence of pointer coming out of the time machine the pointer value will develop to a value that equals half the value of the final value that it encountered. We can represent this development as the continuous deformation of line I into line L. This development is fully continuous. A point $<x,y>$ on line I represents the initial position x of the (young) pointer and the position y of the older pointer as it emerges from the time machine.

A point $<x, y>$ on line L represents the value x that the pointer should develop into given that it encountered the older pointer emerging from the time machine set at position y. Since the pointer is designed to develop to half the value of the pointer that it encounters, the line L corresponds to $x=1/2y$. We have consistency if there is some point such that it develops into that point, i.e. if there is some point $<x,y>$ on line L such that $x=y$. However, there is no such point: lines L and C do not intersect. Thus there is no consistent solution, despite the fact that the dynamics is fully continuous.

Of course if 0 were a possible value L and C would intersect at $<0,0>$. This is surprising and strange: adding one point to the set of possible values of a quantity here makes the difference between paradox and peace. One might be tempted to just add the extra point to the state-space in order to avoid problems. After all, one might say, surely no measurements could ever tell us whether the set of possible values includes that exact point or not. Unfortunately there can be good theoretical reasons for supposing that some quantity has a state-space that is open: the set of all possible speeds of massive objects in special relativity surely is an open set, since it includes all speeds up to, but not including, the speed of light. Quantities that have possible values that are not bounded also lead to counter examples to the presented fixed point argument. And it is not obvious to us why one should exclude such possibilities. So the argument that no constraints are needed is not fully general.

An interesting question of course is: exactly for which state-spaces must there be such fixed points. We do not know the general answer.

The General Possibility of Time Travel in General Relativity

Time travel has recently been discussed quite extensively in the context of general relativity. Time travel can occur in general relativistic models in which one has closed time-like curves (CTC's). Travelling along such a curve, one would never exceed the speed of light, and yet after a certain amount of (proper) time return to a point in space-time that one previously visited. Or, by staying close to such a CTC, one could come arbitrarily close to a point in space-time that one previously visited. General relativity, in a rather straightforward sense, allows time travel: there appear to be many space-times (compatible with the fundamental equations of General Relativity) in which there are CTC's. Space-time, for instance,

Frank Arntzenius and Tim Maudlin

could have a Minkowski metric everywhere, and yet have CTC's everywhere by having the temporal dimension (topologically) rolled up as a circle. Or, one can have wormhole connections between different parts of space-time which allow one to enter 'mouth A' of such a wormhole connection, travel through the wormhole, exit the wormhole at 'mouth B' and re-enter 'mouth A' again. Or, one can have space-times which topologically are R4, and yet have CTC's due to the 'tilting' of light cones (Gödel space-times, Taub-NUT space- times, etc.)

General relativity thus appears to provide ample opportunity for time travel. Note that just because there are CTC's in a space-time, this does not mean that one can get from any point in the space-time to any other point by following some future directed timelike curve. In many space-times in which there are CTC's such CTC's do not occur all over space-time. Some parts of space-time can have CTC's while other parts do not. Let us call the part of a space-time that has CTC's the 'time travel region' of that space-time, while calling the rest of that space-time the 'normal region'. More precisely, the 'time travel region' consists of all the space-time points p such that there exists a (non-zero length) timelike curve that starts at p and returns to p. Now let us start examining space-times with CTC's a bit more closely for potential problems.

Two Toy Models

In order to get a feeling for the sorts of implications that closed timelike curves can have, it may be useful to consider two simple models. In space-times with closed timelike curves the traditional initial value problem cannot be framed in the usual way. For it presupposes the existence of Cauchy surfaces, and if there are CTCs then no Cauchy surface exists. (A Cauchy surface is a spacelike surface such that every inextendible timelike curve crosses it exactly once. One normally specifies initial conditions by giving the conditions on such a surface.) Nonetheless, if the topological complexities of the manifold are appropriately localized, we can come quite close. Let us call an edgeless spacelike surface S a *quasi-Cauchy* surface if it divides the rest of the manifold into two parts such that a) every point in the manifold can be connected by a timelike curve to S, and b) any timelike curve which connects a point in one region to a point in the other region intersects S exactly once. It is obvious that a quasi-Cauchy surface must entirely inhabit the normal region of the space-time; if any point p of S is in the time travel region, then any timelike curve which intersects p can be extended to a timelike curve which intersects S near p again. In extreme cases of time travel, a model may have no normal region at all (e.g. Minkowski space-time rolled up like a cylinder in a time-like direction), in which case our usual notions of temporal precedence will not apply. But temporal anomalies like wormholes (and time machines) can be sufficiently localized to permit the existence of quasi-Cauchy surfaces.

Given a timelike orientation, a quasi-Cauchy surface unproblematically divides the manifold into its *past* (i.e. all points that can be reached by past-directed timelike curves from S) and its *future* (ditto *mutatis mutandis*). If the whole past of S is in the normal region of the manifold, then S is a *partial Cauchy surface*: every inextendible timelike curve which exists to the past of S intersects S exactly once, but (if there is time travel in the future) not every inextendible timelike curve which exists to the future of S intersects S. Now we can ask a particularly clear question: consider a manifold which contains a time travel region, but also has a partial Cauchy surface S, such that all of the temporal funny business is to the future of S. If all you could see were S and its past, you would not know that the space-time had any time travel at all. The question is: are there any constraints on the sort of data which can be put on S and continued to a global solution of the dynamics which are different from the constraints (if any) on the data which can be put on a Cauchy surface in a simply connected manifold and continued to a global solution?

It is not at all surprising that there might be constraints on the data which can be put on a locally space-like surface which passes through the time travel region: after all, we never think we can freely specify what happens on a space-like surface and on another such surface to its future, but in this case the surface at issue lies to its own future. But if there were particular constraints for data on a partial Cauchy surface then we would apparently need to have to rule out some sorts of otherwise acceptable states on S if there is to be time travel to the future of S. We then might be able to establish that there will be no time travel in the future by simple inspection of the present state of the universe. As we will see, there is reason to suspect that such constraints on the partial Cauchy surface are non-generic. But we are getting ahead of ourselves: first let's consider the effect of time travel on a very simple dynamics.

The simplest possible example is the Newtonian theory of perfectly elastic collisions among equally massive particles in one spatial dimension. The space-time is two-dimensional, so we can

179

represent it initially as the Euclidean plane, and the dynamics is completely specified by two conditions. When particles are travelling freely, their world lines are straight lines in the space-time, and when two particles collide, they exchange momenta, so the collision looks like an 'X' in space-time, with each particle changing its momentum at the impact.[1] The dynamics is purely local, in that one can check that a set of world-lines constitutes a model of the dynamics by checking that the dynamics is obeyed in every arbitrarily small region. It is also trivial to generate solutions from arbitrary initial data if there are no CTCs: given the initial positions and momenta of a set of particles, one simply draws a straight line from each particle in the appropriate direction and continues it indefinitely. Once all the lines are drawn, the worldline of each particle can be traced from collision to collision. The boundary value problem for this dynamics is obviously well-posed: any set of data at an instant yields a unique global solution, constructed by the method sketched above.

What happens if we change the topology of the space-time by hand to produce CTCs? The simplest way to do this is depicted in figure 3: we cut and paste the space-time so it is no longer simply connected by identifying the line $L-$ with the line $L+$. Particles 'going in' to $L+$ from below 'emerge' from $L-$, and particles 'going in' to $L-$ from below 'emerge' from $L+$.

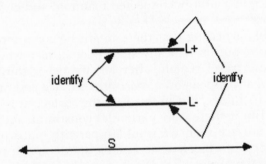

Figure 3. Inserting CTCs by Cut and Paste

How is the boundary-value problem changed by this alteration in the space-time? Before the cut and paste, we can put arbitrary data

[1] Multiple collisions are handled in the obvious way by continuity considerations: just continue straight lines through the collision point and identify which particle is which by their ordering in space.

on the simultaneity slice S and continue it to a unique solution. After the change in topology, S is no longer a Cauchy surface, since a CTC will never intersect it, but it is a partial Cauchy surface. So we can ask two questions. First, can arbitrary data on S always be continued to a global solution? Second, is that solution unique? If the answer to the first question is *no*, then we have a backward-temporal constraint: the existence of the region with CTCs places constraints on what can happen on S even though that region lies completely to the future of S. If the answer to the second question is *no*, then we have an odd sort of indeterminism: the complete physical state on S does not determine the physical state in the future, even though the local dynamics is perfectly deterministic and even though there is no other past edge to the space-time region in S's future (i.e. there is nowhere *else* for boundary values to come from which could influence the state of the region).

In this case the answer to the first question is *yes* and to the second is *no*: there are no constraints on the data which can be put on S, but those data are always consistent with an infinitude of different global solutions. The easy way to see that there always is a solution is to construct the minimal solution in the following way. Start drawing straight lines from S as required by the initial data. If a line hits $L-$ from the bottom, just continue it coming out of the top of $L+$ in the appropriate place, and if a line hits $L+$ from the bottom, continue it emerging from $L-$ at the appropriate place. Figure 4 represents the minimal solution for a single particle which enters the time-travel region from the left:

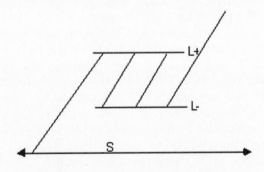

Figure 4. The Minimal Solution

The particle 'travels back in time' three times. It is obvious that this minimal solution is a global solution, since the particle always travels inertially.

181

But the same initial state on S is also consistent with other global solutions. The new requirement imposed by the topology is just that the data going into $L+$ from the bottom match the data coming out of $L-$ from the top, and the data going into $L-$ from the bottom match the data coming out of $L+$ from the top. So we can add any number of vertical lines connecting $L-$ and $L+$ to a solution and still have a solution. For example, adding a few such lines to the minimal solution yields:

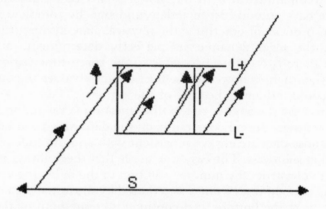

Figure 5. A Non-Minimal Solution

The particle now collides with itself twice: first before it reaches $L+$ for the first time, and again shortly before it exits the CTC region. From the particle's point of view, it is travelling to the right at a constant speed until it hits an older version of itself and comes to rest. It remains at rest until it is hit from the right by a younger version of itself, and then continues moving off, and the same process repeats later. It is clear that this is a global model of the dynamics, and that any number of distinct models could be generating by varying the number and placement of vertical lines.

Knowing the data on S, then, gives us only incomplete information about how things will go for the particle. We know that the particle will enter the CTC region, and will reach $L+$, we know that it will be the only particle in the universe, we know exactly where and with what speed it will exit the CTC region. But we cannot determine how many collisions the particle will undergo (if any), nor how long (in proper time) it will stay in the CTC region. If the particle were a clock, we could not predict what time it would indicate when exiting the region. Furthermore, the dynamics gives us no handle on what to think of the various possibilities: there are no probabilities assigned to the various distinct possible outcomes.

Changing the topology has changed the mathematics of the situation in two ways, which tend to pull in opposite directions. On the one hand, S is no longer a Cauchy surface, so it is perhaps not surprising that data on S do not suffice to fix a unique global solution. But on the other hand, there is an added constraint: data 'coming out' of $L-$ must exactly match data 'going in' to $L+$, even though what comes out of $L-$ helps to determine what goes into $L+$. This added consistency constraint tends to cut down on solutions, although in this case the additional constraint is more than outweighed by the freedom to consider various sorts of data on $L+/L-$.

The fact that the extra freedom outweighs the extra constraint also points up one unexpected way that the supposed paradoxes of time travel may be overcome. Let's try to set up a paradoxical situation using the little closed time loop above. If we send a single particle into the loop from the left and do nothing else, we know exactly where it will exit the right side of the time travel region. Now suppose we station someone at the other side of the region with the following charge: if the particle should come out on the right side, the person is to do something to *prevent* the particle from going in on the left in the first place. In fact, this is quite easy to do: if we send a particle in from the right, it seems that it can exit on the left and *deflect* the incoming left-hand particle.

Carrying on our reflection in this way, we further realize that if the particle comes out on the right, we might as well send *it* back in order to deflect itself from entering in the first place. So all we really need to do is the following: set up a perfectly reflecting particle mirror on the right-hand side of the time travel region, and launch the particle from the left so that—*if nothing interferes with it*—it will just barely hit $L+$. Our paradox is now apparently complete. If, on the one hand, nothing interferes with the particle it will enter the time-travel region on the left, exit on the right, be reflected from the mirror, re-enter from the right, and come out on the left to prevent itself from ever entering. So if it enters, it gets deflected and never enters. On the other hand, if it never enters then nothing goes in on the left, so nothing comes out on the right, so nothing is reflected back, and there is nothing to deflect it from entering. So if it doesn't enter, then there is nothing to deflect it and it enters. If it enters, then it is deflected and doesn't enter; if it doesn't enter then there is nothing to deflect it and it enters: paradox complete.

But at least one solution to the supposed paradox is easy to construct: just follow the recipe for constructing the minimal solution, continuing the initial trajectory of the particle (reflecting it the mirror in the obvious way) and then read off the number and trajectories of the particles from the resulting diagram. We get the result of figure 6:

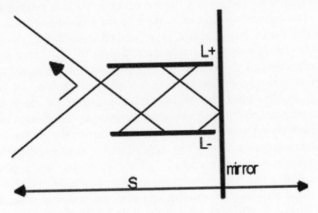

Figure 6. Resolving the 'Paradox'

As we can see, the particle approaching from the left never reaches $L+$: it is deflected first by a particle which emerges from $L-$. But it is not deflected *by itself*, as the paradox suggests, it is deflected by another particle. Indeed, there are now *four* particles in the diagram: the original particle and three particles which are confined to closed time-like curves. It is not the leftmost particle which is reflected by the mirror, nor even the particle which deflects the leftmost particle; it is another particle altogether.

The paradox gets it traction from an incorrect presupposition: if there is only one particle in the world at S then there is only one particle which could participate in an interaction in the time travel region: the single particle would have to interact with its earlier (or later) self. But there is no telling what might come out of $L-$: the only requirement is that whatever comes out must match what goes in at $L+$. So if you go to the trouble of constructing a working time machine, you should be prepared for a different kind of disappointment when you attempt to go back and kill yourself: you may be prevented from entering the machine in the first place by some completely unpredictable entity which emerges from it. And once again a peculiar sort of indeterminism appears: if there are many self-consistent things which could prevent you from entering, there is no telling which is even likely to materialize.

So when the freedom to put data on $L-$ outweighs the constraint that the same data go into $L+$, instead of paradox we get an embarrassment of riches: many solution consistent with the data on S. To see a case where the constraint 'outweighs' the freedom, we need to construct a very particular, and frankly artificial, dynamics and topology. Consider the space of all linear dynamics for a scalar field on a lattice. We will depict the space-time lattice as a directed graph. There is to be a scalar field defined at every node of the graph, whose value at a given node depends linearly on the values of the field at nodes which have arrows which lead to it. Each edge of the graph can be assigned a weighting factor which determines how much the field at the input node contributes to the field at the output node. If we name the nodes by the letters a, b, c, etc., and the edges by their endpoints in the obvious way, then we can label the weighting factors by the edges they are associated with in an equally obvious way.

Suppose that the graph of the space-time lattice is *acyclic*, as in figure 7.

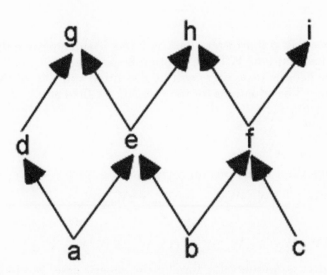

Figure 7. An Acyclic Lattice

It is easy to regard a set of nodes as the analog of a Cauchy surface, e.g. the set $\{a, b, c\}$, and it is obvious if arbitrary data are put on those nodes the data will generate a unique solution in the

Frank Arntzenius and Tim Maudlin

future.[2] If the value of the field at node a is 3 and at node b is 7, then its value at node d will be $3W_{ad}$ and its value at node e will be $3W_{ae}$ + $7W_{be}$. By varying the weighting factors we can adjust the dynamics, but in an acyclic graph the future evolution of the field will always be unique.

Let us now again artificially alter the topology of the lattice to admit CTCs. One of the simplest such graphs is depicted in figure 8: there are now paths which lead from z back to itself.

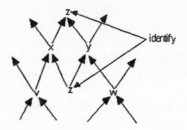

Figure 8. Time Travel on a Lattice

Can we now put arbitrary data on v and w, and continue that data to a global solution? Will the solution be unique?

In the generic case, there will be a solution and the solution will be unique. The equations for the value of the field at x, y, and z are:

$$x = vW_{vx} + zW_{zx}$$
$$y = wW_{vy} + zW_{zy}$$
$$z = xW_{xz} + yW_{yz}.$$

Solving these equations for z yields

$$z = (vW_{vx} + zW_{zx})Wxz + (wW_{wy} + zW_{zy})W_{yz}$$

or

$$z = (vW_{vx}W_{xz} + wW_{wy}W_{yz})/ (1 - W_{zx}W_{xz} - W_{zy}W_{yz}),$$

which gives a unique value for z in the generic case. But looking at the space of all possible dynamics for this lattice (i.e. the space of all possible weighting factors), we find a singularity in the case where $1 - W_{zx}W_{xz} - W_{zy}W_{yz} = 0$. If we choose weighting factors in just

---

[2] The dynamics here is radically non-time-reversible. Indeed, the dynamics is deterministic in the future direction but not in the past direction.

186

this way, then arbitrary data at v and w cannot be continued to a global solution. Indeed, if the scalar field is everywhere non-negative, then this particular choice of dynamics puts ironclad constraints on the value of the field at v and w: the field there must be zero (assuming W_{vx} and W_{wy} to be non-zero), and similarly all nodes in their past must have field value zero. If the field can take negative values, then the values at v and w must be so chosen that $vW_{vx}W_{xz} = -wW_{wy}W_{yz}$. In either case, the field values at v and w are severely constrained by the existence of the CTC region even though these nodes lie completely to the past of that region. It is this sort of constraint which we find to be unlike anything which appears in standard physics.

Our toy models suggest three things. The first is that it may be impossible to prove in complete generality that arbitrary data on a partial Cauchy surface can *always* be continued to a global solution: our artificial case provides an example where it cannot. The second is that such odd constraints are not likely to be generic: we had to delicately fine-tune the dynamics to get a problem. The third is that the opposite problem, namely data on a partial Cauchy surface being consistent with *many* different global solutions, is likely to be generic: we did not have to do any fine-tuning to get this result. And this leads to a peculiar sort of indeterminism: the entire state on S does not determine what will happen in the future even though the local dynamics is deterministic and there are no other 'edges' to space-time from which data could influence the result. What happens in the time travel region is constrained but not determined by what happens on S, and the dynamics does not even supply any *probabilities* for the various possibilities. The example of the photographic negative discussed in section 3, then, seems likely to be unusual, for in that case there is a *unique* fixed point for the dynamics, and the set-up plus the dynamical laws *determine* the outcome. In the generic case one would rather expect *multiple* fixed points, with no room for anything to influence, even probabilistically, *which* would be realized.

It is ironic that time travel should lead generically not to contradictions or to constraints (in the normal region) but to *underdetermination* of what happens in the time travel region by what happens everywhere else (an underdetermination tied neither to a probabilistic dynamics or to a free edge to space-time). The traditional objection to time travel is that it leads to contradictions: there is no consistent way to complete an arbitrarily constructed story about how the time traveler intends to act. Instead, though, it appears that the problem is underdetermination: the story can be consistently

Frank Arntzenius and Tim Maudlin

completed in many different ways. Let us now discuss some results regarding some slightly more realistic models that have been discussed in the physics literature.

Slightly More Realistic Models of Time Travel

Echeverria, Klinkhammer and Thorne (1991) considered the case of 3-dimensional single hard spherical ball that can go through a single time travel wormhole so as to collide with its younger self.

The threat of paradox in this case arises in the following form. There are initial trajectories for the ball such that if such a trajectory

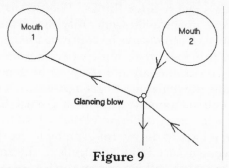

Figure 9

is continued assuming that the ball does not undergo a collision prior to entering mouth 1 of the wormhole, it will exit mouth 2 so as to collide with its earlier self prior to its entry into mouth 1 in such a way as to prevent its earlier self from entering mouth 1. Thus it seems that the ball will enter mouth 1 if and only if it does not enter mouth 1. Of course, the Wheeler-Feynman strategy is to look for a 'glancing blow' solution: a collision which will produce exactly the (small) deviation in trajectory of the earlier ball that produces exactly that collision. Are there always such solutions?[3]

---

[3] One might hope that fixed point theorems can be used to prove the existence of solutions in this type of cases too. Consider, for instance, a fixed initial state of motion I of the ball. Then consider all the possible velocities and locations and times at which such a ball could enter mouth 1 of the wormhole. Each such triple will determine the trajectory of that ball out of mouth 2. One can then look at the continuation of the trajectory from state I and that from state s, and see whether these trajectories collide. Then one can see for each possible triple whether the ball that starts in state I will be collided into mouth 1, and if it is, with which speed at what location and at which time this will occur. Thus given state I, each triple maps onto another triple $<v',x',t'>$. One might then suggest

188

Echeverria, Klinkhammer & Thorne found a large class of initial trajectories that have consistent 'glancing blow' continuations, and found none that do not (but their search was not completely general). They did not produce a rigorous proof that every initial trajectory has a consistent continuation, but suggested that it is very plausible that every initial trajectory has a consistent continuation.

In fact, as one might expect from our discussion in the previous section, they found the opposite problem from that of inconsistency: they found underdetermination. For a large class of initial trajectories there are multiple different consistent 'glancing blow' continuations of that trajectory (many of which involve multiple wormhole traversals). For example, if one initially has a ball that is travelling on a trajectory aimed straight between the two mouths, then one obvious solution is that the ball passes between the two mouths and never time travels. But another solution is that the younger ball gets knocked into mouth 1 exactly so as to come out of mouth 2 and produce that collision. Echeverria *et. al.* do not note the possibility (which we pointed out in the previous section) of the existence of additional balls in the time travel region. We conjecture (but have no proof) that for every initial trajectory of A there are some, and generically many, multiple ball continuations.

Friedman *et. al.* 1990 examined the case of source free non-self-interacting scalar fields travelling through such a time travel wormhole and found that no constraints on initial conditions are imposed by the existence of these time travel wormholes. In general there appear to be no known counter examples to the claim that in 'somewhat realistic' time-travel space-times with a partial Cauchy surface there are no constraints imposed on the state on such a partial Cauchy surface by the existence of CTC's. (See e.g. Friedman and Morris 1991, Thorne 1994 Earman 1995, Earman and Smeenk 1999.)

How about the issue of constraints in the time travel region? *Prima facie*, constraints in such a region would not appear to be sur-

---

appealing to a fixed point theorem to argue that there must be a solution for each initial state I. However, in the first place the set of possible speeds and times are open sets. And in the second place there can be multiple wormhole traversals. Thus the relevant total state-space of wormhole mouth crossings consists of discretely many completely disconnected state-spaces (with increasing numbers of dimensions). So standard fixed point theorems do not apply directly. It should be noted that the results that have been achieved regarding this case do make use of fixed points theorems quite extensively. But their application is limited to certain subproblems, and do not yield a fully general proof of the lack of constraints for arbitrary I.

prising. But one might still expect that there should be no constraints on states on a spacelike surface, provided one keeps the surface 'small enough'. In the physics literature the following question has been asked: for any point p in T, and any space-like surface S that includes p is there a neighbourhood E of p in S such that any solution on E can be extended to a solution on the whole space-time? With respect to this question, there are some simple models in which one has this kind of extendibility of local solutions to global ones, and some simple models in which one does not have such extendibility, with no clear general pattern. (See e.g. Yurtsever 1990, Friedman et. al. 1990, Novikov 1992, Earman 1995, Earman and Smeenk 1999). What are we to think of all of this?

Even If There are Constraints, So What?

Since it is not obvious that one can rid oneself of all constraints in realistic models, let us examine the argument that time travel is implausible, and we should think it unlikely to exist in our world, in so far as it implies such constraints. The argument goes something like the following. In order to satisfy such constraints one needs some pre-established divine harmony between the global (time travel) structure of space-time and the distribution of particles and fields on space-like surfaces in it. But it is not plausible that the actual world, or any world even remotely like ours, is constructed with divine harmony as part of the plan. In fact, one might argue, we have empirical evidence that conditions in any spatial region can vary quite arbitrarily. So we have evidence that such constraints, whatever they are, do not in fact exist in our world. So we have evidence that there are no closed time-like lines in our world or one remotely like it. We will now examine this argument in more detail by presenting four possible responses, with counterresponses, to this argument.

Response 1. There is nothing implausible or new about such constraints. For instance, if the universe is spatially closed, there has to be enough matter to produce the needed curvature, and this puts constraints on the matter distribution on a space-like hypersurface. Thus global space-time structure can quite unproblematically constrain matter distributions on space-like hypersurfaces in it. Moreover we have no realistic idea what these constraints look like, so we hardly can be said to have evidence that they do not obtain.

Counterresponse 1. Of course there are constraining relations between the global structure of space-time and the matter in it. The Einstein equations relate curvature of the manifold to the matter distribution in it. But what is so strange and implausible about the constraints imposed by the existence of closed time-like curves is that these constraints in essence have nothing to do with the Einstein equations. When investigating such constraints one typically treats the particles and/or field in question as test particles and/or fields in a given space-time, i.e. they are assumed not to affect the metric of space-time in any way. In typical space-times without closed time-like curves this means that one has, in essence, complete freedom of matter distribution on a space-like hypersurface. (See response 2 for some more discussion of this issue). The constraints imposed by the possibility of time travel have a quite different origin and are implausible. In the ordinary case there is a causal interaction between matter and space-time that results in relations between global structure of space-time and the matter distribution in it. In the time travel case there is no such causal story to be told: there simply has to be some pre-established harmony between the global space-time structure and the matter distribution on some space-like surfaces. This is implausible.

Response 2. Constraints upon matter distributions are nothing new: for instance $E=\text{div}(\rho)$ constrains field/particle distributions on space-like hypersurfaces. This is not implausible divine harmony. Such constraints can hold as a matter of physical law. Moreover, if we had inferred from the apparent free variation of conditions on spatial regions that there could be no such constraints we would have mistakenly inferred that $E=\text{div}(\rho)$ could not be a law of nature.

Counterresponse 2. The constraints imposed by the existence of closed time-like lines are of quite a different character from the constraint imposed by $E=\text{div}(\rho)$. The constraints imposed by $E=\text{div}(\rho)$ on the state on a space-like hypersurface are i) local constraints (i.e. to check whether the constraint holds in a region you just need to see whether it holds at each point in the region), ii) quite independent of the global space-time structure, iii) quite independent of how the space-like surface in question is embedded in a given space-time, and iv) very simply and generally stateable. On the other hand, the consistency constraints imposed by the existence of closed time-like curves i) are not local, ii) are dependent on the global structure of space-time, iii) depend on the location of the space-like surface in question in a given space-time, and iv) appear not to be simply stateable other than as the demand that the state on that space-like surface embedded in such and such a way in a given space-time, do not lead to inconsistency. On some views of laws (e.g. David Lewis' view) this plausibly implies that such constraints, even if they hold, could not possibly be laws. But even if one does not accept such a view of laws, one could claim that the bizarre features of such constraints imply that it is implausible that such constraints hold in our world or in any world remotely like ours.

Response 3. It would be strange if there are constraints in the non-time travel region. It is not strange if there are constraints in the time travel region. They should be explained in terms of the strange, self-interactive, character of time travel regions. In this region there are time-like trajectories from points to themselves. Thus the state at such a point, in such a region, will, in a sense, interact with itself. It is a well-known fact that systems that interact with themselves will develop into an equilibrium state, if there is such an equilibrium state, or else will develop towards some singularity. Normally, of course, self-interaction isn't true instantaneous self-interaction, but consists of a feed-back mechanism that takes time. But in time travel regions something like true instantaneous self-interaction occurs. This explains why constraints on states occur in such time travel regions: the states 'ab initio' have to be 'equilibrium states'. Indeed in a way this also provides some picture of why indeterminism occurs in time travel regions: at the onset of self-interaction states can fork into different equi-possible equilibrium states.

Counterresponse 3. This is explanation by woolly analogy. It all goes to show that time travel leads to such bizarre consequences that it is unlikely that it occurs in a world remotely like ours.

Response 4. All of the previous discussion completely misses the point. So far we have been taking the space-time structure as given, and asked the question whether a given time travel space-time structure imposes constraints on states on (parts of) space-like surfaces. However, space-time and matter interact. Suppose that one is in a space-time with closed time-like lines, such that certain counterfactual distributions of matter on some neighborhood of a point p are ruled out if one holds that space-time structure fixed. One might then ask 'Why does the actual state near p in fact satisfy these constraints? By what divine luck or plan is this local state compatible with the global space-time structure? What if conditions near p had been slightly different?'. And one might take it that the lack of normal answers to these questions indicates that it is very implausible that our world, or any remotely like it, is such a time travel universe. However the proper response to these question is the following. There are no constraints in any significant sense. If they hold they hold as a matter of accidental fact, not of law. There is no more explanation of them possible than there is of any contingent fact. Had conditions in a neighborhood of p been otherwise, the global structure of space-time would have been different. So what? The only question relevant to the issue of constraints is whether an arbitrary state on an arbitrary spatial surface S can always be embedded into a space-time such that that state on S consistently extends to a solution on the entire space-time.

But we know the answer to that question. A well-known theorem in general relativity says the following: any initial data set on a three dimensional manifold S with positive definite metric has a unique embedding into a maximal space-time in which S is a Cauchy surface (see e.g. Geroch and Horowitz 1979, p 284 for more detail), i.e. there is a unique largest space-time which has S as a Cauchy surface and contains a consistent evolution of the initial value data on S. Now since S is a Cauchy surface this space-time does not have closed time like curves. But it may have extensions (in which S is not a Cauchy surface) which include closed timelike curves, indeed it may be that any maximal extension of it would include closed timelike curves. (This appears to be the case for extensions of states on certain surfaces of Taub-NUT space-times. See Earman and Smeenk 1999). But these extensions, of course, will be consistent. So properly speaking, there are no constraints on states on space-like surfaces. Nonetheless the space-time in which these are embedded may or may not include closed time-like curves.

Counterresponse 4. This, in essence, is the stonewalling answer which we indicated at the beginning of section 2. However, whether or not you call the constraints imposed by a given space-time on distributions of matter on certain space-like surfaces 'genuine constraints', whether or not they can be considered lawlike, and whether or not they need to be explained, the existence of such constraints can still be used to argue that time travel worlds are so bizarre that it is implausible that our world or any world remotely like ours is a time travel world.

Suppose that one is in a time travel world. Suppose that given the global space-time structure of this world, there are constraints imposed upon, say, the state of motion of a ball on some space-like surface when it is treated as a test particle, i.e. when it is assumed

193

Frank Arntzenius and Tim Maudlin

that the ball does not affect the metric properties of the space-time it is in. (There is lots of other matter that, via the Einstein equation, corresponds exactly to the curvature that there is everywhere in this time travel worlds.) Now a real ball of course does have some effect on the metric of the space-time it is in. But let us consider a ball that is so small that its effect on the metric is negligible. Presumably it will still be the case that certain states of this ball on that space-like surface are not compatible with the global time travel structure of this universe.

This means that the actual distribution of matter on such a space-like surface can be extended into a space-time with closed time-like lines, but that certain counterfactual distributions of matter on this space-like surface can not be extended into the same space-time. *But note that the changes made in the matter distribution (when going from the actual to the counterfactual distribution) do not in any non-negligible way affect the metric properties of the space-time.* Thus the reason why the global time travel properties of the counterfactual space-time have to be significantly different from the actual space-time is not that there are problems with metric singularities or alterations in the metric that force significant global changes when we go to the counterfactual matter distribution. The reason that the counterfactual space-time has to be different is that in the counterfactual world the ball's initial state of motion starting on the space-like surface, could not 'meet up' in a consistent way with its earlier self (could not be consistently extended) if we were to let the global structure of the counterfactual space-time be the same as that of the actual space-time. Now, it is not bizarre or implausible that there is a counterfactual dependence of manifold structure, even of its topology, on matter distributions on spacelike surfaces. For instance, certain matter distributions may lead to singularities, others may not. We may indeed in some sense have causal power over the topology of the space-time we live in. But this power normally comes via the Einstein equations. But it is bizarre to think that there could be a counterfactual dependence of global space-time structure on the arrangement of certain tiny bits of matter on some space-like surface, where changes in that arrangement by assumption do not affect the metric *anywhere in space-time in any significant way.* It is implausible that we live in such a world, or that a world even remotely like ours is like that.

Let us illustrate this argument in a different way by assuming that wormhole time travel imposes constraints upon the states of people prior to such time travel, where the people have so little mass/energy that they have negligible effect, via the Einstein equation, on the local metric properties of space-time. Do you think it more plausible that we live in a world where wormhole time travel occurs but it only occurs when people's states are such that these local states happen to combine with time travel in such a way that nobody ever succeeds in killing their younger self, or do you think it more plausible that we are not in a wormhole time travel world? [4]

Quantum Mechanics to the Rescue?

There has been a particularly clear treatment of time travel in the context of quantum mechanics by David Deutsch (see Deutsch 1991, and Deutsch and Lockwood 1994) in which it is claimed that quantum mechanical considerations show that time travel never imposes any constraints on the pre-time travel state of systems. The essence of this account is as follows.

A quantum system starts in state $S1$, interacts with its older self, after the interaction is in state S_2, time travels while developing into state S_3, then interacts with its younger self, and ends in state S_4 (see figure 10).

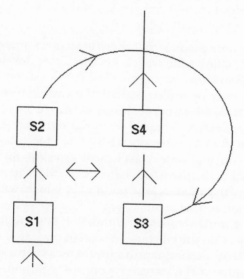

Figure 10

[4] This argument, especially the second illustration of it, is similar to the one in Horwich 1987, pp 124–8. However, we do not share Horwich's view that it only tells against time travel of humans into their local past.

Frank Arntzenius and Tim Maudlin

Deutsch assumes that the set of possible states of this system are the mixed states, i.e. are represented by the density matrices over the Hilbert space of that system. Deutsch then shows that for any initial state S_1, any unitary interaction between the older and younger self, and any unitary development during time travel, there is a consistent solution, i.e. there is at least one pair of states S_2 and S_3 such that when S_1 interacts with S_3 it will change to state S_2 and S_2 will then develop into S_3. The states S_2, S_3 and S_4 will typically be not be pure states, i.e. will be non-trivial mixed states, even if S_1 is pure. In order to understand how this leads to interpretational problems let us give an example. Consider a system that has a two dimensional Hilbert space with as a basis the states $|+>$ and $|->$. Let us suppose that when state $|+>$ of the young system encounters state $|+>$ of the older system, they interact and the young system develops into state $|->$ and the old system remains in state $|+>$. In obvious notation:

$|+>_1|+>_3$ develops into $|->_2|+>_4$.

Similarly, suppose that:

$|+>_1|->_3$ develops into $|+>_2|+>_4$,
$|->_1|+>_3$ develops into $|->_2|->_4$, and
$|->_1|->_3$ develops into $|+>_2|->_4$.

Let us furthermore assume that there is no development of the state of the system during time travel, i.e. that $|+>_2$ develops into $|+>_3$, and that $|->_2$ develops into $|->_3$.

Now, if the only possible states of the system were $|+>$ and $|->$ (i.e. if there were no superpositions or mixtures of these states), then there is a paradox. There is no initial state compatible with this dynamics. For if $|+>_1$ interacts with $|+>_3$ then it will develop into $|->_2$, which, during time travel, will develop into $|->_3$, which inconsistent with the assumed state $|+>_3$. Similarly if $|+>_1$ interacts with $|->_3$ it will develop into $|+>_2$, which will then develop into $|+>_3$ which is also inconsistent. Thus the system can not start in state $|+_1>$. Similar reasoning shows that one can not start in state $|->_1$. So there is no initial state consistent with this dynamics.

But, says Deutsch, in quantum mechanics such a system can also be in any mixture of the states $|+>$ and $|->$. Suppose that the older system, prior to the interaction, is in a state S_3 which is an equal mixture of 50% $|+>_3$ and 50% $|->_3$. Then the younger system during the interaction will develop into a mixture of 50% $|+>_2$ and 50% $|->_2$, which will then develop into a mixture of 50% $|+>_3$ and 50% $|->_3$, which is consistent! More generally Deutsch uses a fixed point theorem to show that no matter what the unitary development during interaction is, and no matter what the unitary development during time travel is, for any state S_1 there is always a state S_3 (which typically is not a pure state) which causes S_1 to develop into a state S_2 which develops into that state S_3. Thus quantum mechanics comes to the rescue: it shows in all generality that no constraints on initial states are needed!

One might wonder why Deutsch appeals to mixed states: will superpositions of states $|+>$ and $|->$ not suffice? Unfortunately such an idea does not work. For instance, let us assume that state S_3 is the superposition $1/\sqrt{2}|+>_3 + 1/\sqrt{2}|->_3$. One might then wish to claim that initial state $|+>_1$ when it encounters $1/\sqrt{2}|+>_3 + 1/\sqrt{2}|->_3$, will develop into superposition $1/\sqrt{2}|+>_2 + 1/\sqrt{2}|->_2$, and that this in turn will develop into $1/\sqrt{2}|+>_3 + 1/\sqrt{2}|->_3$, as desired. However this is not correct. For initial state $|+>_1$ when it encounters $1/\sqrt{2}|+>_3 + 1/\sqrt{2}|->_3$, will subsequently develop into the entangled state $1/\sqrt{2}|->_2|+>_4 + 1/\sqrt{2}|+>_2|->_4$. In so far as one can speak of the state of the young system after this interaction, it is in the mixture of 50% $|+>_2$ and 50% $|->_2$, not in the superposition $1/\sqrt{2}|+>_2 + 1/\sqrt{2}|->_2$. So Deutsch does need his recourse to mixed states.

This clarification of why Deutsch needs his mixtures does however indicate a serious worry about the simplifications that are part of Deutsch's account. After the interaction the old and young system will (typically) be in an entangled state. Although for purposes of a measurement on one of the two systems one can say that this system is in a mixed state, one can not represent the full state of the two systems by specifying the mixed state of each separate part, as there are correlations between observables of the two systems that are not represented by these two mixed states, but are represented in the joint entangled state. But if there really is an entangled state of the old and young systems directly after the interaction, how is one to represent the subsequent development of this entangled state? Will the state of the younger system remain entangled with the state of the older system as the younger system time travels and the older system moves on into the future? On what space-like surfaces are we to imagine this total entangled state to be? At this point it becomes clear that there is no obvious and simple way to extend elementary non-relativistic quantum mechanics to space-times with closed time-like curves. There have been more sophisticated approaches than Deutsch's to time travel, using technical machinery from quantum field theory and differentiable manifolds (see e.g. Friedman *et al.* 1991, Earman and Smeenk 1999, and references therein). But out of such approaches no results anywhere near as clear and interesting as Deutsch's have been forthcoming.

How does Deutsch avoid these complications? Deutsch assumes a mixed state S_3 of the older system prior to the interaction with the younger system. He lets it interact with an arbitrary pure state S_1 younger system. After this interaction there is an entangled state S' of the two systems. Deutsch computes the mixed state S_2 of the younger system which is implied by this entangled state S'. His demand for consistency then is just that this mixed state S_2 develops into the mixed state S_3. Now it is not at all clear that this is a legitimate way to simplify the problem of time travel in quantum mechanics. But even if we grant him this simplification there is a problem: how are we to understand these mixtures?

If we take an ignorance interpretation of mixtures we run into trouble. For suppose that we assume that in each individual case each older system is either in state $|+>_3$ or in state $|->_3$ prior to the interaction. Then we regain our paradox. Deutsch instead recommends the following, many worlds, picture of mixtures. Suppose we start with state $|+>_1$ in all worlds. In some of the many worlds the older system will be in the $|+>_3$ state, let us call them A-worlds, and in some worlds, B-worlds, it will be in the $|->_3$ state. Thus in A-worlds after interaction we will have state $|->_2$, and in B-worlds we will have state $|+>_2$. During time travel the $|->_2$ state will remain the same, i.e turn into state $|->_3$, but the systems in question will travel from A-worlds to B-worlds. Similarly the $|+>_2$ states will travel from the B-worlds to the A-worlds, thus preserving consistency.

Now whatever one thinks of the merits of many worlds interpretations, and of this understanding of it applied to mixtures, in the end one does not obtain genuine time travel in Deutsch's account. The systems in question travel from one time in one world to another time in another world, but no system travels to an earlier time in the same world. (This is so at least in the normal sense of the word 'world', the sense that one means when, for instance, one says 'there was, and will be, only one Elvis Presley in this world'.) Thus, even if it were a reasonable view, it is not quite as interesting as it may have initially seemed.

Conclusions

What remains of the killing-your-earlier-self paradox in general relativistic time travel worlds is the fact that in some cases the states on edgeless spacelike surfaces are 'overconstrained', so that one has less than the usual freedom in specifying conditions on such a surface, given the time-travel structure, and in some cases such states are 'underconstrained', so that states on edgeless space-like surfaces do not determine what happens elsewhere in the way that they usually do, given the time travel structure. There can also be mixtures of those two types of cases. The extent to which states are overconstrained and/or underconstrained in realistic models is as yet unclear, though it would be very surprising if neither obtained. The extant literature has primarily focused on the problem of overconstraint, since that, often, either is regarded as a metaphysical obstacle to the possibility time travel, or as an epistemological obstacle to the plausibility of time travel in our world. As we have discussed, using responses and counterresponses, it is not entirely clear that it is indeed an epistemological or a metaphysical obstacle. It is true that our world would be quite different from the way we normally think it is, if states were overconstrained given the time travel structure. If anything, underconstraint seems even more bizarre to us than overconstraint. However, time travel is quite strange to begin with, and it does not appear to be a terribly strong additional argument against time travel that it has strange consequences.

Bibliography

Deutsch, D. 1991. 'Quantum mechanics near closed timelike curves,' *Physical Review D* **44**, 3197–217.
—— and Lockwood, M. 1994. 'The quantum physics of time travel', *Scientific American*, March 1994, 68–74.
Earman, J. 1972. 'Implications of causal propagation outsider the null cone,' in *Foundations of Space-Time Theory, Minnesota Studies in the Philosophy of Science*, Vol VII, Earman, J., Glymour, C. and Stachel, J. (eds), pp 94–108. Minneapolis, University of Minnesota Press.
Earman, J. 1995. *Bangs, Crunches, Whimpers and Shrieks: Singularities and Acausalities in Relativistic Spacetimes*. New York: Oxford University Press.
Earman, J. and Smeenk, C. 1999. 'Take a ride on a time machine,' Manuscript.
Echeverria, F., Klinkhammer, G., and Thorne, K. 1991. 'Billiard ball in wormhole spacetimes with closed timelike curves: classical theory,' *Physical Review D*, Vol 44 No 4, 1077–99.
Friedman, J. *et. al.* 1990. 'Cauchy problem in spacetimes with closed timelike lines,' *Physical Review D* 42, 1915–30.
Friedman, J. and Morris, M. 1991. 'The Cauchy problem for the scalar

Frank Arntzenius and Tim Maudlin

wave equation is well defined on a class of spacetimes with closed time-like curves,' *Physical Review letters* **66**, 401–4.

Geroch, R. and Horowitz, G. 1979. 'Global structures of spacetimes,' in *General Relativity, an Einstein Centenary Survey*, Hawking, S. and Israel, W., eds.

Gödel, K. 1949. 'A remark about the relationship between relativity theory and idealistic philosophy,' in *Albert Einstein: Philosopher-Scientist*, edited by P. Schilpp, pp. 557–62. Open Court, La Salle.

Hocking, J., and Young, G. 1961. *Topology*. New York: Dover Publications.

Horwich, P. 1987. 'Time travel,' in *Asymmetries in time*. Cambridge: MIT Press.

Malament, D. 1985a. '"Time travel" in the Gödel universe,' *PSA* 1984, Vol 2, 91–100. Asquith, P. and Kitcher, P. editors. Philosophy of Science Association, East Lansing, Michigan.

—— 1985b. 'Minimal acceleration requirements for "time travel" in Gödel spacetime,' *Journal of Mathematical Physics* **26**, 774–77.

Maudlin, T. 1990. 'Time Travel and topology,' *PSA* 1990, Vol 1, 303–15. Philosophy of Science Association, East Lansing, Michigan.

Novikov, I. 1992. 'Time machine and self-consistent evolution in problems with self- interaction,' *Physical Review D* 45, 1989–1994.

Thorne, K. 1994. *Black Holes and Time Warps, Einstein's Outrageous Legacy*. W.W. Norton: London and New York.

Wheeler, J. and Feynman, R. 1949. 'Classical electrodynamics in terms of direct interparticle action,' *Reviews of Modern Physics* 21, 425–34.

Yurtsever, U. 1990. 'Test fields on compact space-times,' *Journal of Mathematical Physics* **31**, 3064–78.

Freedom from the Inside Out

CARL HOEFER

0. Introduction

Since the death of strong reductionism, philosophers of science have expanded the horizons of their understandings of the physical, mental, and social worlds, and the complex relations among them. To give one interesting example, John Dupré has endorsed a notion of *downward causation*: 'higher-level' events causing events at a 'lower' ontological level. For example, my intention to type the letter 't' causes the particular motions experienced by all the atoms in my left forefinger as I type it. The proper explanation of the motions of an atom at the tip of my forefinger primarily involves my intentions, rather than (for example) the immediately preceding motions of other nearby atoms, or any other such particle-level events.

While this is a natural enough idea on the face of it, such downward causation has seemed to be in tension, or outright conflict, with another compelling intuition, which Dupré calls *causal completeness*.

'This is the assumption that for every event there is a complete causal story to account for its occurrence. Obviously enough, this is a view of causality the roots of which are to be found in the soil of determinism. The paradigm of a complete causal story is the sufficient (and perhaps even necessary) antecedent condition provided by a deterministic causal explanation. However ... [since microphysics seems likely to be indeterministic], it is important to consider the indeterministic analogue of deterministic causal completeness. It is not hard to see what this should be. The basic idea is that there should be some set of antecedent conditions that together determine some precise probability of the event in question.' (Dupre 1993, pp. 99–100)

As Dupré points out, belief in some such doctrine as causal completeness underlies the attraction many philosophers still feel for reductionism, despite the latter's untenability in any form stronger than mere supervenience.

It is causal completeness that is at the heart of the age-old

201

dichotomy between free agency and physical determinism. For if determinism is true, there is a prior, sufficient cause of my fingertip's atoms' motions: the earlier state of the physical world. 'Earlier' could mean mere moments ago, or it could mean at some time before I was born. Given this prior, sufficient cause, my intentions seem idle and epiphenomenal; they are there, to be sure, but they are *just as much* caused by this prior physical state of affairs; my 'free' will seems then a hollow joke.

But determinism is not necessary for the threat of causal completeness to free agency to arise. For reasons that Kant first realized, indeterminism at the microphysical level does not seem to help. The randomness, if any, in microscopic phenomena does not seem to 'make room' for free will, but rather only replaces a sufficient physical cause with (at least in part) blind chance. The presumption in favour of *upward* causation and explanation (from microphysical to macrophysical) that comes with causal completeness is what cuts free agency out of the picture, whether this causation is deterministic or partly random.

Philosophical subtlety has thus put our freedom in double jeopardy.[1] Some philosophers of a pluralist/empiricist bent (Cartwright and Dupré for example) respond by saying that they trust the evidence of common sense more than such philosophical subtleties. Maybe there are really no laws of nature at all, in the strict sense; maybe causation at the micro-physical level deserves no priority over causation in the form of human agency. At any rate, on any viable concept of *evidence*, they say, the evidence in favor of free will is stronger than the evidence for universally true physical laws.[2]

On this last point, I think they are wrong: we do have very strong evidence for universal, exceptionless laws of nature. But fortunately, skepticism about true, universal laws of nature is not necessary to derail the apparent challenge to free agency coming from causal completeness. All that is needed is a proper understanding of *time*— what it is in the physical world, what it is in human affairs, and how they are related. Given the proper understanding of time, we will

[1] There is of course a long tradition of philosophers responding to this apparent threat by arguing for the compatability of freedom and determinism, when the former is properly understood. For what follows, I need not enter into these debates. See Fischer (1994) for a comprehensive and robust defense of (a form of) compatibilism.

[2] Dupré does in fact say exactly this, in his paper 1996. Cartwright has not discussed free will explicitly, to my knowledge, but her views about laws, causation and evidence seem to fit well with this response.

see that freedom and determinism are compatible—compatible in a much more robust sense than has ever been thought possible.[3]

1. The Two Times

'Time' means one thing in physics, and something quite different in everyday human affairs. McTaggart first described the distinction clearly, and gave the two times names: A-series time and B-series time.

A-series time is the time in which we live our lives. There is the *past*, the *present* (the 'now'), and the *future*; and the present 'moves' inexorably into the future leaving more and more of our lives behind us. B-series time is by contrast 'static': time is a linear ordering (or partial ordering), typically represented by a line on which each point represents an instant of time, but no point is distinguished as 'now'. (See figure 1.) *Things* may change in B-series time, by having one set of properties at one point, and a different set of properties at a later point. But time itself does not 'change' or 'move'. Physics seems to describe the world entirely in B-series terms, and to have no need of A-series concepts such as *present* and *future*. Indeed, many philosophers believe that physics since Einstein's 1905 relativity theory is outright *incompatible* with the A-

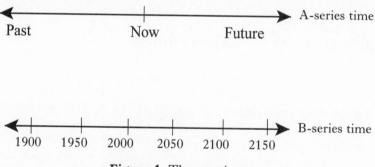

Figure 1. The two times.

[3] On a topic such as freedom of the will, it is too much to hope that any proposal can be completely novel. In section 4 I link my proposal to Kant's reconciliation of freedom and determinism. Further, as I recently discovered, Peter Forrest (1985) has defended free will along lines similar in many respects to those developed here. There are however quite substantial differences, and in particular Forrest does not bring considerations about *time* into play in his account.

series.[4] Regardless of whether this is correct or not, it is still true that physics does not *require* A-series time notions, and seems to find a natural fit only with B-series time. (A possible exception to this is in quantum mechanics, but only under the most bizarre (many-world) or idealistic (consciousness-collapse) interpretations.)

When space is combined with B-series time explicitly, as Minkowski first did in 1908, we get a description of the world as a whole, with four dimensions. This is what we do in drawing 'Minkowski diagrams' in relativity theory, but it works equally well from the perspective of Newtonian physics. Either way, philosophers have found it useful to think of the world, consisting of 3 spatial dimensions and one (B-series) temporal dimension, as a 'block universe' (figure 2).

In the block universe, time is certainly to be singled out as *different* from the three spatial dimensions—in terms of the laws (if any), the metrical structure(s) giving spatial and temporal distances between events or world-points, and so on. Likewise, at least over the part of the block accessible to our observations, the two *direc-*

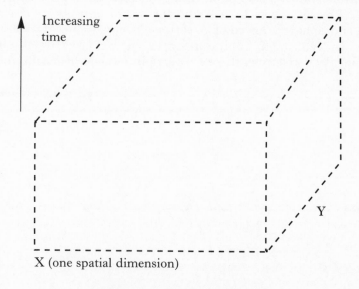

X (one spatial dimension)

Figure 2. The block universe.

[4] The reason is that the A-series seems to require a privileged way of dividing events into those happening *now*, vs. those in the past or future, which is effectively a privileged notion of absolute simultaneity. Special relativity, as standardly interpreted, is incompatible with an absolute standard of simultaneity.

tions of time (past-directed / future-directed) are distinguishable. But what is not to be found is an ontological separation of parts of the block into past, present and future. This striking fact means that events of 1000 years in Earth's future are, in terms of reality or existence, no different from the events (*now*) of your reading these words, or the events of last week.

This notion is hard to grasp, and feels threatening to us as free agents. It has even been advanced, incorrectly, as a vindication of fatalism. For, viewing ourselves and our actions from within the A-series perspective, we think of future events as *open* in some real sense, to be determined (partly) by *our* choices. But in the block, all events are equally real, those in your far future no different from those in your past.[5] This 4-D block world that physics offers us *seems* impossible to reconcile with this agent-centred, A-series-embedded perspective.

I will now argue that in fact, matters are just the opposite of how they seem. The very 'timelessness' of the 4-D block (in an A-series sense) leaves us free to *reject* the customary view that *past* events determine present choices. From the B-series perspective there is no reason to think of past → future determination as more important or real than future → past determination. And, even more to the point, one can equally view a set of events in the *middle* as determiners of both past and future events.

This is exactly what we should do. Our *free* actions, intentions, thoughts etc., in the middle of the block universe, are *part* of what determines how the rest of the block shall be. In order to make the point as clearly as possible, I will first discuss things under the assumption of some standard, Newtonian-style determinism. The idea here is that given the complete state of affairs 'at a time' in the universe (i.e., all physical facts specified on a time slice or thin sandwich), plus the true laws of nature, all earlier and later physical events are logically determined.[6] Weaker forms of determinism can

[5] See Horwich (1987) *Asymmetries in Time* for the correct refutation of the argument for fatalism ('logical' fatalism) based on the block universe.

[6] See Lewis (1994) for an explication of determinism in terms of possible worlds, and Earman (1986) for detailed discussion of the difficulties of defining and assessing determinism in various physical theories. The strong 'Newtonian-style' determinism I am assuming for the moment turns out, as Earman shows, to be best captured not in Newtonian physics but rather in Special-relativitstic physics. For the discussion to follow, I am assuming bi-directionality of determinism. This is assured by time-reversal invariant physical laws, but this condition is not needed. For example, Callender (2000) argues that QM is not time-reversal invariant. Under a Bohmian interpretation, it is nevertheless bi-directionally deterministic.

be defined, but they pose, *prima facie*, less of a problem for free agency.[7] Later I will come back to freedom in a causally complete but probabilistic world.

2. Freedom from the Inside Out

Determinism tells you that the state of the world at a time determines all the rest, past and future, but it doesn't tell you *which* slice, if any, explains or determines all the rest. The challenge to free will from determinism has not come from the physics, but rather from the unholy marriage of deterministic physics with our A-series view of time. The worry we have is that a *past* slice (long in the past, maybe even the 'initial conditions' of the universe if there are such) determines our actions *now*. We never think of a now-slice (including the voluntary actions we perform now) determining what happened in the past. Why not? There are two reasons. First, we unconsciously assume a metaphysical picture that is A-series based and incompatible with the block universe: we think of the past as 'real', fixed or determinate, the present as also 'real' (or becoming so), but the future as 'indeterminate' or 'open'. And as the zipper of the now moves into the future, it's the future that is getting determined, not

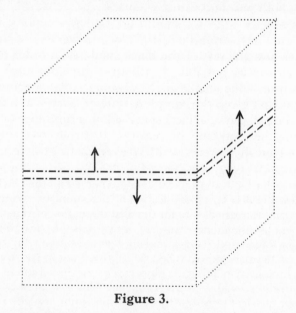

Figure 3.

[7] See section 2.1 below for further discussion of this point.

the past. Once one unearths this lurking metaphysical picture, its irrelevance becomes obvious. Physics has no truck with any of it, and (as noted before) is probably incompatible with it, when understood as applying to physical events *per se*. From the B-series or block-universe perspective, there is no reason to think of the past as determining the present and future, rather than vice-versa, and so on.

The second reason is more interesting. When we consider the idea of events in a time slice *now* physically determining the past, we become nervous because it looks as though we are positing *backward causation*. So if I assert that my actions, now, are free and explained or determined only by my own will; and that in a deterministic world, that may entail consequences about the past, but so what?; it looks as though I am positing backward causation, and giving myself the power to affect the past. And this is thought to be unacceptable on solid *physical* grounds, independent of any A-series/B-series considerations. In many presentations of the incompatibility of determinism and free will, this worry about affecting the past comes out explicitly: saying 'I could have done otherwise' is analysed as tantamount to saying 'I could either have caused a law of nature to be violated, or changed the past.'[8] Laying to rest this worry that freedom with determinism must involve either unacceptable backward causation or 'changing the past' will be the first task of the next section.

The idea of freedom from the inside out is this: we are perfectly justified in viewing our own actions *not* as determined by the past, *nor* as determined by the future, but rather as simply determined (to the extent that this word sensibly applies) *by ourselves, by our own wills*. In other words, they need not be viewed as *caused* or *explained* by the physical states of other, vast regions of the block universe. Instead, we can view our own actions, *qua* physical events, as primary explainers, determining—in a very partial way—physical events outside ourselves to the past and future of our actions, in the block. We adopt the perspective that the determination or explanation that matters is from the *inside* (of the block universe, where we live) *outward*, rather than from the *outside* (e.g. the state of things on a time slice 1 billion years ago) *in*. And we adopt the perspective of downward causation, thinking of our choices and intentions as primary explainers of our physical actions, rather than letting microstates of the world usurp this role. We are free to adopt these

---

[8] For example, see van Inwagen (1975). For a thorough and illuminating treatment of the challenge to free will from determinism, see Fischer (1998).

perspectives because, quite simply, physics—including our postulated, perfected deterministic physics—is perfectly compatible with them.

As I said before, exploring the consequences of these perspectives and defending them against apparent problems will occupy most of the rest of the paper. But the key to the defense has already been explained, and needs repeating. The notion of *past* events determining and explaining *future* events, and the opposite direction (or an 'inside-out' direction) of explanation being somehow wrong or suspect, arises completely from an unholy marriage of A-series time with deterministic physics. The mistake is natural and understandable, because of the way the A-series dominates our lives and our thinking, especially causal/explanatory thinking. It remains nevertheless a mistake. A deterministic physics gives us *logical* relations of determination, not a unique *temporal* relation of determination. In the block universe one can view a slice now, or a future slice, or a future $1/2$-block, or the past $1/2$-block 'before' now, as logically determining the rest.[9] These logical relations however are not in any interesting sense *explanatory*, nor even *causal*. Physics does not pick any one out as more important than the others, and indeed, equally allows us to ignore all of them when it comes to thinking about causation and explanation in things that matter in our lives, leaving room for downwards causation, as we will see below.

This is not the way we are accustomed to thinking of determinism. We usually stay in our A-series perspective on the world, tacitly conflate determination with causal explanation[10], and there we are, mired in the apparent incompatibility of determinism with our actions' being explained by our choices. A first antidote to this mistake is firmly to keep in mind that physical determinism belongs in the B-series world of physics alone. To break the conflation between determination and causal explanation, it helps to remember that deterministic physics equally allows future → past determination, but it does not thereby tell us that the future *causally* explains the past. The full antidote can only come by exploring the consequences of an 'inside-out' perspective on determination, and making sure that they are acceptable both physically and for common sense.

2.1 Past –> future determinism only? Above I said that weaker forms of determinism than the full time-symmetric Newtonian type we have been assuming pose, *prima facie*, less of a threat to free will. But do they really? In particular, does my argument for freedom

---

[9] Always assuming the truth of the deterministic laws, of course.

[10] Often the conflation is explicit, as the phrase "causal determinism" indicates.

from the inside out still have plausibility, if what physics gives us is past → future determinism but *not* future (or middle) → past determinism? At first blush, it might seem that the plausibility of the perspective on offer is undermined. A closer look remedies this misapprehension.

'Past → future determinism only' means that the future → past relationships allowed by the laws are one-many, while the past → future relationship is one-one. These relationships are still, however, *logical* rather than causal or explanatory. As long as our physics remains fully expressable in terms of B-series time, and has no need of A-series time, the one-way character of their determinism does *not* mean that the past is 'fixed' in some sense *vis a vis* future events. Nor do past events become somehow 'logically prior' to present and future events in the block. It is true that we can say that the past (plus the laws) entails our present actions, and can not any longer make the same claim regarding the future (which claim, psychologically, perhaps helps break the grip of the idea that these determination relationships render us unfree.) But this change does *nothing* to weaken the claim that the physical world's time is B-series time, in which past, present and future events all have the same ontological status. It does *nothing* to re-assert the notion that the past is 'fixed, done, and beyond our control'. In short, because this hypothesized weaker form of determinism does not re-impose an A-series metaphysics of time on us, it does not at all undermine the perspective of freedom from the inside out.

In fact, in terms of the worries for this perspective that we are about to explore, past → future only determinism reduces their strength. We are about to consider worries that arise if we consider our free actions as prime, explanatory starting-points, having consequences toward both past and future. But as just noted, under past → future only determinism, the present—past relationship is one-many rather than one-one. So whatever the constraints our free actions place on the past turn out to be, in principle they will be *weaker* than they would under full, bi-directional determinism. The comment made at the end of §1 was correct: the challenge to free will posed by weaker forms of determinism *is* in fact weaker.

3. Causation and Consequences

Can this 'inside-out' perspective be held, though? Does it not make the mistake of claiming that our actions now have causal consequences toward the past? The answer is 'No'. From the inside-out

Carl Hoefer

perspective, our freely chosen actions place *constraints* on what the past and future can be like, but the constraints are astonishingly weak, both toward the future and (especially) toward the past.

To discuss the question in more detail, let's assume that a human action (including the perceived surroundings of the agent's context) is a physical event *type* that has innumerable instantiations at the microphysical level. We assume, in other words, that there is some ill-defined and probably infinite set of microphysical state-types that are 'good enough' to count as a supervenience base for my typing 't' in the assumed context. In doing so, we are doubtless assuming a more reductionist picture than is likely to be true, but this is needed in order to make the apparent challenge as strong as possible.[11]

3.1 Consequences toward the past

If I freely choose to type this letter, 't', the choice in its context entails that some one of this enormous number of micro state-types shall be, and that is all. The constraints this places on how the past should be, even (say) the past of only one minute earlier, are probably either trivial or non-existent. Thinking of the constraints toward the future helps illustrate the weakness in either direction.

In his famous 1908 paper on causation, Russell pointed out that no cause ever *guarantees* the following of the customary effect – unless we inflate what we count as the cause to make it identical to a time-slice of the whole state of the world over a huge region of space. I reach for the 't' key, I depress it; will a 't' appear on the screen microseconds later? Typically, of course, yes; but not as a matter of logic (plus the laws), unless we rule out all possible interferences that could intervene and prevent the effect. (Think of every way that the computer might malfunction, or the power be cut, or a black hole whiz through your CPU at exactly the right time, ...)

The same goes toward the past: in terms of logical determination, our actions have little or no necessary consequences about what the past shall be like, outside of what is already presupposed in describ-

---

[11] Here I am giving the benefit of the doubt to supervenience on the microphysical, and interpreting it relatively strongly. The idea is that, although there can be no conceptual reduction of 'Carl types the letter 't' on his laptop' to the language of microphysics, it is nevertheless the case that at least God could say, if you showed him a microstate, whether or not it is good enough to count as 'Carl typing the letter 't' on his laptop' (or C for short), in the context.

ing the context. At the microphysical level the constraint is just that earlier microphysical states have to be logically consistent with a microstate of the correct type (i.e., one corresponding to my typing a 't') obtaining, at the time and place that it does. If the microstates we are positing cover, for example, a spatial area of 10 metres radius, then any given microstate logically entails the earlier microstates (i.e., toward the past) over an ever-shrinking spatial region, which vanishes 'after' a time period exactly equal to the time that light takes to travel 10 metres. (See diagram 4.) Specifying the microstate over a region of space and a slice or sandwich of time, in other words, logically determines the past and future microstates only over symmetric past- and future-pointing 'light cones' which exist only for an absurdly short period of time. All this is so, assuming Special Relativity's restriction on the velocity of physical things. If we remove that restriction, then the regions of past and future logical determination vanish entirely. And when we recall the huge (probably infinite) number of microstates that can serve as basis for a macroscopic event (my typing the 't'), the logical determination toward the past is correspondingly decreased. (When I freely choose to type the 't', I do not thereby choose to actualize a *particular* microstate!)

Despite the correctness of all this in logical/physical terms, we

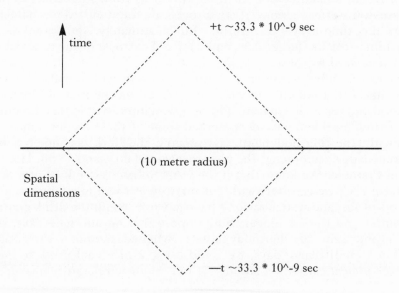

Figure 4. Space-time regions determined by events on hypersurface of 10m radius.

211

nevertheless have to acknowledge that the region of 'practical determination' of the state of things, toward the future, is usually much greater. There are pervasive and fortunate circumstances in the physical world that allow it to be the case that interferences such as Russell noted are rare, and that we are usually successful in producing the effects that we want toward the future. After all, usually my computer is functioning perfectly, there are no black holes or meteors or laser bolts heading toward me, etc. So usually, when I type 't', a 't' appears and stays there for a while. We are able, fortunately, to make things be the way we wish at the macro-level, more or less completely – depending on what we're aiming for—and for a goodly amount of time. If the same thing were true toward the past, then if freedom from the inside out were the case, we should have the ability to freely choose to make past events be the way we wish (most of the time, to some limited extent). This would quickly lead to paradoxes of the time-travel variety. For example, having observed the word 'example' on my screen for the past minute, I could (it seems) now take some action that causes the screen to be blank for the *past* minute. This means either postulating a 'changing of the past'—which is incoherent, or at the very least takes us outside of the block-universe perspective we have been assuming – or mysterious interventions that prevent us from succeeding in our backward-effect actions. (Banana peels are the standard mechanism, in the time travel literature). But fortunately, the same thing (ability to cause large-scale, enduring effects most of the time) is *not* true toward the past.

Temporally asymmetric features of our world make it very unlikely that our free actions leave 'traces' on the past of a macro-level and repeatable nature. Philosophers interested in the 'direction of time' problem have documented some of these circumstances in depth: the thermodynamic asymmetry, the 'fork' asymmetry, the knowledge asymmetry, the radiative asymmetry, and so on. Here is an example. We know that if we want to have a drink be at a uniform 2°C, we can start with our mixture at room temperature, add lots of ice, and wait. We don't have to worry about the drink getting hotter and the ice bigger. But suppose that on alternate days, the Second Law of thermodynamics switched temporal directions. Then on alternate days, we could cause a nice cool drink to *have been present* earlier, by adding ice to a room-temperature mixture.[12]

---

[12] Here I am glossing over all the thorny problems about whether human bodies could live under such a reversal of thermodynamic asymmetry, and whether the perceived flow of time would not then reverse as well.

But things being how they are, thermodynamically, we can't do anything of the sort. I can add ice to the mix, but nothing at all is then entailed about the past features of the drink—even assuming the absence of external influences. It might have sat there for a day, at equilibrium; or it might have had ice in it two hours ago; or it might have been quite hot; and so on.

It appears that our inability to produce causal effects toward the past is largely due to (1) these pervasive asymmetries in physical phenomena; and (2) the nature of our conscious experience and of sensation, which are either 'in', or somehow produce, the A-series, flowing time of common sense.[13] I regard these as very puzzling and unresolved issues; fortunately they do not need to be resolved for our purposes here. What matters is that our free actions, while they may have logical *consequences* about the past because of determinism (of a highly disjunctive nature, and for a trivial amount of time), do not have to be thought of as causally *bringing about* large-scale features of the past, or as explaining them.

Finally, notice that if all this was incorrect, the traditional picture would be in trouble also. Suppose we decided that, on the assumption of freedom from the inside out, we *would* in fact be able to effect noticeable backward causation. In that case, merely rejecting the perspective of freedom from the inside out would not automatically make this backward causation go away! Sticking with the same deterministic physics, the physically possible worlds with the backward-causation events would *still* be physically possible even if we stuck to thinking of determinism as a past -> future relation. The human actions producing backwards effects would still be *physically* possible. So if backward causation is a worry for one perspective, it should be a worry for both. Further constraints on physically possible worlds would have to be added to eliminate the threat, and their justification would not be from physics alone. But let's leave this concern for now, and carry on assuming that backward causation is not a worry.

3.2 Harmony

Granting this, one still might have some worries about *harmonisation*—about whether all the different actions we believe ourselves to be able to freely choose, can really fit together (a) with each other and (b) with the past as we know it (i.e., the macroscopically

---

[13] See Horwich (1987) and Price (1996) for extended discussion of temporal asymmetries.

described, known past) under determinism. One wonders whether billions of humans, all exercising free will, over the course of millenia, shouldn't be expected to generate enough consequences toward the past to generate contradictions—despite the weakness and disjunctive nature of the consequences of each act taken on its own. My freely chosen actions don't just have to harmonise with my immediate past; they have to harmonise with your immediate past and everyone else's, and they all have to be able to be fit together into a consistent past history of the world. The worry here is this: how do we know that there is always *at least one* microstate of the whole past that is compatible with the consequences (toward the past) of all the freely willed actions of all agents in history? Might it not be, instead, that once the free choices of (say) 4 billion humans are conjoined, then the possible choices of the rest of humanity are either removed (only one overall microstate is compatible) or severely constrained (each of us has few genuine choices available to us)? Given that everything has to fit together in such a way as to not violate the physical laws, one may worry that there needs to be a pre-established harmony (or, better: a harmony simpliciter—the 'pre' is misleading), and that because of this, we really are not free to do all sorts of things after all.

We know, of course, that all *actual* choices in fact fit together harmoniously; this is our starting assumption, that a deterministic microphysics holds sway over all actual events. So this harmony worry really has to do not just with actual choices, but the *alternative* choices we think we could have made: our freedom to do otherwise. This then brings us to the heart of the issue of the compatibility of freedom and determinism: the counterfactuals we believe, the could-have-done-otherwise's.

When I type the letter 's' I may think that I could have chosen to type a 'z' instead, in keeping with my nationality. And I think I could have done so, *with the past being, macroscopically, just the way I know it to be*. But can I really? Or is it instead the case (though we can't of course see why) that for me to type that 'z' instead, the past would have to have been different *macroscopically* (e.g., I would have had to have had corn flakes for breakfast instead of toast)?

The qualifier 'macroscopically' is absolutely crucial here. For note that although we are sticking to a block-universe perspective when it comes to real physics, and hence not supposing that the actual physical state of the world this past morning is somehow ontologically privileged over present or future states, nevertheless in terms of *our actions as we conceive them*, there *is* an important asymmetry. We think of ourselves as beings with a certain history, in a physical world with its own history, and our actions as arising freely *given* (or despite) all that.[14] And if this perspective was not in fact sustainable, then the compatibility of freedom with determinism I am after would not be possible after all.[15] I think I have freedom of the following kind: even given that the past history of the world is, macroscopically, as I (and indeed every other agent) knows it to be, I can either type the 's' or the 'z' (depending on which I choose). Can the past and our present actions, *as well as those we don't choose but think we could*, all fit together harmoniously in the way this conception of freedom demands? Can everything harmonize as well as harmonise?

Part of the response to this worry is what has already been explained: that logically each person's free actions entail only (at most) that one of an enormous set of past microstates obtain, and that only over a time-span that is vanishingly small. The time-asymmetry of typical physical events further rules out that there should be macro-scale consequences toward the past under 'typical' circumstances. If each person's free actions entails practically nothing about the past, it is plausible that all persons' actions conjoined should be able to fit together consistently. Moreover, of course, looking at the actual world from the block-universe perspective, all human actions *do* fit together consistently. So we have one example of a universe where it all works. The worry of course is that *only* one such, or very few such worlds are possible given the laws and the contextual/historical circumstances of our free choices. But what reason can we have for this worry?

[14] Here I am implicitly offering a criticism of one standard way (Lewis') of analysing counterfactual statements. Lewis, who seems inexplicably wedded to the A-series in all his metaphysics, supposes that in most uses of counterfactuals we mean to hold the past fixed—and I agree. But for Lewis this means the *physical* past in all its gory microphysical detail; so if determinism is true, it takes a miracle to get the if-had-done-otherwise scenario started. But why hold the past fixed in microphysical detail? What matters for action is the macroscopic past, that we know about empirically. When only that is fixed, I suggest, we don't need miracles to postulate various different actions and their likely future consequences.

[15] In this case, we would have to live with the threat to freedom posed by causal completeness, or take up a different compatibilist picture, such as that of Fischer (1994). He argues that the freedom-relevant sense of control over one's actions is 'guidance control', which does not require the ability to have done otherwise.

If anything, it seems that evidence points strongly the other way. I can test my free will right now, in the very typical circumstance of a person typing on a computer in a small room. I type various letters, randomly. Think of each letter struck as a run of an experiment. The experiment is simply to see whether all sorts of letter-producing choices, in a very normal physical context, starting from macroscopically near-identical initial conditions, can fit together consistently into one history. And the result is clear: they can.[16] Extending this idea further, we can regard much of what happens in an everyday life as providing similar evidence for harmony between a given, fixed macroscopically-described past and multiple present choices. I go to the 4th-floor cafeteria every day, and the menu on offer is always the same; but my choices vary.

Someone gripped by the harmony worry here will say that all this shows nothing. For each letter typed and each lunch selected may *not* be in fact freely chosen, but rather determined by the requirement of there being a globally consistent history (even when only some of the past, macroscopically described, is held as fixed). I find this worry very implausible, verging on the paranoid. The idea is that somehow, the deterministic physics we are assuming allows a world that is (toward the past) macroscopically like ours, in which I type 't' here, but does not allow one in which I type 'q' in that same place. Remember, we are not concerned with the actual past history of the world in all its microscopic detail; that *does*, of course, determine the present including that typing of 't'. We have set aside this traditional problem by adopting the perspective of freedom from the inside out. Instead we are here only concerned with whether there should be a physically possible world similar to actuality in some gross, macroscopic ways, and in which I (or my counterpart, if you like) types 'q'. How could it be the case that physics makes room for the one, but not for the other?

The harmony worry thus boils down to this: that our posited deterministic physics may allow vastly fewer possible worlds than we can imagine, so few that our normal conception of the could-have-done-otherwise is mistaken. And so few that what *seems* like good evidence for multiple choices in a given context (such as the evidence described above) is in fact not good evidence: there are

---

[16] The point in this thought experiment is to keep the macroscopically-described initial conditions as much identical as possible: not only the room, lighting, etc. are the same, but also my intention—namely, to type a letter at random.

very few physically possible worlds like ours, even though at least one of them (i.e., ours) happens to contain an abundance of misleading evidence in favour of freedom. Without having a genuinely adequate deterministic physics in hand to examine, there may be no way fully to resolve this doubt. There might be no way even if we did have the true physics in hand. But I am moved by the intuition that in *any* recognizable deterministic microphysics, there will be *so many* different micro-level world histories, there has to be more than enough scope for freedom as we normally conceive it.

3.3 Indeterministic microphysics

When we turn to considering freedom from the inside out under the assumption that an indeterministic microphysics holds in our world, things become simpler in one sense, and more complicated in others. Intuitively we expect the apparent challenge to freedom posed by such an underlying physics—always less clear-cut than the challenge from determinism—to dissolve more easily. Nevertheless, care is required in thinking through the possibilities under indeterminism.

Again we insist on downward causation, and the need for *past* history (at the micro-level) to conform to the constraints set by the free choices of agents. Again we suppose that there is a past micro-state compatible with my typing 't' now, but also a macroscopically identical micro-state (which may or may not be different!) compatible with my typing 'q' instead. But now the constraint is only that these micro-histories must be consistent with our merely probabilistic laws. Surely this is a looser set of constraints, and hence an easier context in which to maintain freedom?

Perhaps, but this does not follow immediately and trivially from the mere *idea* of an indeterministic microphysics. First of all, notice that in a formal sense determinism could fail (and indeterminism reign) without the challenge to free action changing significantly. Suppose, for example, that it remains the case that the state of the world (over the relevant region) a million years ago makes each and every one of our actions have a probability greater than 99·999%. I submit that this does not alter the force of the traditional incompatibilist argument that we are unfree very much. But things could be worse still; it might be that in fact our actions are all 100% necessitated by the past of 1 million years ago. Suppose that indeterminism holds only in this weak sense: once every 3 million years, an atom of hydrogen pops into existence at a random location in the universe; and this last happened 2.5 million years ago. Otherwise, events follow iron deterministic laws. This scenario posits what is, in some formal sense, an indeterministic world; but in essence things are just the same as under 'pure' determinism.[17]

But recall that we are advocating freedom from the inside out. It is not necessary to maintain that we are only *loosely* constrained by the past, to maintain that we have freedom. Instead we simply maintain that the constraint goes the other way around. The past is (partly) constrained by our choices. How will this partial constraint play out under an indeterministic microphysics? Again, as above, it is not possible to make definitive pronouncements without having the physical laws before us (and it might be practically impossible even then). Plausibility considerations are the best we can do.

Prima facie it seems plausible that an indeterministic microphysics, which allows (by definition) multiple futures branching from a single past, should allow greater room for freedom than a deterministic microphysics. We intuitively picture a 'branching tree' structure of possibilities, and think of the forks as corresponding to our free choices. The scenarios sketched above show us that we cannot automatically assume this is so. What matters, then, are the following questions: does our indeterministic microphysics allow various worlds corresponding to a variety of free actions we can undertake (in a given context) that all share an *identical* **or** *macroscopically identical* past? And does it do so for all of our free actions together, so that they harmonize appropriately?

What is needed, then, is the same as in the case of determinism: a rich variety of physically possible worlds, so that we can take the actual history as one among many similar possible histories, whose actuality is explained (in part) by all our free choices. We need to be able to say that, generally, we *could* have done otherwise in the circumstances where we normally believe this; this might or might not imply that the past would have had to be different at the micro-level. The 'might or might not' in the previous sentence is what distinguishes an indeterministic microphysics from a deterministic set of laws. Those who equate indeterminism with automatic room for freedom are assuming that these four words can be replaced with 'would not'. But this cannot be taken for granted.

What can be taken for granted is just the set of considerations developed above in section 3.2. An indeterministic microphysics might have a richer variety of worlds than a deterministic micro-

[17] These brief remarks are meant to counteract a common tendency in the free will literature, that of conflating indeterminism with a sort of 'anything goes' conclusion about what actions are physically possible given a fixed (micro- and macro-) past.

physics; but for all we know, it might not. To be the correct laws for *our* world, it must allow a great deal of variety—including the phenomena adduced in §3.2 as evidence that we should not worry about harmony problems. In the end, then, the situation seems to be the same as in the deterministic case.

4 Clarification of an Old Idea

Let me recap the main features of the notion of freedom from the inside out. We carefully distinguish the true story of the *physical* world as it is in itself, which is that of a block universe with only B-series time, from the world of everyday *experience* and *action*, which is wholly within A-series time. Physical determinism, if true at all, is true of the block universe with its B-series time, and implies no explanatory priority of the past over the future, or of future over past, or of the middle over the far past and future. It is therefore open to us to conceive of our actions as genuinely free, only *properly* explained by our desires, beliefs and intentions despite being *logically* determined by vast states of the world at other times.

While I have not seen this idea put forth in any modern discussion of free will and determinism, I must confess that I believe the first philosopher to advocate it was not me, but Kant. Kant famously defended a metaphysical picture that postulated a Newtonian/deterministic physical world, but also claimed that rational beings were *genuinely* the authors of their own free actions. How Kant thought he could reconcile these two theses is rarely discussed in a satisfactory way. A typical (and unsatisfactory) way of reading Kant's suggestions on this point is to read him as claiming that, in purely rational/intellectual terms, a person *qua* transcendental being should be considered the author of his/her own actions, at least for the purposes of praise and blame. But there are also cryptic comments about the whole of a person's life actions being but a single phenomenon, and a strong suggestion that the non-temporality of the noumenal world is what allows us to think of a person's will as the genuine source of their actions, despite determination by past events in the *phenomenal* (A-series) world. Here are some passages from the *Critique of Practical Reason:*

'... Repentance is entirely legitimate, because reason, when it is a question of the law of our intelligible existence (the moral law), acknowledges no temporal distinctions and only asks whether the event belongs to me as my act, and then morally connects it with the same feeling, whether the event occurs now or is long since past. For the sensuous life is but a single phenomenon in the view of an intelligible consciousness of its existence (the consciousness of freedom) ... [and] must be judged not according to natural necessity which pertains to it as appearance but according to the absolute spontaneity of freedom.' (LWB translation, p. 102)

'... [despite the determination of a person's actions], we could nevertheless still assert that the man is free. For if we were capable of another view ... i.e., if we were capable of an intellectual intuition of the same subject, we would then discover that the entire chain of appearances, with reference to that which concerns only the moral law, depends upon the spontaneity of the subject as a thing-in-itself, for the determination of which no physical explanation can be given.' (LWB translation, p. 103)

In other words, Kant suggests, the agent as a noumenal being should be considered as the source and genuine explainer of his/her own free actions, even though *qua* physical things *in* time their actions are determined by earlier physical events.

Kant did not have McTaggart's distinction at his disposal. If we bring it to bear on Kant's metaphysical picture, we can clarify (and correct) that picture as follows. The block universe is the realm of things in themselves, i.e., the world *in itself*, not *as experienced by consciousness*. For Kant, 'time' meant A-series time, and that is indeed restricted to conscious/rational experience. Physics, which does try to describe the world in itself (contra Kant's epistemic restrictions), needs only B-series time, i.e., a structure of relations among events that *underlies* and is partly isomorphic to A-series time. Rational agents can be understood as the ultimate explanatory sources of their own free actions[18]; the rest of the noumenal world , i.e., the rest of the block universe, must simply be such as to accommodate those actions. The only real mistake Kant made was in the locus of determinism: he thought it must be a feature of the world of experience, due to the necessary conditions of possible experience. In fact determinism is *no part* of our experience of the world, and if true at all, is only true at the subtle level of ultimate particles. Nevertheless Kant seemed to have the fundamental point right:

---

[18] At this point one perhaps wants to hear more about the positive characterization of freedom that should accompany the negative picture (i.e., sketch of how the physical world leaves us *room* for freedom) developed above. I will not try to sketch or defend any positive account, but I am attracted to the basic idea we find in Kant: free action in the highest sense is action that springs not from mere desire, but rather from something intellectual, a concept of the good.

when agents are conceived as 'things in themselves' (i.e., as rational beings rather than as merely physical objects), their free actions are quite compatible with overall physical determinism, because those actions can be thought of as *outside* the time series (i.e., the A-series with its allegedly fixed past) and hence *not* unfree despite being 'determined' by physical events lying to the past of them.

Whether or not this is really close to what Kant had in mind, I think it is what we should believe to be the case, if our world is causally complete. Free action and causal completeness *are* compatible after all, and not in the (arguably) weak sense offered by traditional forms of compatibilism. You have choices, and you make them. Because of determinism, your choices (like any events) place constraints on what the world's history can be. But the direction of determiniation (and, for most free actions, correct explanation) is *from* your choices *to* the ways the physical world can be—both toward the past and the future.

This picture of freedom from the inside out is more Idealistic than some will find comfortable. Take a God's-eye perspective on the block universe, and ask the question (Q): why are things as they are in it? A 21st-century materialist is comfortable with this sort of answer: 'Well, you see, there was this Big Bang at the beginning, and after that things just sort of bump around in the ways permitted by the laws of nature, and that leads to the whole history.' But this answer (a) is infected with the A-series view of time, (b) seems to presuppose an eliminativist picture of human thought and action, and (c) begs the question "Why was the Big Bang just so and not otherwise?" (a) is a mistake, (b) is at least dubious, and (c) is the lump under the carpet which, if you try to flatten it, leads to moves in all sorts of unpleasant directions (theology, Cosmic Anthropic Principles, and so on).

I prefer the picture that starts with what we *feel* so strongly that we really have: freedom to act in a variety of ways. This picture places some constraints—probably only very weak ones – on what an answer to this ultimate question (Q) can look like, if one is possible at all. It is Idealistic, in that the constraints involve giving rational agents priority over trivia such as the physical micro-state of vast regions of space-time (past or future). But this is a form of Idealism that most of us can learn to live with. Appropriately, it is McTaggart's distinction that helps us see that it is not nearly so strange as it may at first appear.

Carl Hoefer

References

Dupre, John 1993. *The Disorder of Things* (Harvard University Press).
Dupre, John 1996. 'The Solution to the Problem of Free Will', *Philosophical Perspectives*, **10**, 385–402.
Fischer, John *The Metaphysics of Free Will* (Blackwell, 1994)
Forrest, Peter 1985. 'Backward Causation in Defence of Free Will', *MIND*, 210–17.
Horwich, Paul *Asymmetries in Time* (MIT Press, 1987).
Kant, Immanuel. *The Critique of Practical Reason*, trans. Lewis White Beck, Bobbs-Merrill Company, 1956.
Price, Huw *Time's Arrow and Archimedes' Point* (Oxford University Press, 1996).
Russell, Bertrand 'On the Notion of Cause', Address to the Aristotelian Society, reprinted in *Mysticism and Logic* (Allen & Unwin, 1917).
van Inwagen, Peter, 'The Incompatibility of Free Will and Determinism', *Philosophical Studies* **27**, 185–99.

On Stages, Worms, and Relativity*

YURI BALASHOV†

Abstract

Four-dimensionalism, or perdurantism, the view that temporally extended objects persist through time by having (spatio-)temporal parts or stages, includes two varieties, the worm theory and the stage theory. According to the worm theory, perduring objects are four-dimensional wholes occupying determinate regions of space-time and having temporal parts, or stages, each of them confined to a particular time. The stage theorist, however, claims, not that perduring objects have stages, but that the fundamental entities of the perdurantist ontology *are* stages. I argue that considerations of special relativity favor the worm theory over the stage theory.

1. Introduction

Recent work on persistence over time has produced a more fine-grained inventory of views than we had a few years ago. Although there are still two major rival accounts of persistence on the market: three-dimensionalism (3D, endurantism) and four-dimensionalism (4D, perdurantism), distinct varieties of each view have now been identified. For example, philosophers who think that ordinary material objects endure—that they are wholly present at all times at which they exist—now explicitly include those who prefer to run this position together with a certain theory of time, namely *presentism* (roughly, the view that only the present exists),[1] and those who

* I am grateful to Michael Rea and Theodore Sider for valuable comments on earlier drafts. An ancestor of this paper was read at the conference on 'Time, Reality, and Experience' (The London School of Economics, September 2000). My thanks to the audience, and especially to Simon Saunders and Steve Savitt, for very helpful critical discussions. The work on this paper was supported by a junior faculty grant from the University of Georgia Research Foundation.

† Department of Philosophy, 107 Peabody Hall, The University of Georgia, Athens, GA 30605,USA. yuri@arches.uga.edu

[1] See, e.g., Merricks (1995, 1999), Hinchliff (1996), Zimmerman (1998), Craig (2000), Markosian (forthcoming), and references to earlier work therein. Prior's classic (1970) should be specifically mentioned.

223

deny this link between the theory of persistence and the philosophy of time.[2] Similarly, four-dimensionalists who think objects perdure—persist by having different temporal parts at different times—comprise those who think that this position presupposes *eternalism* (the idea that all moments of time are on the same ontological footing)[3] as well as those who argue against this connection.[4]

Another important distinction, which has emerged within the perdurantism camp, is between the *worm* theory and the *stage* theory—the distinction with which I am concerned in this paper. The worm theory features an ontology of 4D wholes (spatio-temporal 'worms') occupying determinate regions of spacetime. Such entitied have parts, or stages, each of them confined to a particular time (an instant or interval). The stage theorist, on the other hand, claims, not that perduring objects have stages, but that the fundamental entities of the perdurantist ontology *are* stages.[5]

In the next section, I attempt to draw the distinction between the worm and the stage theories more precisely while explaining what makes both of them varieties of four-dimensionalism. Then I offer an argument defending worms over stages. The argument is based on considerations of special relativity and requires, as a prerequisite, restating the stage view in the relativistic context. It will be convenient to start with the classical framework, that of neo-Newtonian spacetime, and then show what modifications are to be made in the stage theory in effecting a transition to special relativistic (Minkowski) spacetime.

Although I do not embark, in this paper, on the task of defending four-dimensionalism as a whole against three-dimensionalism, I believe that a somewhat similar argument could be applied to this purpose.[6] My strategy presupposes the eternalist framework: it

---

[2] See, e.g., Mellor (1981), Haslanger (1989), van Inwagen (1990), Rea (1998).

[3] Most four-dimensionalists are eternalists. Merricks (1995), who is a three-dimensionalist, and Carter and Hestevold (1994), who maintain a neutral position, have nonetheless argued for the link between perdurantism and eternalism.

[4] Brogaard (2000) defends presentist four-dimensionalism. Not being presentist four-dimensionalists themselves, Lombard (1999) and Sider (2001, §3.4), have shown that this combination is consistent.

[5] The stage theory has recently been elaborated and defended by Sider (1996, 2000, 2001) and Hawley (2002). References to earlier works can be found therein. The paradigm worm theorist is probably Heller (1990).

[6] See, in this connection, Balashov (2000a, 2000b).

takes the 4D spacetime manifold of point events to be existing in the fundamental tenseless sense and is not concerned to defend this framework against presentism. One reason is that this paper takes relativity seriously, and I agree with many writers[7] that anyone who takes relativity seriously cannot take presentism seriously. At the same time, I believe, contrary to some,[8] that taking relativity seriously does not automatically force one into four-dimensionalism, let alone a particular variety of it. One has to produce a substantive argument to this effect.

2. Stages versus Worms

Both the stage and the worm theorists are four-dimensionalists because both agree that temporally extended objects persist through time by having temporal parts (stages) (cf. Sider 1996, 433). This sets them against the paradigm three-dimensionalist who plainly

---

[7] See, e.g., Savitt (2000), Callender (2000), Saunders (forthcoming), and Sider (2001, §2.4).

[8] Earlier work on persistence did not always draw a clear distinction between four-dimensionalism, a particular ontology of material objects, and eternalism or the 'block-universe' view, which is primarily a view about time and the nature of events. See, e.g., Taylor (1955). Since special relativity undoubtedly favours the latter, some writers were too quick to conclude that it automatically favours the former as well. This link is implicit in Quine (1950, 1987). Recent contributions to the persistence debate have gone a long way towards dismantling this alleged package deal. See, in this connection, Rea (1998), Balashov (1999, 2000a, and 2000c), Sider (2001). Craig, a presentist endurantist, concedes that 'Embracing spacetime realism does not ... commit one automatically to ... four-dimensionalism or perdurantism' (2001, 94n), but he contradicts himself elsewhere: 'Spacetime realism [i.e., the view that all events populating the 4D spacetime manifold tenselessly exist on the same ontological footing] raises a host of problems due to its *entailment* of the doctrine of perdurance ...' (2000, 124–5, my emphasis; cf. 2001, 192); 'If one is a spacetime realist, then, barring conventionalism, things must have spatio-temporal parts' (ibid., 202n68); 'A consistent spacetime realist will ... view objects as spatio-temporal entities which perdure' (2001, 94n54). Craig's reasons for thinking (in the end) that the combination of endurantism with eternalism is inconsistent remain unclear to me, especially given that this combination is widely accepted on the basis of a view of predication known as Adverbialism (see Johnston 1987, Lowe 1988, Haslanger 1989, van Inwagen 1990, Rea 1998). More on Adverbialism below.

denies that the notion of temporal part makes good sense when applied to objects (rather than, say, events).[9]

Furthermore, both the stage and the worm theorists typically believe in temporal stages as well as 4D wholes. Indeed, a chief contemporary advocate of the stage theory, Theodore Sider, accepts such wholes because they are aggregates of stages.[10] And worm theorists usually accept stages on the ground that the latter are parts of what they take to be the central entities of their ontology. What is, then, the difference between the two views?

As Sider notes (1996, 433), 'spacetime worms are [not] what we typically call persons, name with proper names, quantify over'—and attribute temporary properties to, one might add. Stages come closer to filling this bill.[11] To illustrate, consider the famous problem of temporary intrinsics. How can one and the same object—say,

[9] By far, the strongest expression of this attitude belongs to van Inwagen who has said of temporal parts: 'I simply do not understand what these things are supposed to be, and I do not think this is my fault. I think no one understands what they are supposed to be, though of course plenty of philosophers think they do' (1981, 133).

[10] 'At one level, I accept the ontology of the worm view. I believe in spacetime worms, since I believe in temporal parts and aggregates of things I believe in' (Sider 1996, 433).

[11] Hawley (2002, Ch. 2) describes the difference between the worm and stage views similarly:

According to [the worm] theory, persisting objects like bananas and tennis balls are four-dimensional, and they satisfy certain predicates with respect to certain times because of the properties of their temporal parts. Alongside [the worm] theory, there is space for an alternative account of persistence, one which retains the four-dimensional metaphysics of perdurance theory whilst rejecting [the worm theory's] claims about predication. ... According to [the] stage theory, nothing is wholly present at more than one moment, so endurance theory is false. But [the] stage theory also claims that the satisfiers of sortal predicates like 'is a banana' and 'is a tennis ball' are momentary things, the very things which instantiate ordinary properties like *being yellow, being spherical* or *being banana-shaped*.

Consider the series of momentary stages whose sum is what [the worm] theorists think of as the tennis ball. According to [the] stage theory, when we talk about the tennis ball with respect to different times, we talk about different stages in that series, and each of those stages is a tennis ball. The tennis ball at one moment is spherical, and the squashed tennis ball at another moment is not spherical: the spherical tennis ball and the non-spherical tennis ball are different objects.

a poker—instantiate contrary properties at different times, such as being hot at t_1 and cold at t_2? To solve this problem, the worm theorist attributes hotness to the t_1-stage of the poker worm and coldness to its t_2-stage. But it is the poker worm, not its stages, that should properly be called the poker in the worm ontology. Clearly, the 4D poker cannot instantiate temporary intrinsics simpliciter. It can only do so derivatively, via its temporal parts, or stages. Thus it is unable to do what the enduring poker can, according to the *presentist* three-dimensionalism, do quite naturally: by instantiating hotness simpliciter at t_1 and then (next morning) instantiating coldness simpliciter at t_2. Now this advantage is lost as soon as one rejects presentism in favour of eternalism. In the eternalist setting, the endurantist has to replace the simple properties *hot* and *cold* by their time-indexed counterparts, *hot-at-t$_1$* and *cold-at-t$_2$* (Indexicalism) or to replace the having of the usual properties simpliciter by their temporally qualified having (Adverbialism).[12] All things being equal, it would be nice to avoid trading the intuition about the having of temporary intrinsics simpliciter for the (arguably unavoidable) rejection of presentism. And that is what the stage view does. In saying that the poker is hot at t_1, the stage theorist ascribes the usual (not time-indexed) property *hotness* to the poker (i.e., the t_1 poker stage) simpliciter.

This example demonstrates the difference between the two varieties of four-dimensionalism and suggests that, assuming eternalism, the stage theory has an edge over both endurantism and the worm view vis-à-vis the problem of temporary intrinsics. Sider further argues that the stage theory offers the best unified solution to the paradoxes of material constitution and coincident entities (1996; 2001, §5.8).

There is a price to be paid for these gains. To account for persistence and change, the stage theorist is hard-pressed to adopt a temporal version of the counterpart theory. The poker is hot tonight, but it will be cold tomorrow morning. But the poker tonight is just a poker stage confined to a certain time. How can *it* survive till tomorrow and be cold then? Only by bearing a temporal counterpart relation to another poker stage. The latter has a simple property *being cold*, but it is the former, tonight stage (which, remember, *is* the poker, on the stage theory) that has, vicariously, the temporal

---

[12] For discussions of Indexicalism and Adverbialism, see Lewis (1986, 202–204, 1988), Johnston (1987), Lowe (1988), Haslanger (1989), van Inwagen (1990), Merricks (1994), Rea (1998), Balashov (1999, 2000a, 2000c), Lombard (2000), Hawley (2002).

property *being cold tomorrow*. The analogy to the modal counterpart theory is obvious.

Those who are happy with the modal counterpart theory should welcome the stage view as part of the package deal. Others, of course, will consider this kind of commitment unattractive. But one need not be a modal counterpart theorist to adopt the stage theory. The temporal counterpart relation is a this-wordly affair, and realism about other times and their denizens is not nearly as exotic as full-blown realism about possibilia. Furthermore, transtemporal aggregates of shorter-lived entities are familiar (e.g., from the pervading experience of temporally extended events, such as football games and symphony concerts) in a way transworld aggregates of possibilia are not.

In light of the claimed advantages of the stage view, it should be given careful consideration, along with other views of persistence. My eventual goal is to compare the stage and worm theories in the relativistic context. This will require some preliminary work.

3. Local and Global Stages

The first thing to appreciate is that the notion of stage admits of a *global* interpretation. More precisely, local object stages populate and share global *world* stages.

According to the stage theory, various pieces of furniture in my office are so many furniture stages. I can refer to them collectively when I say, for example, that they overcrowd the room. What does it mean, speaking stage-theoretically? It means that each of these things (two chairs, three book cases, a desk, etc.) taken individually—each thing stage, that is—belongs to the room stage and shares this larger stage with other things and with me (that is, my stage). Similarly, the room stage belongs to the building stage, which itself belongs to the campus stage (if there is such a thing). Everything on the planet Earth populates the Earth stage, which inhabits the Solar system, which, in turn, inhabits the Galaxy, and so on. All local object stages, in short, share a global stage cutting across the entire world. In fact, such a global stage *is* the world. Or, to borrow an expression from Shakespeare and Sider (1996, 433), 'all the world's a stage.'

Let us call objects (themselves stages, of course) populating and sharing some global stage *stage mates*, by analogy with Lewis's world mates. Consider an example (Figure 1). Descartes in 1620 (i.e., the 1620 stage of Descartes[13]) and Galileo in 1620 are stage mates because they share the 1620 global stage, which is the entire world in 1620. They also share this *temporal world* with Kepler, but not with Tycho Brahe. The reason is that the 1620 world stage contains a Kepler stage, namely his 1620 stage, but it does not include any stage of Brahe. This cosmologist does not exist in 1620. On the other hand, Descartes in 1600 (i.e., his 1600 stage) and Galileo in 1600 share a global stage with both Kepler and Brahe (i.e., with their corresponding stages). All four are stage mates; they coexist in a single temporal world.

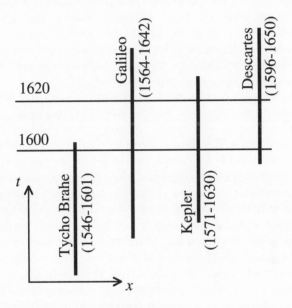

Figure 1.

[13] 'The 1620 stage of Descartes' refers ambiguously to a year-long Descartes' stage and to his momentary stage at a certain time in 1620. Similarly with 'the 1620 world (or global) stage'. Hawley argues that stages must be instantaneous: they 'need to be as fine-grained as possible change, and thus they must be as fine-grained as instants, in order to account for possible change in position' (2002, Ch. 2). Sider's works exploit the instantaneous sense too, and I will do the same in my analysis. I will also restrict my consideration to point-like objects having no extension in space. The reader will appreciate that nothing important turns on these idealizations. But they do simplify the discussion significantly.

The notions of existence and coexistence in a temporal world require some comment.[14] It may be objected that the only concept of existence relevant to the 4D framework is the atemporal notion that all spacetime entities, worms and stages alike, exist as parts of the single reality, that of the 4D spacetime manifold. If that is the case, then the distinction made above between Brahe's existence in 1600 and his non-existence in 1620 holds no water. In the basic atemporal sense, Brahe's existence just means his existence in 1600, 1590 and in general at all times between 1546 and 1601. Put in more explicit stage-theoretic terms, what is asserted here is the existence of Brahe's stages in 1546–1601 and non-existence of his stages at other times. The same applies to Descartes, Galileo, and others. But all these cosmologists (i.e., cosmologist stages) coexist with each other as sharing the same 4D spacetime world, and of course they coexist with everything else that ever existed, exists or will exist in the entire history of the universe. All such entities are in the single domain of quantification of the theory.

I agree that this atemporal concept of sharing the single space-time manifold has its role to play in the 4D framework. But I think it becomes rather trivial, hence useless, when applied to stages as opposed to worms. The basic sense in which complete 4D worms share the same world, or coexist, is indeed the broad atemporal one: they all coexist by populating the same 4D spacetime manifold. But the stage ontology invites a different notion of sharing a world. Stages are confined to particular times rather than being spread over intervals of time. The stages' world is a world stage. It is true but trivial that all stages populate the single 4D manifold and, hence, all coexist. But that is not the issue with which we are primarily concerned when we talk about, refer to, and quantify over stages. A more important notion of coexistence pertinent to stages relates to global stage sharing. In the broad but trivial sense, I (i.e., my current stage) share the single world with George W. Bush (his current stage) and Napoleon (e.g., his 1815 stage). But in our discourse we are inclined to draw a distinction between such cases. And in drawing such a distinction, we are getting at the sense of the coexistence relation such that I bear this relation to Bush but not to Napoleon. This non-trivial notion of coexistence implies a correlated and temporally loaded notion of existence to go along with it. The latter is brought to the forefront when I state, in all seriousness, that Bush *still* exists but Napoleon does so *no longer*. Obviously, both the

---

[14] This comment was prompted in large part by very useful discussions with Ted Sider and Mike Rea.

non-trivial notion of coexistence and the accompanying notion of existence relevant to the stage theory have to do with the sharing of a single temporal world, or a global world stage, by local objects.

Yet one might have doubts about the possibility of accommodating what appear to be two distinct concepts of existence in a single ontology: the universal concept and the restricted one confined to particular global stages. To dispose of such doubts, an analogy with modal realism could be helpful. As noted by Lewis, to quantify correctly over possibilia and, in general, to do justice to the modal discourse, the modal realist needs two different quantifiers: one ranging over the contents of the entire collection of possible worlds and the other restricted to a particular such world (see Lewis 1986, 3, 5–7, and elsewhere). Any two objects populating the Lewisian multi-universe coexist in the broad sense, but those belonging to different worlds do not coexist in the restricted sense. An inhabitant of our world can state, with ontological seriousness, that alien objects do not actually exist (meaning their non-existence in our world). The distinction drawn above between the broad and restricted concepts of (co)existence in the 'temporal multi-universe' (i.e., in the complete four-dimensional spacetime manifold, which can be foliated into families of world stages) parallels the Lewisian distinction between the two quantifiers. The first ranges over all stages of all objects while the second is restricted to stage mates—just as the Lewisian special quantifier is confined to world mates. In fact, the first distinction has more intuitive appeal, as it allows the stage theorist to give due respect to familiar differences, such as that between our coexistence with Bush and our lack of coexistence with Napoleon, whereas rather esoteric intuitions are required to recognize the realm of possibilia in the first place. Nonetheless, the parallel is useful as it brings out, once again, important similarities between the modal and temporal discourses.

With this distinction in mind, we can provide a stage-theoretic analysis for much of ordinary discourse about temporally qualified existence and coexistence. Start with a simple observation that the 1620 stage of Descartes coexists with the 1620 stage of Kepler, but not with his 1615 stage. The first, but not the second pair of stages are stage mates, that is, share a single global stage, or temporal world. Such basic relations among local stages can be used to analyse many familiar locutions.

- The stage-theoretic analysis of 'In 1620, Descartes coexisted with Kepler and Galileo but not with Brahe' would go along the following lines: the 1620 stage of Descartes coexists (in the narrow sense)—or shares a global stage (a temporal world)—with some stage of Kepler and some stage of Galileo but with no stage of Brahe. (Note the tenseless mode of present-tense verbs in the analysans here and below.)

- As already noted, 'Brahe did not exist in 1620' means that no stage of him exists then.
- 'Descartes, Kepler, Galileo, and Brahe were contemporaries' translates into the statement that some stages of Descartes, Kepler, Galileo, and Brahe are all stage mates, for example, their 1600 stages.
- 'Descartes, Kepler, Galileo, and Newton (1642–1727) were contemporaries at some point or other but not all at once' translates into the statement that some stage of each of them shares a single temporal world with some stage of another or with some stages of some others, but no single global stage contains stages of all of them.
- 'Neither Descartes nor Kepler was a contemporary of Ptolemy' means that no stage of Ptolemy shares a temporal world with any stage of Descartes or Kepler.

Although this framework is transparent enough, some of its features should be noted, as they will play a role in the subsequent discussion.

1. The relation of coexistence in a single temporal world—the stage mate relation—is not a set of dyadic relations between members of pairs of objects (i.e., their stages), but a single *many-place* relation among n-tuples of objects. Descartes, Kepler, Galileo, and Brahe coexisted in 1600, not because six dyadic relations obtain between members of pairs of their stages, but because a single four-place relation obtains among all four.

2. Temporal worlds (global stages) hosting local stages of objects can be individuated by very minimal amounts of their contents. Given a single stage of a single object—for example, Descartes in 1620—the global stage representing the whole temporal world containing him is uniquely fixed: the world in 1620. To put it differently, Descartes' local 1620 stage can be uniquely *extended* to the global 1620 world stage.

3. If a collection of stage mates coexist with O1—that is to say, if the original collection and O1 are related by an n-place stage mate relation—and also coexist with O2 (in the same sense), then that collection coexists with both O1 and O2; which is to say that the original collection supplemented by O1 and O2 are related by an

$n+1$-place stage mate relation. Thus Descartes in 1600 and Galileo in 1600 coexist with Kepler (his 1600 stage); these cosmologists bear a three-place stage mate relation to each other thereby sharing the 1600 world. Furthermore, Descartes in 1600 and Galileo in 1600 coexist in the same sense with Brahe (his 1600 stage). Not surprisingly, Descartes in 1600 and Galileo in 1600 coexist with *both* Kepler and Brahe by bearing a four-place relation to their corresponding stages and thereby populating the 1600 world. Let us call this feature of the stage mate relation *non-contextuality*. The full meaning of this term will become clear later on.

4. As Descartes grows older he finds himself in temporal worlds with *progressively older* stages of Kepler and Galileo. (Regrettably, some of those later worlds do not contain Brahe.) In this sense, the stage mate relation is *chronologically well behaved*.

5. The above analysis is classical. It exploits the intrinsic geometry of pre-relativistic (Galilean, or neo-Newtonian) spacetime. The classical spacetime manifold can be uniquely foliated into a family of hyperplanes of simultaneity indexed by the absolute time of Newtonian physics. Every such hyperplane cuts across an entire temporal world. In fact every hyperplane *is* a world or, more precisely, the geometrical locus of a temporal world. Each local stage finds itself on one of the hyperplanes. And the extension of a local to a global stage is achieved by drawing a unique hyperplane of simultaneity through that stage. Figure 1 illustrates these observations.

Classical spacetime provides a rather friendly environment for the stage ontology by making the stage mate relation non-contextual and chronologically well behaved. These benefits are easily overlooked because we normally take pre-theoretical considerations underlying them for granted. These benefits, however, are lost in the transition to special relativity. In the remainder of the paper I shall argue that, on plausible formulations of the stage theory in relativistic (Minkowski) spacetime, one has to surrender non-contextuality and chronologically good behavior of the stage mate relation.

Before we do it, however, let us turn briefly to the worm view and indicate that it suggests a different analysis of the situation considered earlier. On the worm theory, Descartes, for example, is a 4D object (a 1D world line in Figure 1, in which two spatial dimensions are suppressed and, in addition, Descartes and others are taken to be idealized point-like objects) and the same is true of Galileo, Kepler and others. Although one could sensibly talk about their stages and various relations among them, this talk is not ontologically significant in a sense in which the stage theorist's talk of stages

Yuri Balashov

is. Ordinary objects, on the worm view, are not stages but worms; the relations among their stages are derivative from more fundamental relations among the 4D wholes. When asked, 'How many great cosmologists are there?' the stage theorist will take this to be an incomplete question about cosmologist stages and the appropriate answer will require additional information about the time of evaluation. There are, for example, three great cosmologists in existence in 1620 and four in 1600. The basic objects of the stage ontology populate global stages; their common world, recall, is a stage. The basic objects of the worm ontology, on the other hand, populate the entire 4D spacetime reality. When asked, 'How many great cosmologists are there?' the ontologically serious worm theorist should regard this as a complete question that is primarily about perduring wholes, and she will have to list all the great 4D cosmologists—past, present, and future. The list will include Ptolemy as well as Hubble, in addition to Galileo, Kepler, Brahe, and Newton.[15] Now of course, the worm theorist is free to talk about cosmologist stages as well, when confronted with the question 'How many great cosmologists were there in 1620?' And here, she could adopt the stage theorist's approach to local and global stages and their relations described above. But far from considering such relations to pertain to the very essence of existence and coexistence, the worm theorist should regard them as mere *perspectival restrictions* of the more fundamental relations holding among what she takes to be perduring objects—total 4D entities in the spacetime manifold. Thus she would say that, from the perspective of 1620, Kepler but not Tycho coexists with Galileo and Descartes, because the appropriate relation obtains between the 1620 stages of Kepler and Galileo but not between the latter and the 1620 stage of Tycho (there is no such stage), whereas Galileo and Descartes' common 1600 perspective includes both Kepler and Tycho. These relations are underwritten by the spacetime relations among the corresponding 4D objects populating a single neo-Newtonian 4D world. As already noted, in the end all such objects are equally 'world mates.' It normally behooves the worm theorist, but very rarely the stage theorist, to adopt the God's eye view of the universe.

To take a spatial analogy, consider a depot in the yard of a huge museum of natural science, which stations trains bearing the names of prominent cosmologists and natural philosophers (Figure 2). The tourists sitting in the middle cars of 'Descartes' and the front cars of 'Galileo' will see each other's trains and 'Kepler' between

---

[15] Cf. Sider on counting worms in §6 of his 1996 paper.

234

them (Perspective 1). (Let's pretend that the cars are made of glass or at least have sufficiently large windows to enable the tourists to see through.) One could imagine them saying, 'Look, there is "Kepler" over there. Why didn't they put "Tycho" as well? He was, after all, just as great!' The tourists in the back cars of 'Descartes' and the middle cars of 'Galileo,' on the other hand, have a better sense of historical justice: both 'Kepler' and 'Tycho' are in place (Perspective 2). But of course, the vision of the tourists is always perspectivally restricted and, hence, incomplete. To get the full sense of historical justice, one would need to take the bird's eye view of the depot.

These perspectival considerations do not seem especially important in the classical case. The news they bring—that the 1620 perspective is different from the 1600 one—is reassuring to all (the stage and worm theorists alike) but not particularly illuminating. As we shall see shortly, the situation is more complicated in the relativistic case.

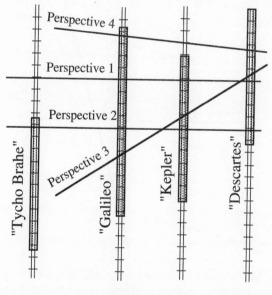

Figure 2.

4. Stages in Minkowski Spacetime

To make a transition to the relativistic case, one should first of all take care to replace the notion of temporal stage with a more general and relativistically acceptable notion of *temporal-like* stage.[16] A global temporal-like stage is simply a 3D hyperplane in spacetime. It is similar to a classical momentary global stage in that it corresponds to a particular time in a given reference frame; but it requires two separate indices for its individuation: a frame and a time in that frame. Two indices, instead of just one, as in the classical case, are needed because of the absence, in the relativistic framework, of the frame-invariant concept of time. Time by itself is not enough to identify such a stage: one has to know in what frame the time is measured.

Figure 3 features various momentary global 3D temporal-like stages in Minkowski spacetime. (Since two spatial dimensions are suppressed in this figure, the stages become 1D lines; but one should not forget that in reality, they are three-dimensional.)

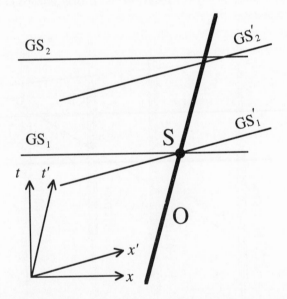

Figure 3. Momentary global stages in Minkowski spacetime. GS_1 and GS_2 correspond to times in frame (x,t) whereas GS_1' and GS_2' correspond to times in (x',t'). The local temporal-like stage S of object O belongs to both GS_1 and GS_1'.

---

[16] This term was suggested in conversation by Steve Savitt. As will become clear immediately below, a temporal-like stage is a temporal stage in a particular reference frame.

In the foregoing, we have drawn useful parallels between Lewis's possible worlds and classical global stages. Now we should note an important dissimilarity between the former and relativistic global stages construed as above. Any two Lewisian possible worlds are entirely distinct: no object can exist in more than one such world. On the contrary, any two global temporal-like stages corresponding to different frames of reference *intersect*. Consequently, a single local object can in principle belong to more than one temporal-like world—that is, to more than one global stage. In fact, unless specific restrictions are imposed on the construction of global stages from local ones, any object belongs to an infinite number of worlds.

Just like global temporal-like stages, local ones are also individuated by two indices. This becomes especially important for spatially extended objects. In Figure 4, global stages GS_1 and GS_2 contain two temporal-like stages of the planet Earth. They cut the 4D world volume of the Earth at different angles in spacetime and intersect one another along a two-dimensional circle. (Because one spatial dimension is suppressed in Figure 4, this intersection looks like a one-dimensional line.)

Such 'crisscrossing' becomes less significant for local temporal-like stages of idealized point-like objects (remember that this idealization is adopted throughout most of the paper), such as particle C

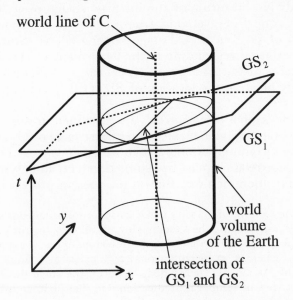

Figure 4. The Earth and its temporal-like stages in Minkowski spacetime.

at the center of the Earth (Figure 4). Its temporal-like stages could in principle be uniquely labeled by just one parameter, for example, the proper time associated with the rest frame of the particle.

5. Global Stage Sharing in Minkowski Spacetime

Let us now turn to the question of how objects can share a global stage in Minkowski spacetime. Here one should be open-minded, as it is difficult to decide in advance what form the stage mate relation must take in the relativistic framework. It is natural to assume that the intrinsic geometrical structure of Minkowski spacetime gives us more flexibility than the rather rigid and unsophisticated geometry of neo-Newtonian spacetime. Hence, it is best to be maximally unprejudiced, consider all the options available, and be prepared to let the chips fall where they may.

For the purpose of discussion, it will be convenient to begin with a non-starter. Suppose there are just two objects, O_1 and O_2. Under what conditions can O_1 share its particular stage, say S^1_1, with *some* stage of O_2? Clearly, there should be a single global stage—a single temporal-like world containing S^1_1 and some stage of O_2. And there are an infinite number of such global stages. Is any one of them distinguished? Not in virtue of the intrinsic structure of Minkowski spacetime alone. But given this structure *and* the instantaneous state of motion of O_1, one global stage hosting S^1_1 is naturally privileged—the one corresponding to the hyperplane of simultaneity in the rest frame of O_1. In Figure 5, it is GS^1_{rest}. As long as we know the velocity of O_1 at the location of S^1_1, GS^1_{rest} is uniquely determined.[17]

But if the 'global extension' of S^1_1 is defined in this way, it will not, in general, be a global extension of any stage of O_2 and, hence, will not be a common temporal-like world of O_1 and O_2. Indeed, the stage mate relation must be symmetrical, O_1 and O_2 must figure in its specification on a par. But on the present proposal, this, in a

[17] Does the concept of velocity make sense for instantaneous stages? One might think not, because the specification of velocity requires the specification of the object's positions at an infinitesimal but still extended interval of time, whereas an instantaneous stage exists at a single time (in a given frame). As already mentioned, however, the stage theory adopts a counterpart view of temporal predication. On that view, an instantaneous stage S located at position x at time t (in a particular frame) has all sorts of temporal properties, including such properties as *being at $x+dx$ at $t+dt$*. Thus an instantaneous velocity can be attributed to it.

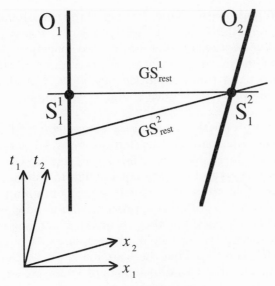

Figure 5.

great majority of cases, is impossible to satisfy. A global stage such as GS^1_{rest}, distinguished from the point of view of O_1, will not, in general, be distinguished from the viewpoint of O_2. O_1 and O_2 can share a global stage defined as above only if they are at rest with respect to each other. And such cases are extremely rare. If O_1 moves relative to O_2, the global extensions of their stages are 'at an angle' and thus no global stage can be their common stage (Figure 5). Such objects can never be stage mates and, therefore, can never populate a single temporal-like world.[18]

It is clear, on reflection, that linking global stages to the state of motion of local objects was simply a leftover of the classical view. In the classical case, two object stages shared a global stage whenever they were *co-present* to one another. And co-presence simply meant existing at the same time, the universal Newtonian time of classical physics. By abandoning this latter notion—by making time frame-dependent—special relativity prevents one from associating onto-

---

[18] A point duly appreciated by Sider (2001, §5.8) in his discussion of how to make the stage view consistent with relativity. Sider's vocabulary and agenda there are, however, rather different from mine and his proposal to relativize the truth value of tensed utterances about stages to the rest frame of the speaker is of no help in handling the ontological issues surrounding the notion of coexistence in the stage world.

logical commitments with coordinate time and simultaneity. But relativity puts something else in their place: the frame-invariant notion of *spacelike relation*, or separation. Two spacetime points are spacelike related just in case there is a reference frame in which they are simultaneous. And this existential fact is itself absolute: if it obtains in any legitimate reference frame, it obtains in every such frame.

This suggests a proposal to ground the stage mate relation in the objective relation of spacelike separation between local object stages. In Figure 5, local stages S^1_1 and S^2_1 of, respectively, O_1 and O_2 are spacelike related and that may be enough to ensure that they are stage mates—that there is a global stage containing both of them, for example, GS^1_{rest}. In this approach, a common global stage is not required to be specific to either O_1 or O_2. It can be just one of the many legitimate (i.e., spacelike) hyperplanes that could be drawn through S^1_1 and S^2_1. That there are many others can be seen as soon as one recalls that two dimensions of space are suppressed in Figure 5.

The extension of this schema to more numerous collections of object stages requires caution. Suppose there are five (or more) local stages of five (or more) objects, all pairwise spacelike related. In general, there will be no spacelike hyperplane that can be drawn through all of them. Indeed, five or more points in a four-dimensional space do not always lie on a single hyperplane.[19] But one should not infer from this that five or more objects could not in general be stage mates in Minkowski spacetime. Instead, one should adopt a more charitable approach to the (temporally-qualified) notion of coexistence in the stage ontology.

The approach just considered starts with a collection of local stages and then goes on to assert their coexistence (or the lack of it, as the case may be) in a single global stage. But there is no more reason to do things in this order in the relativistic case than in the classical case. In the latter case, we do not begin with, say, the 1620 stage of Descartes, the 1620 stage of Galileo, and the 1615 stage of Kepler, only to conclude that they do not coexist in any single temporal world. That they don't is, no doubt, good news but it is hardly enlightening. A more sensible strategy is to fix attention on a particular stage of Descartes, say his 1620 stage, and then pose the question as to what *objects* it coexists with. It coexists with Galileo and Kepler in virtue of bearing a (classical) stage mate relation to

[19] Just as four or more points in a more familiar three-dimensional space do not always lie on a single plane.

their corresponding 1620 stages, and it does not coexist with Brahe, because there is no Brahe stage in 1620. Most objects in our world come to be and cease to exist. And that is a matter of significance to us when we say that we (that is, our current stages) coexist with Bush but not with Napoleon.

Similarly, one should not be obligated to start with an arbitrary collection of stages in Minkowski spacetime, only to discover that its members could not (in virtue of the above-mentioned geometrical considerations) be stage mates. Instead, one ought to start with a particular object of interest O at a certain time t in its life career (which is none other than *proper time* intrinsic to the object and measured in its rest frame) and then pose the question as to what objects it coexists with. Other objects enter into such a relation of coexistence with O at t by having stages that bear a single many-place stage mate relation to each other and to S_t, the stage of O at t. On this approach, O at t turns out to coexist (as it should) with what we would pre-relativistically count as its 'contemporaries' and not coexist with any of its 'predecessors.'

The notion of a relativistic 'contemporary' is, of course, different from its classical counterpart. Classical contemporaries exist at the same moment of a single time, the absolute Newtonian time. No such concept is available in the relativistic framework. But there is a good substitute. Each 'contemporary' of O at t is a *certain age*, the age in question being measured by the proper time of that 'contemporary.' In the end, this enables all relativistic 'contemporaries,' including O, to enter into the relation of coexistence with each other on a par. Thus, the 30-year old Data, the 46-year old Captain James T. Kirk, and the 65-year old Captain Jean Luc Picard are 'contemporaries' of each other: their corresponding stages are stage mates. On the other hand, Klingon Trevor is the relativistic predecessor of all of them: none of his stages shares a temporal-like world with any stage of the first three (Figure 6).

Notably, the same 30-year old Data is also a 'contemporary' of the 40-year old Captain Kirk and the 55-year old Captain Picard. This is a consequence of the latitude allowed by relativistic spacetime. It may look surprising but is surely tolerable. I show below that other features of the relativistic stage mate relation are more pernicious. Before doing it, however, it may be useful to note that the relativistic account developed here gives the right result in the *classical limit*, which is surely a good sign.

The limiting property of scientific theories constitutes the gist of the *correspondence principle*, governing the relationship between an old and a new theory: the former should be (in some sense) a limit-

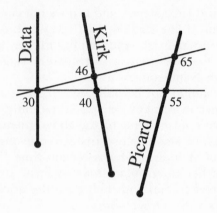

Figure 6.

ing case of the latter when the domain of application is restricted to that covered by the old theory. Thus classical mechanics is a limiting case of relativistic mechanics for velocities much smaller than the speed of light or, alternatively, in the limit $c \to \infty$. Although the validity of the correspondence principle has been called in question by the advocates of incommensurability and related ideas in the post-positivist philosophy of science, it is still used in the foundations of physics as a helpful heuristic device. (Witness recent discussions of the classical limit of different interpretations of quantum mechanics.)

Be this as it may, the classical limit of the relativistic stage mate relation is clearly the old classical relation of existing at the same moment of absolute time. Applied to Descartes and his ilk—objects moving with small relative velocities and separated by small distances—the relativistic analysis simply recovers Figure 1, in which the outsides of the light cones collapse into absolute hyperplanes of simultaneity, thereby forcing all global stages (generally inclined at various angles) to become horizontal. The latitude referred to above evaporates in this limit: Descartes in 1620 has the uniquely-aged Galileo and Kepler as his contemporaries.

6. Contextuality

We are, however, interested in precisely those features of the relativistic stage mate relation that deviate from the classical features. Some such features are unwelcome. It is now time to investigate them. Begin with *contextuality*. Object O at t (i.e., its t-stage, S_t) coexists with O_1 and with O_2 but *not* with *both*: there is no single temporal-like world containing S_t and some stages of both O_1 and with O_2 (Figure 7). One might wonder, however (and rightly so), why there *should* be such a single world, given that O_2 is in the *absolute future* of O_1. O_1 may be Captain Kirk's great-grandfather and O_2 his great-grandson. It would be rather strange for anyone to be a 'contemporary' of both.

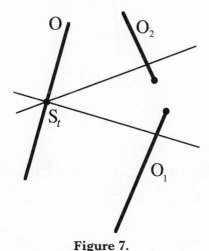

Figure 7.

But the problem is easily reproduced by separating O_1 and O_2 wide enough in space (Figure 8). There we have a situation in which O_1 *does* coexist with O_2 at a given point of its life career (some of their stages share a global stage, e.g. GS*), and O at t coexists with O_1 and O_2 but *not with both*.

In fact, a stronger result obtains. Suppose all three objects are entities that come to be and cease to exist. Then given their suitable locations in spacetime, they may coexist pairwise at *some point or other* of their life careers: all three may have stages that bear dyadic stage mate relations to each other. But this does not guarantee that they coexist *all together*. The failure of such mutual coexistence occurs in cases in which no selection of the stages of the three objects can be unified by a single triadic stage mate relation. Thus

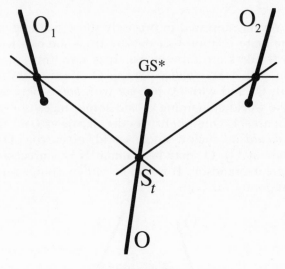

Figure 8.

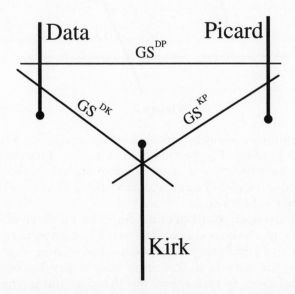

Figure 9. Kirk coexists with Data: they have stages sharing the global stage GS^{DK}. The same is true of Kirk and Picard, and of Picard and Data. But there is no single global stage containing stages of all three.

it may be the case that Data coexists with Captain Kirk, Captain Kirk coexists with Captain Picard, and the latter coexists with Data. Taken pairwise, they all share temporal-like worlds with each other. Taken all together, however, they don't share any single temporal-like world (Figure 9). The same is true of a quadruple of objects. Any three of them may coexist but this does not entail the coexistence of all four. (Considerations of space prevent me from illustrating such a case.)

This result is easily extended to more numerous collections of objects. Take a suitably situated group of n objects with finite life spans, such as Star Trek civilizations, that are all created and destroyed. Add two more such objects. It may be the case that the entire initial collection coexists with them taken separately but not with both taken together—even if those two objects, in addition, coexist with each other. A more involved case would include, say, 1000 Star Trek civilizations $C_1, \ldots C_{1000}$ and three more: C^*_1, C^*_2, and C^*_3. All members of the latter group coexist with each other and *any pair* of them coexists with all the members of the first group, $C_1, \ldots C_{1000}$. And yet, all 1003 do not coexist. (Again, I leave these cases without illustration.)

It may be interesting to find out if coexistence (that is, the temporally qualified coexistence grounded in the many-place stage mate relation) of *all n-1-tuples* of objects $O_1, O_2, \ldots O_n$ need not entail the coexistence of the entire collection. But even if this more general result does not hold, the situation is frustrating enough. Coexistence in the relativistic stage world turns out to be partitioned in a most peculiar way bearing the mark of contextuality. Facts about coexistence among members of a collection of objects, however numerous, become sensitive to what other objects are taken into account. Such facts do not 'add up' properly.

Contextuality of coexistence in the stage world should not be confused with the breakdown of transitivity. First, coexistence in a temporal-like world is a *many-place* relation, not a dyadic one. Furthermore, even if consideration is restricted to pairs of objects, contextuality and the lack of transitivity are distinct features. It is true that coexistence between members of pairs of objects in the relativistic stage world is not transitive: coexistence of O_1 with O_2 and of O_2 with O_3 does not entail coexistence of O_1 with O_3. Contextuality, on the other hand, means that coexistence between members of *all* such pairs does not entail coexistence among members of the *whole triple*, O_1, O_2 and O_3.

Why should the stage theorist be bothered by contextuality, but not so much by the lack of transitivity? One reason is that transitivity of coexistence fails even in the classical stage world. I coexist with my father (some of our stages are classical stage mates) and he coexists with my grandfather. But I don't coexist with my grandfather. But the classical relation of coexistence is free of contextuality. If my father, my grandfather, and I coexist pairwise then we coexist all together. We do not find this remarkable because we simply take it for granted. But for the stage theorist, something important is at stake here.

Indeed, stages live in stage worlds; their common world is a global stage. *That* is what they share—just as objects in Lewis's ontology share a particular possible world. In a trivial sense, the latter also share the entire collection of Lewisian worlds. But that sense is irrelevant, nothing significant turns on it. All the important features of that ontology, including the modal properties of objects, are grounded in the facts about what objects belong to what worlds. The fact that every object also belongs to the whole collection of worlds bakes no bread. Similarly, the stage theorist should take the facts about what object stage belongs to what temporal world—and what other stages it shares that world with—as the ground of all the important properties exhibited in the stage 'multi-universe.' These include the temporary properties of objects, the account of change they undergo, and the ways they interact with each other. The fact that all stages of all objects trivially share the single 'multi-universe' occupying the entire spacetime manifold is simply too coarse-grained to add anything significant to the picture.

In short, the stage theory must recognize existence in a temporal (or temporal-like) world and sharing such a world as primary categories of its ontology. But then it is natural to expect such categories to obey some reasonable 'calculus.' And they certainly do so in the classical case, where the stage mate relation is grounded in absolute simultaneity among local stages. Minkowski spacetime suggests a *bona fide* candidate to do a similar job, the relation of belonging to a single spacelike hyperplane, which adequately recovers its pre-relativistic counterpart in the classical limit and is, as we saw, partly successful. The problem with it is that it stumbles upon a simple rule that is, intuitively, part and parcel of the concept of coexistence: if A coexists with B, B coexists with C, and C coexists with A, then A must coexist with B and C.

To be sure, these considerations do not go as far as to refute the stage theory. Rather, they indicate what price this theory has to pay in the transition to relativity. And that is only part of the price. Besides being contextual, coexistence in the relativistic stage world is not well behaved chronologically.

7. Chronology

Let's start with an unproblematic case. The 30-year old Data coexists with the 35-year old Captain Kirk and the 40-year old Captain Picard: they share a common global stage GS_1. As Data grows older and reaches the age of 35, he happens to coexist with a *younger* Captain Kirk, who just turned 32, and a younger, 33-year old Captain Picard: they share a common global stage GS_2 (Figure 10).

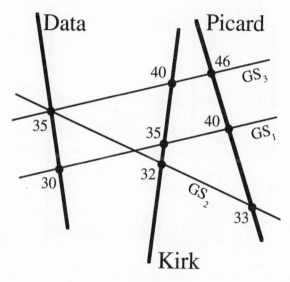

Figure 10.

This, however, is not particularly disturbing. At any moment in his life, Data belongs to an infinite number of temporal-like worlds. The fact that one can pick out a chronologically ill-behaved series of such worlds (e.g., the sequence of GS_1 and GS_2) should not be held against the stage view, as long as another, chronologically well-behaved series *is available*. And it is surely available in the case under consideration; for example, the series including GS_1 and GS_3. The latter global stage, GS_3, features the 35-year old Data, and the correspondingly older Captain Kirk and Captain Picard. One is not saddled with the unpalatable sequence of GS_1 and GS_2, because there is no reason to allow one to exploit the latitude inherent in relativistic spacetime *frivolously*, by sequencing global stages at will. The availability of chronologically well-behaved series of global stages is all that the Star Trek biographer needs to tell a sensible story about the life careers of the three famous characters and their relations to each other.

But there are cases where a chronologically well-behaved series of temporal-like worlds is *not* available and there is no escape from a disturbing conclusion that ageing results in being a contemporary of progressively younger companions. Such a case is represented in Figure 11.

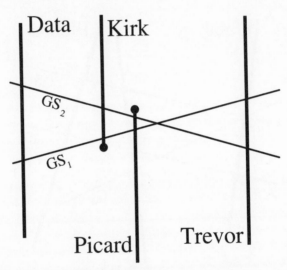

Figure 11. SG_1 and SG_2 form a sequence of global stages that is chronologically well-behaved for Data, Kirk, and Picard. But given the configuration of these objects in spacetime, any such sequence inevitably picks out progressively (or rather regressively) younger stages of Trevor.

Here the most one can do is to identify a chronologically well-behaved series of global stages including the correspondingly ageing Data, Kirk, and Picard, for example, SG_1 and SG_2. Adding Trevor to the picture, however, turns the series into a bad one. As Data, Kirk, and Picard *all* grow older, they find themselves in worlds with the younger and younger Trevor. And that is not the worst possible scenario yet. With some modifications, one could make progressively ageing Data, Kirk, and Picard *unavoidable contemporaries* of, first, Chief Trevor, next the 15-year old Cadet Trevor, then the newly born Klingon baby just named Trevor, and eventually, Trevor's great-grand-grandfather!

This is surely an unwelcome result. Along with contextuality, it brings out the difficulties of formulating the coexistence relation in the relativistic stage world.

8. Discussion

Why is the worm theory not afflicted with the same or similar problems? Because the worm ontology presupposes a different notion of coexistence. All 4D worms coexist with each other in the Minkowski world. This does not mean that one cannot pose temporally sensitive questions about the coexistence of their various parts. But the answers to them do not get at the basic sense of coexistence essential to the worm ontology. They are always restricted to a particular *perspective* in spacetime, just as the answers to similar questions were restricted to a purely temporal perspective in the classical framework.

The perspective in question is associated with a hyperplane drawn through the location of a given temporal-like part of a 4D object. Return to Figure 8 but read it differently now. The figure represents three 4D objects, O, O_1, and O_2—three full-blown spatio-temporal worms, all coexisting together in the single spacetime. These objects have parts, or stages, confined to spacetime points, and associated with each such part are infinitely many momentary perspectives on the single spacetime world. Thus the perspectives linked to the t-part of O include those containing some part of O_1 and those containing some part of O_2. As it turns out, there is no perspective containing parts of both O_1 and O_2. The t-part of O is unable to share a perspective with objects O_1 and O_2 taken together. Given an appropriate configuration of the three objects (three worms, that is), a stronger result obtains (cf. Figure 9). Taken pairwise, Data, Kirk, and Picard may share spatio-temporal perspectives with each other. Taken all together, however, they may not. But that is quite different from being unable to share a *world*. In a similar vein, being saddled with a chronologically ill-behaved series of perspectives is rather benign in a way in which being saddled with a correspondingly bad series of temporal-like worlds is not. Every such world constitutes an appropriate habitat for an object-stage, but not for an object-worm. Indeed, temporal-like worlds are something in which the objects of the stage ontology live and coexist with each other. The objects of the worm ontology, on the other hand, live and coexist in the much bigger world, the entire Minkowski spacetime. Their more fine-grained temporal characteristics are a matter of perspectivalism, not existence.

Perspectivalism of this sort should not be surprising as it is a general feature of our perception of the world. Tourists sitting in 'Descartes' can look out the window at various angles and thus get different perspectives on other trains. Some tourists see 'Kepler' between themselves and 'Galileo' (Perspective 3 in Figure 2), others don't (Perspective 4). This is anything but surprising and has nothing to do with the real existence of 'Kepler.'

We can view a house from various vantage points and take its pictures. In general, such pictures look very different; in particular, they feature different two-dimensional shapes of the whole construction and its different parts. Such representations are inevitably incomplete, because they are perspectivally restricted, and some do not 'add up.' One of them may feature the kitchen and the living room, another the kitchen and the bedroom, and the third the kitchen and the bedroom. There may be no representation featuring all three rooms together, but that is just what is to be expected. In fact, nothing could be more natural than such incompleteness and 'contextuality' inherent in spatial perspectivalism. And of course, these features have nothing to do with existence. Every one knows that the real house out there is three-dimensional, and its 3D invariant configuration, complete in every detail, stands behind all partial 2D representations.

Similarly, the objective 4D configuration of worms in the single spacetime stands behind all stage-restricted perspectives. In this sense, it may not be too far off the mark to say that worms are, after all, primary and stages secondary.

References

Balashov, Yuri 1999. 'Relativistic Objects,' *Noûs* **33** (1999): 644–62.

—— 2000a. 'Enduring and Perduring Objects in Minkowski Space-Time,' *Philosophical Studies* **99**, 129–66.

—— 2000b. 'Relativity and Persistence,' *Philosophy of Science* **67**, S549–S562.

—— 2000c. 'Persistence and Space-Time: Philosophical Lessons of the Pole and Barn,' *The Monist* **83**, 321–40.

Brogaard, Berit 2000. 'Presentist Four-Dimensionalism,' *The Monist* **83**, 341–56.

Callender, Craig 2000. 'Shedding Light on Time,' *Philosophy of Science* **67**, S587–S599.

Carter, W. R. and Hestevold, H. S. 1994. 'On Passage and Persistence,' *American Philosophical Quarterly* **31**, 269–83.

Craig, William Lane 2000. *The Tenseless Theory of Time: A Critical Examination*. Dordrecht: Kluwer.

Craig, William Lane 2001. *Time and the Metaphysics of Relativity*. Dordrecht: Kluwer.

Haslanger, Sally 1989. 'Endurance and Temporary Intrinsics,' *Analysis* **49**, 119–25.

Hawley, Katherine 2002. *How Things Persist*. Oxford: Clarendon Press.

Heller, Mark 1990. *The Ontology of Physical Objects: Four-dimensional Hunks of Matter*. Cambridge: Cambridge University Press.

Hinchliff, Mark 1996. 'The Puzzle of Change,' in J. E. Tomberlin, (ed.), *Philosophical Perspectives* 10. Oxford: Basil Blackwell, pp. 119–36.

Johnston, Mark 1987. 'Is There A Problem About Persistence?' *Proceedings of the Aristotelian Society*, Supplement **61**, 107–35.

Lewis, David 1986. *On the Plurality of Worlds*. Oxford: Blackwell.

—— 1988. 'Rearrangement of Particles: Reply to Lowe,' *Analysis* **48**, 65–72.

Lombard, Lawrence 1999. 'On the Alleged Incompatibility of Presentism and Temporal Parts,' *Philosophia* **27**, 253–60.

—— 2000. 'The Lowe Road to the Problem of Temporary Intrinsics,' presented at the Pacific Division Meetings of the APA (April 2000).

Lowe, E. J. 1988. 'The Problem of Intrinsic Change: Rejoinder to Lewis,' *Analysis* **48**, 72–77.

Markosian, Ned (forthcoming), 'A Defense of Presentism,' in Dean Zimmerman (ed.), *Oxford Studies in Metaphysics*, vol. 1.

Mellor, D. H. 1981. *Real Time*. Cambridge: Cambridge University Press.

Merricks, Trenton 1994. 'Endurance and Indiscernibility,' *Journal of Philosophy* **91**, 165–84.

—— 1995. 'On the Incompatibility of Enduring and Perduring Entities,' *Mind* **104**, 523–31.

—— 1999. 'Persistence, Parts, and Presentism,' *Noûs* **33**, 421–38.

Prior, Arthur N. 1970. 'The Notion of the Present,' *Studium Generale* **23**, 245–48.

Quine, W. V. O. 1950. 'Identity, Ostension, and Hypostasis,' *Journal of Philosophy* **47**, 621–33.

—— 1987. 'Space-Time,' in *Quiddities*. Cambridge, MA: Harvard University Press, pp. 196–199.

Rea, Michael 1998. 'Temporal Parts Unmotivated,' *The Philosophical Review* **107**, 225–60.

Saunders, Simon (forthcoming), 'Why Relativity is Contrary to Presentism,' in Craig Callender (ed.), *Time, Reality, and Experience*. Cambridge: Cambridge University Press.

Savitt, Steven 2000. 'There's No Time Like the Present (in Minkowski Spacetime),' *Philosophy of Science* **67**, S563–S574.

Sider, Theodore 1996. 'All the World's a Stage,' *The Australasian Journal of Philosophy* **74**, 433–53.

—— 2000. 'The Stage View and Temporary Intrinsics,' *Analysis* **60**, 84–88.

—— 2001. *Four-Dimensionalism. An Ontology of Persistence and Time*. Oxford: Clarendon Press.

Yuri Balashov

Taylor, Richard 1955. 'Spatial and Temporal Analogies and the Concept of Identity,' *The Journal of Philosophy* **52**, 599–612.
Van Inwagen, Peter 1981. 'The Doctrine of Arbitrary Undetached Parts,' *Pacific Philosophical Quarterly* **62**, 123–37.
—— 1990. 'Four-dimensional Objects,' *Noûs* **24**, 245–55.
Zimmerman, Dean (1998. 'Temporary Intrinsics and Presentism,' in Peter van Inwagen and Dean Zimmerman, (eds), *Metaphysics: The Big Questions*. Oxford: Blackwell, pp. 206–19.

On Becoming, Cosmic Time and Rotating Universes[1]

MAURO DORATO

Abstract

In the literature on the compatibility between the time of our experience and the time of physics, the special theory of relativity has enjoyed central stage. By bringing into the discussion the general theory of relativity, I suggest a new analysis of the misunderstood notion of becoming, developed from hints in Gödel's published and unpublished arguments for the ideality of time. I claim that recent endorsements of such arguments, based on Gödel's own 'rotating' solution to Einstein's field equation, fail: once understood in the right way, becoming can be shown to be both mind-independent and compatible with spacetime physics. Being a needed *tertium quid* between views of time traditionally regarded as in conflict, such a new approach to becoming should also help to dissolve a crucial aspect of the century-old debate between the so-called A and B theories of time.

1. Introduction: the shift from STR to GTR and the centrality of becoming

In the literature on the relationship between the time of our experience and the time of physics, the special theory of relativity (STR) has curiously but undoubtedly played a major role. On the assumptions that

(i)   becoming (the 'flow of time') is the essential feature of experienced time;

[1] I thank J. Butterfield, C. Callender, R. Clifton, J. Faye, M. Piazza and the audience at LSE and Vancouver for helpful comments and suggestions on previous drafts of this paper. S. Savitt deserves a special mention, for our frequent exchange via e-mail helped me to formulate my views in a clearer way. Despite some criticism that here I raise to his previous, thought-provoking work, he has now independently come to defend views about temporal becoming that are very close to mine, as is evident from the paper in this collection.

253

Mauro Dorato

(ii) *objective* (i.e. *mind-independent*) becoming presupposes an *ontological* difference between *present* and *future* events or state of affairs;

(iii) the geometrical structure presupposed by STR is a necessary constraint that physical time in general must meet,

a solution to the problem of the definability of becoming in Minkowski spacetime has also been regarded as the main way to solve the question of the compatibility between the time of physics and the time of our experience.[2]

However, while (i) and (ii) above can be regarded as plausible, (iii) should strike us as suspicious, especially when it is used to claim that *if* Minkowski spacetime cannot make room for any sort of 'ontological difference' mentioned in (ii), *then* becoming must be considered to be mind-dependent. An endorsement of the truth of the antecedent of this conditional is usually assumed to have consequences also for the *philosophy* of time one should adopt. For instance, to the extent that a commitment to a mind-independent becoming is regarded as the *essential* tenet of the so-called *A* (or 'dynamic') theories of time, those of their *B* ('static') rivals that treat past, present and future events as being *ontologically on a par* would be vindicated by the geometrical requirements of Minkowski spacetime.[3] On the contrary, if some sort of primitive relation of becoming—appropriately *relativized* to points or worldlines—could be defined in terms of the structure of Minkowski spacetime, the compatibility between becoming and STR would be demonstrated, and no choice between the *A* and the *B* theories of time would be possible only on the basis of physics.

To an unbiased reader, however, such an exclusive worry with STR should appear as puzzling, and in need of a justification. True enough, Minkowski spacetime is the standard, flat spatiotemporal arena for contemporary quantum field theories. However, since in the presence of gravitating matter STR does *not* yield an accurate description of physical reality, *it cannot be viewed*—as (iii) obviously

---

[2] See Rietdijk [1966], Putnam [1967], Stein [1968, 1991], Weingard [1972], Godfrey-Smith [1979], Maxwell [1985], Dieks [1988], Clifton and Hogarth [1995], Dorato [1996, 2000], Rakic [1997], Tooley [1997], and Savitt [2000] among others.

[3] For a recent survey on the debate between the A and the B theories of time—whose formulation dates back to McTaggart [1908]—see Le Poidevin [1998]. For reasons that will become clear in the following, rather than referring to the debate by using the misleading terms 'tensed' and 'tenseless' theories of time, I prefer the more neutral 'A' and 'B' theories of time.

presupposes—as a *fundamental physical theory*. Considering that within the general theory of relativity (GTR), STR has only a '*tangential*' *validity*,[4] why should we assume that the properties of time that are characteristic of the latter theory also apply to the former? *More generally, why should we assume that time has the* same *properties across different physical theories?*

Notably, Weyl [1918, p. 220], Eddington [1920, p. 163], Jeans [1936] and Gödel [1949a] were all aware of the fact that the special relativistic limitations *vis à vis* the absence of a *distinguished, global time order* can be regarded as a 'local phenomenon'. In fact, the presence and the actual distribution of matter in the large-scale structure of the universe may «largely destroy the equivalence of different observers, and distinguish some of them from the rest, namely those which follow in their motion the mean motion of matter» (Gödel [1949a, p. 559/1990, p. 204]). Unfortunately, in much of the recent literature such an important point seems to have been lost.[5] One of the main aims of this paper is to redress the balance, by relocating the discussion about becoming and physical time in the more appropriate context of GTR and of cosmological models in general.[6]

Besides having being too absorbed by the infinitesimal, 'tangential' features of Riemannian spacetimes, I think it is fair to add that the philosophical literature has never yielded a clear and convincing analysis of the rather obscure notion of becoming, something which has contributed to generate a widespread—but, in my opinion, totally ungrounded—belief in the incompatibility between the time of physics and the time of our experience. Such an obscurity has also affected the formulations of the two major theories that have divided the analytic 20th century philosophy of time. As it is should be clear from the above presentation, I take it that the real contention between the 'A' and the 'B' theories of time does *not* concern

---

[4] The pun of 'tangential' refers to the validity of STR in planes that are tangent to each point of a Riemannian manifold of GTR. The pun is in Savitt [2000].

[5] Saunders [1996] offers a brief discussion of cosmic time in the context of Gödel's argument, and defends a relational view of tenses with which this paper is in complete agreement, though he would probably disagree with the view of becoming presented here. Yourgrau's [1991], Savitt's [1994] and Earman's [1995] contributions will be discussed below.

[6] Of course, GTR might end up being a phenomenological, derived theory as well. However, until a reasonably agreed upon quantum theory of gravity is available, we can assume that GTR *is* a fundamental physical theory.

Mauro Dorato

the truth conditions of tensed sentences (as Faye [1989] and Mellor [1998] have it), or the relational *versus* the monadic nature of tenses (as Horwich [1987] among others has it). In spite of the obvious importance of these questions, in the following I will take for granted that the crucial, still open rift between the two camps concerns *the nature of change and the mind-independence of becoming.*[7] Especially within the recent attempts at grounding a quantum theory of gravity, time seems to have lost the independence it had acquired with respect to change in the complex historical path that led from Plato to Newton (see Smith [2000, p. 928–9]), and today it seems appropriate to regard the notion of time as being inextricably linked to that of change.

Given the importance of a correct understanding of becoming for this project, I plan to begin by proposing a new analysis of such a notion, to be regarded, on the wake of Gödel [1949a], simply as the *successive occurrence* (coming into being) *of tenselessly conceived facts or events* (§2). Armed with such a much needed *tertium quid* between the traditional ontological requirements of the A and the B theories of time, I will then show that *both* Gödel's argument against the reality of time based on his famous 'rotating universes', *and* its recent endorsement by Savitt [1994], *fail* (§3 and §4). Despite the fact that physics in principle cannot yield a *sufficient* condition for the *tenseless coming into being of events at instants of cosmic time* which becoming consists in, I claim that the cosmological model currently adopted by physicists is completely consistent with it and with the requirements of experiential time, once the latter has been correctly explicated. Finally, by showing that my explication of becoming is faithful to our pre-theoretical intuitions about it and does not run into notorious paradoxes entailed by 'the moving now', I conclude with a simple argument in favour of its objectivity (§5).

2. The nature of becoming and Gödel's argument for the ideality of time

Gödel's argument against the reality of time, which appeared in Schilpp's volume in honour of Einstein (Gödel [1949a]), is based on

---

[7] Here I follow Tooley [1997], who has convincingly argued that granting (as I do) (1) that the truth-conditions of tensed sentences are given by tenseless sentences and (2) that tenses are relations, does not yet solve the problem of becoming and of the ontological status of future events, which is what I am after here.

the discovery of a new solution to Einstein's field equation, notoriously encompassing the existence of *closed timelike curves* (Gödel [1949b]). The argument is important not only for the conclusion it—unsuccessfully, as we will see—tries to support, but much more for the brilliant analysis of controversial philosophical notions that it provides; from this point of view, it has certainly *not* received the attention it deserves.[8] Besides Yourgrau's pioneering work on Gödel's philosophy of time [1991, 1999], which had the great merit of taking into account also Gödel's unpublished material, there are as of now *two* conflicting reconstructions of Gödel's argument for the ideality of time, Savitt's [1994] which endorses it, and Earman's [1995, pp. 194–200], which rejects it, and somehow considers it unworthy of much attention.

Part of the neglect of this argument in comparison to the question of time travel, also raised by Gödel's model, can be explained by the fact that Gödel's argument is incomplete and 'gappy' to say the least, as it appears to be centred around the cryptic claim that *since there is no objective lapse of time in his rotating universe, there is no objective lapse of time in our world either*, the main difference between the two models depending only on the way matter is *contingently* distributed and moves. More specifically, in our universe, unlike Gödel's, matter is not everywhere rotating (as Gödel put it, «the compass of inertia does *not* rotate around galactic matter»), *though the physical laws given by Einstein's equations are the same*, as Gödel's model satisfies them. Interestingly, Gödel discovered that the lack of rotation is sufficient to define a global temporal order (see Malament [1995, p. 263]), since the congruence of worldlines of matter corresponding to the major mass points of the universe can be compared to the strands or the fibres of a rope representing spacetime. Absence of twisting, which corresponds to null rotation, is sufficient to slice through the rope with a plane which is orthogonal to every fibre of the rope and *the collection of all such planes is called 'cosmic time'*.

To philosophers of space and time, it is indeed reassuring to find out that Gödel's interest in general relativity was *philosophical* in origin, as his mathematical work on time «was spurred by his interest in Kant's philosophy of space and time rather than by his frequent talks with Einstein», which in any case began only in 1942 (Wang [1995], p. 216). In fact, in his 'Lecture on rotating universes' [1990, p. 274], Gödel himself tells us that he was motivated to find

---

[8] Though Stein [1970] had already stressed its philosophical significance.

Mauro Dorato

his new 'rotating solutions' to Einstein's field equation to rebut an argument due to Jeans [1936], in which it is maintained that the general theory of relativity has re-established the possibility of an 'objective lapse of time'.[9]

In order to thoroughly understand the argument I am about to present below, two terminological points are appropriate. First, it is important to keep in mind that the notion of change that Gödel introduces in the argument is *at variance* with much of the analytic tradition in the philosophy of time, since it requires *an objective coming into existence of facts or events* (this coming into existence he calls: 'the lapse of time'). While within such a tradition *change* presupposes just the possession of two incompatible properties exemplified by the same *perduring* entity at two different times, Gödel's notion of change is tantamount to an objective coming into being, and is to be regarded as an *essential* feature of the time of our experience. In a passage in the manuscript B2, where Gödel summarizes the result of his investigation into the structure of time in STR [1995, p. 236], he writes «what remains of time in (special) relativity theory as an objective reality inherent in the things neither has the structure of a linear ordering nor the character of flowing or allowing of change. Something of this kind, however, *can hardly be called time* (my italics)». In other words, according to Gödel, *time is real only if both a linear ordering and an objective lapse exist independently of observers.*

The second remark is that in the published piece [1949a], he defends also the converse claim that change presupposes an objective lapse of time. These two claims together imply that time is real *if and only if* a change in the existing is real. This equivalence eliminates the charge of circularity in the first three premises of the argument below, and justifies in particular its first premise (0), which in the published paper has no textual support, but is obviously assumed for the sake of the conclusion about the ideality of time.

Whenever possible, each premise of the argument—whose reconstruction owes much to both Earman's and Savitt's—is supported by textual quotations from Gödel's published work [1949a]. Partial conclusions deduced from previous premises are in bold types:

---

[9] The English word used by Gödel, 'lapse' comes from the Latin *labi*, which means to flow. So lapse of time is equivalent to flow of time, in the way to be clarified below.

GÖDEL'S ARGUMENT AGAINST THE REALITY OF TIME

Part I

(0) Time is real only if change is real.

(1) Change is real only if there exists an objective lapse of time. «change becomes possible only through the lapse of time» (1949a, p. 558/1990, p. 202)

(2) Time is real only if there exists an objective lapse of time [from (0) and (1)]

(3) «The existence of an objective lapse of time means or at least is equivalent to the fact, that reality consists of an infinity of layers of 'now' which come into existence successively» (1949a, p. 558/1990, p. 202).

(4) Reality consist of an infinity of layers of 'now' which come into existence successively only if spacetime admits of a global time function (*cosmic time*).

(5) Time is real only if spacetime admits of a global time function [from (2), (3) (4)]

(6) Gödel's rotating-model M, *qua* solution to Einstein's field equations, is a physically *possible* model, and despite the presence of closed timelike curves (circular time) and looming grandfather paradoxes, cannot be ruled out *a priori*.

(7) Since for every x in M, x chronologically precedes itself, M does not possess a global time function.

(8) In the physically possible world M, time is ideal [from (5) (6) (7)]

Part II

(9) The main, contingent, non-lawlike difference between M and our universe is given by the (probable) absence of a net rotation of matter, which implies the existence of cosmic time in our world

(10) ?

(C) Time in ideal also in our universe

Two obvious questions must be answered in order to see whether Kant's theory of an ideal (transcendental) time is really vindicated by Gödel's rotating universes, as the Austrian logician had it: (i) is the first part of the argument valid? (ii) if it is, how do we bring its

Mauro Dorato

conclusion to bear on the status of time in *our* universe, which does not seem to show any rotation of the kind required by Gödel's model (the second part of the argument)? The second question is clearly linked to the problem of filling the premise (10).

3 The first part of Gödel's argument

The unanimous opinion of commentators is in favour of the conclusion of part I of the argument, which proves that in Gödel's universe time is ideal, or mind-dependent. However, some of the premises in my reconstruction, which differs from Savitt's and Earman's, might be regarded as controversial.

For instance, and firstly, it could be objected that (1)—and therefore (2)—are not plausible, as they imply the dubious theory of an *absolute change in what exists*, rather than an ordinary, *qualitative* change *of* what already (tenselessly) exists, as in 'the party *became* boring' or 'the traffic light became red'. *Absolute change* in this sense is what Gödel called 'a change *in the existing*', already distinguished from *qualitative change* by C. D. Broad long ago: «To 'become present' is, in fact, just to 'become', in an absolute sense; i.e., to 'come to pass' in the Biblical phraseology, or, most simply, to 'happen'. Sentences like 'This water became hot' or 'This noise became louder' record facts of qualitative *change*. Sentences like 'This event became present' record facts of 'absolute becoming'» [Broad 1938, p. 280]. To counter this first objection to Gödel, it is then important to keep in mind that 'change' as used in premise (0) refers to *absolute* change (absolute becoming) in Broad's sense, to be carefully distinguished from a *qualitative* change of events losing the (pseudo-attribute of) 'being future' and becoming present.

Secondly, it might be objected that (2) implies the dubious 'moving now' conception of time (see Earman [1995] and Savitt [1994, p. 468]), since it is always possible to ask 'how fast does the absolute change in what exists occur?' However, as anticipated earlier, I argue that the claim that instantaneously conceived events (or facts) 'come into existence' at a certain time (the 'objective lapse of time' in the above argument) is simply equivalent to the claim that *they mind-independently occur at that time*. Consequently, Gödel's locution 'events come into existence successively' should really be read simply as 'events *(mind-independently) take place one after the other at their time of occurrence*'.

In a word, as I interpret it, the objective lapse of time or the '*change the existing*' referred to by Gödel amounts to the rather non-metaphysical, almost self-evident claim that if 'event E occurs (or, equivalently, tenselessly exists) at time t', at a later or earlier time t'', other events occur (exist)[10]. This means that, at time t', the set of existing events includes events *other than* those existing at t''. With this stipulation, our language regimented in a logical way would have a domain of quantification for each time, containing only those entities that then exist.

To come now to the charge that an objective coming into being, or the 'flow (lapse) of time' as it is interpreted here, implies the fallacious 'moving now', note that one could simply point out that the absolute change in what exists is no ordinary change, and as such, *it does not conceptually depend* on other notions as the latter does.[11] The reason why it is *simply meaningless* to ask 'how fast does such a change in the existing occur?' is given by the fact that the notions that are synonymous of becoming or 'coming into existence', namely 'occurring' or 'happening', *are not further analysable*; in any case, they don't presupposes a perduring entity and a pair of incompatible properties possessed by the same entity at different times as the qualitative notion of change does. It is only in the ordinary sense of change—the qualitative change of, say, a *piece of iron* becoming *rusted*—that one can talk about *the rate* of change, since any change *in* time can be slow or fast (a slow aging or rusting, a fast aging or rusting). Of a change *of* time, one cannot even say that *it occurs*— though it can be regarded it as a feature of the universe quite independent of our minds—since, *strictly speaking*, it is only events that can occur at times, and their succeeding one another at different times is *not* an event, if the latter is defined as an instantaneous entity as is customary in relativity.

A third objection a tenseless theorist of time might have against (1) above is that it ignores the tenseless aspect of time. According to the tenseless theorist, events are mind-independently *before* one another, even though they *are given in block*, because they don't become, or don't come into being or cease to exist (*the block universe*). In a word, for certain B theorists like Mellor and Faye, tenseless temporal relations—and therefore, in a sense, time—are real even if the lapse of time usually advocated by the A camp (i.e., the coming into existence of events) is mind-dependent, so that (2) is false.

---

[10] 'Exist' here is meant in a tenseless sense, given by 'existing at a time'.

[11] This is the line also taken by Savitt in his contribution to this volume. As a matter of fact, we arrived independently at the importance of carefully distinguishing *absolute* change from ordinary qualitative change in Broad's sense.

Mauro Dorato

As a reply to this third criticism, note that even if we changed (2) above by requiring that

(2)′ Time is real only if the distinction between before and after is mind-independent (objective),

a tenseless theorist would still have a harsh destiny in M. Given the existence of closed timelike curves for any point of Gödel's spacetime, an observer whose spatiotemporal carrier coincided with a segment of such curves would have no justification for claiming that *beforeness or afterness* is mind-independent. Events of type E that she would experience as being before events F, on a closed timelike curve would also be such that F is before E, so that, in such a Gödelian world, *temporal betweenness* would seem the only objective relation «inhering in events». Consequently, as Kant had it, in Gödel's universe it would be plausible to assume that time as we experience it emerges from the relation of our faculty of perception with the «things in themselves», which established the conclusion of the first part of the argument.

In order to give further arguments in favour of premise (2), it is of paramount importance to keep in mind that when Gödel refers to 'time', he always means 'the time of our experience', or «what everybody understood by time before relativity theory existed» (1990, manuscript C1, p. 247). In particular, this implies that, in any case, premise (1)—and (2)—*do not purport to say something about physical time or the metaphysics of time in general, but only about mental, experienced time.* Considering that the overarching purpose of Gödel's paper is to re-evaluate Kant's theory of time and show that it is not only compatible with relativity but even vindicated by it— as is also clear from the opening paragraphs of the two manuscripts preceding [1949a]—premise (1) needs no justification from the moving-now conception of time, as Earman speculates [1995, p.199]. Premise (1) is assumed only to prove that if spacetime does not make room for a necessary condition for *objective* (mind-independent) coming into being, namely cosmic time, Kant's thesis about the ideality of time would be correct, *against the prevailing opinion of 20th century philosophers of space and time.*[12]

---

[12] 'Prevailing', however, does not mean all: witness the contemporary theoretical physicist Rovelli, and the way he concludes his overview of the problem of time in quantum gravity: «If *time* is the order of the changes in the states of the systems, and if the state of a system is a relational notion, one that has meaning only if referred to an observer, can there be time outside the observer/observed relation? Is perhaps time precisely what emerges from this observer/observed relation? Is time precisely such a relation?». Rovelli [1997, p. 217].

On Becoming Cosmic Time and Rotating Universes

A fourth controversial point of the first part of Gödel's argument might concern the condition of *globality*: one could object that in the spacetime of general relativity, such a condition may not be necessary to the existence of a lapse of time, and therefore question premise (4) above. One could conceive a local, mind-independent coming into being along single worldlines also in a Gödelian universe, not matched by analogous phenomena at a cosmic scale. Likewise, the absence of an invariant, global time order in STR could be compensated by a worldline-dependent becoming, as is proposed by Clifton and Hogarth [1995].

In the same fashion, for example, Boltzmann thought that the universe could be in a global state of thermal equilibrium, while some regions, large as a cluster of galaxies, could be characterized by gigantic, rare fluctuations, due to which, for some billions of years, observers would reckon an increase of entropy, and therefore some sort of objectively irreversible phenomena (Boltzmann [1896-98/1964]). Would we deny that entropy grows in those regions simply because at a larger scale, both spatially and temporally, the universe is in equilibrium? I doubt it. But then, why can't we say that some sort of local becoming takes place in a mind-independent way?

Gödel would probably object that by admitting a local coming into being, where 'local' here has the same sense it had in Boltzman's 'pockets of increasing entropy lasting for eons', we would make a change in the existing—the lapse of time—*relative* to particular worldlines, i.e., to *some possible observers* living in a galaxy. And then, he would add: «The concept of existence (...) cannot be relativized without destroying its meaning completely» [1949a 559/1990, 223, fn. 5].

However, note that if we cannot relativize the concept of existence, an examination of the impact of the special and the general theory of relativity on our ordinary notion of time would be meaningless since, *independently of relativistic considerations*, such a relativization is implicit in the very idea of a lapse of time even according to Gödel. In our experience, as he wrote, *we often assert of the same event that «it exists and it does not exist, at two different instants of time»*. Furthermore, without such a relativization, we would be subject to some form of McTaggart's paradox about events being present (existent) and non-present (non existent) *at the same time*. These remarks are of paramount importance, since not only do they entail that a relativization of tenses is necessary, but also that it does not lead us to a view of becoming that is too deflated to be worth having (see Callender [1997, p.118]). Elsewhere (Dorato [1995]), I

263

have argued that there cannot be a *future* event in an absolute sense, since an event can count as future only relatively to some present event or other, and human existence appears always temporally located and perspectival, that is, experienced at each instant of time from the perspective offered by that instant. Here, let it suffice to say that, beyond the possibility it offers of re-establishing a compatibility with physical time, the main reason why one wants to defend such a perspectival, relational understanding of existence in time is that without it we could not make room and explain our capacity to literally *bring about a future event* by acting in the present: 'making things happen' presupposes that events that are yet to occur and are brought about by our efforts do not (tenselessly) exist relatively to the moment of action. If they did, our action and our experience of passage would be both illusory, and utterly unexplainable.

Granting the possibility of relativizing the concept of existence in this sense, a much more plausible defence of the condition of globality is that, by rejecting it at least in the context of Gödels's spacetime, we would make the lapse of time non-intersubjectively valid: «in whatever way one may assume time to be lapsing there will always exist possible observers to whose experienced lapse of time no objective lapse corresponds (in particular possible observers whose whole existence objectively would be simultaneous)» (Gödel 1949a 561/ 1990, 205-6). Gödel here refers to hypothetical observers O_1, whose worldlines lie *beyond* a certain critical point P of his spacetime model, characterized by the fact that the light cones at P are *tangent* to the hyperplane of simultaneity determined by those observers (call them O) that are located in the conventionally chosen axis of rotation of Gödel's universe. Since, beyond P, O_1's closed *worldlines belong to a hypersurface of simultaneity* determined by O, O_1's *whole* existence along the circular time-like curve would be simultaneous *with a particular instant* in O's existence.[13] In view of this peculiarity of Gödel's spacetime, I take that in the context of the argument under discussion it is plausible to grant Gödel's implicit condition of globality, in such a way that an objective lapse of time must be a lapse for all *possible* observers (worldlines) of the spacetime. In a word, making a reasonable 'equation' between a possible observer and a worldline, within Gödel's cosmological model the *objectivity of becoming must imply its intersubjective validity*.

We can therefore conclude that if we lived in Gödel's universe,

---

[13] For a vivid representation of this situation, I refer the reader to the picture in Malament [1985]. See also Savitt [1994, note 10].

we should be Kantian about time, since both the difference between earlier and later and that between present and future would be mind-dependent.

4 The second part of Gödel's argument: why the epistemic defence fails

How does the valid conclusion of the first argument impinge on the way we should understand time in *our* universe, where the distribution of matter is different? There are two possible interpretations of Gödel's argument, an *epistemic* one and a *metaphysical-modal* one, pointing to the necessary grounding of cosmic time in the laws of nature. Here I will limit myself to the former interpretation, which is essentially due to Yourgrau [1991] and Savitt [1994]. Not only is this choice motivated by the fact that it has generated more discussion than the latter, but also by the remark that the metaphysical interpretation has unanimously been regarded as being extremely difficult to justify.

Suppose, with Savitt [1994], that in a physically possible Gödelian model, there are inhabitants like ourselves measuring a *local time* t_L in the local «compass of inertia», in such a way that whenever x temporally precedes y *for any two events* in the galaxy where the Gödelians live, $t_L(x) < t_L(y)$. Then it could be argued that the direct experience of time of the Gödelians is exactly like ours. On the basis of this remark, Savitt has thus reconstructed Gödel's reasoning:

(10) it is possible to have direct experience of time just like ours in a universe in which (as in M) there is no objective lapse of time;   [recall (8)]

(11) such an experience provides the *only* reason to suppose that there is an objective lapse of time in our universe;

(12) **«our direct experience of time provides no reason to suppose that there is an objective lapse of time in our universe»**   [from 10 and 11]

(13) **«Since there is no objective lapse of time in M, there is *no reason* to suppose that there is an objective lapse of time in our universe»** (Savitt [1994, p. 468]).
[from 8 and 12]

This reconstruction has the undeniable merit of being faithful to the text, as it is probably spells out what Gödel had in mind when

Mauro Dorato

he wrote: «if the experience of time can exist without an objective lapse of time, no reason can be given why an objective lapse of time should be assumed at all.» (Gödel [1949a, p. 561/1990, pp. 205–206]).

Such an epistemic interpretation of Gödel's argument had already been anticipated, somewhat more concisely but less perspicuously, by Palle Yourgrau: «Since the actual world is lawlike compossible with the Gödel universe, it follows that our direct experience of time is *compatible* with its ideality (assuming with Gödel, its ideality in the Gödel universe). But if even *direct experience* is inadequate to establish the existence of intuitive time—that is, not merely (relativistic) causal or cosmic time, but genuine, successive time that lapses or passes—*then nothing further* will suffice» (Yourgrau [1991, p. 53]). In a word, Yourgrau-Savitt's *epistemic* argument weakens Gödel's attempted conclusion, as it amounts to *shifting the burden* of proof to the defenders of the reality of the time of our experience.

The latest attempt at an evaluation of the gist of this argument is Earman's, who, in the appendix to the chapter 6 of his [1995], examines Yourgrau's version as is reported above and rejects it—he does not discuss Savitt [1994], as the paper was probably in press. Earman tells us that «*apart from our experience, we have all sorts of evidence that lend strong support to the inference that we do not inhabit a Gödel type universe, but rather a universe that fulfills all of the geometrical conditions necessary for an objective lapse of time.*» [1995, p. 199].

Unfortunately, it seems to me that Earman has misconstrued Gödel's argument and Yourgrau's main point. The crux of Gödel's argument is *not* that our scientifically tutored experience, together with inferences to theoretical structures, *does not suffice* to establish that we live in a universe endowed with *cosmic time*, as Earman seems to have it. Rather, Gödel's point, as correctly reconstructed by Yourgrau and Savitt, is that after the discovery of the rotating solutions to Einstein's field equation, *our experience alone* (without the help of independent arguments) *is not sufficient for objective becoming, i.e., for establishing the existence of a mind-independent lapse of time.* Since in the quotation above Earman himself explicitly recognizes that cosmic time would be a merely *necessary* condition for an objective lapse of time, he cannot be interpreted as denying premise (11) above, namely that we have independent evidence for becoming *because* we have scientific evidence (as we do) for the existence of cosmic time. Consequently, if a realist about time and becoming wants to attack Gödel's argument, she must pick up Savitt's challenge, and discuss his two premises, namely (10) and (11).

Starting with the former, could the experience of the Gödelians be identical to ours? If we grant this point, obviously we deny that there exists a *necessary* link between what we experience and the structure of objective, cosmic time also in the *actual* world, and it may seem that Savitt's premise, to a certain extent, simply *begs the question*. The point, however, is not that such a premise is question begging, but rather that *since* the logical and physical possibility of time travel is needed by Savitt for Gödel's universe not to be ruled out *a priori*, it is certainly available to an antikantian (a realist about time) to claim that *it is at least physically possible* that the experience of time of the 'Gödelians' be very much *unlike* ours.[14]

Savitt might perhaps defend his premise by invoking well-known technological difficulties entailed by time travel. Observers living in Gödel spacetime would presumably share our technological problems concerning the amount of acceleration and fuel needed to voyage into the past (Malament [1985]), and would not *actually* be travelling into the past, though it would be *physically possible* for them to do so. Moreover, we have to keep in mind that Savitt's premise (10) merely relies on the *physical possibility of their experiencing time exactly as we do, and this point is not touched by the mere possibility of time travel.*

If time travel in this context is a red herring, there is another difficulty that stands in the way of our accepting (10): to say that it physically possible for local observers living in Gödel's spacetime to experience time as we do implies that it is physically possible for such observers *to fail to see any trace of the future.* This is highly doubtful, however, since it is certainly physically possible for them *not* to be screened off from causes that are *later* than their effects, exactly because they live in a universe in each point of which a closed timelike curve can always be found! One can even argue that in Gödel spacetime *there must be traces of the future*, since even if the Gödelians' psychological arrow is directed along one direction of time, and that direction is picked out as *the* direction of time, some later events along that direction will have to be regarded as indirectly causing events in the observers' present. So, especially if such observers live along timelike 'loops' whose diameter is not very large,[15] we can conclude that their experience of time would be relevantly different from *ours*, and Savitt's basic premise would

[14] Of course, Savitt acknowledges that after a bit of scientific development, the gödelians might discover that there is no cosmic time in their universe, i.e., no necessary structure for the existence of an *objective* lapse of time [1994, p. 467].

[15] This remark was raised by Joos Uffink during the discussion of the paper.

have to be abandoned. At this point, he might retort that for observers living on very large causal loops, causes that are later than their effects would be very improbable, and the technological difficulties of travelling into the past might just make their experience indistinguishable from ours.

Leaving to the reader the difficult task of judging who is going to score on this uncertain point, let me strengthen my objection to Savitt's argument by considering that also premise (11) is debatable: is our 'direct experience of time' the only argument to believe in the objectivity of the lapse of time? Clearly, an evaluation of this claim depends on how to understand 'our experience of time', in particular the ambiguous and vague word 'experience'. If Savitt means to claim that no argument in defence of an objective coming into existence is ever likely to come from physics ('experience' meant in a very wide sense, encompassing scientific knowledge), I think we must agree, because cosmic time cannot be regarded as *sufficient* for objective becoming. Furthermore, it is certainly not among physics' aims to yield a distinction between physical systems or entities that are *actual* at a certain time and systems that are merely *possible*, and precisely this distinction is needed for becoming. Consequently, in his argument 'experience' must mean 'scientifically untutored experience'. However, even in this restricted sense, 'experience' can have two interpretations, a *broad* and a *narrow* one.

In a broad sense, one could refer to 'experience' as it is coded in ordinary language, particularly in those concepts—possibly *a priori* for the individual but *a posteriori* for the species—that have been acquired during our evolutionary history and that are tested, say, in experiments within the so-called *naive physics*. These 'concepts' (time included) must possess some sort of *adaptive value*, in the sense that they must enable us to cope with the environment in a successful way, despite their approximation and possible lack of precision for purposes of the scientific description of the world. If we interpret 'experience' in such a *broad evolutionary, not purely psychological, sense*, we may even grant Savitt's premise (11), by remarking at the same time that the adaptive value of our naive concepts of 'object' and 'property' may justify some sort of general, defeasible 'folk realism', telling us that such objects and their properties are *prima facie* real. Rather than calling into question and 'eliminate' what Sellars [1962] used to call 'the manifest image' (the world of our experience), we may temporarily adopt its ontology, *until conflicts with the 'scientific image' force us to abandon it.* On this hypothesis, however, why doubt that there is something mind-independent that our experience of time is about, *if in our model of the universe no scientific fact is in direct conflict with it*? In *our* universe, unlike *Gödel's*, one *can* be a folk realist about becoming *since a necessary condition for it—cosmic time—*is indeed *satisfied*. In this line of argument, rather than arguing directly for the reliability of our experience of time, one could begin by defending, indirectly, some sort of folk realism, which would then support in a non-ad-hoc way also our 'natural belief' in objective becoming, once conflicts with known physical theories are shown to be absent.

If, on the other hand, 'experience' is given a *narrower, purely psychological* reading, isn't it quite hazardous to deny, at the present moment, that *any future philosophical* arguments constructed to prove the reality of the lapse of time must fail? For instance, Tooley [1997] has recently given an important argument in favour of the unreality of the future based on causation, not on our 'psychological' experience. How can we exclude that forthcoming and more sophisticated arguments will succeed without calling into question our mental set-ups?

In sum, I don't mean to suggest that Savitt's reconstruction of Gödel's argument is not interesting and persuasive, but only that it is *not conclusive* to establish the mind-dependence of becoming or the ideality of time in the sense of Kant. In the remainder of the paper, I will pick up Savitt's challenge (recall the shift of the burden of proof) by defending the mind-independence of a somewhat 'deflated', minimalist and *tenseless* notion of becoming, which concerns our experience only in the broader, non-psychological sense mentioned above. As we are about to see, such a notion is nevertheless a satisfactory explication of our intuitive notion of time

5. Becoming as real occurrence of events and facts

My suggestion is to explicate, or rather simply *equate* becoming with the notion of 'taking place' or 'occurring', which is also the natural way to understand *change* in Broad's absolute, non-qualitative sense referred to above:

Def: *Becoming is real if and only if events successively and mind-independently take place at their own proper time of occurrence.*[16]

[16] Interestingly, the etymology of 'event' betrays an original, revealing image of motion through space, as the word comes from the Latin verb *advenire*, literally 'to arrive', 'to come to', which is then extended metaphorically to temporal matters to mean 'to occur', 'to happen', where such happenings *are changes*.

Mauro Dorato

Given that it is non-controversial to grant that for an event to *occur at a time* just means for it to *exist at that time*, the task that still remains is to show that the proposed, minimalistic equivalence between 'coming into existence at time t' (Gödel's change) and 'occurring (existing) at that time' captures the essential features of our pre-theoretical intuitions about becoming and the passage of time.

The solution we are after is simple if we identify the lapse of time with the view, dearest to our intuition, that the 'present coincides with the existing'. By relativizing this claim to a time t, we get that at t only events simultaneous with (present at) t exist, where 'existence' is here understood in a relational, tenseless sense, given by 'existence at a date/time'. Capturing this intuition in our explication of becoming is therefore indispensable to make the latter adequate, and it seems to me that Gödel has understood this essential point better than any other philosopher before or after him. Consider the following, precious but strangely neglected quotation: «For that time elapses and change exists means [...] that at any moment of time only a certain portion of the facts composing the world exists objectively (and different portions at different moments)» [Gödel 1995, p. 235]. Provided that the notion of occurring at a certain proper time is mind-independent—why deny that 'things occur' and 'events happen' without our taking notice of them?—the thesis *that only the present exists* (even formulated in the relativized way seen above) *is sufficient to claim that events and facts come into existence (and cease to exist) mind-independently.*

In fact, *how can two temporally separated events* coexist in a tenseless sense *if, at any instant of (cosmic) time t, only events occurring at t exist (at that time)?* For any two temporally separated, instantaneous events e and f, the earlier of the two must cease to exist when the other comes into being, provided that 'event e comes into being (into existence) at t' (tenseless becoming) simply means 'e occurs or happens at t' or 'e is present at (simultaneous with) t'. The first, essential question we must face, then, is whether, and in what sense, events can be said to *coexist tenselessly* in the same possible world (spacetime), or alternatively, which arguments we have to defend the view that only what occurs at t exists at that time. The other problem is to show that such a relational, tenseless view of becoming is a *faithful* explication of our experience of time and passage. Let us examine these two issues in turn.

The argument to defend the view that at time t only what then occurs exists as of that time may run as follows. For simplicity, imagine a universe in which time has a discrete ordering, composed only of instants 1 and 2, with two causally connectible, instantaneous events, E_1 and E_2, occurring at those temporally separated instants. At t_1, E_2 trivially doesn't exist (both in a tenseless and in a tensed sense of 'existence'), simply because, by definition, E_2 *occurs at the different time* t_2![17] In fact, if 'occurring at t' and 'existing at t' must be regarded as perfectly interchangeable, *tenseless* expressions, it follows that at time t_1, E_2 does not exist, otherwise E_2 would exist *at all times* (that is, in our simplified model, it would exist also at t_1), which is absurd. Therefore, since at time t_1 E_1 exists (occurs) and E_2 doesn't (in the perfectly acceptable tenseless sense seen above), one can safely assume that E_2 *comes into being at* t_2, by simply happening or taking place at that time. Conversely, since E_1 exists (occurs) only at t_1, at t_2 it *ceases to exist*, since at that time E_2 is the only existing event.

By defending such *a tenseless and relational* view of becoming, one can readily join Williams [1951] in arguing that the *flow* of time interpreted in a *literal* sense is inconsistent, because of notorious difficulties with questions like 'how fast does the present flow'? Of course, renouncing this view is certainly not a sacrifice, because the explication of becoming proposed here—by broaching this problem we come to the second issue anticipated above—does indeed save two essential tenets of the commonsensical view of time:

(i) At any instant of time, only what is present at that time exists, since both the past and the future at that time don't exist (both in the tensed sense of existence, given by 'existing now' and in a perfectly acceptable tenseless sense, given by 'existence at a date/time')[18];

(ii) an absolute change in what exists can be regarded as objective, since it coincides with the successive coming into being (occurring) of events either (a) at different instants of a global, cosmic time, if the latter is indeed available, or (b) at instants of a local, proper time along a particular worldline.

I argue that such a successive coming into being of events at different moments of time is *the mind-independent, objective core* lying behind the *subjective sense of literal passage of one time over another*,

---

[17] For the purpose of rebutting charges of fatalism allegedly entailed by the tenseless view of time, this point has been correctly noted already by Oaklander [1994, 1998]. However, I think that he has not drawn its philosophical consequences for the view that he himself defends about becoming (he is against it).

[18] The fact, urged by Savitt, that other senses of tenseless existence are on the ground ('existing at all times' is one) is irrelevant in our context.

Mauro Dorato

which, admittedly, is engendered by our memory of events that don't exist any more and our anticipations of events that are yet to happen, fused together in a unique but continuously changing present experience. The changing of such an experience can be explained only by the successive coming into being of events and states of affair at their time of occurrence.

It is in this sense that I think that such a minimalist view of becoming, that in the literature has never been clearly formulated, can be regarded as a *tertium quid* between, and therefore as a *dissolution* of, some of the main contentions between the two camps (the 'A' and the 'B') in which the analytic philosophy of time of the 20th century has been divided. Despite the fact that tensed sentences have tenseless truth conditions—as urged by Mellor [1981] and Faye [1989]—becoming must be regarded, *contrary to the typical B-theorists' view*, as a *mind-independent* feature of the universe.[19] At any instant of a cosmic or local time, tenselessly conceived events and facts do come into being as objectively as it gets, for the simple reasons that at any instant of time, only events occurring at that instant exist (in the two senses seen above), and such events do not occur all at once, but in succession. Furthermore, once we realize that it does not make sense to ask how fast events do come into being, because coming into being at t just means occurring at that time and not existing before, the ghost of the infinite regress, imported by misleading metaphors of motion through space of a reified now, vanishes.

Incidentally, we should note that the view that mind-independent occurring (on the part of events) is sufficient for becoming is not completely new, since it has been *implicitly* defended by authors that are usually identified as arch-enemies of becoming, like Eddington: «events do not happen, they are just there and we come across them» [1920, p. 51), and Weyl «the objective world simply is, it does not happen» [1949, p. 116]. I claim that these oft-quoted passages, whose true meaning has escaped us, are the only coherent formulations of a becomingless world, i.e., a world in which events literally *don't occur*, but simply *are*.

It should be obvious why both Weyl and Eddington defended this view with respect to STR. Given that in this theory the temporal order is only *partial*, events that are usually defined, as in Kim's

---

[19] For a number of B-theorists defending the mind-dependence of the difference between past, present and future, see Russell [1915], Grünbaum [1963], Faye [1989], and Mellor [1998]. Not all B theorist defend the mind-dependence of becoming: J. Butterfield (private communication) is an exception.

theory [1976], by a *triple* constituted by a substance, a property and *a* (coordinate) *time*, would have to be regarded as having an identity which depends on an arbitrary choice of an inertial frame. In this case, it may appear more plausible to assume, as Eddington and Weyl did, that events don't occur at all, but simply are, or tenselessly coexist in the block view of the universe. If my reading of those oft-quoted passages is correct, these two philosophers had already realized what I am urging here, namely that for the reality of change and of temporal becoming, the reality of 'occurrence' *suffices*. This, in its turn, implies that as soon as we grant that in a general relativistic spacetime endowed with a *global* time order events can objectively and mind-independently occur in succession, we thereby introduce a change in what is real at different instants of time for the reasons given above, and therefore a tenseless form of becoming at a cosmic time *t*. It is certainly more difficult to defend a local, worldline-dependent becoming in the Minkowskian setting, since the present there does not extend in space but must be identified with a point (the here-now). However, this is the topic for a different paper.

6 Conclusion

Even if the argument above in favour of becoming were not judged to be conclusive, what matter most for my purpose is that the adoption of a relativized and tenseless notion of becoming yields a coherent alternative to its mind-dependence and to the block view. We can adopt *the view from no-when* of the block universe, a God's eye point of view, which describes entities that are temporally extended *sub specie aeternitatis*, or we can resort to a relationist, perspectival description of reality, which refers existence to a particular 'point of view' or instant of time. If both are compatible with know physical theories, the choice between them can be only be a matter of overall coherence with what else we know about the universe.

The reasons to prefer the latter view are not only pragmatic, i.e., given by the fact that we *are* temporally located beings. The former view, by regarding the difference between *present* and *future* events as identical to the difference between *here* and *there*, makes our experience of time utterly unexplainable, and in principle not describable in physicalistic or even naturalistic terms. In fact, how can I act to produce or bring about a future event *e* if *e* coexists (tenselessly) with the time of my action in the same sense in which

Mauro Dorato

a past event exists? Within the perspectival, relationist option, causation *can* be regarded as an ontologically loaded notion: from the perspective of a region R, where my present action is located, events occurring in the later region R' don't exist (tenselessly or tensedly), and an event in R (my action) literally *brings about* those in R' *by causing them.*

If what I am trying to argue is correct, it follows that a somewhat deflated version of objective becoming must be reintroduced, one that is equivalent to the notion that events mind-independently occur at a certain proper time and place. If the proper time of a single, fundamental particle (observer) can be extended to a cosmic time as in standard Robertson-Walker cosmologies, becoming can be regarded as being independent of the varying lapses of time associated to different timelike curves, and, as such, it passes the test of intersubjective validity. *If* there is a perfectly legitimate sense in which physical events belonging to any relativistic spacetime (also Minkowski's) exist only at their proper time and place of occurrence—no interpretation of relativity forces us to abandon this trivially simple remark—it should be clear why this view of becoming entails some sort of *rapprochement* between the so-called static view of time and the dynamic view: the only existing facts are tenseless (facts at times), but their becoming or coming into being at instants of cosmic or local time is a *real, though physically unexplainable feature of the universe.*

References

Boltzmann, L. 1896–1898. *Vorlesungen über Gastheorie*, transl. by S. Brush [1964], *Lectures on Gas Theory. 1896–1898*. Berkeley: University of California Press.

Broad, C. D. 1938. *Examination of McTaggart's philosophy*, Cambridge: Cambridge University.

Callender, C. 1997. 'Review of M. Dorato's *Time and Reality*, Bologna, Clueb 1995', *British Journal for the Philosophy of Science*, **48**, 117–20.

Clifton, R. and Hogarth, M. 1995. 'The Definability of Becoming in Minkowski Spacetime', *Synthese*, **103**, 355–87.

Dieks, D. 1988. 'Discussion: Special Relativity and the Flow of Time', *Philosophy of Science*, **55**, 456–460.

Dorato, M. 1995. *Time and Reality*, Clueb, Bologna.

—— 1996. 'On Becoming, Relativity and Non-separability', *Philosophy of Science*, **64**, 585–604.

—— 2000. 'Becoming and the Arrow of Causation', *Philosophy of Science*, Supplement to vol. 67, **3**, S523–534.

Earman, J. 1995. *Bangs, Crunches, Whimpers and Shrieks. Singularities and Acausalities in Relativistic Spacetimes.* Oxford: Oxford University Press.

Eddington, A. S. 1920. *Space, Time and Gravitation.* Cambridge, Cambridge University Press.

Faye, J. 1989. *The Reality of the Future*, Odense, Odense University Press.

Gödel, K. 1949a. 'A Remark About the Relationship Between Relativity Theory and Idealistic Philosophy', in P. A. Schilpp (ed.), *Albert Einstein: Philosopher-Scientist*, La Salle IL: Open Court, pp. 557–62, reprinted with corrections and additions in Gödel (1990).

—— (1949b. 'An Example of a New Type of Cosmological Solution of Einstein's Field Equations of Gravitation', *Review of Modern Physics*, **21**, 447–50.

—— (1990. *Collected Works*, S. Feferman *et. al.* (eds), Vol. 2, Oxford: Oxford University Press.

—— (1995. *Collected Works*, S. Feferman *et. al.* (eds), Vol. 3, Oxford: Oxford University Press.

Godfrey-Smith, W. 1979. 'Special Relativity and the Present', *Philosophical Studies*, **36**, 233–44.

Grünbaum, A. 1963. *Philosophical Problems of Space and Time*, New York: A. Knopf.

Horwich, P. 1987. *Asymmetries in Time*, Harvard Mass.: The Mit Press.

Jeans, J. 1936. 'Man and the Universe', Sir Stewart Alley Lecture, in *Scientific Progress*, New York: The McMillan Company, pp. 13–38.

Kim, J. 1976. 'Events as property exemplification', in Brand M. and Walton D. (eds), *Action Theory*, Dordrecht: Reidel, pp. 159–77.

Le Poidevin, R. (ed.) (1998. *Questions of Time and Tense*, Oxford: Oxford University Press.

Malament, D. 1995. 'Introductory Note for *1949b*' in Gödel (1995), *Collected Works*, S. Feferman *et. al.* (eds), Vol. 3, Oxford, Oxford University Press, pp. 261–69.

Maxwell, N. 1985. 'Are Probabilism and Special Relativity Incompatible?', *Philosophy of Science*, **52**, pp. 23–43.

McTaggart, J. 1908. 'The Unreality of Time', *Mind,* **68**, pp. 457–74.

Mellor, D. H. 1997. *Real Time II*, London: Routledge.

Oaklander, N., and Smith, Q. (eds) (1994. *The New Theory of Time*, New Haven: Yale University Press.

Oaklander, N. 1998. *Freedom and the New Theory of Time*, in Le Poidevin, R. (ed.) (1998. *Questions of Time and Tense*, Oxford: Oxford University Press.

Padgett, A. 1992. *God, Eternity and the Nature of Time*, New York: St. Martin's Press.

Putnam, H. 1967. 'Time and Physical Geometry', *The Journal of Philosophy*, **64**, pp. 240–47.

Quine, W. v. O. 1987. 'Space-time', in *Quiddities*, Harvard University Press: Harvard Mass.

Rakic, N. 1997. 'Past, present and future and special relativity', *British Journal for the Philosophy of Science*, **48**, 257–280.

Mauro Dorato

Rietdijk, C. 1966. 'A rigorous proof of determinism derived from the special theory of relativity', *Philosophy of Science*, **33**, 341–44.

Rovelli, C. 1997. 'Half-way through the woods: Contemporary Research in Space and Time', in J. Earman and J. Norton (eds), *The Cosmos of Science*, Pittsburgh: University of Pittsburgh Press, pp. 180–224.

Russell, B. 1915. 'On the Experience of Time', *Monist*, **25**, 212–33.

Saunders, S. 1996. 'Time, Quantum Mechanics and Tense', *Synthese*, **107**, 19–53.

Savitt, S. 1994. 'The Replacement of Time', *Australasian Journal of Philosophy*, **72**, 463–474.

—— (2000. 'There's No Time Like the Present (in Minkowski spacetime)', in D. Howard (ed.), *PSA 98*, part II, Supplement to volume 67, **3**, S563–S573.

Sellars, W. 1962. 'Philosophy and the Scientific Image of Man', in R. Colodny (ed.), *Frontiers of Science and Philosophy*, Pittsburgh: University of Pittsburgh Press, pp. 35–78.

Smith, Q. 2000. 'Review of Philip Turezsky's *Time*', *The British Journal for the Philosophy of Science*, **51**, 27–933.

Stein, H. 1968. 'On Einstein-Minkowski spacetime', *Journal of Philosophy*, **65**, 5–23.

—— 1970. 'On the Paradoxical Time-Structure of Gödel,' *Philosophy of Science*, **37**, 589–601.

—— 1991. 'On Relativity Theory and Openness of the Future', *Philosophy of Science*, **58**, 147–67.

Tooley, M. 1997. *Time, Tense and Causation*, Oxford: Oxford University Press.

Wang, H. 1995. 'Time in Philosophy and in Physics from Kant and Einstein to Gödel', *Synthese*, **102**, 215–34.

Weingard, R. 1972. 'Relativity and the Reality of Past and Future Events', *British Journal for the Philosophy of Science*, **23**, 199–221.

Weyl, H. 1918. *Raum-Zeit Materie*, Berlin, J. Springer.

Williams D. 1951. 'The Myth of Passage', reprinted in R. Gale (ed.) 1967, *The Philosophy of Time*, New York: Anchor Books, pp. 98–116.

Yourgrau P. 1991. *The Disappearance of Time*, Cambridge: Cambridge University Press.

—— 1999. *Gödel meets Einstein*, New York: Open Court.

How Relativity Contradicts Presentism

SIMON SAUNDERS

Introduction

But this picture of a 'block universe', composed of a timeless web of 'world-lines' in a four-dimensional space, however strongly suggested by the theory of relativity, is a piece of gratuitous metaphysics. Since the concept of change, of something happening, is an inseparable component of the common-sense concept of time and a necessary component of the scientist's view of reality, it is quite out of the question that theoretical physics should require us to hold the Eleatic view that nothing happens in 'the objective world'. Here, as so often in the philosophy of science, a useful limitation in the form of representation is mistaken for a deficiency of the universe (Black, 1962).

The theory of relativity has excited more philosophical commentary, and exerted more influence in mainstream philosophy, than any scientific theory, with the possible exception of Newton's theory of gravity. But it is a remarkable fact that its influence on metaphysics proper has been somewhat marginal. That is probably a testimony to the anti-metaphysical attitude that characterized so much philosophy in the last century, certainly in the Anglo-American tradition, and certainly among more scientifically-minded philosophers. Although the hey-day of logical empiricism is long-since past, philosophers of physics have continued to remain cool to metaphysics. Since they remain the ones best suited to explain the implications of relativity theory for the philosophy of time, if they find no interesting links between these disciplines, metaphysicians are unlikely to look for them.

I make this observation (and I promise to say no more in this vein) because relativity theory, and specifically the special theory of relativity, does I believe have a simple and direct bearing on a perennial question in the philosophy of time. It would, I believe, *settle* this question, were special relativity the whole of the story. I shall say something about the broader perspective of quantum theory and general relativity at the end.

Simon Saunders

What traditional question does special relativity decide on? It is whether reality—what exists—is a four-dimensional web of world-lines (a 'block universe'), or something less. There are competing versions of what this 'something less' might be, but they are variations on what I shall call *presentism*, the view that only the present is real. The argument is simple, and I will state it with the minimum of technicality. Although, I say, it has been largely ignored, versions of it have been stated before; it was stated in brief by Gödel,[1] and at great length by Putnam[2]. But this latter version of the argument has been roundly condemned by Stein. This dispute between Putnam and Stein is in fact well-known in the philosophy of physics literature, but insofar as there is a consensus on it, it is that Stein was in the right.[3] I will come on to this dispute in due course.

Presentism

'Presentism', as I shall understand it, is the thesis that *the present is all that exists*. But this needs some unpacking. It is intended to be something more than a platitude, and surely the present is all that exists *now*, as the future is all that *will* exist, and the past all that *did* exist. Who will argue with these claims?

One way to get clearer on the presentist thesis is to say that it is meant tenselessly; that the copula in the sentence 'the present is all that exists' is not itself tensed. But that is a doubtful manoeuvre. Very often the presentist will go on to deny that there is any mean-

---

[1] For Gödel the point was obvious; he immediately went on to consider the situation in Einstein's theory of gravity, specifically in the light of his rotating universe solutions to the field equations of general relativity. The latter argument has been carefully analysed by a number of authors: see Stein (1994), Earman (1996), and Savitt (1997).

[2] Putnam (1967); versions of it were also stated by Rietdijk (1966) and Maxwell (1986), and these Stein has also criticized; but their interests were a little oblique to our topic, and their handling of it more muddled. Rietdijk's treatment, in particular, was just careful enough, and just muddled enough, to be conclusively refuted (see Torretti 1983, pp. 250–51l; see also Landsberg 1970 p. 1146–47). I shall confine myself almost entirely to Putnam's argument, and to Stein's response to it (Stein 1978, 1991).

[3] Among those who have endorsed Stein's objections to Putnam's argument, see Clifton and Hogarth (1995), Dickson (1998 pp. 165–73), and Shimony (1993), with qualifications). So far as I know only Callender (1998) has expressed any real reservations; but see also Saunders (1996, 1998).

278

ingful, irreducibly tenseless use of 'is', at least when it comes to the physical world; and that *passé* Mellor and others, it is equally possible to give tensed truth conditions for tenseless sentences as tenseless ones for tensed. Exercises in the philosophy of language do not seem to be settling anything.

But nebulous though it is, there is surely something about the presentist's position which is perfectly clear: it is intended to be a thesis about what to count as real. It is a realist thesis. It is a claim about temporal reality which is supposed to hold independent of our state of knowledge or beliefs. We and our works are not what the thesis is about; the presentist is making a claim about reality, not about what we know or say about it.

The claim can also be put in negative terms, as the view which is opposed to the tenseless view of time (according to which all events exist on a par, regardless of whether we consider them as past, present, or future). On the tenseless view, talk of events as past, present or future is really talk about ourselves, of the relation of events to how we are momentarily arranged. The word 'now' is like the word 'here'; mention of 'future' and 'past' is like pointing this way and that way in space.

That is all that is needed to bring out the conflict with special relativity. If presentism is a thesis about ontology, and says that existence consists of a three-dimensional spatial reality; if, in elaboration of this thesis, it opposes the tenseless view of time, and denies that talk of events as past, present or future is elliptical talk about the relation of events to our momentary selves: then it contradicts special relativity. It contradicts it in the sense that it implies that special relativity is badly deficient as a fundamental theory of the world.

Of course special relativity is an empirical theory. One might take the view that presentism is concerned with a level or reality which is beyond the reach of experimental methods.[4] But I do not grant that physics is so limited in scope, or that metaphysics can find anything deeper. But I will not argue for either of these claims here.

How Relativity Contradicts Presentism

The difficulty posed by special relativity is extremely simple. According to presentism, all that is physically real is the present—a

---

[4] For a metaphysician who hovers uncomfortably between this view, and the view that anyway relativity does not contradict presentism, see Smith (1993 pp. 2–4).

system of physical events all of which are simultaneous with each other. No other events are real. Precisely what this system of events may be, *now*, as I snap my fingers, may not be known to me; but there is a fact of the matter as to what it is, and it is a universal fact which embraces us all. It is an intersubjective reality—now, as a snap my fingers—and it is a reality which contains us only as an incidental part. But even if one knew all that there is to know, consistent with special relativity, one would not be able to say what this system of events might be. According to presentism, therefore, special relativity is radically deficient as a description of reality. It is blind to the sequencing of what is physically real.

There is no such problem in the Newtonian case. There, knowing all there is to know, the set of events simultaneous with this event—as I snap my fingers—is unambiguously defined. It is all and only those events absolutely simultaneous with it. In that theory there is postulated a relation, absolute simultaneity, which partitions events into disjoint classes, namely instants of time. It does so democratically: no one event of each class is singled out in the definition of the partition. To be precise, this relationship of absolute simultaneity is reflexive, symmetric and transitive, so instants of time are equivalence classes of events. This relation, moreover, plays a crucial role in the subsequent definition of the dynamical laws of motion (and of suitable initial data for those laws); it could hardly play a more fundamental role in Newton's theory. And we ourselves, and our momentary and spatial arrangements, are manifestly incidental to its definition; we are incidental to what each reality consists in. Newtonian theory, gratifyingly for the presentist, is attentive to what is physically real. Not so special relativity.

The argument is so simple that it speaks for itself. No technical result is needed: it is of the essence of the theory of special relativity that absolute simultaneity as such does not exist. Everyone knows that there is nothing else to replace it—there is no other nontrivial symmetric and transitive relation intrinsic to Minkowski space. Of course, making reference to the matter content of spacetime as well, there may well be methods for defining a partitioning of spacetime into spaces (for defining global instants, as required by presentism), but none of them are likely to claim any fundamental status. It is unlikely that any can be taken seriously, if we are concerned with the definition of the totality of what is physically real. Only given a matter distribution of exceptional symmetry—for example, a stream of particles all moving inertially, with zero relative velocities—would a slicing of spacetime into spaces at different times (a *foliation* of spacetime) be obviously privileged. The presentist will *literally* need a river for there to be time, according to his metaphysics.[5]

One need only consider the realistic candidates to see the difficulty. Given any one inertial (straight) worldline, one can define a natural slicing of Minkowski space into spaces at different times, namely into the set of (parallel) timeslices orthogonal to it. But how can the whole of reality—what is physically real—depend on a *single* worldline? *What* is this thing which has this special privilege— or *who* is it—that has this extraordinary status? In fact, from a physically realistic point of view, there are no objects which always move inertially. Nor, in an infinite universe, does anyone know how to construct such a world-line: one cannot define the centre of mass of the universe as a whole if it is infinite; and one cannot make do with any part of it without privileging that part. Why *that* part, and not some other? Even in the finite case the option of the centre of mass is not very attractive, involving as it does messy and arbitrary conventions (there is no unique definition of the centre of mass frame in the finite case, again in contrast to the situation in Newtonian theory). The presentist cannot be neutral on this score; to suppose it can be settled by convention is precisely to take the view that what is real—the breaking down of spacetime into spaces at different times—is not of fundamental import, but a matter of convenience, a matter of convention. That is precisely what the *tenseless* theory says. This is not an option available to the presentist.

In the general case, and in an infinite universe, in practise one seizes on a segment of a particular worldline or worldtube of some body (or bodies slowly moving with respect to each other). At any point of it a spacelike hyperplane can be constructed to which it is orthogonal. If approximately inertial, a family of hyperplanes can be constructed which are non-intersecting, at least locally. This is the technique used in positional astronomy: Ephemeris Time is precisely such a system for partitioning events in the history of the solar system into spaces at different times (more precisely, it is a based on the relative configurations of the Earth-Moon-Sun

---

[5] For a more general criterion, less dependent on symmetry, suppose that hypersurfaces are defined as everywhere orthogonal to the integral curves of the four-velocity field of the fluid. Then the fluid had better be irrotational (lacking 'twist'), if the surfaces are not to intersect. (For a simple geometric illustration, think of a twisted rope; it cannot be cut so as to cut each strand of it orthogonally.) Gödel was led to his rotating universe solutions to the Einstein field equations by considerations of just this sort: see Malement (1994).

system). By its means, if there ever does come into being a community of astronauts in space, moving about the solar system, it will still be possible to agree on what events in whose lives get to take place at the same time. The criteria will be public and intersubjective. No particular person will be singled out in counting what is real (of what belongs to which moment in time). But the community as a whole is singled out. The Earth-Moon-Sun system acquires a very special status. As the basis for the criterion of what is real, it is parochial. It will hardly do for metaphysics. It is as embarrassing as Newton's hypothesis as to what is really at absolute rest (the centre of mass of the Solar System). What is so special about the Earth, Moon and Sun?

The presentist has little option but to hold out for some as yet unknown criterion for determining what is physically real—for splitting Minkowski spacetime into spaces at different times. Special relativity, the presentist must conclude, is radically incomplete. But the alternative view is that progress in physics has counted against presentism. Physical theories were once compatible with it, but then they were not.

The Dispute Between Putnam and Stein

This argument is I believe unassailable, but it is similar to Putnam's, and Putnam's has been roundly condemned. On what grounds?

First Putnam's argument. He considers what he calls 'the view of the man on the street'. It is the same as presentism: it is the view that 'all (and only) things which exist now are real'. Putnam now assumes:

> I. I-now am real. (Of course, this assumption changes each time I announce that I am making it, since 'I-now' refers to a different instantaneous 'me'.)
>
> II. At least one other observer is real, and it is possible for this other observer to be in motion relative to me. (Putnam 1967 p. 240.)

He also assumes what he calls 'the principle that There Are No Privileged Observers':

> III. If is the case that all and only the things that stand in a certain relation R to me-now are real, and you-now are real, then it is also the case that all and only the things that stand in the relation R to you-now are real. (*ibid* p. 240).

Putnam gives no argument for this principle, and in his subsequent use of it only transitivity is explicitly mentioned; but by the letter of III it is clear that R must also be symmetric. And so it should be, if of all the events which are real, no one of them is to be privileged. If not, then if we start from a fiduciary event x (there is at least one real event, by I), and define the others that are real as those which stand in relation R to x, then the set $\{y:Rxy\}$ that we end up with cannot also be defined by starting with another element of this set. In other words, each set will have to be specified by the relationship R and a particular element of it (not any element of it); so for each set one element of it would have to be privileged. Likewise if R is symmetric but not transitive. Since R is surely reflexive, 'no privilege' exactly forces R to be an equivalence relation. When the elements in question are events in the lives of observers—person-stages—the principle is 'no privileged person-stages'. ('No privileged observers' has a better ring.)

Finally, Putnam requires:

IV. R is definable in special relativity.

The similarity of Putnam's argument to the one I have given should be perfectly clear. Indeed, given a partitioning of Minkowski space M, one can always define an equivalence relation in its terms. Let the timeslices of M—the partitions—be labelled by a parameter t, denote $\{M_t\}$. Then R is the co-membership relation

$$R=\{<x,y>; \exists t \text{ such that } x \in M_t \text{ and } y \in M_t\}. \tag{1}$$

It is obviously an equivalence relation, and, given $\{M_t\}$, it is obviously definable in special relativity. The question that remains is how the partitioning of Minkowski space was arrived at. If by a relationship on M—essentially reversing the procedure just sketched—then we are back to Putnam's approach. But whatever the method, a principle analogous to III will apply. I would add that not only can it not privilege any particular person, but it had better not privilege any particular community, either. A metaphysics which is explicitly community bound is not worthy of the name.

Putnam considered only partitions defined by a relationship R, not the more general case. A quick result follows on the narrow reading of IV, that R must be defined in terms of the *geometry* of M. Then, trivially, there are only the two equivalence relations, $\{<x,y>;x,y \in M\}$—all events are real—and $\{<x,y>;x=y\}$—only the fiduciary event x is real. If these are the only possibilities, it is not hard to see which we should choose.

But Putnam did allow that R may be defined by reference to the matter distribution. The result still follows, failing any special symmetries, but whilst intuitively plausible it is harder to prove. Putnam did not prove it.[6] He only considered the most obvious candidates for it, in particular Einstein synchrony, denote *Ein*; this obviously fails, because for points on an arbitrary collection of timelike lines it is neither symmetric nor transitive. He also considered the worldline-independent relation of past causal connectibility, denote *Con*. Let $x \leq y$ iff x is in or on the past light cone of y; then *Con* is the relation $\{<x,y>;x \leq y\}$. Although reflexive and transitive, it is not symmetric. This too is of no use to the presentist.

Putnam did not put it in quite these terms, however. In this latter part of his paper, where he introduced *Con*, he spoke rather of truth-values of statements, not of the reality of events. He considered *Con* in this context, as the suggestion that only statements about events in the lower half of my light-cone have a truth value. Of this he remarked:

> This last move, however, flagrantly violates the idea that there are no Privileged Observers. Why should a statement's having or not having a truth value depend upon the relation of the events referred to in the statement to just one special human being, me? (ibid. p. 246)

The point is not entirely self-evident. A statement may fail to have a truth value because it may fail to refer to anything, and whether or not a statement refers (and what it refers to) may well depend on whether it has a relation to a particular human being—so much is true of any statement containing an explicit or implicit indexical. And Putnam did not make it clear that one can hardly insist on his requirement III, of 'No Privileged Observers', as it was originally stated, in this new context, for no-one will demand *symmetry* in this case. By shifting to the question of what statements have truth-values, it is surely intended that we include statements referring to past events as well as to present ones. Putting it in non-linguistic terms, it is not the thesis of presentism, but rather the the thesis that *only the present and the past is real*. Call it 'possibilism'[7] If defined by a

---

[6] It is an immediate corollary of the result of Clifton and Hogarth (1996), namely that in the absence of symmetries, there is no worldline-dependent relation which is so much as transitive. Perversely, they took this to lend support to Stein's argument, rather than Putnam's (for it generalizes Stein's proof that *Con* is the only intrinsically-definable nontrivial transitive relation on M; see below).

[7] In line with Savitt's terminology (Savitt 1998).

relation, the possibilist will obviously not want it to be symmetric. If an earlier event is real in relation to a later one, that should not imply that the later one is real in relation to the earlier. Given possibilism, we should not expect to obtain a democracy of timelike-separated observers.

But possibilists will still insist on the remaining requirement built into III, that if you are real to me, then what is real to you is real to me as well. Transitivity is necessary here as before. And now one might be lulled into thinking that transitivity is *sufficient* for possibilism: that possibilism differs from presentism only in that it demands a weaker version of III.

The waters are now seriously muddied, for of course transitivity is *not* enough for possibilism. The constraint is operating, here as before, that what is present—meaning, according to possibilism, what is the *boundary* of all that is physically real—is an intersubjective and non-parochial affair. But this latter constraint can no longer be imposed by formal conditions on R, if R relates all and only the events which the possibilist considers as real.

Were transitivity all that is required by the possibilist, the relation *Con* would be just the ticket. This is exactly Stein's response to Putnam: it is enough to define a relation 'already happened', and it is enough if this relation is transitive and definable in terms of the intrinsic geometry of M (reflexivity as before can be stipulated). *Con* does the job. Stein made this clear in his first paper on the subject (Stein 1968, p. 5); in his second he went on to prove that *Con* is essentially the only such transitive relation on M (Stein 1991).

As for Putnam's error, Stein located it in the passage just cited:

The answer is that 'having or not having a truth value', in this question, must be understood classically to mean 'at a given time' ... but 'at a given time' is not a relativistically invariant notion, and the question of definiteness of truth value, to make sense *at all* for Einstein-Minkowski space-time, has to be interpreted as meaning 'definiteness at a given space-time point' (or event)—to be vivid, 'definiteness for me now'. The 'Privileged Observer' (or, rather, privileged event) is—in effect—named in the question, and therefore has every right to be considered germane to the answer. Putnam's objection has an exact analogue, whose inappropriateness is plain, in the pre-relativistic case; namely, the question 'why should a statement's having or not having a truth value depend upon the relation of the events referred to in the statement of just one special time, *now*?' (Stein 1968 p. 15).

Simon Saunders

According to Stein, Putnam presupposes notions that are simply not available in special relativity. He has failed to take note of the changed situation in that context, that 'definiteness to the present' has to be replaced by 'definiteness at a given space-time point'. Clearly, on making this replacement, one cannot rule out reference to a particular point, no more than in the non-relativistic case can one rule out reference to a particular instant.

All well and good, but clearly this changed situation is simply *no longer hospitable* to presentism. In the pre-relativistic case 'an instant' is a public reality, on which all who were included in it could intersubjectively agree. It offered room enough for an account of the whole of reality (it was a *plausible* reality, at least for some). But nothing like this can be said of a spacetime point. If this is really all that special relativity provides, short of the whole of Minkowski spacetime, we have no option but to opt for the latter. If it is true that 'the now' can only be a spacetime point—as Stein seems to imply—then presentism is *obviously* untenable. A single point in spacetime *cannot* be all that is physically real.

Stein is in fact perfectly indifferent to presentism.[8] He makes this clear in the paragraph that follows:

> ... in Einstein-Minkowski space-time *an event's present is constituted by itself alone*. In this theory, therefore, the present tense can never be applied correctly to 'foreign' objects. This is at bottom a consequence (and a fairly obvious one) of our adopting relativistically invariant language—since, as we know, there is no relativistically invariant notion of simultaneity. The appearance of paradox only confirms that the space-time of Einstein and Minkowski is quite different from pre-relativistic space-time. (*ibid.* p. 15)

The tenseless point of view is so natural that it is not even worthy of comment: *of course* the present of an event is constituted by itself alone; what else is one to think in special relativity! Stein is not concerned with the metaphysical thesis of presentism. He is impatient with talk of the view of the man in the street—he finds it curious that special relativity should be held hostage to that—because for Stein, it is a *fairly obvious consequence* of relativity theory that an event's present is constituted by itself alone (the second of the two trivial equivalence relations). *Obviously* the presentist's position is

---

[8] Compare Torretti (1983 p. 250): 'Each event is (tenselessly) real and determinate, in this absolute sense, as its own worldpoint. No tensed, frame-independent statement can add to it or detract from its reality...' I do not believe that the presentist, or anyone even loosely associated with presentism, can agree with this statement.

untenable, given special relativity. Precisely so; the only question is why Stein disputed Putnam's conclusions.

There is one more respect in which the shift of topic, to possibilism and definiteness of truth value, may have led to confusion. What is the status of future contingencies? Rietdijk advanced an argument similar in certain respects to Putnam's, but used it to conclude that special relativity implies *determinism*. Almost twenty years later, and without reference to either Putnam or Rietdijk, so too did Maxwell. It was this that prompted Stein's second paper on the subject, in which he proved that Con was essentially unique. It was titled 'On Relativity Theory and the Openness of the Future'. Clifton and Hogarth's generalization of this result, to include worldline-dependent relations (in the absence of symmetries), was entitled 'The Definability of Objective Becoming in Minkowski Spacetime'. Black shifted without comment from the view that reality is a 4-dimensional whole, to the view that change is unreal; Shimony, approvingly citing Stein's response to Putnam, was concerned to deny that change was illusory. Evidently there are two further questions at stake in all this: one, whether indeterminism is consistent with special relativity, and two, whether the tenseless view of time is committed to the view that change, or becoming, is unreal. But one can answer these questions either way and yet reject presentism;[9] Putnam made no mention of either of them.

The one clear respect in which Stein flatly denies a step in the argument as I have given it is this:

> ... in effect what he calls the principle of No Privileged Observers just requires R to be an *equivalence relations*. But such a requirement has in fact no connection with the privilegedness of observers; and it is moreover extremely inappropriate to Einstein-Minkowski space-time—in which (unlike pre-relativistic space-time, with its temporal decomposition) *there are no intrinsic geometrical partitions into equivalence classes at all, besides the two trivial ones*... (*ibid.* p. 19)

Stein denies that to partition a set into classes by means of a relation, in such a way that each class can be defined independent of the

---

[9] The presentist, of course, may disagree; so too will 'A-theorists', who find compelling McTaggart's argument that the B-series is inadequate to the description of change. I have more sympathy for Maxwell's claim, that special relativity poses problems for indeterminateness (see my 1996, 1998, for further discussion).

choice of any particular element of that class, the relation must be an equivalence relation. I say he is mistaken.[10]

How might *Con* be used to define a partitioning of Minkowski space? There is a near neighbour to it which does the job quite easily. Let $x \preceq y$ iff x is on the surface of the past light-cone to y. Define *Berk* as the relation $\{<x,y>; y \preceq x\}$. Berkeley's criterion, indeed, was that to be real (to x) is to be seen (by x, so to be on the past light-cone to x).[11] Let us now partition up M into disjoint sets in the obvious way, as a nesting of lightcones. We do not obtain a foliation in this way, for the partitions are not spacelike surfaces, but put that aside. The real difficulty is that each partition has a distinguished point—the apex of each cone—and the partitioning as a whole clearly distinguishes a unique timelike line—the locus of these distinguished points. Such is the price for using a relation which is not an equivalence relation. Now suppose this partitioning has the metaphysical significance accorded to it by the presentist: a given one of them is to define the whole of what is physically real, a mater on which all will agree. So what is this worldline—the worldline of *what* or of *whom*—that is to have this extraordinary significance? It can hardly be one of the obvious candidates from the tenseless point of view (one's own worldline, or the worldline of the earth, or of the centre of mass of the sun, earth and moon), wherein no ontological significance resides (for on the tenseless point of view the fundamental ontological reality is the whole of Minkowski space, and everything in it). We have been over this before

On the tenseless view, all events are real; the significance of the partitioning is quite different. If asked which relationship gives the 'correct' partitioning, the answer will depend on how the question is construed. *Berk* is a natural candidate, but so is *Ein*—in each case referred to a particular timelike line. If the question is construed as what to count as the past, or what to count as the present, most of us

---

[10] Compare Sklar, '... why one should think that such a doctrine of "No Privileged Observers" would lead one immediately to affirm the transitivity of "reality for", given that one has already relativized such previously nonrelative doctrines as that of simultaneity, is beyond me.' (Sklar 1981 p. 130). The answer is that Putnam's aim was exactly to show that once 'simultaneity with' is relativized in a way which is non-symmetric, and non-transitive, then 'reality for' must be relativized similarly: in which case it is unacceptable.

[11] Of course Berkeley was not proposing that all that exists is what is visible to a unique x—a unique and particular event in space and time; rather, he proposed that it is what is visible to God.

will settle for a foliation of spacetime, on which we can reach community-wide consent. It is *Ein*, and Ephemeris Time, that we will choose.[12]

Prospects for Presentism

Putnam made mistakes in his argument, but that does not explain its reception. Dickson has diagnosed the fault with it—as we have seen Stein says the same—as the sheer *inappropriateness*, in special relativity, of Putnam's assumptions; that 'before special relativity can have anything to say about the doctrines in question, they must be expressed in a language that is meaningful in a relativistic context' (Dickson p. 170). Stein's sympathy with Carnap's philosophy is well-known (Carnap was committed to the doctrine of incommensurability long before Kuhn): evidently it retains its appeal for Dickson as well.

But we can meet this objection head-on. The requirement of intersubjectivity is certainly relativistically meaningful. The inference from that to the requirement that R be an equivalence relation was independent of spacetime considerations altogether. To infer from that that there must exist a privileged foliation to Minkowski spacetime is precisely to spell out the doctrine in relativistically invariant terms. The fact that this doctrine is then ruled out by special relativity was precisely Putnam's point.

At the other extreme is the deflationary, commonsensical reading of presentism, along the lines sketched by Savitt and Moratio. According to them, it is obvious that the past did exist, that the future will exist, and that only the present is (presently) real. What, I wonder, is obvious to them? That only my momentary self is (presently) real? That what is (presently) real is what is related by *Ein*? Or is it *Con*, or is it *Berk*? They may of course reply that it makes no difference which, but that is not a deflationary reading of anything.

Somewhere in between is *quietism*, the view that special relativity cannot adjudicate on the matter unless supplemented by some form or other of verificationism (Sklar 1981). So it was with Einstein's elimination of ether; his approach to special relativity was explicitly verificationist, and only given this could he conclude that the ether did not exist. Indeed, the presentist has only to suppose that there is, in fact, a unique resting frame, albeit that no measurement can tell us what it is: this is the foliation he has been after all along.

[12] For a recent defence of the virtues of *Ein* over *Berk*, see Sarkar and Stachel (1999).

He can claim it serves an explanatory function in physics as well, citing Lorentz, for whom it was a 'matter of taste', and citing Bell, for whom it was the best way 'to teach the subject.'[13] But here I think Stein is exactly right when he says (Stein 1991 p. 155) that if it is verificationism that is needed, to do away with an absolute 'up' in the face of rotational symmetry, then it is a form of it that is perfectly defensible, that we should all of us embrace: the form of it which eliminates an absolute state of rest in the face of the relativity principle. And, obviously, one can draw the same conclusion on the basis of a *realist* view of Minkowski space (not of course available to Einstein *circa* 1905).

I have maintained that presentism is a substantive position that places clear demands on the theory of special relativity. They are demands which I do not think can be met, consistent with that theory. This fact needs to be clearly appreciated, if there is to be movement on this subject. Movement there is, as soon as we consider the wider perspective of Einstein's theory of gravity, and dynamics proper.

Of course general relativity, just like the special theory, is committed to the principle of arbitrariness of foliation. Nevertheless, for an important class of spacetime models—*hyperbolically complete* spacetimes, for which the Cauchy problem is soluble—there is a natural definition of a global foliation, which has a number of desirable, dynamical properties. It is essentially unique; it is what is actually used in numerical calculations in geometrodynamics; it also has links to a number of open theoretical questions, particularly questions concerning the nature of scale in the classical theory.

I give this example, called *York time*,[14] after its discover James York, not because I am convinced it is fundamental, in classical theory, but as an example of the new avenues that are opened up as soon as one considers gravitational dynamics proper.[15] Certainly

---

[13] This, the so-called 'Lorentz pedagogy', has recently been defended by Brown and Pooley (2001); but in their view it is not committed to the view that any one frame of reference is truly the resting frame; they suppose that the forces which yield the contraction and dilation effects may be explanatory, even if there is no fact of the matter as to what they really are.

[14] For a simple exposition of its uses in Hamiltonian formulations of general relativity, see Wald (1984).

[15] And to repair my unhappy neglect of it in my (1996). The class of hyperbolically-complete spacetimes is of course only a sector of the full theory, and there are already problems with this in the quantum case, if black-hole evaporation is anything to go by; but it is an important sector all the same, and black-hole evaporation equally causes problems for unitarity.

none of the arguments I have given here tell against it. And ultimately, of course, one must look to a quantum theory of gravity, where the interpretation of time in canonical approaches to quantization is anyway in dispute. If one throws into the equation the foundational problems of quantum mechanics, and the evident difficulty, in that context, of defining a Lorentz-covariant stochastic dynamics,[16] it is clear that here there is everything to play for. But we are not about to make progress with any of these fields if the metaphysics of presentism, in the most simple case of classical special relativity, is still in dispute. In this most simple case, I have argued, it can finally be laid to rest.

References

Bell, J. 1987. 'How to Teach Special Relativity', in *Speakable and Unspeakable in Quantum Mechanics,* Cambridge University Press: Cambridge.

Black, M. 1962. 'Review of G. J. Whitrow's "The Natural Philosophy of Time"', *Scientific American,* CCVI, pp. 181–2.

Brown, H. and O. Pooley 2000. 'The Origin of the Spacetime Metric: Bell's "Lorentzian Pedagogy" and its Significance in General Relativity', in *Physics Meets Philosophy at the Planck Length,* C. Callender and N. Huggett, (eds), Cambridge University Press: Cambridge.

Callender, C. 1998. 'Shedding Light on Time', *Philosophy of Science* (*Proceedings*), **67**, S587–S599.

Clifton, R. and M. Hogarth 1995. 'The Definability of Objective Becoming in Minkowski Spacetime', *Synthese,* **103**, 355–87.

M. Dickson 1998. 'Digression: The Block-Universe Argument', in *Quantum Chance and Non-Locality,* Cambridge University Press: Cambridge.

Earman, J. 1996. *Shrieks, Bangs, Whimpers and Grunts,* Oxford University Press: Oxford.

Gödel, K. 1949. 'A Remark About the Relationship Between Relativity Theory and Idealistic Philosophy', in *Albert Einstein, Philosopher-Scientist,* A. Schilpp, (ed.), Open Court, La Salle.

Landsberg, P. T. 1970. 'Time in Statistical Physics and Special Relativity', *Studium Generale,* **23**, pp. 1108–59.

Malement, D. 1994. 'Commentary', in *The Collected Papers of Kurt Gödel,* Vol. 3, S. Fefferman, J. Dawson, W. Goldfarb, C. Parsons and R. Solovay, (eds), Oxford University Press: Oxford.

---

[16] See my (1996) for illustrations of the difficulties, and the reasons why they do not arise in the Galilean-covariant case. For the difficulty in generalizating the pilot-wave theory to the relativisic case, see my (1999); the latter are less directly linked to the foliation-arbitrariness, however.

Maxwell, N. 1985. 'Are Probabilism and Special Relativity Incompatible?', *Philosophy of Science*, **52**, 23–43.

Putnam, H. 1967. 'Time and Physical Geometry', *Journal of Philosophy*, **64**, 240–47, reprinted in *Philosophical Papers*, Vol. 1, Cambridge University Press, Cambridge, 1975.

Rietdijk, C. 1966. 'A Rigorous Proof of Determinism Derived from the Special Theory of Relativity', *Philosophy of Science*, **33**, 341–4.

Sarkar, S. and J. Stachel 1999. 'Did Malament Prove the Non-Conventionality of Simultaneity in the Special Theory of Relativity?', *Philosophy of Science*, **66**, 208–20

Saunders, S. 1996. 'Time, Quantum Mechanics, and Tense', *Synthese*, **107**, 19–53.

Saunders, S. 1999. 'The "Beables" of Relativistic Pilot-Wave Theory', in *From Physics to Philosophy*, J. Butterfield, and C. Pagonis, (eds), Cambridge University Press: Cambridge.

Saunders, S. 1998. 'Tense and Indeterminateness', *Philosophy of Science (Proceedings)*, **67**, S600–611.

Savitt, S. 1994. 'The Replacement of Time', *Australasian Journal of Philosophy*, **72**, 463–74

Savitt, S. 1998. 'There's No Time Like the Present (in Minkowski Space-time)', *Philosophy of Science (Proceedings)*, **67**, S563–574.

Shimony, A. 1993. 'The Transient Now', in *Search for a Naturalistic World View*, Vol. 2, Cambridge University Press: Cambridge.

Sklar, L. 1981. 'Time, Reality, and Relativity', in *Reduction, Time and Reality*, R. Healey, (ed.), Cambridge University Press: Cambridge.

Smith, Q. 1993. 'Introduction', in *The New Theory of Time*, J. Oaklander and Q. Smith, (eds), Yale University Press: Newhaven.

Stein, H. 1968. 'On Einstein-Minkowski Space-Time', *Journal of Philosophy*, **65**, 5–23.

Stein, H. 1991. 'On Relativity Theory and the Openness of the Future', *Philosophy of Science*, **58**, 147–67.

Stein, H. 1994. 'Commentary', in *The Collected Papers of Kurt Gödel*, Vol. 3, S. Fefferman, J. Dawson, W. Goldfarb, C. Parsons and R. Solovay, (eds), Oxford University Press: Oxford.

Torretti, R. 1983. *Relativity and Geometry*, Pergamon Press: Oxford.

Wald, R. 1984. *General Relativity*, Chicago University Press: Chicago.

Can Physics Coherently Deny the Reality of Time?

RICHARD HEALEY

0. Introduction

The conceptual and technical difficulties involved in creating a quantum theory of gravity have led some physicists to question, and even in some cases to deny, the reality of time. More surprisingly, this denial has found a sympathetic audience among certain philosophers of physics. What should we make of these wild ideas? Does it even make sense to deny the reality of time? In fact physical science has been chipping away at common sense aspects of time ever since its inception. Section 1 offers a brief survey of the demolition process. Section 2 distinguishes a tempered from an extremely radical form that a denial of time might take, and argues that extreme radicalism is empirically self-refuting. Section 3 begins an investigation of the prospects for tempered radicalism in a timeless theory of quantum gravity.

1. How Physics Bears on the Reality of Time

Let me begin with a quotation:

> Time by itself does not exist. Time gets its meaning from the objects: from the fact that events are in the past, or that they are here now, or they will follow in the future. It is not possible that anybody may measure time by itself; it may only be measured by looking at the motion of the objects, or at their peaceful quiet.

This quote is from Lucretius's *De Rerum Natura*. It illustrates the fact that, for a long time now, there have been philosophers who have doubted the reality of time. But if that is indeed a fact, then it seems such doubts must have been misplaced after all! Does that mean it is simply incoherent to doubt the reality of time? I think not. But it does mean that anyone expressing such doubts has three tasks. The first task is to make clear just what *feature* of time it is whose reality is questionable. The second task is to show how we can get along with a concept of time that lacks that feature. The third task is to explain how we mistakenly came to believe in a time with that feature.

Take Lucretius as an example. He is not denying the existence of events, of temporal relations between them such as simultaneity, earlier and later, of a distinction between past, present and future, of change, or of motion. He may not even be denying the existence of temporal congruence relations—that a definite interval of time elapses between events. Perhaps he is merely claiming that we have only two ways of *measuring* the duration of such an interval. We can correlate its beginning and end with events in some more or less regular motion, treated as a clock; or we can simply estimate its duration by reference to our own internal 'sense of time'. At most then, Lucretius is denying the existence of moments of time distinct from events that occur at them, and of an absolute temporal metric, independent of actual physical or mental 'clocks' suited to measure it. To make good his denial, he must show how we can describe and explain our observations and experiences if there are really no such temporal structures. And he owes us an account of how we came to be fooled into believing in them.

Newton described the concept of time he was to employ in his physics in his famous Scholium to the *Principia*. This was richer in structure than that of Lucretius, incorporating not only an absolute temporal metric, but apparently also an ontology of temporal moments, existing independently of any events that may or may not occur at them. Newton even endorsed the common sense idea that time *flows*. But though this idea may well have had significant heuristic value for him in developing the mathematical framework in which to construct his theories (the calculus), it plays no essential role in the final structure of those theories. The great predictive and explanatory success of Newtonian physics seemed to establish the reality of the other features of Newton's time. In retrospect this proved a high water mark for the reality of time in physics from which it has been receding ever since.

In the nineteenth century, Boltzmann's attempts to find a mechanical basis for the physical irreversibility inherent in the second 'law' of thermodynamics highlighted the temporal reversibility of Newtonian mechanics, and indeed of all then known fundamental physical laws. This seemed to show that the distinction between earlier and later was accidental rather than a matter of fundamental physical law. Whether this is so remains controversial to this day. But even if there are temporally asymmetric fundamental physical laws, it is unclear to what extent these can account for the pervasive temporal asymmetries we observe in physical processes. Boltzmann went further, speculating that the manifest asymmetry between past and future was not itself a fundamental feature of time, but rather a reflection of the contingent asymmetries in physical processes, at least in our region of the universe. The idea is that in so far as these processes underlie the operation of our mental as well as physical lives, it is ultimately this feature of our physical situation that accounts for the perceived difference between past and future, which is not, therefore, a real feature of time itself.

Early in the 20th century, Einstein's theories of relativity undermined other features of common sense as well as Newtonian time. It came to be recognized that the temporal interval between non-coincident events is not an invariant quantity, but depends on the state of uniform motion to which one refers those events. If the events happen in such a way that a material particle could travel from one to the other, then the time interval between them is relative to the trajectory of such a particle: in that sense, time intervals are only locally defined. If the events are space-like separated, so not even light (in a vacuum) could travel from one to the other, then even their time *order* must be relativized to a state of uniform motion: this is the famous relativity of simultaneity. Accepting it means acknowledging that for space-like separated events simultaneity, earlier and later are not two place but three place relations, between a pair of events and a state of motion. This presents serious problems for any conception of time according to which a single present moment separates the past from the future, since the Minkowski space-time of special relativity (unlike that of Newton) does not in itself determine which distant events are to count as present.

At least Minkowski space-time permits one (somewhat arbitrarily) to define a global present moment—most naturally as a hyperplane of simultaneity in some chosen frame. But the space-time associated with a generic mass-energy distribution in general relativity will contain no such hyperplanes, and may not even contain a single global 'time-slice' (a space-like hypersurface with no boundary). As is well known, Kurt Gödel found a novel solution to the field equations of general relativity with no global time-slice and used its existence as a premise to mount a controversial argument for the unreality of time. He argued that time is unreal in so far as there can be no objective lapse of (global) time in Gödel space-time. But we have strong evidence that the space-time of our universe differs from Gödel space-time precisely in the crucial respect that it does indeed possess a global foliation into time-slices. This not only allows for the possibility of an objective lapse of global time in our universe.

It also seems to guarantee that our universe changes, and indeed expands, as time passes. For we have strong evidence that the spatial geometry and matter distribution of our universe differ in just this way on each time-slice, no matter how these slices are defined! However, there is a very different view of how general relativity treats time. Adopting this alternative view would void any guarantee of a changing universe, and replace it with the radical denial that there is any real physical change in a universe described by general relativity. The alternative view has been advocated not just by some physicists but also recently by the philosopher John Earman (forthcoming). At first glance, it may seem merely perverse to recommend that we adopt an alternative interpretation of general relativity with such radical implications for the nature of time and change. But such an interpretation can seem quite natural, or even inevitable, from a certain perspective.

This perspective emerges from attempts to create a quantum theory of gravity by applying standard quantization techniques to general relativity. Such attempts have been beset for forty years or more by severe conceptual as well as technical problems, including the notorious 'problem of time in quantum gravity'. Here is one way of stating that problem. Because of the vanishing of the Hamiltonian, the quantum gravity analog to the Schrödinger equation (the Wheeler-DeWitt Equation) implies that the wave-function(al) that supposedly describes the evolution of space and its contents never changes! This problem then comes back to haunt classical general relativity. For the basic strategy behind many attempts to quantize that theory has been to begin with a constrained Hamiltonian formulation, in which the theory is taken to describe the dynamics of space and its contents, rather than as corresponding to a collection of models of matter distributions in space-time. But in such a formulation, it seems that the genuine physical quantities of classical general relativity are all constants of the 'motion'—their values do not change! This raises two fascinating philosophical questions: Why do we experience change in such a Parmenidean universe?' and 'Is it even coherent to suppose that an *experience* of change might be an *illusion*?' I want to come back to these questions after completing this initial survey of ways in which physical theorizing bears on the purported reality of time.

As I have explained, relativity threatens the reality of various features of Newtonian and common-sense time such as the absoluteness of simultaneity and of temporal ordering of all events, the absoluteness of temporal duration, and the existence of a unique global division of events into past, present and future.

Quantum mechanics, on the other hand, seems quite conservative in its attitude toward time. Both non-relativistic quantum mechanics and relativistic quantum field theories simply assume some fixed space-time background—be it that of Newton, Minkowski or a curved general relativistic space-time. Such conservatism has even been thought to go over into a positively reactionary attitude toward time. I shall give three examples.

All fundamental theories known to Boltzmann were time-symmetric in this sense: If the models of the theory contained a motion from state S_1 at time t_1 to state S_2 at time t_2, then they also contained a 'time-reversed' motion from S^T_2 at time t_1 to S^T_1 at time t_2, where S^T indicates the so-called time-reversed state corresponding to state S (e.g. S^T might be a state of a bunch of Newtonian particles in which these particles have the same positions but oppositely directed momenta to what they have in state S). While requiring a slightly more subtle notion of time-reversal, relativity theory did not affect this general feature of physical theories. But with quantum mechanics the situation is more complicated. The time-dependent Schrödinger equation is the fundamental dynamical equation of non-relativistic quantum mechanics. It has been taken to be time-reversal invariant, but this is true only if one requires the time-reverse of the wave-function describing the state of a system to be given by taking its complex conjugate as well as replacing t by $-t$. This may he justified by claiming that the empirical content of the theory is exhausted by transition probabilities from one state to another, and the suggested requirements ensure that these are time-reversal invariant. But this claim is controversial. Moreover, the quantum measurement process seems to introduce a fundamentally time-asymmetric element into the theory through the notorious 'collapse of the wave-packet'. Craig Callender (2000), for one, has argued that a thorough analysis of quantum mechanics reveals that it is *not* a time-reversal invariant theory. If that's right, then the theory reintroduces the distinction between earlier and later into physical theory at a fundamental level.

Naive versions of the collapse postulate in quantum mechanics take it to occur at an instant, even though prior to collapse the wave had significant amplitude over a wide region. Any such physical process could he instantaneous in only one frame. If all collapses occur instantaneously in a single frame, then the collapse postulate picks out a preferred frame as a matter of physical law, in violation of the principle of relativity. Such violation could be extremely hard to demonstrate experimentally because of decoherence effects, and so cannot be taken to be in conflict with existing evidence supporting

Richard Healey

the principle of relativity. The existence of such a preferred frame would motivate an argument for additional temporal structure in Minkowski space-time (or a general relativistic space-time) corresponding to an absolute quasi-Newtonian time over and above the relativistic times appropriate to (relativistic) reference frames in various states of motion in that space-time. The presence of such structure could be taken to reinstate absolute simultaneity and a global distinction between the past, present and future of an event. Similar conclusions may be drawn from a Bohmian account of violation of Bell inequalities, involving information travelling from one wing of an Aspect-type apparatus to the other at an arbitrarily fast speed in some unique, privileged reference frame—a frame that is experimentally undetectable, thus preserving the principle of relativity at an empirical level. Maudlin (1994), for one, seriously entertains such an account.

As a third and final example of an attempt to draw a reactionary conclusion about the real features of time from quantum mechanics, consider John Lucas's recent appeal to quantum mechanics to locate the flow of time at a fundamental level in physical theory. I quote:

> There is a worldwide tide of actualization—collapse into eigenness—constituting a preferred foliation by hyperplanes (not necessarily flat) of co-presentness sweeping through the universe—a tide which determines an absolute present ... Quantum mechanics ... not only insists on the arrow being kept in time, but distinguishes a present as the boundary between an alterable future and an unalterable past. (Butterfield, ed. (1999), p. 10)

Lucas believes that real quantum-mechanical collapse reinstates not only absolute simultaneity, but also real tense, i.e. an objective but constantly changing distinction between past, present and future corresponding to the objective passage of events from potentiality to actuality (or nonactuality). If he's right, then quantum physics has finally come up with the cash to back Newton's promissory note in his reference to the flow of time!

But this was counterfeit coinage concealed in the metaphysician's sleeve. Even if quantum mechanical 'collapse into eigenness' were to occur on a global time-slice this would require at most an absolute time in the sense of a privileged foliation by such slices. The fact that the state on a slice is not determined by those on earlier slices in no way precludes the actual determinateness of states at all time(-slice)s. An opponent who denies the metaphysical reality of tense could even point to a sense in which 'collapse into eigenness' renders the past more open than the future. For while a state may collapse into any one of a discrete set of eigenstates of the measured observable, such a post-collapse eigenstate is compatible with each of a continuous infinity of non-orthogonal pre-collapse states!

Quantum mechanics is a distraction from the battle over the reality of tense, which is more properly fought on metaphysical ground. Radical deniers of tense such as Mellor (1981) would argue that Lucas's 'worldwide tide of actualization' falls prey to McTaggart's (1908) notorious argument for the unreality of time. For the kind of change Lucas takes quantum mechanics to underwrite—an event's changing from potential to actual (or counterfactual) with the passage of time—is an example of what Mellor called 'McTaggart change'. The radical response to Lucas is to agree with McTaggart that the idea of such change is simply incoherent, though fortunately not required for things to undergo the less metaphysically loaded kind of change we, as well as quantum physicists, suppose them to.

If I'm right, then quantum mechanics alone neither establishes nor poses any threat to the reality of time. But things change (if anything does!) when one tries to come up with a quantum theory of gravity. It turns out to be very hard to fit even *ordinary* change into the resulting framework of thought. And some (notably Julian Barbour) have given up the attempt and simply declared that change, motion, indeed time itself are all ultimately illusory.

2. The Perils of Parmenides

Before plunging into the details of canonical quantum gravity and the constrained Hamiltonian approach to general relativity as a gauge theory, I want to step back to survey the ground that needs to be covered by anyone who wishes to use these details to argue for the unreality of time, or at least of change.

Here is the basic situation. Any theory of gravity, quantum or classical, is a physical theory. We have no reason to believe this, or any other physical theory, without evidence. The evidence for any physical theory is empirical: it consists, ultimately, in the results of observations and experiments. Whatever physical form these take, they must give rise to experiences in scientists who perform them if they are to serve their epistemic purpose. Such experiences will be events—at least mental if not also physical. For there to be such events, it must be possible to make sense of the idea that they occur

Richard Healey

in time—that the *earlier* mental state of an observer was a state of ignorance, while his or her *later* mental state was a state of knowledge (at least in a weak sense of that term). Moreover, at least in the typical case, a physical theory is confirmed by testing its *predictions*—statements made *at an earlier time* in ignorance of their truth-value and then checked by making observations *at a later time*. Both the formulation of a prediction and the performance of a subsequent observation to test it are *acts*—events of a particular kind involving different intentional states that the observer is in at different times. It follows that the testing of a prediction presupposes the possibility of *change*—in the mental state of an observer, if not also in the physical state of the world that he or she is observing.

All these points are blindingly obvious. But note what follows from them. There can be no reason whatever to accept any theory of gravity—quantum or classical—which entails that there can be no observers, or that observers can have no experiences, some occurring later than others, or that there can be no change in the mental states of observers, or that observers cannot perform different acts at different times. It follows that there can be no reason to accept any theory of gravity—quantum or classical—which entails that there is no time, or that there is no change. Now it is important to note that it does not follow that no such theory can be *true*. But any such theory would have the peculiar feature that, if true, there could be no reason to accept it. To borrow a term from Jeff Barrett (1999), any such theory would be *empirically incoherent*. It follows that no argument that concludes that time, or at least change, is unreal, and which starts from the assumption that some theory of gravity—quantum or classical—is true, can have any empirical basis. In the case of a quantum theory of gravity, this negative conclusion may not come as a surprise. Not only do we not currently have any convincing quantum theory of gravity, but the prospects for finding evidence to support any such theory are at best distant. But classical general relativity is a different matter: we take ourselves to have considerable evidence supporting this theory, especially following careful analysis of the binary pulsar studied by Hulse and Taylor. But if general relativity, correctly interpreted, implies the nonexistence of time, or of change, then we must be wrong to take this evidence to support the theory after all. For the correct interpretation of this supposed evidence must undercut its epistemic credentials. Put bluntly, a radically timeless interpretation of general relativity entails the impossibility of performing any of the experiments and observations, the

300

performance of which we ordinarily take to provide our reasons to believe that theory. Such an interpretation makes the theory empirically self-refuting.

Now I want to suggest that things may not he entirely hopeless for a contemporary Parmenidean. His strategy must he to embark on an ambitious reconstruction project—the project of coming up with serviceable replacements for those temporal concepts—implicit as well as explicit—which, as currently understood, presuppose the existence of time and change at a fundamental level. A glance at the history of science reveals a number of similar reconstruction projects necessitated by advances in fundamental physics, some more radical than others. As has often been noted, these have typically involved the 'demotion' of some concept, formerly assumed to pick out some fundamental element of physical reality, to something more anthropocentric. The up/down distinction and the distinction between motion and rest both came to be relativized to particular states, and so to be naturally associated with the perspective of an observer in such a state. With relativity, the same thing happened to spatial and temporal intervals, and also to energy and momentum. So-called secondary qualities like colours and sounds came to be regarded not as fundamental properties of objects and events, but rather as corresponding to a humanly convenient way of categorizing those things in response to fundamental properties such as the wavelengths of light and sound that they reflect or emit. There is a tradition of describing such conceptual displacements in radical terms. Galileo famously contributed to this tradition when he said in *The Assayer*

> I think, therefore that these tastes, odours, colours, etc. so far as their objective existence is concerned, are nothing but mere names for something which resides exclusively in our sensitive body, so that if the perceiving creatures were removed, all of these qualities would be annihilated and abolished from existence. But just because we have given special names to these qualities, different from the names we have given to the primary and real properties, we are tempted into believing that the former really and truly exist as well as the latter.

I place contemporary Parmenideans in the same radical tradition as Galileo. Detecting the need for a conceptual shift in our temporal concepts in the light of contemporary physics, they characterize that shift in eliminativist terms. Noting the consequent failure of our standard temporal vocabulary to mark out any fundamental temporal facts, they take our assertions employing this vocabulary to be massively in error. They take the view that the denial of time and/or change is merely the honest acknowledgment of this error.

But even with regard to secondary qualities like colours and sounds this radical approach is not the only way to go, and it may not be the best way. Even if we acknowledge that the colour of an apple is not among its most fundamental physical attributes, distinguishing Red Delicious from Granny Smiths by colour is extremely convenient given the contingencies of human colour vision and ambient lighting conditions. There continue to be good reasons for deploying colour concepts which allow that Red Delicious apples are red even when the lights are out, and would continue to be red even 'if the perceiving creatures were removed'. A less radical response to a scientifically induced conceptual shift is desirable for practical purposes, and in this case it is certainly available. We know it is available because we successfully avail ourselves of it on a daily basis. But this transcendental argument from practice conceals an important scientific and philosophical question: 'How is the human practice of making what we call colour discriminations possible if colour is not a fundamental property of physical objects?' Any account of colour that denies that colour is a fundamental property of physical objects owes us at least a sketch of an answer to this question. And any such account that entails that the question is unanswerable is *ipso facto* unacceptable.

Physical science has had the resources to provide such a sketch since the seventeenth century. The details have been significantly modified as the account has become more sophisticated since Newton's classic investigations on the nature of light and colours. But the sketch is still broadly as follows. We see a red apple when ambient light is reflected from its surface to our eye. The surface of the apple has intrinsic physical properties (describable without mentioning colour) that dispose it preferentially to reflect certain components of the ambient light incident on it while absorbing others. The reflected light therefore has a different composition than the ambient light: again, this composition is describable in physical terms without mentioning colour. Light with this different composition is disposed to elicit a characteristic sensation when it enters the open eye of a human with normally functioning visual and neural systems. An English speaker experiencing this sensation has acquired the ability to apply the term 'red' to objects like apples that elicit it in normal viewing circumstances, along with other discriminatory and inferential abilities associated with his or her possession of the corresponding concept. Thus while a fundamental physical account—of apples, the light they reflect, and the human who sees them—need include no mention of colour, it does not follow that apples have no colour. Rather, that account explains our abilities successfully to deploy colour concepts like *red* in ordinary circumstances, and thereby legitimizes this application. It licenses the claim that Red Delicious apples really are red, even though redness is not a fundamental physical property.

The central claim of a contemporary Parmenidean is that time, or something basic that presupposes time (such as change), is in effect a secondary quality. The claim is that, like colour, time and/or change is not a fundamental feature of the world. And just as Galileo went on to deny the objective existence of the secondary quality of colour, so too a contemporary radical Parmenidean denies the objective existence of time and/or change. But while agreeing with Galileo about the importance of the primary/secondary quality distinction, the philosopher Locke may be read rather as drawing a distinction between two kinds of objective properties. On this reading, the primary qualities of an object are those that figure in a fundamental (corpuscularian) account of its nature: the secondary qualities arise from complex arrangements of matter in particular circumstances that dispose it to affect our senses in certain characteristic ways. This suggests a moderate, neo-Lockean, alternative to the radical contemporary Parmenidean who simply denies the reality of time and/or change. It is to accept that time and/or change is a secondary quality, but to go on to explain how it arises from some more fundamental features of the world in particular circumstances that explain both why we experience our world as temporal and why we are warranted in so describing it. I think the contemporary Parmenidean would be wise to take this suggestion seriously. Only in this way can he or she rescue the physical theory that supposedly grounds Parmenideanism from empirical incoherence.

A claim that time or change is a secondary quality requires some initial clarification if it is to seem defensible. What is time or change supposed to be a secondary quality *of*? This question reads such claims too literally: what matters is being secondary, not being a quality. One may explicate the claim that time is a secondary quality as follows. Qualitative and quantitative temporal relations such as being earlier than or occurring two weeks after are to be understood not as external relations but as relations that hold, when they do, by virtue of intrinsic properties of objects including their relata. Barbour calls these objects 'Nows': a Now is something like an instantaneous global state of the universe in relative configuration space. The intrinsic properties of Nows may be compared, and if all the Nows have the right kinds of intrinsic properties, then it will follow that certain events bear one another relations corresponding to qualitative and quantitative temporal relations such as being earlier than or occurring two weeks after. The claim then is that when such temporal relations obtain between a pair of events, they do so only by virtue of the nontemporal properties of all the Nows. This is a deeply Leibnizean picture, in which neither time nor temporal relations are literally qualities, even though both arise from what may be considered primary qualities of Nows.

A second difficulty is presented by the inclusion of *state of motion* in lists of primary qualities, beginning with Locke. For motion clearly requires change. Indeed, Aristotle took any kind of change in the properties of a substance to be a sort of motion, taking what we call motion to correspond merely to change of place, or local motion. But if motion is a primary quality, then change cannot be a secondary quality, and nor can the time it presupposes.

This difficulty does not present a serious challenge to the thesis that time and change are secondary qualities. To resolve it, it suffices to note that the set of primary qualities should not be taken to be defined by any fixed list. What should appear on a list of primary qualities at any stage in the development of science are just those properties and relations that science then takes to be fundamental. Thus a list of the primary qualities of elementary particles today would include such things as electric charge and intrinsic spin. Indeed contemporary physicists have playfully added what they call 'colour' and 'flavour' to their list of primary qualities of quarks, confident that after Galileo and Newton no-one could confuse these with the colour and flavour of Red Delicious apples! Physics long ago abandoned the corpuscularian restriction of primary qualities to those observable or 'conceivable' (i.e. imaginable) in ordinary middle-sized objects.

The fact that motion is historically taken to be a primary rather than a secondary quality does not refute the view that time and/or change is a secondary quality.

I hope these considerations have at least made conceptual space for claims to the effect that change and the time it presupposes are secondary qualities. But so far we have seen no reason why reflection on contemporary physics should motivate anyone to try to occupy that space.

3. The Timelessness of Canonical Quantum Gravity

In the canonical quantization approach to a quantum theory of gravity pioneered by Dirac, one begins with a formulation of general relativity as a constrained Hamiltonian system, and proceeds to quantize the theory by following a standard prescription that works well when applied to other theories like electromagnetism. If one starts with the usual variables (rather than Ashtekar's new variables), then one ends up with the Wheeler-Dewitt equation. The equation itself is very complex, and may not even be well-defined mathematically. I know of no realistic solutions to the full equation (though Smolin (2001), p. 40 claims to have found some), but approximate solutions have been found to simplified versions of the equation at least in restricted circumstances (e.g. by Hawking and Hartle). What would a solution look like? It would be a complex-valued function whose arguments are 3-dimensional spatial geometries with matter fields defined on them. Hartle and Hawking call a cosmological solution a 'wave-function of the universe'. If this is indeed analogous to an ordinary quantum mechanical wave-function, then the square of its absolute value should associate a probability to each value of its arguments. But this raises two related problems. It is unclear what these are probabilities of: and whatever they are probabilities of, those probabilities don't change with time since there simply is no time parameter in the equation (it is like a 'time-dependent' Schrödinger equation with a zero Hamiltonian operator). One might expect a solution to the equation to yield answers to questions like 'What is the probability of finding the system with such-and-such matter fields and spatial geometry if these were measured at time t?' But since the equation itself contains no time parameter, any answer to such a question can only be independent of the value of t. This would make sense if the state of the system in fact never changed with time. One kind of Parmenidean takes this to warrant the denial of change at a fundamental level in any system described by the Wheeler-Dewitt equation: I shall call this character a *changeless Parmenidean*. But there is an even more radical Parmenidean who concludes not merely that any system described by the Wheeler-Dewitt equation is in fact devoid of change, but rather that the absence of any time parameter in the equation shows that there is in fact no such thing as time. The idea is that, rather than having the same answer for all values of t, a question of the form 'What is the probability of finding the system with such-and-such matter fields and spatial geometry if these were measured at time t?' has a false presupposition—that there are times

Richard Healey

to which 't' may refer! I shall call this even more extreme Parmenidean a *timeless Parmenidean*. Both Parmenideans are now committed to the kind of reconstruction project I outlined in the previous section.

I now want to focus on the Parmenidean views of two physicists: Carlo Rovelli and Julian Barbour. I am indebted to John Earman (forthcoming) for his exposition of Rovelli's views, as well as to Rovelli (1991). I take Barbour's book *The End of Time* and his (1994a,b) as my source for his views. Rovelli's idea of 'evolving constants' may suggest that he is a changeless Parmenidean—denying change but not time, while it is natural to take Barbour to be a timeless Parmenidean. But in the end I think they are both timeless Parmenideans, though Barbour's Parmenideanism is still the more radical.

In a constrained Hamiltonian formulation of dynamical theory, it is normal procedure to require that genuine physical quantities be gauge invariant, i.e. that they commute with all the (first-class) constraints. This requirement is motivated in part by consideration of examples of theories such as classical electromagnetism in which there are independent reasons to conclude that quantities that are not gauge invariant (such as the electromagnetic potentials) are indeed unobservable, while gauge invariant quantities (such as electromagnetic fields) are observable. In general relativity (or indeed any diffeomorphism-invariant dynamical theory) the requirement of gauge invariance implies that the only genuine quantities are those that commute with the Hamiltonian constraints. But since the Hamiltonian constraints generate the time-evolution of the system, it follows that the only genuine physical quantities in such a theory are constants of the 'motion'! We have a 'frozen' dynamics: no genuine physical quantity changes. This looks like changeless Parmenideanism. Note that this conclusion has been arrived at purely at the *classical* level, even though one main reason to employ the constrained Hamiltonian formulation of a dynamical theory is as a prelude to quantizing that theory.

Rovelli's idea of 'evolving constants' can also be explained at the classical level. The idea is that, for many constrained Hamiltonian systems (including diffeomorphism-invariant ones), there will be some parameter which can be thought of as a 'clock' variable—think, perhaps, of the radius of the expanding universe in a spatially compact model of general relativity. Now this parameter will not itself be gauge invariant, and nor will some other quantity in whose 'evolution' one might be interested (say, a parameter corresponding to the density of matter in that universe). But one can construct a continuous family of gauge invariant quantities corresponding, for example, to 'density of matter-at universe radius R', for varying R. Now each of these is a genuine physical quantity, and while each individual quantity is constant, the 'evolution' of the universe's matter density may be taken to he reflected in the continuously varying values of these quantities with varying R. We have the illusion of change while everything really stays the same!

But how can we explain our experience of change by appeal to such evolving constants? Earman (forthcoming) suggests two ways to go. The first would be simply to postulate some primitive human faculty which lets us interpret the difference between two constant quantities such as 'matter density d_1 at R_1' and 'matter density d_2 at R_2' as an instance of change. The second, and perhaps more promising, would be to show how the physics of the objects and our psychology combine in such a way that we represent the world as filled with change despite the fact that no genuine physical quantity changes. Both these strategies strike me as hopeless. More importantly, I don't think Rovelli himself would be tempted to pursue either strategy. My reason for saying this is that it seems to me that while Rovelli is indeed aware of the need to somehow explain the temporal character of our experience, and in particular our experience of change, he himself does not introduce his evolving constants to that end. His primary concern is to arrive at a quantum theory of gravity by some canonical quantization technique. The evolving constants are introduced not to explain our illusion of change in a changeless world, but to provide a substitute for time in a fundamentally timeless theory. They are there to help us to do fundamental physics, not to explain the temporal character of our experience. How then are we to do that? Here Rovelli appeals to a different tactic. Two quotes are highly relevant

> An accepted interpretation of [the disappearance of the time coordinate from the Wheeler-DeWitt equation] is that *physical* time has to be identified with one of the internal degrees of freedom of the theory itself (*internal time*). (1991, p. 442)
> ... we do not address the problem of the existence of an exact internal time in general relativity. Instead, we assume, first, that a way to obtain an approximate description of the world as we see it (with time) can be extracted from the theory, second, that this description is valid only within the approximation. (p. 443)

As I understand him, he believes that the task of accounting for the temporal character of the world as we experience it is to be undertaken in three stages. The first stage is to develop a coherent (and hopefully empirically successful!) quantum theory of gravity. The second is to apply this to derive the existence of some kind of internal time *as an approximation in a classical limit*. And the final stage is to use this approximate internal time to account for the temporal character of the world as we experience it—since such experiences are inevitably going to occur only under circumstances in which the approximation of the classical limit is valid. Now Rovelli himself says that 'The physical hypothesis that we put forward is the absence of any well-defined concept of time at the fundamental level'. (p. 442) This makes him a timeless Parmenidean in my terminology. It would be consistent with his program to develop a quantum theory of gravity which contained nothing remotely like time, as long as an approximate time could be retrieved from this theory in the classical limit. But (he thinks) it turns out that the best way of aiming for a quantum theory of gravity is to use 'evolving constants' associated with 'clock parameters' as technical substitutes for the fundamental time that is missing from that theory. I can see nothing in the programme that requires these 'evolving constants' to play any role in retrieving an approximate internal time in the classical limit. And it is this latter project which is eventually supposed to make the connection with our temporal experience, not the project in which he is initially engaged in constructing a quantum theory of gravity which will have this limit. Of course, we philosophers await the successful completion of the former project before we can be satisfied that the hoped-for quantum theory of gravity is not merely internally consistent but also empirically successful. For, as I stressed in the previous section, we can have no empirical reason to believe such a theory if it cannot explain even the possibility of our performing observations and experiments capable of providing evidence to support it. And in the absence of convincing evidence for such a theory we have no good reason to deny the existence of time as a fundamental feature of reality.

Barbour explicitly denies the existence of time. Once more, his denial is intimately connected to his attempts to make sense of the Wheeler-DeWitt equation. Unlike Rovelli, he makes no mention of 'evolving constants', but he does make considerable efforts to show how what is, for him, our *illusory* experience of time arises. His basic explanatory device is that of what he calls a 'time-capsule'. This is a highly-structured 'Now'. Recall that for Barbour, Nows of various kinds and multiplicities constitute the basic furniture of the world. To get an idea of what a Now is supposed to be, one is supposed to think initially in temporal terms. In those terms, a Now corresponds to an instantaneous relative configuration of the universe. But of course, Nows are neither instants nor contained in any independently existing time: they just exist atemporally. Most Nows are not time-capsules. But amongst the vast number of Nows are a few whose internal structure contains a representation of an entire sequence of other Nows—a sequence that, when appropriately ordered in accordance with the internal properties of each represented Now, comes to represent what looks like a possible *history*. These are the time-capsules. Barbour's central idea is that experiencing such a time-capsule gives rise to the (misleading) belief that it does indeed represent the sequence of events that have actually occurred, so that the 'history' apparently represented in the time-capsule in fact occurred as a unique sequence of events in time.

A solution to the Wheeler-DeWitt equation assigns probabilities to all Nows, and Barbour conjectures that it must do so in such a way as to enormously favour those that correspond to time-capsules. He offers little support for this conjecture, and this lacuna has been highlighted as the weak link in his argument by Jeremy Butterfield (forthcoming) in his review of Barbour's book. But let's assume that the conjecture turns out to be true. How would this establish Barbour's claim to have accounted for our experiencing a literally timeless world as temporal?

The truth of the conjecture would leave most of the needed reconstruction still to be carried out. The task is to show how, in a fundamentally timeless world composed ultimately only of Nows, it is possible for there to be observers who naturally experience that world as temporal—as having a history and incorporating motion and change. To do this it would be necessary to explain why observers in a timeless world have experiences of particular kinds, including experiences of motion, apparent memories of past events, observations of mutually consistent apparent records of past events, and so on. That is what the high probability of time-capsules is supposed to do. Barbour cannot begin to explain the *character* of our experience until he has first explained how a timeless world can contain *observers* capable of *having experiences* with any character at all. The explanation has to start from the Nows, since Barbour takes everything else to he composed of, or supervenient upon, these. The first step, then, must be to provide a reconstruction of observers in terms of Nows. Ordinarily we think of observers as enduring embodied things that maintain their identities *through time*. If we are wrong to think of observers in this way, how can we think of them?

This is only the first of many basic questions to which Barbour owes us an answer if he is to carry off a successful reconstruction of our temporal experience from timeless elements. We need to be told what it is for an observer to have different experiences at different times without assuming the independent existence of such times. We need to know what it is for a particular Now to be actual rather than merely possible. And we need to understand what the probabilities generated by a solution to a timeless Wheeler-DeWitt equation are probabilities of; and how their concentration on time-capsules helps to account not only for the general character of our temporal experience, but also for those special experiences of scientists capable of confirming the theory of quantum gravity on which the whole reconstruction project rests.

In my judgment Barbour's published works do not provide clear, consistent and satisfactory answers to these questions. But they do contain the materials for a charitable interpretation of his project that might do so. It is in this constructive spirit that I offer the following answers on Barbour's behalf.

Begin with Barbour's 'many-instants' interpretation of quantum theory, and of quantum cosmology in particular. This agrees with Everett that there is no physical wave collapse. Barbour supposes that the solution to a Wheeler-DeWitt equation for our universe assumes a WKB form over a significant region of the whole space of relative configurations, with a semi-classical factor representing its gross features, and a quantum factor associated with the finer details of it structure. He conjectures that the solution's probability density is sharply peaked on time-capsules, each apparently recording in its configuration a history of the development of the gross features of the universe. Moreover, these time-capsules are supposed to be arrayed along what may be called 'streamers' in relative configuration space in such a way that those in any particular streamer cohere with one another, in two senses. Each time-capsule in a streamer itself contains multiple (almost) mutually consistent apparent records of the universe's prior development. And the capsules in a streamer may be ordered in a sequence whose elements apparently record a single history of the gross features of the universe up until successively later stages in its development.

Within this framework we may begin to answer the questions posed earlier. Begin with the modal status of the Nows. The time-capsules in each streamer collectively portray an apparent history of a world, with relatively minor inconsistencies in their individual representations of that history. The time sequence of a history is portrayed by virtue of the nested time-capsules' representations: hence temporal relations are not external relations between real events, but relations between portrayed events determined by internal relations among the time-capsules that portray them. An event counts as actual relative to a streamer just in case it figures in the apparent history the streamer portrays: a Now counts as actual relative to that streamer if and only if it contributes to the portrayal of the apparent history. In both cases actuality is indexical. The apparent histories portrayed in distinct streamers are like David Lewis's possible worlds. No apparent history is any more real than the others. In this sense all possible worlds are equally real (or unreal)! All Nows are real. Since only those Nows within a streamer contribute to a possible world, there is a sense in which only these Nows are possible—the rest are impossible, though still real! A residual vagueness attaches to all these categories, since the sharp peaking of probability that defines the streamers leaves these with 'tails' of low probability. This modal vagueness is ontological rather than conceptual or linguistic, and constitutes a provocative and potentially problematic consequence of the view.

An observer is basically a physical object whose structure permits the formation of internal records in the configurations of its 'memory'. In the case of human observers, some of these internal neurological record states determine the contents of experience and conscious memory. Any enduring physical object is taken to be constituted by, or at least to have its states supervenient upon, appropriate events portrayed by the Nows in a streamer. So now we have our observers, and human observers with experiences. Any human experience is determined by that human's neurological state at a particular Now. A person will have different experiences at different Nows. Some of these will include representations of others, integrated in such a way as to be experienced as having happened earlier. Others will be integrated in such a way as to be experienced as perceived motion.

Streamers 'branch' in global configuration space. This induces branching of the possible worlds they portray and of physical objects, including observers, in such worlds. We suppose that the relative multiplicities of Nows of each type reflect the probabilities derived from a solution to the Wheeler-DeWitt equation. Consider a physicist about to perform a quantum measurement. The physicist and his environment are in a possible world portrayed by a streamer in universal configuration space. Many different streamers branch off from the Now that includes the physicist's experience as he is about to perform the experiment—at least one streamer for every possible measurement outcome. The Wheeler-DeWitt probabilities give the relative numbers of streamers corresponding to each possible outcome. The physicist's experiential state contains

Richard Healey

no information fixing which of these streamers portrays the 'future history' of him and his environment. But the Wheeler-DeWitt probabilities may be used to condition his expectations, by yielding the probability that the streamer portraying the state he now experiences also portrays this rather than that outcome of his measurement. This finally gives empirical content to the Wheeler-DeWitt probabilities. These do not specify the probability of a particular Now being real, or actualized, or even of its being experienced as actual. Instead, when conditionalized, they yield the probability that an apparent history will continue in one way rather than another. Finally we see how it is that an observer can come to have experiences of a kind capable of confirming the theory of quantum gravity that entails a Wheeler-DeWitt equation which issues in a timeless probability density on the space of global relative configurations. It is striking that experiences whose apparent content so misleads one about the course of history may nevertheless come to provide evidential support for a theory that predicts them. In this respect the view involves a radical reinterpretation of the content of experience in the tradition of Galileo's defence of Copernicanism by reinterpreting our experience of a 'stationary' earth.

This sketch of a Barbourian account of experience is radically incomplete and slurs over problems sufficiently serious to justify extreme scepticism about the feasibility of the whole reconstruction project. It is best to think of it, not as a defence of Barbour's view, but rather as an exploration of conceptual possibilities. As such, it serves as an illustration of the radical moves that may be required before adopting an interpretation of a theory of quantum gravity that demotes time to secondary quality status if one is to avoid rendering that theory empirically incoherent.

Let me summarize my discussion of the prospects for attempts to establish timeless Parmenideanism by reflection on the canonical approach to quantum gravity. Rovelli acknowledges the need for a timeless quantum gravity to explain the temporal character of the world as we experience it, but he has a quite different motivation for introducing his 'evolving constants'. While Barbour portrays himself as a radical timeless Parmenidean, he has made serious efforts to explain what he takes to be our *illusion* that we inhabit a temporal world. But his efforts still fall short of what would be needed to do that. Moreover, a successful explanation of our experience of a temporal world on the basis of a fundamentally timeless theory cannot establish this experience as wholly *illusory*. For our only evidence for such a theory must come from experience of a temporal world.

Can Physics Coherently Deny the Reality of Time?

Now we have no current empirical evidence for any theory of canonical quantum gravity. But we do take ourselves to have considerable evidence supporting *classical* general relativity. This makes it interesting to examine a recent argument by John Earman (forthcoming) in support of an interpretation of classical general relativity according to which there is no change in fundamental physical magnitudes.

As I read him, Earman's argument against change in the general theory of relativity (GTR) comes in two versions. The first begins by noting that GTR is superficially indeterministic in the following sense. A complete specification of the metric and matter fields on and to the past of a time-slice S that is a Cauchy surface fixes the development to the future of S only up to a diffeomorphism d that reduces to the identity on and to the past of S: if $m_1 = \; < M, g, T >$ is a solution to the field equations, so is $m_2 = \; < M, d^*g, d^*T >$, where d^* is the drag-along corresponding to the diffeomorphism d. The argument continues by recommending adoption of a suggestion by Bergman (1961) that genuine observables be restricted to diffeomorphism-invariant quantities. Such quantities do not discriminate between m_1 and m_2, which may consequently be regarded as physically equivalent, thereby neutralizing the threat of indeterminism. But this restriction turns out to imply the apparently absurd conclusion that there can be no change in local physical quantities, as long as these are built up from Bergmannian observables.

The obvious response to this argument is to accept the absurdity of its conclusion, and to treat it as a *reductio* of Bergmann's suggested restriction on observables. One can still regard m_1 and m_2 as equivalent representations of a single physical situation if one takes their diffeomorphically related geometric objects (such as d^*g, g) to represent the same physical quantities. From this perspective, the choice of d^*g (say) in m_2 rather than g in m_1 to represent the space-time metric is fundamentally no different than the choice of one coordinate system rather than another in which to represent the components of g. Both are merely choices among alternative mathematical representations of the same physical reality. In each case, connecting the representation to observation requires coordinating mathematical objects to directly presented physical objects and processes. Different choices simply require different coordinations. The physical determinism of GTR may be secured without adopting Bergmann's suggested restriction on observables.

It is interesting that it was Bergmann who made this suggestion, since he was an influence behind the constrained Hamiltonian formulation of GTR, and it is to this formulation that Earman's second version appeals. The second version advocates a different, though related, restriction on observables. This time, it is maintained that a genuine observable must be gauge invariant, in the sense of commuting with all first-class constraints. Since the Hamiltonian constraints generate motion, it follows that any such observable will be a constant of the motion, again apparently implying that there is no change in any genuine physical quantity. But despite its initial plausibility within the constrained Hamiltonian framework, the new restriction on observables is controversial. In particular, its applicability to the Hamiltonian constraints has been rejected by Kuchar (1992, 1999) and others. And even its initial plausibility depends on adopting the constrained Hamiltonian formulation of GTR—A formulation that is strictly optional prior to quantization, and only one of several frameworks in which physicists have struggled to develop a quantum theory of gravity.

Another argument (not offered by Earman) appeals to the ontology of GTR. Our common sense notion of change requires an object that endures while having different properties at different times. But no such enduring objects are postulated by a field theory like GTR. Hence there can be no common-sense change in a general-relativistic world.

This argument fails also. While GTR does not itself postulate enduring things, neither does it exclude them. In some models of GTR, classical fields are distributed in such a way as to provide just the right kinds of spatio-temporal continuity to connect up what may consequently be regarded as succeeding stages of enduring objects that supervene on them. Moreover, GTR can be taken to underwrite causal links between these stages even though it does not itself make causal claims. In these circumstances, even though GTR by itself does not entail the existence of enduring things, it makes room for their existence. Moreover, changes in the properties of such objects from earlier to later time-slices are naturally taken to supervene on variations in underlying fields. Property change is not only compatible with GTR: GTR nicely accounts for the possibility of property change.

The standard interpretation of classical general relativity as a space-time theory without restrictions on observables does allow for the existence of enduring physical objects like tables, chairs, planets, stars, you and me. Moreover, this interpretation allows for the possibility of change, including those changes in the world and our mental states that we take to ground our reasons for confidence in general relativity. Any interpretation that cannot allow for our possession of this evidence is *ipso facto* inferior, whatever other advantages it may seem to have. I have found wanting two arguments based on alternative interpretations that involve restrictions on what can count as observable. But if such an argument were to succeed it could not rationally convince us to adopt a changeless-Parmenidean interpretation of the theory absent an adequate account of what we take to be the changes that warrant our acceptance of the theory in the first place. If experiments turn out to warrant belief in general relativity only interpreted as an indeterministic theory, then, surprising as it may seem, we should believe that the world is described by an indeterministic general relativity. The only alternative would be to suspend belief in one of our best theories altogether. The role of the philosopher of physics as intellectual conscience of the practicing physicist does not license such a sweeping condemnation.

References

Barbour, J. 1994a. 'The timelessness of quantum gravity: 1. The evidence from the classical theory', *Classical and Quantum Gravity* **11**, 2853–73.

—— 1994b. 'The timelessness of quantum gravity: 11. The appearance of dynamics in static configurations', *Classical and Quantum Gravity* **11**, 2875–97.

—— 2000. *The End of Time: the Next Revolution in Physics* (New York: Oxford University Press).

Barrett, J. 1999. *The Quantum Mechanics of Minds and Worlds* (New York: Oxford University Press).

Bergmann, P. G. 1961. 'Observables in General Relativity', *Reviews of Modern Physics* **33,** 510–14.

Butterfield, J. (ed.) 1999. *The Arguments of Time* (New York: Oxford University Press).

—— (forthcoming), 'The End of Time?', to appear in *British Journal for Philosophy of Science*.

Callender, C. 2000. 'Is Time "Handed" in a Quantum World?', *Proceedings of the Aristotelian Society* **121**, 247–69.

Earman, J. (forthcoming), 'Thoroughly Modern McTaggart: Or What McTaggart Would Have Said If He Had Learned the General Theory of Relativity', to appear in *Philosophers' Imprint*, http://www.philosophersimprint.org

Kuchar, K. 1992. 'Time and the Interpretation of Quantum Gravity', in G. Kunsatter, D. Vincent and J. Williams, (eds), *Proceedings of the 4th Canadian Conference on General Relativity and Relativistic Astrophysics:* 211–14. (Singapore: World Scientific).

—— 1999. 'The Problem of Time in Quantum Geometrodynamics', in Butterfield (ed.) (1999).

Richard Healey

McTaggart, J. E. M. 1908. 'The Unreality of Time', *Mind* **17**, 457–74.

Maudlin, T. 1994. *Quantum Non-Locality and Relativity*. (Oxford: Blackwell).

Mellor, D. H. 1981. *Real Time* (Cambridge: Cambridge University Press).

Rovelli, C. 1991. 'Time in quantum gravity: An hypothesis', *Physical Review D* **43**, 442–56.

Smolin, L. 2001. *Three Roads to Quantum Gravity*. (New York: Basic Books).

Rememberances, Mementos, and Time-Capsules

JENANN ISMAEL

Time Capsules and Presentism

I want to consider some features of the position put forward by Julian Barbour in *The End of Time*[1] that seem to me of particular philosophical interest. At the level of generality at which I'll be concerned with it, the view is relatively easy to describe. It can be arrived at by thinking of time as decomposing in some natural way linearly ordered atomic parts, 'moments', and combining an observation about the internal structure of moments with an epistemological doctrine about our access to the past. The epistemological doctrine, which I'll call 'Presentism', following Butterfield, is the view that our access to the past is mediated by records, or local representations, of it. The observation is that the state of the world at any moment has the structure of what Barbour calls a 'time capsule', which is to say that it constitutes a partial record of its past, it is pregnant with interrelated mutually consistent representations of its own history.

When he speaks of time capsules, Barbour has in mind things like tracks formed in a cloud chamber when a decaying nucleus emits an α-particle,[2] footsteps in the sand made by a passerby, or fossil records of prehistoric animals. But to get a grip on what time capsules look like in cases that approach realistic complexity, you should think of something like Proust's *Rememberance of Things Past* conceived not as an historical novel, but as a description of the intrinsic structure of a single moment. For the book is not really about the past, but about the traces that it has left on the present, and what it gets exactly right is the way in which each temporal part of one's conscious life is a kind of Barbourian time capsule. Each living moment has written into it, into its *intrinsic* structure, a representation of times that preceded, replete with *their* internal representations of those that preceded *them,* and theirs of those that preceded them, and so on, potentially *ad infinitum.*[3]

[1] London: Weidenfeld and Nicholson, 1999.
[2] The Mott-Heisenberg analysis of α-decay is his explicit model.
[3] My present experience is coloured by memories, including memories of myself remembering, and the way those memories coloured experience under them.

Jenann Ismael

Barbour, as I said, isn't so literary about it, but part of the appeal of his position is that it gets something right about the structure of a life, and something right about our *experience* of time. Each moment is at least as richly structured as Proust's novel; every moment contains within it its very own *Rememberances of Things Past*. The way to picture McTaggart's B-series[4] is not as a sequence of structureless points, but a stack of novels, each as thick as Proust's, and each containing a kind of Proustian representation of those that precede it.

Combine this insight into the internal structure of the parts of time, with Presentism, and a gap opens up between the records and what they are supposed to be records *of* (i.e., between the past and the present representations of it)[5] that Barbour exploits (and that Bell first recommended to followers of Everett to do so) to reconcile the appearance of historical continuity (i.e., the *appearance* that the present state of the world arose as the product of continuous evolution from earlier states) with its non-actuality.[6] From an epistemological perspective, the gap was always there—it was always possible to call into question the accuracy of our historical records—(Russell made the point with his remark that for all we know, the world was created three seconds ago, replete with fossils, and history books, memories, and all the rest of it)—but it is exacerbated in the context of quantum mechanics for reasons I'll say below.

Now, go back to the stack of Proust volumes. The time capsule structure of each means that it contains a representation of the volumes that precede it, but there is nothing in the picture—and nothing in particular, in the *internal* consistency of the various volumes in the stack—that keeps us from stacking volumes that are inconsistent *with one another*, i.e., that *mis*represent earlier representations of historical events, and misrepresent them precisely as

[4] 'The Unreality of Time', *Mind*, New Series, 68, Oct. 1908. McTaggart distinguished two series in which events were ordered, an A-series, which ordered them in terms of their relations to the present moment, and a B-series, which ordered in terms of their unchanging, eternal, temporal relations to one another.

[5] No restriction on the form such records take is presumed; photographs, recordings, footprints in sand, traces in memory...

'But what is the past? Strictly, it is never anything more than we can infer from present records. The word "record" prejudges the issue... we might replace "records" by some more neutral expression like "structures that seem to tell a consistent story".' (Barbour, op. cit., p. 33)

[6] 'Quantum Mechanics for Cosmologists', in *Speakable and Unspeakable in Quantum Mechanics*, Cambridge University Press, Cambridge (1987), p. 117–38.

318

being consistent with their own depiction thereof. What we've really got, so far as constraints on the consistency of the picture go, is a set of novels horizontally stacked, potentially disagreeing about historical events, but representing themselves *as* in accord. And the discrepancy is undiscoverable so long as we are epistemically trapped within the pages of a particular novel, forever creating new records of old records, and of relations between old records and what they are records of, but never in a position to compare any record directly with the event it purports to record. We have no way of establishing the reliability of the mechanisms that generate records of past events that doesn't itself make use of those mechanisms. The circle of justification is inescapable, and it is vicious.

The insight in Bell's recommendation to Many Worlds theorists that they relinquish continuous trajectories, is that this kind of structure, internal to the parts of time, places virtually no restrictions on the external relations *between* them. We can give a completely consistent description of a universe constituted by a set of time capsules, arranged in a McTaggartian B-series, containing internally consistent representations of their own histories but inconsistent *with one another*, and inconsistent, moreover, with the actual history, jointly constituted by the lot of them. But Barbour takes things one step further, and, in a bold Leibnizian move, kicks away even the external relations between the time capsules, so that there is not, in actuality, any history at all. In Barbour's picture, time capsules bear one another internal relations of similarity and accord, but there is no external dimension in which they are collectively ordered.[7] There are not really any genuinely external relations between time capsules, none that don't supervene on their internal properties.

Moments, in this picture, are elements in a grand configuration space, like the worlds in Lewis' modal universe; there *is* no time-like dimension constituted by them collectively and misrepresented by them individually. An order can be reconstructed *within* each moment by stacking together internal *representations* of others, using a procedure that works by comparing their intrinsic structures.[8] But that, according to Barbour, is only an internal surrogate,

---

[7] Just as, in a Leibnizian universe, there is not any genuinely external dimension in which the monads are ordered; spatial relations, such as they are, arise from relations among the intrinsic properties of monads. This is why I call the move Leibnizian.

[8] The procedure identifies places across time in a way that minimizes resulting overall motion of bodies, and it turns out that both Newtonian time, and time in General Relativity are explicitly definable in this way from the dynamical evolution of the universe.

compatible with the non-existence of any real, external time. All that there is, on this view, are the various instantaneous configurations of the universe,[9] replete with their interior 'records' of other instantaneous states, arranged in a relative configuration space by a similarity relation expressed by Barbour's best-matching procedure.[10]

There are a huge number of details, and they matter, but that, if I understand it, is the broad vision. What our physics, properly understood, gives us, according to Barbour, is a ψ-function sitting timelessly in a relative configuration space, defining a probability distribution that clusters on time capsules[11], with the *appearance* of temporality arising from structure internal to the capsules. The view is a temporal analogue of Leibnizian monadism. Whereas, for Leibniz, space arose from purely internal relations among monads, each of which contains an internal representation of itself *as* located in a real space (i.e., in a network of external relations among spatially extended systems), for Barbour, time arises from purely internal relations among monads, each of which contains a representation of itself *as* located in real time.

What puzzles one about the picture is the question of why, having gone so far, Barbour stops where he does? What reason could he have, by his own lights, for supposing the universe contains anything more than a single time capsule? It's the same puzzlement one feels, in a Many Worlds universe, about what the other worlds are *there* for, or in a Leibnizian universe about why one should suppose that there are *multiple* monads. The problem, in each case, is that once you have written all worldly structure into one part of the universe, you are left with nothing for the other parts to *do* (except, perhaps, if this is a proper sort of occupation—*get represented,* and the thing about the other time capsules in a Barbourian universe is that they don't even do *that* very well). It's as though Barbour replaced windows with paintings of external landscapes, and then insisted on keeping the landscapes, denying even, that they were faithfully depicted.[12]

---

[9] All those ascribed a non-zero amplitude by the quantum state.

[10] E.g.: is time atomic? How big is the smallest time-capsule? Endless technical details, and questions of motivation.

[11] Barbour is up-front about the conjectural nature of the assumption that the ψ-function will end up clustering on time-capsules; the position could fall on this purely technical consideration.

[12] At least in the case of monads, their internal structure really *does* reflect the actual network of relations, though it turns out that they are internal.

Suppose we parted ways with Barbour on this question and held that the universe consists of a solitary Barbourian time capsule: a single temporal monad. It would be hard to say, in that case, what remains of Barbour's denial of the reality of time. It is an essential part of the view, crucial to its empirical plausibility, that time capsules have an internal surrogate for time (i.e., parts that represent parts of time, and that can be ordered by a best-matching procedure into a representation of history), and the question is, what is missing in a universe that consists of a single capsule, to make one want to describe it as a time-less one? What distinguishes it from an ordinary McTaggartian B-series? And if nothing, why would one describe a view that holds that the universe consists in a whole big bunch of these as one that denies the existence of time? Isn't it rather a temporally **rich** universe? What this puts pressure on is the very difficult analytic question, raised by any view that denies the reality of time, of what it is, exactly, for time to exist.

I can think of a couple of things that might make one resist describing the single capsule universe as an ordinary temporal reality. One is that while a time capsule has an internal time, it is not itself extended in time. It is like a book with parts that represent parts of time, but that are not themselves arranged *in* it. The second is that the gappiness of historical records in a time capsule universe has to be given an ontological interpretation. The history of such a universe has to be as spotty as our records of it; if there is nothing in its occurrent state to determine the precise moment between two times, t and t*, that an α-particle is emitted from a radioactive atom, then there *was* no such moment (although it will still be correct to say that the particle was emitted, and indeed emitted between t and t*).[13]

Both considerations seem too esoteric to underwrite the denial of the existence of something that plays such a central role in so much of our thinking about the physical world. And Barbour, in any case, holds firmly to the existence of all time capsules assigned a non-zero probability by the ψ-function. His reason is this:

'I believe all of Platonia is "there", not just a single time capsule, because there is then at least some chance of explaining why I experience this instant (because it is one of many to which the wave function of the universe gives a high probability). So the mere fact that I experience this instant with properties that (in

---

[13] Suppose that t is the time at which we prepared the particle, that t* is the instant, 5 seconds later, at which it is first detected outside the nucleus, and that there is nothing to place the emission event at any moment between t and t*.

Jenann Ismael

principle if my scheme is correct) theory predicts allows me to conclude that the others must be experienced too.'[14]

I'm not sure what to make of this, but I'll let Barbour have the last word, and turn to a couple of features of the general metaphysical picture that make it interesting from a philosophical perspective.

Temporal Leibnizianism

The first is something I have already noted: the Leibnizian structure of the Barbourian universe. Leibniz' and Barbour's pictures both make something of the fact, which is both a consequence of our physical theories, and a salient feature of our experience of the world, that every part of space and time has written into its material contents—i.e., into the structure of the concrete bodies, and the waves it contains, into the memories of the people that occupy it, and the books and sounds they produce—variously complete and variously faithful representations of other parts.

Our physical theories provide us with increasingly detailed accounts of natural mechanisms that give rise to this kind of structure (theories of wave-propagation that tell us how waves carry structure from one part of space to another; neurophysiological theories that tell us how world-representing structure gets built into the wet stuff between our ears, theories we can add to our practical understanding of how to build the structure in our heads into our material surroundings). It is something that Bohm calls attention to repeatedly, and that plays a central role in his own philosophy;

'consider ... how on looking at the night sky, we are able to discern structures covering immense stretches of space and time, which are in some sense contained in the movements of light in the tiny space encompassed by the eye (and also how instruments, such as optical and radio telescopes, can discern more and more of this totality, contained in each region of space).'[15]

And rather than reify the global structure in each of the parts, Barbour and Leibniz both deny the existence of anything over and above the parts, and think of temporality and spatiality, respectively,[16] as emerging from internal relations among, or structure internal to,

[14] Personal communication.
[15] 'Quantum Theory as an Indication of a New Order' in *Wholeness and the Implicate Order*, Routledge, New York (1980), p. 149.
[16] Or, in Barbour's case, the appearance of it.

322

the parts. Barbour does with time essentially what Leibniz does with space, and what Bohm does with space-time. There are differences, to be sure: Barbour takes time as the basic structure, denies the existence of genuine temporal relations between time-capsules, and doesn't place restrictions on the internal relations among them. Leibniz takes space as the basic structure, and denies the existence of spatial relations (conceived non-reductively as genuinely *external* relations between monads), but places strong consistency constraints on internal relations among them.[17,18] Bohm takes space-time as the basic structure, conceives of spatio-temporal relations as full-fledged, external relations between point-like events, and has much that is new, and very interesting, to say about the particular way in which global structure is locally represented. But all of them have in common the basic construction of a whole constituted by parts that contain (variously complete and variously accurate) representations of it.

Memories and mementos

The second thing I want to consider is the relationship between Barbour's metaphysical view and quantum mechanics. The insight Barbour took from Bell was that one can deny that the actual history of the world is continuous, while explaining the *appearance* of continuity by pointing to quantum mechanisms for the creation of consistent records. The idea was that once you've got all this past-representing structure written into the present, acknowledged that knowledge of the past is mediated by knowledge of present past-representing structures, and accepted a quantum-mechanical account of how such structures (i.e., records) are produced, you realize that the appearance of consistency (which is to say, a positive result for measurements to check the accuracy of our records of the past) places virtually no constraints on the actual relations between those records and the past, or even, indeed, among those records themselves. The history of the world may jump around as discontinuously as you please from one moment to the next, without any threat to the appearance of continuity, and without any way of dis-

[17] The internal structures of monads have to be unfolding in sync with one another in a way that gives rise to the impression of a common external cause.

[18] The other difference, of course, is that Barbour describes his view as a denial of the reality of time, where Leibniz describes his as a view about the true nature of space.

covering that the physical mechanisms that produce records are anything but what they purport to be: more or less reliable ways of generating faithful representations of past events. Barbour did Bell one better by denying that there *are* trajectories, continuous or otherwise. All that exists, according to him, is the collection of time capsules, and the ψ-function giving their relative probabilities.

Butterfield, in a review of Barbour's book,[19] points out that Presentism, as a philosophical doctrine, isn't inevitable. And that is correct. But it does express the epistemological position in which our *physical* theories (both classical and quantum) cast us, and that gives it something more than the status of an optional, and not especially attractive, philosophical view. We simply *cannot* accept a broadly naturalistic picture of ourselves and deny that our knowledge of distant places and times is mediated by local representations. He also remarks that Barbour's position makes as much sense in classical contexts as in quantum mechanics, and that too is correct, but it leaves out Bell's central insight.[20] It is true in the classical world, as surely as the quantum one, that we are trapped in the present, forever planning new measurements to check results of old ones, but no more able to check whether the new are consistent with the old than whether the old are consistent with what they measure, i.e., forever creating records of past events, and records of the relations between those records and the events they record, with no independent way of ascertaining whether the mechanisms for creating records really *do* that, no way of telling for sure, that is, whether they actually reveal pre-existing consistency.[21]

The twist added by quantum mechanics is that it elevates what was in the classical case a mere epistemic possibility (*viz.*, that

[19] Butterfield, *BJPS*, forthcoming. The article surveys the whole of Barbour's work and situates it with respect to the contemporary philosophical literature about time.

[20] Bell himself dismisses the view on the grounds that it gives rise to scepticism:

"Everett's replacement of the past by memories is a radical solipsism – extending to the temporal dimension the replacement of everything outside my head by my impressions, of ordinary solipsism or positivism. Solipsism cannot be refuted. But if such a theory were taken seriously it would hardly be possible to take anything else seriously." (Bell, *op.cit.*, p. 136).

[21] There are two ways to think of the relationship between records and measurements; you can think of measurements as interactions that create accessible records of not otherwise accessible facts, or you can think of records as the presently accessible results of measurements on the past.

measurements don't simply create records of preexisting facts) to a nomological necessity. The theory actually entails non-canonical relations between measurement results and the events they are suppose to record.[22] Whereas in classical mechanics, the physical laws entail that a photograph, a footprint in the sand, or in general, the position of a pointer observable after measurement can only have arisen by a deterministic process from the preceding events of which they constitute records, in quantum mechanics, the physical laws themselves block any direct backward inference from the result of a measurement to the state of the world beforehand. Whereas in classical mechanics, one cannot deny the faithfulness of records and the reliability of the processes that generate them without denying the physical laws, the laws of quantum mechanics themselves *entail* that records aren't generally reliable. For recording is just a kind of measuring, one that takes the present observable state of the world as a pointer observable in a measurement of its state in the past. And we know that we cannot in general interpret the results of individual quantum mechanical measurements as simple, faithful representations of the state of the measured system.

There is a film in theatres now called *Memento* in which the hero doesn't have a short term memory, and has to rely for his information about the recent past, on various kinds of material artifacts: snapshots, written notes, tattoos, what other people tell him. We think that the fact that we have memories puts us in a better position, but if memories are just tattoos in the brain—i.e. present representations of the past events—the difference is shallow. They are only as reliable as the processes that produce them.

Conceived naturalistically, memory has the same status as perception; both are physical processes that generate local (respectively, present/internal) representations of distant (past/external) states of affairs.[23] Doubt is appropriate if there are occasional, contextual reasons for thinking that the mechanisms aren't functioning normally (things are broken, conditions are non-standard, or some

[22] The only thing we can conclude from the result of an individual measurement is that the measured system is not (or, is with measure zero probability) in an eigenstate of the measured observable with eigenvalue orthogonal to the one observed.

[23] There are philosophical positions (sometimes called 'direct realist') that hold that both perception and memory, are representationally unmediated ways of apprehending external things and the past. So long, however, as we are spatially localized things picking up information about our environments from local causal interactions, Presentism is the epistemology built into our physical theories.

such), but global scepticism is possible only by denying that the mechanisms operate as they are supposed to, i.e., by holding a special, non-standard *theory* about their operation. That is what traditional sceptical possibilities offer; whatever else it is, Descartes' evil daemon is an alternative hypothesis about the mechanisms that give rise to our perceptual states.

The lesson that Barbour took from Bell, and that we can learn from him, is that quantum mechanics provides just the kind of nonclassical account of the generation of records that undermines their general reliability as sources of information about the past. The insight is that in a quantum context, the mechanisms that generate future representations of moments past leave us with something that bears as loose a relation to their source as the post-measurement position of a pointer observable to the pre-measurement value of the measured observable. The hero of *Memento* gets into all sorts of difficulties because his records are generated by unreliable mechanisms (they are produced by people [himself included] and hence dependent for their reliability on the trustworthiness of their producers). If we call records like that 'mementos', we can put the lesson by saying that, where classical physics gave us memories, quantum mechanics gives us only mementos.[24]

Queries

A couple of final questions. There is an irony in the fact that at just the point that Barbour thinks physics has divested itself of all vestiges of temporality, if what I have been suggesting is correct, it actually does a fair job of capturing central features of the *experience* of time. One of the most surprising things about Barbour's view is just how much of our temporal experience can be recovered from structure *internal* to his time capsules.[25] This raises again the question of why Barbour describes his view as a denial of the *reality* of time, rather than an idiosyncratic theory about what time *is*. The question is not inconsequential. It is, of course, in its general form ('What does the world have to be like for time to be real?', or, more

---

[24] Or, a formulation I prefer, the classical world remembers its earlier states, where the present state of the quantum universe is merely a memento of its past.

[25] I have argued, independently that we can even find in the relations among temporally situated representations of time—of which time capsules are instances—something that satisfies McTaggart's desiderata for passage ('The Reality of Time', *ms.*).

pointedly, 'What properties must a physical parameter have to deserve to be called "time"?') the question that confronts the quantum gravity theorist.

Another question that it would be good to hear more from Barbour about has to do with records. Time capsules are records of a certain kind, specifically, structures that encode an appearance of history. But he doesn't give any explicit, intrinsic characterization of what this means. In the classical contexts, we could think of them as structures generated by mechanisms that lend them a kind of natural intentionality; we could say that A is a record of B *iff* B was caused in the right way by A, or, perhaps, if B was typically a reliable sign of a preceding A-occurrence, or if A gave rise to B by a structure-preserving process, or some such thing.[26] The problem is that in a quantum context, reliable covariation is out of the picture, and Barbour forswears external connections, so causal relations, at least as usually conceived, aren't available to him. In virtue of what, by Barbour's lights, does an instantaneous configuration (e.g., a footprint in the sand, a track in a cloud chamber) constitute a record of this or that sort of preceding event.

Questions about what it is for a structure to have representational purport, and to have the particular purport that it does, are notoriously hard; the reason it is fair to demand something more from Barbour in the way of an explicit account is that his central notion is ill-defined without one, and none of the approaches in the literature would seem to serve his purpose.[27] There are some indications in his discussion of the Mott-Heisenberg analysis of α-decay of how it might go, but one would like to see it worked out.

There is a very great deal more to say about the view; I have focused on features that are especially suggestive from a philosophical perspective: in particular, the surprising degree to which our experience of time can be recovered from structure *internal* to its parts, and the insight about the looseness, in a quantum context, of the relationship between the past and our present representations of it. There are other aspects of the position, also of philosophical interest, and a number of deeply perplexing issues, that I haven't

---

[26] There are a variety of accounts in the literature, all presupposing some form of causal determination or nomological covariation.

[27] The derived intentionality of artifacts like linguistic structures, designed with representational **intent** isn't obviously applicable (unless the intent is God's, and Barbour wants to convict him of malice). One might surmise, however, from some of his remarks about consciousness, that Barbour inclines towards some sort of irreducible intentionality derived from their relations to human minds.

touched on (not to mention endless questions, of both a technical and conceptual nature, concerning the physics and the relationship to quantum gravity).[28] It is bound to take some time before the view is fully absorbed, and I am not sure I have understood it entirely, but it seems to me a genuinely *new* position, with deep and acknowledged affinities to Leibnizian monadism, that is bound to repay philosophical attention.

---

[28] There are a whole set of questions, for instance, about what Barbour means when he talks about selves; he speaks sometimes as though he is a self-aware time-capsule, and sometimes as though he thinks he is temporally extended, 'present', somehow, in different time capsules.